Historica...

Library

Historical Association Studies

General Editors: *Muriel Chamberlain, H. T. Dickinson and Joe Smith*

The Historical Association, founded in 1906, brings together people who share an interest in, and love for, the past. It aims to further the study and teaching of history at all levels: teacher and student, amateur and professional. This is one of over 100 publications available at preferential rates to members. Membership also includes journals at generous discounts and gives access to courses, conferences, tours and regional and local activities. Full details are available from The Secretary, The Historical Association, 59a Kennington Park Road, London SE11 4JH, telephone: 0171-735 3901.

Postwar Japan
1945 to the Present

Paul J. Bailey

BLACKWELL
Publishers

First published 1996

2 4 6 8 10 9 7 5 3 1

Blackwell Publishers Ltd
108 Cowley Road
Oxford OX4 1JF
UK

Blackwell Publishers Inc
238 Main Street
Cambridge, Massachusetts 02142,
USA

British Library Cataloguing in Publication Data

A CIP catalogue record for this book is available from the British Library.

Library of Congress Cataloging-in-Publication Data

Bailey, Paul John, 1950–
    Postwar Japan : 1945 to the present / Paul J. Bailey.
        p.   cm.—(Historical Association studies)
    Includes bibliographical references and index.
    ISBN 0-631-18101-6.—ISBN 0-631-17901-1 (pbk.)
    1. Japan—History—1945–   I. Title. II. Series.
DS889.B27   1996
952.04—dc20   96-13662
                                                         CIP

Typeset in 10 on 12 pt Times
by Best-set Typesetter Ltd, Hong Kong
Printed in Great Britain by Hartnolls Limited, Bodmin, Cornwall

This book is printed on acid-free paper

Contents

Author's Note

Abbreviation used in the main text FEER: *Far Eastern Economic Review* (Hong Kong).

Reference to Japanese names in the text is in accordance with Japanese usage, i.e. family name is given first.

Outline Chronology

1945	August	Emperor Hirohito broadcasts surrender speech; General MacArthur arrives in Tokyo as Supreme Commander of Allied Powers (SCAP) to administer the occupation.
	September	Formal Japanese surrender takes place on board the USS *Missouri*; President Truman approves Initial Post-Surrender Policy for Japan.
	October	SCAP issues Civil Liberties Directive; Japanese Communist Party (JCP) legalized; Prince Higashikuni resigns as Prime Minister and is succeeded by Shidehara Kijuro.
	November	MacArthur approves Yasuda plan for the break-up of the *zaibatsu*.
	December	State Shinto Directive separates religion from the state; Trade Union Law guarantees workers the right to organize and strike.
1946	January	Emperor Hirohito formally renounces his divinity.
	April	First postwar elections are held, and women for the first time are allowed to vote and stand as candidates.
	May	Yoshida Shigeru, leader of the conservative Liberal Party, becomes Prime Minister; the International Military Tribunal of the Far East (IMTFE) opens proceedings in Tokyo; height of 'production control' struggles.

	October	SCAP-promoted Land Reform Bill passed.
	November	New constitution promulgated (to be effective in May 1947).
1947	January	MacArthur bans planned general strike.
	April	First elections held under the new constitution; the Japanese Socialist Party (JSP) becomes the largest single party in the lower house; Katayama Tetsu becomes Prime Minister of a socialist-led coalition government; Labour Standards Law passed.
	May	Formal adoption of FEC-230, calling for the dissolution of all excessive concentrations of economic power; Fundamental Law of Education revises the prewar education system.
	December	Deconcentration Law passed and 300 companies are slated for dissolution.
1948	January	Following the Draper Mission, the anti-*zaibatsu* programme is wound down.
	February	Katayama resigns; coalition continues under Ashida Hitoshi, leader of the conservative Democratic Party.
	July	Offensive against labour begins with the ban on strikes in the public sector.
	October	Adoption of NSC 13 in Washington, which places priority on economic revival and political stability in Japan; Showa Denko scandal leads to resignation of Ashida; Yoshida becomes Prime Minister again.
	November	IMTFE hands down its verdicts; seven defendants (including wartime Prime Minister Tojo Hideki) are condemned to death.
	December	The Dodge Plan aims to bring about economic stabilization in Japan and leads to massive unemployment; National Public Service Law denies civil servants the right to strike and engage in collective bargaining.
1949	January	Lower house elections give Yoshida's Liberal Party a plurality of seats.
	May	Reparations programme terminated.
	October	SCAP censorship formally ends.
1949–50		'Anti-red' purge results in the dismissal of

		thousands of left-wing sympathizers from the public sector.
1950	June	Three days before the outbreak of the Korean War, Washington formally urges upon the Japanese government the need for rearmament.
	July	Creation of the National Police Reserve.
1951	April	General Ridgway replaces MacArthur as SCAP.
	September	Peace Treaty signed in San Francisco (to come into effect in April 1952); on the same day the US and Japan sign a Security Treaty allowing for the continued presence of US military bases in Japan.
	October	The Japanese Socialist Party (JSP) splits over the Security Treaty.
1952	April	Japan regains its sovereignty; Yoshida falls in line with US China policy when he signs a treaty recognizing Chiang Kai-shek's regime on Taiwan as the Republic of China.
1953		Further restrictions on labour with strikes banned in the coal and electricity industries; Anti-Monopoly Law modified.
1954	March	US and Japan sign the Mutual Security Assistance Agreement providing for increased American military aid.
	June	Police Law recentralizes police administration.
	July	Defence Laws transform the National Police Reserve into the Self Defence Forces under civilian control.
	December	Yoshida resigns as Prime Minister and is succeeded by Hatoyama Ichiro, a former purged politician and leader of the conservative Democratic Party.
1955	September	Japan is admitted to the General Agreement on Tariffs and Trade (GATT).
	October	The two wings of the Japanese Socialist Party reunite.
	November	The two principal conservative parties merge to form the Liberal Democratic Party (LDP).

1956	June	School Boards Law abolishes local elective local boards and is preceded by massive demonstrations and fights in the upper house.
	October	Normalization of relations with the Soviet Union, although the question of the Northern Territories (Southern Kuriles) remains unsettled.
	November	Hatoyama resigns and is succeeded by Ishibashi Tanzan.
	December	Japan enters the UN.
1957	February	Kishi Nobusuke, another 'depurged' politician, succeeds Ishibashi as Prime Minister.
	May	First elections held since the formation of the LDP, which gains 57.8 per cent of the vote.
	August	Teacher demonstrations in protest against the government's rating system and the reintroduction of moral education into the school curriculum.
	October	Kishi has to shelve Police Duties Amendment Bill due to violent opposition in the Diet.
1959	March	Growing opposition to the revised US–Japan Security Treaty symbolized by the formation of the People's Council for Preventing Revision of the Security Treaty.
	September	The JSP again splits into left-wing and right-wing groups.
1960	January	Kishi leaves for Washington to sign revised Security Treaty; creation of the moderate Democratic Socialist Party (DSP).
	February	The revised Security Treaty is submitted to the Diet for ratification.
	May	Kishi's extension of the Diet session to ensure ratification of the Security Treaty leads to socialist boycott and massive public demonstrations.
	June	President Eisenhower's visit to Japan is cancelled amidst continuing protests against the revised Security Treaty.
	July	Following Kishi's resignation, Ikeda Hayato becomes Prime Minister and promises to improve living standards.

September	Bitter one-year strike at Miike Coal Mine ends.
October	Asanuma Inejiro, leader of the JSP, is assassinated.
1962	Trade memorandum agreement allows for private Japanese trade with the People's Republic of China.
1964	Olympic Games are held in Tokyo; formation of the Clean Government Party (*Komeito*); Sato Eisaku succeeds Ikeda as Prime Minister.
1965	Japan and South Korea normalize relations; Anti-Vietnam War movement begins, spearheaded by the Citizens' Federation for Peace in Vietnam (*Beheiren*).
1966	The Japanese Communist Party (JCP) asserts its independence from both Beijing and Moscow.
1967	In lower house elections the LDP fails to gain more than 50 per cent of the popular vote for the first time, although it remains the majority party in the Diet; Minobe Ryokichi, a candidate of the Left, is elected governor of metropolitan Tokyo; anti-Vietnam War demonstrations and strikes become more frequent; the first pollution lawsuit is brought against a company in Niigata and other lawsuits follow.
1968	Following the departure of the American nuclear-powered aircraft carrier *Enterprise*, Sato announces Japan's Three Non-Nuclear Principles.
1969	Sato–Nixon Communique announces that Okinawa will revert to Japanese control in 1972; in the elections the LDP gains more seats but again fails to obtain more than 50 per cent of the vote.
1970	The US–Japan Security Treaty is automatically renewed despite huge demonstrations; the Diet passes anti-pollution legislation; the novelist Mishima Yukio commits ritual suicide after an abortive appeal to the Self Defence Forces.

1971	Nixon initiative on China taken without consulting Japanese government; further 'shocks' lead to increased duties on Japanese imports to the US and the upward revaluation of the yen; Emperor Hirohito visits Western Europe.
1972	Left-wing terrorist group, the Japanese Red Army, forms links with the Palestinian Popular Front for the Liberation of Palestine and carries out an attack at Lod Airport, Israel, in which 24 people die; Okinawa is returned to Japanese control; Sato resigns and is succeeded by Tanaka Kakuei, a self-made politician; Tanaka visits China and normalizes relations; in the lower house elections both the JSP and the JCP make gains; a number of prefectural and municipal administrations are headed by opposition candidates.
1973	Tanaka's government implements free medical care for the elderly, an innovation pioneered by several progressive local administrations; oil crisis leads to the scaling down of Tanaka's ambitious plans for regional development.
1974	Tanaka's tour of Southeast Asia is met with hostile demonstrations in Thailand, Indonesia and the Philippines; amidst charges of financial wrongdoing, Tanaka resigns and is succeeded by Miki Takeo.
1975	Miki's political reform bills aim, without success, to end factionalism and illegal financial contributions; Emperor Hirohito makes a state visit to the US.
1976	Former Prime Minister, Tanaka Kakuei, is linked to the Lockheed Scandal and is formally indicated (although a judgement is not passed until 1983); in the wake of the scandal the LDP experiences its first split when six members form the New Liberal Club (NLC); Miki is replaced as LDP President and Prime Minister by Fukuda Takeo.

1977	Fukuda aims to woo Southeast Asian countries with his 'Fukuda Doctrine'.
1978	Narita airport finally opens (seven years behind schedule) amidst continuing opposition from local farmers; Sino-Japanese Treaty of Peace and Friendship is signed in Beijing; accession of Ohira Masayoshi to the premiership brings out into the open the bitter factional rivalry between Tanaka Kakuei and Fukuda Takeo.
1979	Fifth summit of seven industrialized countries is held in Tokyo; following the LDP's poor showing in the elections, Fukuda Takeo stands as a candidate for Prime Minister when Ohira refuses to resign; Ohira wins Diet vote and stays on as Prime Minister.
1980	Prime Minister Ohira is forced to call elections after a no-confidence vote in the Diet; during the campaign Ohira dies and is succeeded by Suzuki Zenko; the LDP win a massive sympathy vote.
1981	The Commission on Administrative Reform (*Rincho*) is set up and calls for reduction in public expenditures and privatization.
1982	Nakasone Yasuhiro is chosen as LDP leader and Prime Minister.
1983	In talks with US President Reagan, Nakasone promises to enhance Japan's defence capabilities; Nakasone's government forms a coalition with eight-member New Liberal Club.
1985	Nippon Telephone and Telegraph is privatized; Nakasone and his cabinet worship officially at the Yasukuni Shrine on the anniversary of Japan's surrender in the Second World War; anti-Japanese demonstrations break out in China.
1986	In double elections (for the lower and upper houses) the LDP achieves its best results since 1963; Nakasone earns a one-year extension as LDP leader and Prime Minister; the NLC dissolves and its members return to the LDP fold;

Doi Takako becomes Japan's first female party leader when she succeeds Ishibashi Masashi as leader of the JSP; school textbook revisions lead to further deterioration in Sino-Japanese relations.

1987   Japan National Railways is privatized; Nakasone is forced to withdraw a tax reform bill due to public opposition; for the first time the government cuts the producer rice price; the 1 per cent ceiling on defence expenditures is exceeded for the first time since 1976; Toshiba products are banned from the US for up to five years; Nakasone is succeeded as Prime Minister by Takeshita Noboru.

1988   Takeshita pushes through a revised tax reform bill in the Diet; Recruit Scandal breaks; Finance Minister Miyazawa Kiichi, implicated in the scandal, is forced to resign.

1989   Emperor Hirohito dies and is succeeded by his son Akihito; in the wake of the Recruit Scandal Takeshita steps down as Prime Minister, but his successor Uno Sosuke is soon implicated in a sex scandal; in upper house elections the opposition takes control for the first time; Uno resigns and is succeeded by Kaifu Toshiki; when public sector unions join the National Federation of Private Sector Trade Unions (*Rengo*) the bulk of the labour movement is unified for the first time.

1990   In lower house elections the JSP fails to capitalize on public dissatisfaction with the governing party; Gulf Crisis breaks out and Japan pledges $4 billion to aid the multilateral force in Saudi Arabia.

1991   Kaifu pledges a further $9 billion following outbreak of the Gulf War; after the war Kaifu secures Diet approval for the despatch of SDF minesweepers to the Middle East; Kaifu is succeeded by Miyazawa Kiichi as Prime Minister; Doi Takako steps down as JSP leader.

1992	Further financial scandals involving LDP members; Kanemaru Shin, a key LDP factional leader, is forced to resign his Diet seat after being indicted for financial corruption; The Peacekeeping Operations Bill (PKO) is passed authorizing the use of SDF units abroad for non-combatant purposes; SDF personnel are sent to Cambodia to assist with elections; Hosokawa Morohiro, a former LDP member of the upper house, forms the Japan New Party.
1993	Miyazawa loses parliamentary vote of confidence; LDP dissidents led by Hata Tsutomu and Ozawa Ichiro form the Renewal Party; in lower house elections the LDP loses its majority; Hosokawa becomes Prime Minister of a seven-party coalition government; in his first major Diet speech, Hosokawa publicly apologizes to Asian countries for Japan's actions in the Second World War; Japan's rice market is opened to foreign imports.
1994	Electoral reform bill is passed, to take effect in 1995; Hosokawa resigns following allegations of financial corruption; the short-lived government of Hata Tsutomu is succeeded by a LDP–JSP coalition government headed by a socialist, Murayama Tomiichi; opposition parties in the Diet merge to form the New Frontier Party.
1995	Kobe earthquake results in over 5,000 deaths; a nerve-gas attack on the Tokyo subway, believed to be the work of a religious sect (Aum Shinrikyo), leaves 12 people dead; US–Japan trade dispute over car imports is averted; a watered-down war apology resolution is passed in the Diet on the eve of the 50th anniversary of Japan's surrender.

Introduction

With the ending of the Cold War and the disappearance of the Soviet Union, Japan's relations with its Western partners, particularly the United States, have reached a critical turning-point. A book published by two American writers in 1991, the year in which the 50th anniversary of Pearl Harbour was commemorated in the United States, painted a grim scenario for the future. Entitled *The Coming War With Japan* its authors, G. Friedman and M. Le Bard, argued that with the removal of the Soviet menace the fundamentally different geopolitical interests of Japan and the United States would be laid bare. No longer accepting Japan's privileged economic position as the price it had been obliged to pay for keeping Japan in the 'free world' camp, the United States would contest Japan's economic pre-eminence in Asia. Japan, in turn, would build up its navy to secure vital sea-lanes, thus bringing it into military conflict with the United States in an eerie repetition of the situation during the late 1930s. The authors concluded that the United States would emerge victorious from the resulting struggle because of its superior military power and its ability to cut off a vulnerable Japan from its crucial overseas markets.

Such a sensationalist publication is perhaps only the most extreme example of a phenomenon referred to as 'Japan bashing' by concerned observers in the United States. Beginning with a 1985 article by Theodore White in the *New York Times Magazine* entitled 'The Danger of Japan', American media, business and political opinion has increasingly viewed Japan's emerging status as an economic superpower with suspicion and hostility (Johnson 1988; Miyoshi 1991; Dower 1993b). It is argued that Japan has aggressively and selfishly pursued its own economic interests, capturing markets abroad while refusing to open its own markets to foreign imports. Furthermore, it is claimed, Japan's prosperity has been achieved on the back of the United States: its enlightened occupation policies after the war, its support for Japan's reintegration into the free world economy, its assumption of much of Japan's defence, and its liberal provision of technology gave Japan unique advantages in the postwar era.

'Japan bashing' has been accompanied by the resurrection of fears and stereotypes first enunciated at the turn of the twentieth century when Japan's increasing economic and military power in East Asia prompted warnings of a 'Yellow Peril' on the verge of swamping the Christian West (Iriye 1967; 1972; 1975; Lehmann 1978; Dower 1986). A recently funded CIA report warned of Japan's drive to dominate the world economically, and contrasted its collectivist ethos with the more humane individualist values of the West (FEER, 27 June 1991). Dehumanization of the Japanese during the Second World War has been revived with contemporary references to the Japanese in the Western popular media as 'economic animals' or 'robot-like' salarymen (Dower 1986; 1993b).

Recent book-length accounts in English of contemporary Japan also reflect ambivalent attitudes towards Japan's postwar success, and adopt a very different approach from that taken by E. Vogel in his 1979 book *Japan As Number One*. Vogel's book itself was a reaction against earlier accounts, such as R. Benedict's *The Sword and the Chrysanthemum* (1946) and Z. Brzezinski's *The Fragile Blossom* (1972), which had emphasized the paradoxes of Japanese culture and the problems they posed for Japan's democratic development (Glazer 1975). Vogel insisted that the West had much to learn from Japan in terms of its labour relations, consensual decision-making, commitment to education, the primacy accorded to collective over individual interests, and the positive role of the state. Since then general accounts have been prone to view those very same features highlighted by Vogel in a more negative light and to emphasize the flaws of both Japan's economic success and political system. The very titles of such works indicate such an approach, e.g. *Japan: The Blighted Blossom* (Thomas 1989); *The Enigma of Japanese Power* (van Wolferen 1989). The latter, for example, argues that because power is spread across a number of semi-autonomous bodies which are neither responsible to the elec-

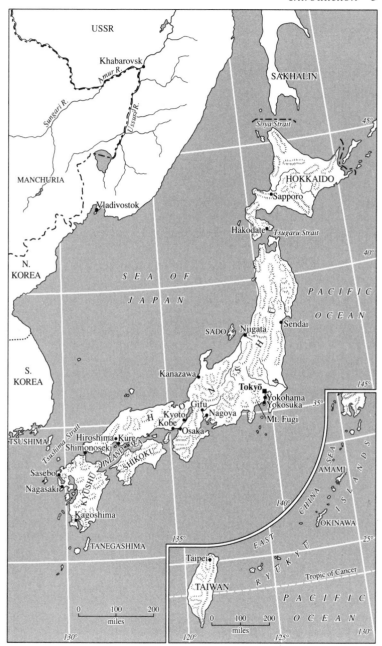

Map 1.1 Modern Japan
Source: Hane (1992)

torate nor subservient to one another, one cannot refer to a Japanese 'state' at all but rather to a 'system'.

At another level, of course, an increasing number of specialist works in recent years have contributed to a more sophisticated understanding of postwar Japan, but it is interesting that they, too, emphasize aspects of Japanese society and politics hitherto overlooked amidst the overwhelming attention paid to Japanese economic success. Thus, Vogel's description of a harmonious society and polity is modified by works that focus on the nature and processes of different kinds of conflict at all levels of Japanese society, from the village and workplace to the national Diet (Krauss, Rohlen and Steinhoff 1984), movements of mass protest against the state involving environmental concerns (McKean 1981; Apter and Sawa 1984), the adverse effects of economic growth (Tsurumi 1988), the ambiguous nature of Japanese democracy (McCormack and Sugimoto 1986), and the obsessions and fears that underpin popular culture (Buruma 1985). On the other hand, the idea that Japan is a 'bureaucratic corporative state' (Scalapino 1989: 107) or that the politico-economic system is to be seen as a giant conglomerate ('Japan Incorporated', a term first coined by *Time* magazine in 1971) (Burks 1981) has been qualified by the description of the Japanese political system as one that encompasses competing group interests within a *changing* elitist structure (Stockwin 1982; Stockwin et al. 1988), or as one that leaves considerable scope for political opposition at the local level (Steiner, Krauss and Flanagan 1980). Political change is also seen as the product of political party responsiveness to shifting public demands rather than brought about by bureaucratic fiat or imposed by an elite consensus (Curtis 1988). Recent works have also characterized the postwar period as one of insecurity, tension and conflict rather than one of stability and consensus (Calder 1988; Dower 1993b). Others stress that democracy in Japan compares favourably with North America and Western Europe, noting the wide acceptance of democratic values and institutions in society, the existence of a free press, and the accepted legitimacy of open public conflict amongst political parties (Ishida and Krauss 1989). Finally, there is an intriguing debate over the precise reasons for, and the nature of, Japan's 'economic miracle' itself, with the description of Japan as a 'capitalist developmental state' in which the bureaucracy played a crucial guiding role (Johnson 1982) being contested by the view that Japan's economic success was more due to the continuing vitality of smaller producers engaged in flexible production techniques (as opposed to large firms engaged in mass production) within a context of decentralization rather than all-embracing regulation (Friedman 1988).

Whatever the complexities of postwar Japan, however, the country's phenomenal recovery from the devastation of war in 1945 and its current position as an economic superpower are undeniable. Between 1949 and 1976, Japan's economy grew 55-fold (Johnson 1982: 6). In 1970, Japan's GNP was already the third largest in the world; by the mid-1970s Japan accounted for 10 per cent of world economic activity, despite the fact that the country occupied just 0.3 per cent of the world's surface and comprised only 3 per cent of the world's population (Tasker 1987: 1). In 1985, the year in which the United States sank into debt for the first time since the First World War, Japan became the world's largest creditor nation (Frost 1987: 31; Hunter 1989: 307). By 1985–6, Japan's per capita GNP (US$17,000) had surpassed that of the United States. In May 1992, the Deutsche Bank's chief economist in Tokyo predicted that by the year 2000 Japan would become the number one economic power overall. Significantly, also, Japan by the early 1990s had become the world's largest aid donor nation (Taira 1993: 168; Cortazzi 1993: 86).

The measure of Japan's economic growth is most graphically illustrated when considering its impact on US–Japan trade. In 1949, Japan's trading deficit with the United States was over 146 billion yen, and Japan at that stage was a net importer of capital (Hunter 1989: 307). In 1952, the year that the American occupation of Japan formally ended, Japan's imports from the United States totalled $768.3 million, while its exports to the United States totalled $234.5 million. In 1965, the balance began to shift; in 1978 the respective figures were $14,790.4 million and $24,914.7 million (Johnson 1988: 134). By the mid-1980s, Japan accounted for one-third of the US trade deficit and financed one-third of its budget deficit (Frost 1987: 9–10). In 1986, the overall US trade deficit was $170 billion, of which $59 billion accrued from trade with Japan (Frost 1987: 13).

Two important aspects of Japan's economic success, however, need to be underlined. First, Japan's growth has depended not so much on exports as on the development of a domestic market. In the late 1960s, for example, exports constituted only 9.6 per cent of GNP. Between 1953 and 1972, Japan had a consistently lower dependency on exports and imports as a percentage of GNP (at constant prices) than France, Germany, Italy and Britain (Johnson 1982: 15–16; Lehmann 1988: 246). Second, at least up until the late 1980s, only 10 per cent of Japan's foreign assets were the product of direct investment in property, factories or companies; the rest accrued from indirect investments in foreign bonds. As a recent study notes, only a small section of Japan's economy until recently has interacted with the rest of the world. Thus, 15 per cent of Japan's GNP in the 1980s was exported, compared to 29 per cent of Britain's GNP and 31 per cent of Germany's GNP, while the largest Japanese companies had 5 per cent of their production overseas compared with 15–20 per cent for their European and American competitors (Tasker 1987: 23).

This situation, however, has been changing in recent years. In the United States, Japanese interests have invested in real estate in California – the Pebble Beach golf course, for example, was acquired for US$800 million in September 1990 (Calder 1990)–and purchased a stake in New York's Rockefeller Centre. In 1989, the Japanese electronics firm Matsushita purchased the film and video producer MCA Universal, while one year later Sony acquired Columbia Pictures. Japanese car manufacturers like Nissan, Toyota and Honda are investing in plant in both the United States and Britain. Fujitsu has acquired an 80 per cent controlling interest in ICL, Britain's sole computer manufacturer.

Japan's current status as an economic superpower should not mask the fact that domestically, too, Japan is at a crossroads. Buffeted by financial scandals, the conservative Liberal Democratic Party (LDP), which had ruled Japan continuously since its formation in 1955, lost its parliamentary majority in 1993 and was replaced by a short-lived coalition government committed to overhauling the electoral system and ending the corrupt money politics of the past. Continued political instability, however, was to lead to an unexpected alliance between the Socialist Party and the LDP, bitter ideological enemies during the 1950s and 1960s. It remains to be seen whether this new socialist-led coalition government can survive long enough (or indeed is willing) to oversee substantial changes in Japan's electoral system. Political uncertainty has been accompanied by uncertainty over both Japan's future role in world affairs and the kind of society that could best usher the country into the twenty-first century. While a widespread cynicism towards the political system and a pervasive feeling of insecurity over the country's perceived economic vulnerability

(Ishinomori 1988) continue to exist, a vociferous minority has begun to insist that Japan needs to take pride in its achievements and break free from what is seen as a subservient relationship with the United States. (This latter view was best expressed by Ishihara Shintaro, a right-wing LDP politician, whose book *The Japan That Can Say No* was published in 1991.) Conservative politicians have harangued the younger generation for not being as hardworking, frugal or diligent as their elders in the 1950s and 1960s. Their solution is to call for a 'leaner and fitter' Japan buttressed by a spiritual revival. Finally, the recent debate over Japan's contribution to the Gulf War has reopened the sensitive issue over the legitimacy and role of Japan's Self Defence Forces as well as broaching the wider question of how Japan's economic influence might be matched by a more assertive political and/or military role in world affairs.

The following chapters will seek to analyse the context within which these debates took place, revealing the conflicts and tensions that accompanied Japan's transformation from a defeated and bankrupted nation occupied by a foreign power to a technologically advanced 'postmodern' society. Before proceeding with the American occupation of Japan in 1945, however, the background to the country's conflict with the West needs to be briefly discussed.

1

The Path to 1945

Japan's defeat in 1945 represented an ignominious end to the modernization drive that was launched after 1868 with the Meiji Restoration, when the feudal regime of the Tokugawa Shogunate (1601–1867) was overthrown by an alliance of disaffected middle-ranking samurai (warrior elite) and court nobles anxious to restore the central political role of the Emperor (Beasley 1972; Huber 1981; Jansen 1989). With the Meiji Emperor (r.1867–1912) as a potent unifying symbol, the new leadership, drawn from the ranks of those samurai who had been the most active in overthrowing the Tokugawa regime, set about creating a centralized state that would break down rigid class distinctions and transform the country into an industrial and military power.

The feudal domains (*han*) were abolished and the country divided into prefectures whose governors were directly appointed by the central government. The feudal lords (*daimyo*) themselves were pensioned off, while the monopolistic privileges of the samurai class were gradually whittled away; hereditary rice stipends, for example, were commuted into lump cash payments and the samurai's military monopoly broken by the creation of a national army comprising peasant conscripts. Restrictions on the sale and purchase of land were removed and feudal land dues (paid in kind) were replaced by a nationally uniform and fixed land tax (paid in cash) based on current land values; the central government was thus ensured a steady flow of revenue from which it was able to finance industrialization (Smith 1988). The government, in fact, took the lead in both promoting manufacturing industry and providing the required transportation and financial infrastructure.

Although many government enterprises were auctioned off into private hands during the 1880s, links between government and business remained close due to personal ties, shared ethos (many of the early Meiji entrepreneurs were from the samurai class) and the practice of government contracts and subsidies for particular enterprises (Smith 1955; Marshall 1967; Crawcour 1989). Finally, a national system of primary schools was created in which values of loyalty to the Emperor, patriotism and discipline were vigorously promoted.

An important motivation that underpinned these modernizing changes was the desire to ward off the threat posed by the Western powers and, ultimately, to seek equality with them. Like China, Japan in the 1850s and 1860s had been compelled to sign unequal treaties which virtually made the country, in the words of one historian, a 'client state' of the West until the 1880s (Beasley 1989a: 306). Such treaties, although not as extensive as those imposed on China, allowed foreigners to reside and enjoy the privilege of extra-territoriality in designated ports as well as stipulating fixed tariff duties on imports into Japan. For the next two decades after 1868 most of Japan's coastal shipping, import–export business and foreign currency exchange operations were monopolized by foreigners (predominantly British). Government policy after 1868 was premised on the basis that Japan needed to emulate the West while at the same time avoiding dependence on it. A striking example of this was the active official encouragement of study abroad in Europe and the United States in order to train native experts to replace as speedily as possible foreign advisers and specialists employed by the Japanese government during the 1870s and 1880s (Jones 1980). Judicial reforms and the implementation of a constitution in 1889 were further examples of the government's willingness to embark on institutional change with the aim of convincing the West of Japan's modern credentials and hence supporting the country's diplomatic efforts to revise the treaties (Lehmann 1982; Beasley 1989b).

In contrast to the approach adopted by some earlier accounts of Japan's modernization process, however, which generally took for granted the smooth transition from feudal backwater to modern nation-state (e.g. Jansen 1965; Ward 1968a), as well as viewing the process from the perspective of government and elites, recent research has looked at society from the bottom up and emphasized the hardships, tension and conflict caused by the imposition of modernizing changes (Hane 1982; Bix 1988) in addition to the far from smooth process by which the government attempted to impose a uniform and Emperor-centred ideology upon the populace (Bowen 1980; Gluck 1985).

Rural unrest was widespread during the 1870s and 1880s, for example; peasants resisted conscription, refused to abandon traditional festivals or to adopt the lunar calendar, and remained suspicious of new schools. More importantly, the land tax of 1873 and the deflation of the 1880s brought added hardships, with many peasants falling into debt and having to mortgage their land. Scattered peasant uprisings, a feature of the late Tokugawa period, continued to alarm the authorities until the end of the 1880s. Samurai opposition, also, was rife. One strand of opposition adopted a reactionary stance and was manifested in armed rebellions against the dismantling of feudal privilege; the last such major rebellion was crushed by the new imperial conscript army in 1877. The other strand embraced political protest, as samurai leaders from some of the former smaller domains, resenting the monopoly of power held by those from the former domains of Choshu and Satsuma (the two domains that had spearheaded the Meiji Restoration), founded political associations and parties after 1873 and called for the immediate election of a national assembly. This 'People's Rights Movement', as it became known, remained active until the early 1880s, helping to popularize notions of popular sovereignty as well as prompting the government to speed up its own plans for a constitution (Vlastos 1989). Recent research has also focused on the exploitation of female textile workers in Japan's early industrialization, as well as on the vital role such workers played in the country's economic growth (Tsurumi 1990). Finally, the imposition of a unified and Emperor-centred state orthodoxy itself in the late nineteenth and early twentieth centuries was a long and complicated process during which a variety of competing ideological visions were always vigorously promoted by bureaucrats, local elites and intellectuals (Gluck 1985).

The cornerstone of the modernization programme was the constitution of 1889, which was to remain intact until 1947. In addition to mollifying critics of the government and impressing upon the West Japan's commitment to the creation of modern institutions, the granting of a constitution was also a logical outcome of the pledge made by Restoration leaders in 1868 to widen political participation and set limits to arbitrary rule. However, the political structure that resulted was a fundamentally unstable one (Mitani 1988). Bestowed upon the people as a 'gift' by the Emperor and promising essential freedoms of belief, thought and association (all of which could be altered or modified according to the law), the constitution allowed for a bicameral Diet, an appointed upper house (House of Peers) and a lower house to be elected on a restricted franchise. The powers of the lower house were limited (it could not initiate legislation, for example), but it could vote on the budget and question government ministers. The latter, moreover, were responsible solely to the Emperor, in whom was clearly located sovereignty. In effect, ministers were to act in the Emperor's name, since it was considered imperative by the framers of the constitution that the Emperor be above politics and hence avoid direct executive responsibility. In order to avoid the monopolization of imperial sovereignty it was parcelled out amongst non-party cabinets, the military, Privy Council and Imperial Household Ministry, all of which existed independently of each other, were directly responsible to the Emperor and could claim to act in the Emperor's name.

Until the first decades of the twentieth century a co-ordinating role was played by the *genro* (senior statesmen), a clique of ex-samurai leaders from Satsuma and Choshu who came to power in the wake of the Meiji Restoration. They were members of the Privy Council, exercised military leadership and served as prime ministers. As the first generation *genro* passed from the scene, and political parties came to contest the appointment of cabinets by a second generation of *genro* in the 1910s and 1920s, the political process became both more fluid and unstable. Although party government became the norm for a brief period in the 1920s, the Diet was only one of a number of competing institutions that insisted on speaking on behalf of the Emperor; these included the military, which often exploited its right to nominate service ministers to bring down cabinets, and the bureaucracy, which had been effectively isolated from any party interference by the *genro*.

In addition to modernization at home Meiji leaders also sought great power status abroad at a time of increasing Western imperialist activity in Asia, which seemed to confirm both the Social Darwinist principles underpinning international relations and the impulse of expansion as the hallmark of a modern nation-state (Jansen 1984; Iriye 1989). Motivated initially by strategic concerns and then by ambitions to secure outlets for future exports and to enhance its economic influence in China, Japan became an imperialist power in its own right by the turn of the twentieth century. After a successful war fought with China in 1894–5, over which country would exert dominant influence in Korea, Japan acquired Taiwan as a formal colony and was granted treaty port privileges in China already enjoyed by the Western powers (Peattie 1988). Subsequent developments confirmed Japan's new-found status as an imperialist power in East Asia. In 1900, Japan participated in the allied expedition to suppress the Boxer Uprising in China; in 1902, a military alliance was signed with Britain to check Russian expansion in Asia; and victory in the Russo-Japanese War of 1904–5 allowed Japan to establish a protectorate over Korea (to be formally annexed in 1910) and to appropriate a former Russian leasehold territory in China (the Kwantung Peninsula in southern Manchuria), which included ownership of the South Manchurian Railway. At the same time Japan was able to revise the unequal treaties signed with the West in the 1850s and 1860s. An agreement with Britain in 1894 provided for the ending of foreign consular jurisdiction in Japan (which took effect in 1899), while full tariff autonomy was regained in 1911.

In less than 50 years, therefore, Japan had become a colonial power in East Asia and a partner in the unequal treaty structure in China. Yet relations with the West remained ambivalent. Already in 1895, following its victory in the war with China, Japan had been compelled to return to China the Liaodong (Kwantung) Peninsula acquired in the peace treaty as a result of diplomatic pressure exerted by Russia, France and Germany (the 'Triple Intervention'). Japan's resentment was not eased by the fact that shortly afterwards Russia obtained the Liaodong Peninsula as a leasehold territory from an increasingly enfeebled China. Although Japan's defeat of Russia in 1905 was initially hailed with enthusiasm in the United States and Britain as the victory of a plucky modernizing state over a backward but dangerously expansionist autocracy, suspicion soon crept in. The United States, itself an expanding Pacific power (having annexed Hawaii and the Philippines by the end of the nineteenth century), began to perceive Japan as a military rival whose hegemonic economic ambitions in south Manchuria threatened to undermine Washington's self-proclaimed Open Door doctrine (which advocated equality of economic opportunity amongst the powers). United States' suspicion of Japan's growing naval and economic power in East Asia was matched by its hostility towards Japanese emigration to Hawaii and California, which often played on racist fears of the 'yellow peril' (Iriye 1967).

Within Japan, too, ambivalence towards the West prevailed. The westernizing craze of the 1870s, during which everything from Western diet and clothing to art and architecture had been enthusiastically championed, gave way in the 1880s and 1890s to a more sober advocacy of selective borrowing on the one hand, and an impassioned plea for a return to traditional values as a means of preserving the 'national essence' on the other (Pyle 1989). An enhanced feeling of national self-confidence after the victories of 1895 and 1905, allied with the suspicion that the West did not fully accept Japan as an equal, meant that civil and military elites were often caught between the desire to abide by the rules of collective informal imperialism in China (Duus 1989) and the imperative of acting autonomously and decisively to protect the country's economic interests there.

Such a dilemma was inextricably linked with equally ambivalent attitudes towards China. For a while in the 1870s a debate occurred over Japan's approach to China – should the two countries join in a united front against the incursions of Western imperialism or should Japan cut itself free from identification with Asia and become a willing partner in the Western imperialist endeavour? Japan's apparently successful modernization drive led to increasing criticism of what was perceived as Chinese backwardness, so that by the 1880s government leaders and intellectuals were arguing that Japan needed to disassociate itself from China and join with the West in expanding its influence there. The Sino-Japanese War of 1894–5, in fact, was portrayed in the Japanese press as a struggle between the forces of progress and reaction. At the same time, however, attitudes towards China were coloured by a Pan-Asianist approach. Initially promoted by conspiratorial ultranationalist organizations, which cultivated personal ties with individual Diet members, military officers and business leaders and urged vigorous Japanese expansion in Asia without deferring to the West, Pan-Asianism implied that Japan had a duty to assist China in its development. Yet the concept was riddled with contradictions. While for some Japanese intellectuals Pan-Asianism underlined the need for genuine co-operation between the two countries, it more often became in the minds of militarists and politicians the rationale for Japan's right to exercise hegemony.

After 1905, when Japan gained a foothold on the Chinese mainland, policy towards China became closely bound up with domestic politics. Although no one questioned the country's gains in south Manchuria there was disagreement on how to preserve such gains, especially after 1911 when the fall of the monarchy in China led to political instability and the gradual breakdown of central control. While party-led governments during the 1920s favoured a policy of co-operation with the West in East Asia and were committed to principles of internationalism (symbolized by Japan's participation in the League of Nations after 1919 and adherence to the treaties signed at the Washington Conference in 1921–2, which guaranteed China's territorial integrity, called for open diplomacy and joint consultation amongst the powers, and prescribed lower naval quotas for Japan in comparison to those of the US and Britain), ultranationalists and elements within the military, particularly amongst units stationed in the Kwantung Peninsula, insisted on vigorous and autonomous expansion on the Chinese mainland. Such demands were often linked to a fierce condemnation of the domestic status quo.

The target of this attack by militarists and ultranationalists was the party-led governments and their business allies. The era of party government (1918–22, 1924–32), during which prime ministers and cabinet members (except for the heads of the service ministries, who continued to be nominated by the army and navy) belonged to the majority party in the Diet, has traditionally been regarded as the culmination of a protracted process of conflict and compromise between the *genro* and party leaders, as the latter sought to enhance their role and influence in the policy-making process (Najita 1967; Duus 1968). A recent study, however, has also emphasized the role of popular discontent in a wider movement of 'imperial democracy' that emerged after 1905 and in which urban workers, tenant farmers, feminists and intellectuals called for constitutional government attentive to the welfare of the people (Gordon 1991).

Yet at their moment of power the established political parties were fatally undermined by a combination of their innate conservatism, corruption, urban and rural unrest, economic crisis, and growing threats to Japan's interests in China. Although universal manhood suffrage was granted in 1925 the parties moved slowly on political and social reform, while personal links with the business conglomerates (the *zaibatsu*) that dominated the economy rendered them vulnerable to charges of corruption. The parties' image was further dented by their seeming inability to attend to the needs of an increasingly impoverished rural population hit by the effects of the Depression in the late 1920s (the collapse of the silk export trade, for example, removed a vital supplementary income for peasants). For ultranationalists and radical army officers (many of whom came from the affected rural areas) the political parties symbolized the general malaise they associated with the cosmopolitanism of parasitic cities, the growing attraction of intellectuals to alien Western ideas of democracy and socialism, and the breakdown of traditional values (emphasizing consensus and harmony) evident in the increasing number of urban strikes and tenant disputes after 1918.

Interestingly, it was bureaucrats within the Social Bureau of the Home Ministry who in the 1920s tended to champion more liberal labour policies with the aim of 'incorporating' workers and guaranteeing smooth industrial relations. These 'social policy bureaucrats' (Garon 1987) were behind proposals for labour union bills, workers' health insurance and conciliation procedures. Much of this legislation was blocked in the Diet by the more conservative of the two main parties, the *Seiyukai*, and during the 1930s, after the fall of party government, social policy bureaucrats emerged as 'renovationist' bureaucrats (*kakushin kanryo*) favouring a more arbitrary and state-oriented corporatism.

Party-led governments in the 1920s were also accused of failing to protect Japan's interests in China, where a growing tide of anti-imperialism calling for an end to unequal treaties and foreign privilege became particularly evident after 1925. In 1926, the Nationalist Party (*Guomindang*) under Chiang Kai-shek and its communist allies launched the Northern Expedition from its bastion in south China to defeat regional militarists, reunify the country and renegotiate the unequal treaties. The threat such developments posed for the Japanese presence in south Manchuria was exacerbated in the view of the Japanese military by the build-up of Soviet strength on the Manchurian border and ostensible Soviet Union support for the Chinese Communist Party. At the same time the Japanese navy, already dissatisfied with the naval restrictions agreed to at the Washington Conference in 1922, was to accuse the government of compromising Japan's naval hegemony in the Western Pacific at the London Naval Conference of 1930, which allowed the United States to attain parity with Japan in heavy cruisers (Crowley 1966).

Ironically, just as ultranationalist condemnation of the rules of informal imperialism (i.e. co-operation amongst the powers in China and the preservation of its territorial sovereignty) was becoming more blatant Japan had emerged, by 1930, as the major foreign presence in China, supplanting Britain in terms of direct investment, trade, the number of firms and numbers of foreign nationals (Duus 1989: 3). Yet it was precisely because Japan stood to lose the most in the wake of a reinvigorated Chinese nationalism (or the disorders arising from a prolonged civil war) that prompted militarists and ultranationalists to champion vigorous and unilateral action in China. At the same time junior army and navy officers formed or joined conspiratorial societies that organized a series of abortive coups in 1930–1 aimed at destroying the political and financial establishment and ushering in what was called a 'Showa Restoration', direct rule by the Emperor ('Showa' was the reign title of Emperor Hirohito, who had ascended the throne in 1926) which would 'cleanse' and unify the country and allow it to fulfil its rightful mission as the 'protector' of China.

The final collapse of party government occurred in 1932 as a result of the Manchurian crisis. In a classic case of 'sub-imperialism' the Japanese Kwantung Army, alarmed that the establishment of a new Chinese government under the Nationalists in 1928 would threaten Japan's treaty privileges in south Manchuria, created a sabotage incident in 1931 that provided the pretext for full-scale military action in Manchuria without the sanction of the civilian government in Tokyo. By 1932, Manchuria was under Japanese control and the puppet state of Manchukuo created. The Japanese government's desperate attempts to allay foreign criticism and rein in the action of the military led to another coup attempt by army officers in Tokyo which resulted in the assassination of the last party prime minister before 1945. Henceforth, cabinets were to be dominated by military leaders and bureaucrats.

During the 1930s governments became more authoritarian, with the military and renovationist bureaucrats increasingly calling for an emphasis on patriotism and unity at home and the implementation of widespread state economic controls in preparation for war abroad. After Japan's withdrawal from the League of Nations in 1933 in protest against international condemnation of Japanese aggression in Manchuria, foreign policy was marked by a desperate search for new arrangements in East Asia that would preserve and consolidate Japanese hegemony, an aim that was explicitly linked to Japan's own national security and economic prosperity (Crowley 1966). In the process, especially after 1936, Japan became increasingly estranged from the Anglo-American powers while fatefully becoming more identified with the Axis powers (Iriye 1987).

Following a local skirmish between Chinese and Japanese troops near Beijing in 1937, Japan launched a full-scale invasion in order, it was hoped, to settle the 'China Problem' once and for all. A New Order in East Asia was proclaimed the following year, envisaging Japanese hegemony over an autarchic bloc that would free the region from the influence of both Anglo-American liberalism and Soviet communism. The attempt was doomed from the start. Although Japanese armies captured the major Chinese cities and occupied large areas of northern and eastern China they did not secure the surrender of Chiang Kai-shek's Nationalist government, which retreated westwards to the province of Sichuan, nor could they suppress a vigorous guerrilla compaign by the Chinese communists from their bases in northwest China. Japanese troops were to remain bogged down in China for the next eight years. Although an ostensibly independent Chinese government was established in Nanjing under Japanese auspices in 1941, it never secured the widespread support of the Chinese people nor, indeed, the various Japanese field armies, which sponsored their own separatist regimes (Bunker 1971; Boyle 1972). At the same time Japan's continued dependence on resources such as oil, tin and rubber from areas outside the East Asian region, notably Southeast Asia (Beasley 1987), prompted increasing calls from the military to advance southwards, which would bring Japan into conflict with both the United States and the European colonial powers.

At home a New Order was also proclaimed, designed to unite all interests and occupation groups in society behind absolute loyalty to the Emperor, the national interest and mobilization for war. Political parties were dissolved in 1940 and replaced by an umbrella organization, the Imperial Rule Assistance Association, while labour unions were abolished and replaced by industrial patriotic units set up at the plant level and overseen by the government-controlled Greater Japan Industrial Patriotic Association. Press and media censorship was tightened, while schools were used to champion increasingly strident ultranationalist doctrines emphasizing the uniqueness and superiority of the Japanese imperial 'family-state'.

Considerable scholarly debate has arisen over the nature of wartime Japan. Maruyama Masao (1963) argued that in contrast to the mass-based fascist movements in Europe, Japan after 1936 witnessed fascism imposed from above, when the dominant Control (*Tosei*) faction within the army – favouring state-controlled economic mobilization for war – allied with the renovationist bureaucrats seeking to unite all interests in society in support of the nation's welfare. Others have underlined the 'traditionalist' content of Japanese fascism, whereby the military was able to manipulate a rural 'premodern collectivist ethic' (Beasley 1990) in securing acquiescence for its policies. Shillony (1981), however, has argued that the continued existence of the Diet (the 1889 constitution was never abrogated), the lack of a *fuhrer*-led mass-based party (the Imperial Rule Assistance Association was never able to fulfil this function), the inability of wartime Prime Minister Tojo Hideki to exert complete control over the military, bureaucracy (which survived intact) and even the judiciary, and the continued influence of the *zaibatsu*, made wartime Japan more of an authoritarian rather than a fascist state. More recent studies (Garon 1987; Gordon 1991), concentrating on the fate of the labour movement in Japan, have pointed to the direct influence that Nazi labour laws had on the measures adopted by bureaucrats and military planners after 1937, as well as the co-opting of labour in support of the repressive and expansionist aims of the military–bureaucratic regime, to demonstrate that Japan in the period 1937–45 did exhibit the features of a fascist state. Nevertheless, the militarist ideal of *ichioku* (one hundred hearts beating as one) was never fully realized during the war, as continuing rural discontent and absenteeism in the factories demonstrated (Dower 1993b: 101–54).

By the summer of 1941 Japan's advance into French Indo-China and the threat posed to the Dutch East Indies brought the country onto a collision course with the United States. The latter had progressively imposed embargoes on the sale to Japan of scrap iron, machine parts and oil, while in protracted negotiations that fateful summer Washington insisted on the withdrawal of Japanese troops from China as a *sine qua non* of an overall settlement, a condition that neither the Japanese government nor the military could accept. The Japanese navy, aware that the country's supply of oil was dangerously limited, urged a pre-emptive strike on the United States' navy at Pearl Harbour to free the way for the occupation of resource-rich Southeast Asia (Iriye 1987).

Following the attack on Pearl Harbour on 7 December 1941 (which, ironically, did not succeed in crippling the US carrier fleet) Japanese armies quickly overran the Dutch East Indies, the British colonies of Hong Kong, Malaya, Singapore and Burma, and the American-controlled Philippines (formerly an American colony, the Philippines had been granted 'commonwealth' status in 1935 with the promise of full independence in 1945). A 'Greater East Asia Co-Prosperity Sphere' was proclaimed, but despite the grandiose rhetoric promising the region freedom from the political and cultural shackles of white colonialism and the creation of a more equal and harmonious order amongst Asian peoples under the all-pervasive benevolence of the Japanese Emperor, the reality was very different. There was no existing blueprint for the implementation of a uniform Japanese administration of the conquered territories, with the result that control was exercised by individual field army commands; co-ordination with Tokyo always remained weak (Beasley 1987). Although some nationalist leaders imprisoned by the former colonial authorities were freed and a limited amount of political activity (under close Japanese supervision) was allowed, it soon became clear that the region was primarily meant to serve Japan's military needs. Resort to conscript labour was widespread and local economies distorted in order to serve Japan's interests (Benda 1967; Lebra 1975; McCoy 1980). Racial harmony was belied by official propaganda, which trumpeted the merits of the Japanese race in bringing salvation to the benighted and backward peoples of Asia.

Once the tide of war in the Pacific had turned against Japan at the end of 1942, even the benefits to Japan of the Greater East Asia Co-Prosperity Sphere gradually diminished. With the shortage of shipping and personnel, and the increasing vulnerability of Japanese convoys to American attacks from the air, the hoped-for bonanza in resources never materialized. By the last months of the war, despite the granting of formal independence to some countries (Burma, Philippines, Indonesia) there was widespread hostility towards the Japanese; mutinies even broke out amongst the army units that had been created by the Japanese military (Lebra 1977).

As American forces captured Japanese-held islands in the Pacific, Japan itself became the target of American aerial bombardment, culminating in the dropping of two atomic bombs on Hiroshima and Nagasaki in August 1945. In the same month the

Soviet Union, reneging on its 1941 neutrality pact with Japan, declared war and quickly overran Manchukuo. The stage was set for Japan's surrender and an extraordinary change of direction in the country's modern history.

2

The American Interregnum (1945–1952)

On 15 August 1945 a war-weary and demoralized Japanese people heard for the first time the voice of their Emperor, Hirohito (r.1926–89), announcing over the radio the country's decision to surrender to allied forces:

> After pondering deeply the general trends of the world, and the actual conditions obtaining to our Empire today, We have decided to effect a settlement of the present situation by resorting to an extraordinary measure. We have ordered our Government to communicate to the Governments of the United States, Great Britain, China and the Soviet Union that our Empire accepts the provisions of their Joint Declaration. . . . Despite the best that has been done by everyone . . . the war situation has developed not nec- essarily to Japan's advantage, while the general trends of the world have all turned against her interest. (Cited in Morris-Suzuki 1984: 184–5)

In archaic and euphemistic court language the Emperor called on the people to 'endure what is difficult to endure, and to suffer what is difficult to suffer' (Shillony 1981: 87), thereby acknowledging that Japan's attempt to create an empire in Asia, an endeavour begun with the invasion of China in 1937, had been an unmitigated disaster for the country. It had also proved catastrophic for the peoples of East and Southeast Asia. As a recent study notes (Dower 1986: 295–6), the official statistics on military casualties overlook the numbers of those who died as a result of forced labour, famine and economic chaos in the wake of the Japanese occupation. At least ten million died in China; 300,000 Indonesian labourers perished; in Vietnam nearly one million died from starvation in 1945 alone as a result of occupation policies; and up to 70,000 Koreans died, victims of either atomic bombings or forced labour while in Japan, or while serving as conscripts in the Japanese army.

Japanese army casualties amounted to over one and a half million, while naval casualties totalled 420,000 dead or missing; in addition, 31,000 merchant seamen were killed in action (Coox 1988: 376–7). The condition of the army was so parlous by the end of the war, moreover, that 81,000 personnel died overseas after the ceasefire and before they could be repatriated (Dower 1986: 298).

More significant, however, was the number of Japanese civilian deaths as a result of air-raids, atomic bombings, mass suicides, hunger and disease. Civilian deaths due to air-raids on the Japanese home islands totalled nearly 400,000 (compared to 300,000 in Germany). Although tonnage dropped on Japan was less than that dropped on Germany, the denser housing in Japanese cities, for the most part built of wood, led to greater casualties. A fire-bomb raid on 9 March 1945, involving the use of 2,000 tons of bombs, left 83,793 dead (Hane 1992: 326), while up to 100,000 perished in Tokyo during the fire-bomb raid of 10 May 1945 (Havens 1978: 176, 181; Ienaga 1979: 199). From November 1944, in fact, bombing raids on Japan forced mass evacuation from the cities. Ultimately, ten million urban residents had to flee to the countryside, and by the end of the war the six largest cities had lost over one-half of their 1940 populations. Nearly 4.25 million people left Tokyo alone during the last year of the war (Havens 1978: 167). The atomic bombs dropped on Hiroshima (6 August 1945) and Nagasaki (9 August 1945) claimed over 200,000 lives; people continued to die well beyond 1945 because of radiation sickness. Between 1986–7, for example, 4,619 died in Hiroshima and 2,539 in Nagasaki (Kanda 1989: xiii).

The traumas, human misery and devastation in the wake of the atomic bombings have been dramatically and poignantly illustrated by interviews with survivors (Kanda 1989), in pictorial art (Dower 1988; 1993b: 242–56) and in Japanese literature, most notably in Ibuse Masuji's (1979) novel *Black Rain*. Drawn from actual records and interviews, the novel provides a horrifying close-up of the atomic impact. Just after the explosion at Hiroshima, for example, the novel's principal protagonist, Shigematsu Shizuma, surveys the scene around him:

The people in the street by the shrine grounds were all covered over their heads and shoulders with something resembling dust or ash. There was not one of them who was not bleeding. They bled from the head, from the face, from the hands; those who went naked bled from the chest, from the back, from the thighs, from any place from which it was possible to bleed. One woman, her cheeks so swollen that they dropped on either side in heavy pouches, walked with her arms stretched out before her, hands drooping forlornly, like a ghost. (Ibuse 1979: 44)

Shigematsu himself has not escaped the impact:

I ran my hands over my face. The left hand came away wet and sticky. I looked and found the left palm had something bluish purple like little shreds of damp paper on it. I stroked my cheek again, and again some sticky substance came off on my hand. (Ibid.: 45–6)

Japanese civilian casualties overseas were also often overlooked in official figures. In Manchuria and China 170,000 civilians are thought to have died. In the context of what one historian (Dower 1986) describes as a racial conflict between the United States and Japan, civilians living on occupied Pacific islands, accustomed to hearing about the bestiality of American troops, committed suicide rather than surrender during the final stages of the war; on Saipan, for example, 10,000 died in this way. Nearer home, on the island of Okinawa (annexed by Japan in 1879) over 100,000 civilians perished in addition to 110,000 troops (Dower 1986: 45, 299; Coox 1988: 376–7; Hane 1992: 330–1; Dower 1993b: 121).

Disease and the prospects of famine were also ever present in the wake of Japan's surrender. Already in 1944, one year before the end of the war, Japan had suffered a 17 per cent reduction in average daily calories per civilian since 1941, compared with a 2 per cent reduction in Britain and gains of 1 per cent and 4 per cent in Germany and the United States respectively (Havens 1978: 130). During the last years of the war people were urged to eat chickweed and thistle, while plans were made to produce pulverized food from potato stems, mulberry leaves, wild plants and the residue of soybeans and peanuts. By June 1946, the inhabitants of Tokyo were receiving in their ration only 150 calories a day, one-tenth of what was required to keep alive and a mere 7 per cent of the prewar intake of 2,260 calories a day (Cohen 1987: 142). The desperate food situation (rice production, for example, was down

32 per cent compared to the prewar average) after the surrender was graphically demonstrated by a judge who resolved to live entirely on his official rations; within months he had died of malnutrition (Morris-Suzuki 1984: 196). Epidemic disease was also a threat. By 1946 there were over 30,000 cases of typhoid on the Japanese home islands.

The American journalist, Mark Gayn, arriving in Japan with the American occupation army, gave a vivid description of the desolation around Yokohama, on the approach road to Tokyo:

> Before us as far as we could see, lay miles of rubble. The people looked ragged and distraught. They dug into the debris to clear space for new shacks. . . . The skeletons of railway cars and locomotives remained untouched on the tracks. . . . Gutted buses and automobiles lay abandoned on the roadside. . . . There was plenty of traffic, but all of it was American and military. The Japanese trudged by, swallowed in the dust, and seeming not to care. (Gayn 1981: 1–2)

The Potsdam Declaration and the Structure of the American Occupation

The formal origins of United States postwar policy towards Japan are usually attributed to the Potsdam Declaration, issued on 26 July 1945 by the United States, Britain and China and which called on Japan to surrender or face 'prompt and utter destruction'. The Declaration made it clear that Japan would be occupied after the surrender until all its war-making potential was destroyed and peace and security established. In the process, Japan was to be divested of its overseas empire, the country's industry was to be restricted sufficiently to prevent rearmament, all obstacles to the development of democratic tendencies were to be removed, and Japanese 'war criminals' were to face trial. The Declaration, omitting specific references to what might be done with the Japanese Emperor, went on to state that the occupying forces would be withdrawn when 'a peacefully inclined and responsible government' had been established (Hane 1992: 335). Crucially, the Declaration also noted that Japan was not to be divided up into zones of occupation, as was to be the case with Germany. As will be noted later, it was assumed, moreover, that the occupation would primarily be an American one.

It was over the precise issue of the Emperor (i.e. no guarantees that the imperial institution would be preserved) that made the Japanese government initially reluctant to accept the terms of unconditional surrender. This, despite the fact that after July 1944, when Prime Minister Tojo Hideki had been compelled to resign, his successors Koiso Kuniaki (July 1944–April 1945) and Admiral Suzuki Kantaro (April–August 1945) had been exploring ways to end the war, including the use of Soviet mediation. Behind this search lay real fears that a prolongation of the war and its increasingly disastrous effects on the lives of the Japanese people would lead to left-wing revolution at home led by army radicals (Shillony 1981; Welfield 1988). Although Washington replied to Tokyo's request for clarification on the Emperor issue that both the Emperor and government would be subject to the occupation authorities and that the 'ultimate form of government would be established by the freely expressed will of the Japanese people' (Hane 1992: 337), there was still deadlock in Tokyo; the army insisted on continuation of the war while Prime Minister Suzuki advised acceptance of the surrender terms. It was the personal intervention of Emperor Hirohito on 14 August 1945 that settled the matter in favour of surrender. Despite a desperate attempt by a few middle-ranking army officers from the imperial guards division in Tokyo on the night of 14 August to destroy the recording of the Emperor's surrender speech, the broadcast went ahead the following day (Large 1992: 126–9).

It is important to note, however, that the broad principles of occupation policy outlined in the Potsdam Declaration represented the culmination of considerable debate amongst US planners concerning postwar policy towards Japan that had begun as early as 1943 (Ward 1987a). An extreme view was that Japan and its people were to be destroyed; such a view drew on wartime racial stereotypes that had portrayed the Japanese as unpredictable primitives and adolescents at best, and as vermin, rodents and apes at worst (Dower 1986). During the war even Roosevelt and Churchill had taken seriously hare-brained racial theories that claimed skull size was proof of Japanese inferiority (Thorne 1978: 7–8, 158–9). An adviser to the State–War–Navy Coordinating Committee (SWNCC), a body set up in December 1944 to co-ordinate future postwar policy, proposed 'the almost total annihilation of the Japanese as a race', while just after the surrender a Democratic senator urged the sterilization of all Japanese (Schaller 1985: 3–4). As

Dower (1986; 1993: 257–85) points out, however, even the extreme stereotypes that had fed race hatred during the war were to be adapted to the new situation of the occupation. Thus, in American journals of the time the wartime simian image of the Japanese became one of a clever, imitative and domesticated pet, while the portrayal of the Japanese as good pupils of their American teachers was an adaptation of the wartime metaphor of the Japanese as children.

The prevailing view, particularly amongst State Department officials with prewar experience or knowledge of Japan such as Joseph Grew (ambassador to Japan 1932–1941), and who together with other prominent public and business people have been loosely described as the Japan Lobby (Schonberger 1989), was that postwar policy towards Japan should be constructive, enabling it to be integrated into the world community as soon as possible. Since they also blamed the Japanese military solely for the war, they urged the retention of the Emperor as a way of ensuring domestic stability and of rallying the support of those liberal elements within Japan that had promised so much in the 1920s before being overwhelmed by an aggressive and jingoistic militarism.

Recent studies (Iriye 1981; Borden 1984) have argued that such views were not unusual given the significant economic ties between Japan and the United States before the war. As late as 1939, for example, the United States accounted for 18.4 per cent of Japan's export trade and 38.7 per cent of its import trade (Hane 1992: 297). The desire to restore that economic relationship clearly influenced those who urged a constructive policy towards Japan. Iriye (1981), in fact, goes on to argue that in the last year of the war there were parallels in American and Japanese thinking (particularly amongst bureaucrats and traditional conservatives such as Yoshida Shigeru, who was to become prime minister during the occupation period) concerning ultimate peace objectives, focused on the desire to resurrect the internationalism of the 1920s. As he remarks (ibid.: 120):

> In essence both sides recognized the need for some modification of the existing arrangements along the lines of mutuality, cooperation, economic development, prosperity, autonomy and self-determination, ideals that went back to the shared Wilsonian internationalism of the 1920s.

In March 1944 the newly formed Postwar Programmes Committee under the State Department reported that it favoured a nearly exclusive American occupation as well as supporting the idea that the Japanese government was to be used and the Emperor retained. Once the country was 'reformed' Japan was to be allowed to rejoin the Asian-Pacific community. Such thinking was confirmed by the plan formulated by the SWNCC's sub-committee on the Far East in April 1945, which again envisaged exclusive American occupation, utilization of the Japanese government, democratization and economic reform (but with no dismantling of heavy industry). The sub-committee supported retaining the Emperor and in fact the original Potsdam Declaration allowed for a constitutional monarchy; the idea was dropped due to fears of a hostile American public opinion as well as to opposition voiced in the Senate and amongst the military, who wanted to leave open the possibility of trying the Emperor as a war criminal.

When General Douglas MacArthur arrived in Japan on 30 August 1945 in his capacity as Supreme Commander for the Allied Powers (SCAP), the question of the Emperor was therefore unresolved. The broad principles outlined in the Potsdam Declaration had also to be fleshed out. How far democratic and economic reform was to be taken, for example, was still a thorny issue. While people like Joseph Grew (Under-Secretary of State 1944–5) argued for minimal change other than the removal of the military, others who were to become involved in the planning or implementation of the occupation (such as T. A. Bisson) insisted that the militarism of the 1930s, far from being an aberration, was a logical outcome of the authoritarian and anti-democratic tendencies that had characterized Japanese politics and society since the end of the nineteenth century. Such tendencies could only be eliminated by deep-seated reforms (Schonberger 1989). Such an idea was also attractive to many New Dealers within as well as outside the State Department – for them the occupation provided a unique opportunity to construct a democratic and more just society.

For the Japanese government, now headed by the Emperor's cousin, Prince Higashikuni, much also remained unclear. In a situation described by the Japanese press as 'one hundred million people in a state of trauma' (Morris-Suzuki 1984: 196) and in which the people had been led to believe by the propaganda of their military leaders that the invading Americans would kill all the men and ship off all the women into prostitution, it was hardly surprising that the enormous relief felt with the ending of the war would be tempered by anxiety and trepidation. In the event, the arrival of MacArthur and the signing of the formal surrender on board the

USS *Missouri* on 2 September 1945 proceeded without mishap. In the ensuing years a bold experiment took place, as an occupying power working through an indigenous government attempted to remould a whole society. It was to be a complex process. Recent research (Borden 1984; Schaller 1985; Ward 1987b; Schonberger 1989), making use of newly available archival material, has revealed how much the Japanese government itself was able to influence the course of events, how Prime Minister Yoshida Shigeru skilfully exploited deep divisions amongst American occupation officials over reform policies, the tussle between MacArthur and Washington over the control and direction of the occupation, and, finally, how closely US policy towards Japan was linked with American strategic and economic concerns in East and Southeast Asia.

In theory, MacArthur was acting on behalf of the allied powers, who were to formulate policies through the eleven-member Far Eastern Commission in Washington. A four-power Allied Council, established in Tokyo in December 1945 and comprising representatives from the United States, the British Commonwealth, the Soviet Union and China, was meant to liaise with MacArthur (Kawai 1960). A recent study (Buckley 1982) also argues that there was substantial British participation in the occupation on the rather flimsy evidence that a small British Commonwealth force (comprising British, Indian, Australian and New Zealand troops) was stationed in Japan alongside the much larger American military presence and that British officials frequently took issue with US policy.

In reality, however, the occupation was entirely run by MacArthur and his American-staffed bureaucracy (referred to as SCAP) reporting directly to his military superiors in Washington (Buckley 1990: 7). Comprising four General and nine Special Staff sections (all headed by military officers), SCAP by 1948 employed over 5,000 people. Two of the most important General Staff sections were Government Section (GS) under Major-General Courtney Whitney, which worked with the Japanese government in drafting legislation and implementing reforms, and the Economic and Scientific Section (ESS) under Major-General William Marquat, which supervised taxation and trade regulations. The Japanese foreign ministry established a Central Liaison Office to mediate between SCAP and the Japanese bureaucracy, while SCAP civil affairs teams (mainly staffed by military officials) were sent throughout the country to oversee local administration.

MacArthur himself remained an aloof figure, rarely emerging from his headquarters in downtown Tokyo or meeting with any Japanese except for the Prime Minister. Theodore Cohen, head of the Labour Division that was to draw up trade union legislation, later remarked, 'For more than five years, with the rarest of exceptions, the only thing MacArthur saw of Japan physically was on the automobile route between the Daiichi Building and his quarters at the American embassy, a distance of about a mile' (Cohen 1987: 66). He was driven, nevertheless, by a crusading zeal to reform Japanese society. In a radio broadcast to the American public on 2 September 1945, MacArthur likened himself to Commodore Perry, whose naval expedition in 1853 had forced Japan to abandon its isolationist stance. Just as Perry's expedition symbolized the beginning of Japan's exposure to advanced Western civilization, so the American occupation in 1945 would provide Japan with a second chance to imbibe the democratic values of the West (i.e. the United States): 'Today, freedom is on the offensive, democracy is on the march. Today, in Asia as well as in Europe, unshackled peoples are tasting the full sweetness of liberty, the relief from fear' (cited in Nishi 1982: 40–1).

It was no coincidence that MacArthur's crusading zeal was accompanied by enthusiastic encouragement of Christian proselytization in Japan. Missionaries were welcomed into Japan and bibles widely distributed. The use of SCAP personnel and resources to encourage Christian proselytizing activities ironically contradicted one of the aims of the occupation's democratizing reforms, the guarantee of religious freedom (Moore 1979). Hopes for a massive Christian conversion, however, were to remain unfulfilled. The number of Japanese Christians as of December 1948 – 342,607 (0.6 per cent of the population) – remained the same as before the war (Nishi 1982: 43). Underpinning MacArthur's idealistic impulse was an enormous condescension towards the Japanese people. Reflecting on the occupation in 1951, MacArthur implied that the Japanese had been content to follow the US because of their slavish mentality of adulating a winner. In the process they could not help but be impressed with American values of justice and democracy, a result that was inevitable because the Japanese were not as 'developed' as their Western counterparts:

If the Anglo-Saxon was, say, forty-five years of age in development, in the sciences, the arts, divinity, culture, the Germans were quite as mature. The Japanese, however, in spite of their antiquity measured by time were in a very tuitionary condition. Measured by the standards of modern civilization, they would be like a boy of twelve as compared with our development of forty-five years. (Cited in Johnson 1972: 9–10)

Although most attention has been focused on the subsequent reforms undertaken by SCAP it should not be forgotten that Japan was under effective American military control, with all the restrictions such a status implied. The 400,000-strong US Eighth Army was stationed in Japan; its numbers fell to 125,000 in 1948 and then increased to 250,000 during the Korean War (1950–2). As will be noted later, the Security Treaty signed between the US and Japan in 1951 allowed for the continued stationing of American troops in Japan and it was not to be until 1957 that their number fell below 100,000 (Johnson 1988: 75–6). Throughout the occupation period foreign visitors to Japan were carefully screened and Japanese overseas travel curtailed.

More significant, however, was the vigorous censorship SCAP imposed on the press, radio, communications (domestic and external) and the cinema. The press, in particular, was singled out. Ironically making use of the very same institutions that had censored the Japanese press during the war (the Police Bureau of the Home Ministry and the Cabinet Information Bureau), SCAP's Civil Intelligence Section ensured that no unfavourable opinion on the occupation and its policies was published (Braw 1991). This included any reference to the fact that SCAP was making decisions on behalf of the Japanese government; rather, SCAP was to be presented as simply giving advice. The five major Tokyo newspapers were soon subject to precensorship and by January 1946 670 newspaper articles had been banned (Nishi 1982: 101). Any discussion of the effects of the atomic bombings was also prohibited, on the grounds that it would imply criticism of the allied powers. Public relief measures for atomic victims were also discouraged by occupation authorities (Kamata and Salaff 1988). The first Japanese manuscripts on the subject were not declassified until January 1949 (Braw 1991: 131) and it was only then that serious research could be undertaken into how to treat survivors of the atomic explosions.

SCAP's Civil and Information Section, in addition to utilizing radio, film and the schools to 'remake' Japanese thinking, was also responsible for the confiscation of prewar Japanese literature that contained military propaganda. Even foreign books translated into Japanese were subject to scrutiny. Erskine Caldwell's *Tobacco Road*, for example, was banned because it depicted the seamier aspects of American society (Nishi 1982: 103). Censorship was not formally ended until October 1949. It should be noted, however, that certain forms of popular culture, in contrast to the cinema or the press, were able to evade censorship quite successfully. By December 1945, for example, SCAP had banned 225 films out of 554 reviewed; many of the films banned were those of the *jidaigeki* (period film) genre depicting the heroic deeds of samurai, and hence guilty in SCAP's view of promoting feudal thinking (Anderson and Richie 1982: 160–3). Yet small-scale itinerant popular theatre (*taishu engeki*), often performed in roofless shacks in the countryside, continued to depict dramatic tales of samurai heroism and loyalty (Ivy 1993: 246).

Finally, throughout the occupation SCAP's Military Intelligence Section (G-2) under Major-General Charles Willoughby, maintained an extensive surveillance on Japanese radicals and communists as well as reporting critically on American reformers within SCAP itself suspected of having pro-communist sympathies. Willoughby, who was to become an adviser to General Franco in the early 1950s, employed former Japanese military intelligence officers and discredited ultranationalists to work on SCAP's behalf (Welfield 1988: 67–9). Even American journalists, such as Mark Gayn of the *Chicago Sun*, ran foul of the occupation authorities when they criticized aspects of the occupation or reported sympathetically on popular demonstrations against the Japanese government.

Occupation Reforms, the Revival of Politics, and the Struggles of Japanese Labour

The agenda for the occupation, known as the 'Initial Post-Surrender Policy for Japan' and approved by President Truman on 6 September 1945, was sent to MacArthur without informing or consulting the allies (in 1947 it was to be formally adopted by the Far Eastern Commission). MacArthur was instructed to implement both punitive measures and democratizing reforms (Livingston, Moore and Oldfather 1973: 7–11). The former included the demobilization of all Japanese armed forces, the carrying out of war crimes trials, the dissolution of the *zaibatsu*, and a purge of all public figures known to have sympathized or worked with the pre-1945 military regime.

The most dramatic of the punitive measures undertaken was the setting up of the International Military Tribunal of the Far East to try high-level military and political leaders on the pattern of the Nuremburg War Crimes Trials that were then being carried out in Germany (Kawai 1960). By the time proceedings opened in May 1946 the question of the Emperor had been resolved. Although the Joint Chiefs of Staff in Washington had instructed MacArthur in November 1945 to gather information and evidence relating to the Emperor's possible war guilt, MacArthur insisted that to put the Emperor on trial would provoke widescale resistance in Japan and would possibly lead to a guerrilla war against the occupying American forces. He also argued that the preservation of the imperial institution would provide the necessary stability at a time of dramatic change. A recent article notes that from the very beginning of the occupation, in fact, both MacArthur and the Japanese government had vested interests in shielding the Emperor from war responsibility; MacArthur wanted to use the Emperor to legitimize occupation reforms, while Japanese government leaders and court officials wanted to preserve the imperial institution (Bix 1995). It was an arrangement with which the Emperor himself was happy to go along, so that the relationship between the occupation authorities and the Emperor was one of 'expediency and mutual protection'. Significantly, in the first opinion poll held on the issue of the Emperor (itself an unprecedented event), 95 per cent of the Japanese people favoured keeping him on the throne (Horsley and Buckley 1990: 15). In January 1946 Emperor Hirohito himself took the step of formally renouncing his divinity and the matter was subsequently laid to rest with SCAP's draft constitution of March 1946, which referred to the Emperor as ceremonial head of state (see later).

During the opening proceedings of the war crimes trial in May 1946 the 11 justices representing the 11 victorious allied nations charged 28 defendants (classified as Class A War Criminals) with crimes against humanity and conspiracy to wage aggressive war. They included 14 generals (one of whom was Tojo Hideki, the wartime prime minister), three admirals and five career diplomats. Konoe Fumimaro, prime minister at the time of Japan's invasion of China in 1937, was also indicted but had committed suicide before he could be brought to trial. The sentences, pronounced in November 1948, prescribed death for seven of the defendants (including Tojo Hideki and Hirota Koki, a prewar foreign minister), life imprisonment for 16 and shorter terms of imprisonment for two wartime foreign ministers (Togo Shigenori and Shigemitsu Mamoru). Two defendants died during the trial while the remaining one (Okawa Shumei, the ultranationalist propagandist) was declared insane (Hane 1992: 345–6). Other trials were carried out at the same time of Class B (high-ranking officers) and Class C (lesser-ranking officers) in Japan and various countries in Southeast Asia (Bowring and Kornicki 1993: 106–7). By the time the trials ended in 1951 over 4,000 had been convicted, of whom 920 were executed.

Of those imprisoned Shigemitsu Mamoru was the first to be released in November 1950. He went on to become foreign minister in 1954 and was able in subsequent years to negotiate with the US government for the release of all those still in prison. As will be discussed later, while there was little public reaction in Japan at the time of the trials and execution of the Tokyo defendants, controversy was to arise in the 1970s and 1980s when some conservative politicians sought to rehabilitate the reputations of Japan's wartime militarists.

Two English-language accounts of the Tokyo War Crimes Trials adopt radically different viewpoints. Brackman (1989), a United Press correspondent who covered most of the proceedings, insisted that the trials were legitimate and the verdicts justified. Citing the opinion of the UN War Crimes Commission in early 1945 that the actions of the Japanese army were not individual and isolated incidents but were 'deliberately planned and systematically perpetrated throughout the Far East and Pacific', Brackman regards one of the key assumptions underpinning the trials (that the political and military leadership were responsible for all atrocities committed by Japanese forces) as entirely correct. Minear (1971), however, as the title of his work suggests, questioned the legality and morality of the trials altogether. In terms of international law he cast doubt especially on the charge levied against the Tokyo defendants of conspiracy to wage aggressive war, a conspiracy that supposedly began in 1928 with the abortive attempt by the

Japanese Kwantung Army to effect a military take-over of Manchuria. Such a charge grossly oversimplified the events of the late 1920s and 1930s. Significantly, the one judge to have a background in international law, Justice Pal of India, issued a dissenting opinion acquitting the defendants on the grounds that no conspiracy had been proved, the rules of evidence had been slanted in favour of the prosecution and that aggressive war was not a crime in international law.

The morality of the trials was also undermined by the fact that in addition to the arbitrary selection of those to be tried (the 26 defendants were chosen from an original total of 250 high-ranking officials in Allied custody) the members of the notorious Unit 731 in Manchuria (euphemistically designated the Water Purification Unit) that had tested plague, cholera, typhoid and frostbite on live, mainly Chinese, prisoners, were never indicted. On the contrary, the US military made use of their expertise in its own work on biological warfare (Ienaga 1979: 188–9; Powell 1980; Welfield 1988: 67–9).

In addition to war crimes trials there was an extensive purge of military officers, government officials, party politicians and business leaders thought to have actively supported or sympathized with the aims of the wartime regime. By May 1948 up to 220,000 had been affected. Crucially, however, the bureaucracy remained virtually intact. Thus, while 80 per cent of military personnel and 16 per cent of the prewar Diet were purged, less than 1 per cent of civil servants were affected (Halliday 1975: 173; Fukui 1988: 181). This has been attributed to SCAP's insistence that a competent and efficient bureaucracy was needed to implement reform, as well as to pre-existing American assumptions that bureaucracies were fundamentally apolitical in nature (Pempel 1987). Many of the renovationist bureaucrats who had served within the labour and police divisions of the prewar Home Ministry continued to serve in public life after 1945. When the Home Ministry was abolished in 1947, in line with SCAP's policy of decentralizing powers, and its functions dispersed amongst various ministries and agencies, prewar labour bureaucrats went on to form the core of the newly created Labour Ministry (Garon 1984; 1987). Significantly, this bureaucratic continuity was particularly noticeable in labour legislation. The drafters of the Trade Union Law of 1945 and the Labour Standards Law of 1947 (see later) were the same people who had been involved in drafting labour union bills in the 1920s.

As before, concern was shown to combine the guarantee of basic union rights with government supervision and control (to ensure, amongst other things, a depoliticized labour movement), a prewar ideal of the renovationist bureaucrats and one with which the American authorities could well identify (Garon 1987). As late as 1969, the vice-minister and key bureau chiefs within the Labour Ministry came from amongst the core group that had entered the Home and Welfare Ministries at the height of the Pacific War, while Nakasone Yasuhiro's cabinet of 1982 contained four veterans of the prewar Home Ministry, all of whom combined experience of labour administration with extensive police work (Garon 1984). Of the 14 Home Ministry bureaucrats in charge of police activity during the 1935–45 period, seven were to serve in the postwar Diet (van Wolferen 1989: 359). In some cases, too, prewar officials in the Home Ministry's Special Police Section (*Tokko*) resigned and were then reassigned to different ministries. The journalist Mark Gayn discovered in September 1945 that the head of a thought police unit before 1945 had been purged one day and reassigned the following day as a liaison officer between the Japanese and a local American army unit (Gayn 1981: 68–9).

Other aspects of the punitive programme, such as the dismantling of heavy industry, the imposition of reparations and the dissolution of the *zaibatsu* monopolies, were shelved or modified. This was due to opposition from a variety of quarters. Japanese political and business elites argued that such measures would further destabilize the economy, making Japan not only permanently dependent on US aid but also vulnerable to communist revolution at home. This argument received sympathetic support from elements within SCAP itself, particularly the Economic and Science Section (ESS) and Military Intelligence Section (G-2), which always remained suspicious of the reformist zeal of SCAP's Government Section (GS), the principal supporters of the anti-*zaibatsu* programme. At the same time various American business and financial interests, especially those that had been heavily involved in the Japanese economy before the war and were anxious to restore profitable trade relationships, condemned the programme as dangerously socialistic and a threat to the revival of a prosperous economy. Finally, and most crucially, changing strategic priorities formulated after 1947 within the State and Defense Departments, which favoured the rehabilitation of the Japanese economy, increasingly dampened Washington's enthusiasm for anti-monopoly legislation. The issue itself was also inextricably linked with the growing tussle between Washington and MacArthur over the direction of occupation policy.

The recommendations of the Pauley Commission in late 1945, for example, calling for the reduction of heavy industrial production (in shipbuilding, steel and chemicals) and the imposition of reparations in the form of large-scale industrial transfers to the rest of Asia (Livingston, Moore and Oldfather 1973: 83–5; Borden 1984: 66) were soon shelved. Pauley had envisaged a radical restructuring of the Japanese economy, which would have resulted in Japan concentrating on food production and light industry interacting with new industrial exporters in Asia (Schaller 1985: 38). The Japanese economy at this time, however, was in a parlous state. Although SCAP's original mandate was simply to prevent disease and unrest, by the spring of 1946 it was already importing 800,000 tons of grain to alleviate the food crisis. Such grain imports contributed to the spiralling costs of the occupation, which totalled $900 million by 1949. The need, therefore, to relieve the American taxpayer, combined with the changing strategic priorities of the American government, would ultimately encourage quite a different approach, that of rehabilitating Japan as an industrial exporter to Southeast Asia (Borden 1984). Eventually, less than 30 per cent of industrial facilities declared surplus by the FEC were dismantled or transferred (Halliday 1975: 177), while the reparations programme itself was officially terminated in May 1949. After 1952, when the occupation ended, Japan would enter into bilateral agreements with various Southeast Asian governments that often tied reparation payments to Japanese overseas aid or loans. By April 1964, Japan had paid out $477 million as reparations to six Southeast Asian countries (Hane 1992: 346).

The most significant modification of the original punitive programme concerned the break-up of monopolies. In November 1945, MacArthur had agreed to the plan put forward by the head of the Yasuda *zaibatsu* for voluntary and limited deconcentration of the *zaibatsu*, the huge trading, industrial and financial conglomerates that had dominated the prewar economy (Livingston, Moore and Oldfather 1973: 78–82). It is estimated, for example, that the ten major *zaibatsu* (including Yasuda, Mitsui and Mitsubishi), through 67 holding companies and over 4,000 operating subsidiaries, controlled 75 per cent of Japan's prewar commercial, industrial and financial activities (Schonberger 1975: 16). The Yasuda plan provided for the dissolution of the major holding companies and the sale of family shares to be supervised by a Holding Company Liquidation Commission. It did not, however, allow for the break-up of the large operating subsidiaries, nor did it firmly guarantee a permanent and wide distribution of *zaibatsu* assets.

The plan was soon superseded by a far more radical approach following the report of the Edwards Mission to Japan in January 1946. The report was adopted by the SWNCC later that year and forwarded to SCAP as an interim directive. It was subsequently submitted to the Far Eastern Commission and formally adopted in May 1947. Known as FEC-230, the report reflected the firm belief of Corwin Edwards (an economist and government adviser on cartels) that the vigorous dismantling of all monopolies (domestic and international) was the key to a revived world economy. Accordingly, he called for the dissolution of all excessive concentrations of economic power. In line with the thrust of the report MacArthur prodded the Japanese government into passing the Anti-Monopoly Law in April 1947 (prohibiting the formation of trusts and interlocking corporate controls, as well as establishing a Fair Trade Commission) and a Deconcentration Law in December 1947. The latter designated over 300 companies for dissolution. At the same time MacArthur pushed ahead with plans for an extensive purge of business leaders.

Ironically, however, by the time the Deconcentration Law was passed Washington had already clearly changed tack. In May 1947 the Assistant Secretary of State, Dean Acheson, reflecting the growing American disillusion with the hopelessly corrupt National-ist regime in China and its prospects for survival against Mao Zedong's communist forces, pointed to the important role Japan would play in East and Southeast Asia as the 'workshop of Asia'; rehabilitation of the Japanese economy would take priority over unnecessary reform. Opposition to MacArthur's programme from both Japanese conservatives such as Yoshida Shigeru (prime min-ister five times between 1946 and 1954 and linked by marriage to the Mitsubishi *zaibatsu*) and the Japan Lobby in the US was given credence by the recommendations of the Draper Mission in early 1948. William Draper, the Under-Secretary of the army and a leading Wall Street banker, urged MacArthur to go slow on the purge and to wind down the dissolution programme.

MacArthur saw this opposition from Washington as a direct attack on his control of occupation policy although, as one historian has pointed out (Schonberger 1989), his championing of 'economic democracy' had as much to do with his presidential ambitions back home. By the end of 1948 MacArthur's influence was on the wane. His attempt to secure the Republican nomination for president in June 1948 was a dismal failure, while his strongest supporters for the dissolution programme within SCAP's Government Section, such as T. A. Bisson (accused of having communist sympathies by SCAP's Intelligence Section), had resigned. Draper's hand-picked Deconcentration Review Board overturned or amended most of the 300-plus reorganization directives issued by the Holding Company Liquidation Commission. Ultimately, only nine corporations were slated for dissolution. Although overall 83 *zaibatsu* companies were broken up and 5,000 companies forced to reorganize (Kawai 1960: 147) the deconcentration programme did not fulfil its original ambitious aims expressed by the Edwards Mission. Many of the former *zaibatsu* were to regroup after the occupation (albeit in different ways), while the Anti-Monopoly Law was to remain ineffective in subsequent years. By 1951, for example, three firms in the pig iron industry accounted for 96 per cent of total output, while three firms in the aluminium industry accounted for *all* output (Schonberger 1989: 107).

Meanwhile, the extent of Washington's changed priorities was seen in the massive economic aid that went to Japan under the EROA (Economic Recovery in Occupied Areas) programme, which totalled $180 million up till June 1949 and supplemented the existing $400 million already spent each year for food and vital supplies (Schaller 1985: 114). Ironically, considering later US–Japan friction in the late 1960s and 1970s over cheap Japanese textile exports to the US, the US Congress also created at this time a revolving fund to allow the purchase of American cotton by Japanese mills, with exports of the finished textiles repaying the loans. The scheme was designed to gear up Japanese industry as well as to provide a convenient outlet for American cotton producers. It was, of course, assumed that Japan's revived economy would take the shape of increased exports of manufactured goods to Southeast Asia; it was never considered likely that Japanese goods would be able to penetrate the Western market (Dower 1993a: 12).

The Initial Post-Surrender Policy for Japan (known as SWNCC 150/4/A) also authorized MacArthur to establish representative government, promote individual liberties, decentralize police powers and encourage a free labour movement. MacArthur accordingly instructed the Japanese government on 4 October 1945 to remove all restrictions on political, civil and religious liberties. Prince Higashikuni resigned the next day and was replaced by Shidehara Kijuro, who had been foreign minister and advocate of co-operation with the West in the 1920s. Shidehara's foreign minister was Yoshida Shigeru, another prewar foreign ministry bureaucrat and an outspoken critic of the military in the 1930s; he had been briefly arrested in April 1945 because of his identification with an anti-militarist group of peers and political party leaders who had urged a diplomatic solution to end the war out of fear that a prolongation of hostilities would increase deprivation at home and hence the possibility of left-wing revolution led by radical army officers (Dower 1979). Yoshida was to emerge as the most powerful politician during and after the occupation, serving as prime minister on five occasions between May 1946 and December 1954. Shortly after Shidehara became prime minister SCAP issued another directive ordering the enfranchisement of women, encouragement of unionization and the liberalization of education. A vigorous revival of politics and the flourishing of an active labour movement quickly followed.

Thousands of political prisoners incarcerated before and during the war were released. The Japanese Communist Party, founded in the early 1920s but never allowed a legal existence, was legalized and party leaders such as Nosaka Sanzo allowed to return from exile (Scalapino 1967: 48–58). The JCP under Tokuda Kyuichi and Shiga Yoshio (who had been imprisoned during the war and never performed *tenko*, ideological conversion) (Steinhoff 1988) quickly reorganized, issuing the first issue of its journal *Akahata* (Red Flag) in October and actively recruiting new members. Membership had never exceeded 1,000 before 1945 but by April 1950 it had grown to nearly 110,000 (Scalapino 1967: 67). The party expressed support for the wide-ranging SCAP reform programme (ironically akin to the approach adopted by enthusiastic New Dealers within SCAP) and also called for both the overthrow of the Emperor system and the establishment of a People's Democracy. While promoting the idea of a united front (under JCP leadership) the party at this time (at its fifth congress in February 1946, for example) stressed the importance of a 'peaceful revolution' based on support for parliamentarianism and reliance on mass organizations. The JCP's increasing influence was to culminate in the election of 35 members in the 1949 elections (polling nearly 10 per cent of the popular vote).

The legalization of the JCP was soon followed by the revival of the prewar political parties. The first to re-emerge was the Japanese Socialist Party (*Nihon shakaito*), formed from among the various left-wing proletarian parties of the 1920s, followed by the Liberal Party (*Nihon jiyuto*) and the Progressive Party (*Nihon shimpoto*, later in 1947 to be called the Democratic Party) – reincarnations of the two principal prewar conservative parties, the *Seiyukai* and *Minseito*, respectively (Curtis 1988). The first postwar elections for the lower house, in April 1946, saw over 300 parties and 2,770 candidates competing for 466 seats (Scalapino and Masumi 1962; Stockwin 1982; Curtis 1988). Such a proliferation of parties was greatly facilitated by a multi-vote, multi-member constituency system (the first and only time it was to be used in Japanese elections), whereby 124 electoral districts returned up to 14 members each and voters had one to three votes depending on how many members a particular district had.

The elections were notable for being the first in which women voted and stood as parliamentary candidates. Voter turnout amongst women was nearly as high as for men (67 per cent to 74 per cent respectively) and 39 women were elected (Paulson 1976: 20; Robins-Mowry 1983: 95). Subsequent elections for the lower house in the next three decades did not build on this achievement. Thus, although voting turnout amongst women came to equal (and surpass) that of men, only nine women candidates won seats in the lower house elections of 1955 (Buckley 1993: 336), while a mere seven women won seats in the 1972 lower house elections, although in 1974 18 women were elected to the upper house (Carlberg 1976: 236–7; Stockwin 1982: 90–1). Ironically, one of the leaders of the women's suffrage movement (dating from the 1920s), Ichikawa Fusae, was purged on the eve of running for the upper house in 1947 because she had visited China in 1940 and spoken in favour of the Greater East Asia Co-Prosperity Sphere. 'Depurged' in 1950, Ichikawa was elected to the upper house in 1953 and served there almost continuously until her death in 1981 (Robins-Mowry 1983: 88). That women were not expected to be involved in politics (despite being given the vote) has been illustrated by a recent study of films made in the immediate postwar period (Hauser 1991). Although such films depicted independent and self-assertive women who questioned the war and the nationalist claims that underpinned it they were essentially apolitical; they criticized the war on social and cultural grounds rather than taking political positions that specifically opposed the government. Like the women depicted in wartime films, their main concerns were protecting the family and community.

The elections of 1946 also produced a virtually new house, with 375 out of the 466 representatives being elected for the first time. The SCAP-imposed purge of all public figures who had supported or been associated with the pre-1945 militarist regime had affected the membership of the political parties (particularly that of the Progressive Party), leaving the way open for former bureaucrats to become party candidates (Curtis 1988). The largest single party to emerge was the Liberal Party (140 seats), followed by the Progressive Party (94 seats) and Socialist Party (92 seats). The leader of the Liberal Party, Hatoyama Ichiro, was purged on the eve of his becoming Prime Minister – he had been Minister of Education in 1931–1934 – and so Yoshida Shigeru, as the new leader of the Liberals, became Prime Minister for the first time in May 1946. Political turmoil, however, was to be the order of the day for the next few years, and it was not to be until the elections of 1949, when Yoshida's Liberals gained 264 out of 466 seats, that a political party would hold an absolute majority in the Diet.

The two most important occupation reforms (and which have remained intact, unlike some of the other reforms) were the promulgation of a new constitution and the implementation of land reform. The new constitution (text in Cortazzi 1993: 188–98) that replaced the 1889 Meiji constitution and which came into force in 1947 was to a large extent imposed on the Japanese (Stockwin 1982), although recent research has stressed significant Japanese input (Ward 1987a). It should also be noted that no public debate (outside the Diet) was allowed during the period of its formulation due to the strict SCAP censorship noted earlier. There was initially no American blueprint, merely a directive sent to SCAP by the State Department in October 1945 referring to the need for responsible government, wider suffrage and executive responsibility; MacArthur himself suggested to Prime Minister Shidehara that the constitution be liberalized. Shidehara, like many conservatives, did not believe that the Meiji constitution needed to be fundamentally revised; in his view it had simply been abused by the militarists during the 1930s.

Nevertheless, the Japanese government, which had already set up an official constitutional revision committee in October 1945, produced a draft constitution of its own in February 1946, known as the Matsumoto Draft (after Matsumoto Joji, the Minister of State without Portfolio). Dissatisfied with this draft, which retained imperial sovereignty, SCAP produced within six days its own draft constitution envisaging far more radical changes. The extraordinary speed with which the draft was drawn up is graphically illustrated by the fact that members of SCAP's Government Section had to search Tokyo libraries for copies of existing Western constitutions (Horsley and Buckley 1990: 17). MacArthur was able to put pressure on the Japanese government by hinting that only a speedy acceptance of the SCAP draft would prevent unwanted interference by the Far Eastern Commission (about to be set up in Washington), which was known to be in favour of indicting the Emperor as a war criminal. Mark Gayn in 1948 also reported that MacArthur threatened to go over the head of the Japanese government and appeal directly to the Japanese people (Livingston, Moore and Oldfather 1973: 19–24).

The SCAP constitution provided for the continued existence of the imperial institution but the Emperor was now to be simply a symbol of state. Sovereignty was attributed to the people through an elected parliament, which was declared to be the highest organ of state power and sole law-making authority; pre-1945 institutions that had been responsible to the Emperor rather than the Diet – the Privy Council, the Imperial Household Ministry, the *genro* system and the War and Naval Ministries – were abolished. Direct cabinet responsibility to the Diet was also stressed; furthermore, the prime minister and the majority of the cabinet had to be Diet members, with the prime minister to be chosen from amongst its own members (i.e. the majority party in the Diet would decide). The constitution also provided for the establishment of a Supreme Court (on the American model) to determine the constitutionality of any law, while courts at all levels were made independent of the Justice Ministry.

During the ensuing discussions, which lasted until August 1946, some important changes were made to SCAP's original draft. An elected *bicameral* rather than the originally proposed unicameral Diet was agreed upon (Baerwald 1987). The lower house, known as the House of Representatives and to be elected normally for a four-year term, was clearly the most influential, having the power to force a cabinet resignation through a non-confidence vote. The 252-member upper house, known as the House of Councillors, had the power to delay legislation from the lower house, although a bill could become law if passed a second time in the lower house by a two-thirds majority. Significantly, however, while the lower house could be dissolved by the prime minister *before* its full term in preparation for new elections (which has happened in most cases since the 1950s) the upper house could not be so dissolved before its full term (six years, with half its membership being re-elected every three years). The voting age was lowered from 25 to 20 years, with the lower house being elected by each voter casting one non-transferable vote in a multi-member constituency (ranging from one to five members) and the upper house being elected from both a national list and multi-member constituencies. The Diet also took the initiative in framing specific provisions of the Constitutional Revision Bill, such as the creation of standing committees within both houses to conduct investigations in relation to government.

Other changes to the original draft included additions to the list of guaranteed rights (proposed by opposition Diet members) that would provide for the people's right to 'minimum standards of wholesome and cultured living' and the 'right and obligation to work' (McNelly 1987). In the area of women's rights, in particular, SCAP officials worked with prominent Japanese women leaders to produce constitutional provisions that were in some ways more extensive than those in the United States (Pharr 1987). Article 14 of the new constitution, for example, guaranteed women's equality and formally prohibited discrimination on the grounds of sex, while article 24 guaranteed marriage by mutual consent as well as equal rights within marriage in terms of property, inheritance and divorce. Such rights were enshrined in the revised Civil Code of 1947, which abolished the patriarchal household system (the *ie*) and for the first time gave the wife legal rights as a juristic person (Paulson 1976: 20; Steiner 1987; Upham 1993: 326), and the Labour Standards Law (1947), which stipulated equal pay for equal work and guaranteed working women 12 weeks' maternity leave. One significant consequence of women's newly granted rights was the increase in the number of women initiating divorce. Most of the 83,869 recorded divorces granted in 1950 (in 1943 there had been 49,705 divorces) were initiated by women (Robins-Mowry 1983: 99). As will be seen later, however, constitutional provisions outlawing gender discrimination at the workplace were not always observed in subsequent practice (Brinton 1993). The same could be said for constitutional provisions prohibiting discrimination against minorities such as the *burakumin* – descendants of outcaste groups associated with occupations that had traditionally been regarded as polluting (e.g. grave diggers, butchers, tanners) (Upham 1993: 327).

Perhaps the most significant example of Diet modification of the original draft concerned Article 9, known as the Peace Clause. Some confusion has arisen over who was responsible for the initial proposal, which renounced war and the threat of force as a means of settling international disputes, as well as prohibiting the development of land, sea and air forces. MacArthur was later to insist that the idea had first been suggested by Prime Minister Shidehara in January 1946 (Stockwin 1982: 179), although recently some scholars have noted that it originated from within SCAP itself, probably its Government Section (McNelly 1987: 79–80; Welfield 1988). As a result of discussions in the Diet two statements, known as the Ashida Amendment (after Ashida Hitoshi, a hawkish member of the Democratic Party) were added to Article 9. The renunciation of war and the threat of force was now preceded by: 'Aspiring sincerely to an international peace based on justice and order', while the ban on armed forces was preceded by: 'In order to accomplish the aim of the preceding paragraph' (Stockwin 1982: 180; McNelly 1987: 92; Welfield 1988: 64–5). Paragraph one could be interpreted to mean that war was to be renounced *only* as the means to settle international disputes (and thus leaving open the possibility of self-defence), while paragraph two could be interpreted as qualifying the ban on armed forces (i.e. it might not apply to defence preparations against aggression). Such an interpretation would later be used to argue that the creation of the Self Defence Forces did not contravene the constitution. Evidence suggests that SCAP at the time understood and approved of this train of thought; indeed, SCAP's Intelligence Section was already recruiting Japanese former military and intelligence personnel with the aim of planning future rearmament (Stockwin 1982; Welfield 1988: 62).

In August 1946 the Constitutional Revision Bill was passed by the lower house and in October 1946 by the House of Peers (thereby voting for its extinction). The new constitution, formally promulgated in November 1946, became effective in May 1947. It has proved to be remarkably resilient despite repeated calls by conservatives during the 1950s for its revision. This was because the majority governing party in the Diet was never able to acquire a two-thirds majority in both houses needed for revision, but also because enthusiasm for revision gradually waned within the ruling party itself (Dower 1993a). Moreover, both the Japanese Left and Right (for different reasons) saw concrete advantages in abiding with the Peace Clause (see chapter three). While some Western scholars believe that the American-imposed constitution merely gave direction to, and reinforced, endogenous forces for change (Ward 1987a; Reischauer 1988), others assert that without the SCAP initiative the Meiji constitution would never have been revised (McNelly 1987; Fukui 1988; Buckley 1990). Whatever the case, the fact that the constitution obtained considerable public support and has remained intact to the present clearly demonstrated a willingness to respond positively to democratic reform.

With the promulgation of the new constitution SCAP also sought to democratize the imperial institution and 'humanize' the Emperor (Bix 1995). Having firmly rejected, on three separate occasions, Emperor Hirohito's suggestion that he abdicate (Large 1992), SCAP was anxious to demystify the Emperor's role and encourage the image of a benign figurehead ruler closely identified with the new democratic order (as if to demonstrate this SCAP was at pains to point out that the Crown Prince now had an American tutor!). A directive of 15 December 1945 abolished State Shinto, which had promoted the fanatical cult of the Emperor (Hardacre 1989) and in January 1946 Hirohito himself renounced his divinity in a public broadcast. Formally titled 'Rescript to Promote the National Destiny', and popularly known as the Declaration of Humanity (*ningen sengen*), the Emperor's broadcast emphasized continuity with the Meiji period, described as a time when Emperor and people had been genuinely united. Later, in June 1947, the custom of bowing towards the palace, universalized in 1937, was abolished.

Symbolically, the Emperor became associated with the new constitution when he personally presented the draft to the Diet. Prime Minister Yoshida, with the clear intention of underlining continuity, also ensured that the constitution was promulgated on the day (3 November) when the Meiji Emperor had been born (Dower 1979: 327–8). Under the constitution the Emperor was to be dependent on Diet appropriations for the budget of the imperial house, while the Imperial Household Agency (created in 1947) was to be attached to the prime minister's office. Finally, between 1946 and 1951, SCAP encouraged the Emperor to embark on highly visible tours of the country, during which his ordinary and awkward appearance and manner contrasted dramatically with his pre-1945 militarist image (Gayn 1981: 137). Although he was sometimes sarcastically referred to in the press as '*Ah-so san*' (Mr 'Is that so?' based on his usual reply to the people he talked with) and was the object of criticism at some mass protest rallies organized by the Communist Party (Gayn 1981: 12), various opinion polls taken at the time indicated that there was overwhelming public support for the imperial institution (Fukui 1988: 169; Large 1992: 143). Ironically, the occasional lampooning of the Emperor in the popular press, portraying him as the comic victim of advisers and politicians, may have served to reinforce the official view that Hirohito had always been an orthodox constitutional monarch (Bix 1995). Hirohito was rarely to be so publicly visible after the occupation, but perceptions of the Emperor would continue to be contentious, with conservatives claiming him as a symbol of state authority, while their critics, anxious to prevent the re-emergence of jingoistic nationalism, would underline the Emperor's role as a symbol of democracy.

The other enduring achievement of the occupation period was land reform. As with constitutional revision, Japanese officials were already working on such an idea, and a Land Reform Bill drafted by the Agriculture and Forestry Ministry was introduced to the Diet *before* SCAP officially raised the issue in December 1945 (Dore 1959). In fact, the Japanese government's Land Reform Bill in a sense represented the culmination of earlier prewar attempts to solve tenancy disputes that became particularly acute after 1918. During the 1920s the government passed conciliation laws and regulations to provide loans for tenant purchase of land, although these had proved largely ineffective (ibid.: 84). In 1941, 53.2 per cent of riceland and 37 per cent of upland were still cultivated by tenants. Nevertheless, a recent study (Dower 1993b: 21) argues that wartime developments after 1941 eroded the authority of landlords as the government began paying tenants directly for their produce.

The government's Land Reform Bill in November 1945 called for the compulsory transfer to cultivators (tenants) of all land owned by absentee landlords, as well as tenanted land owned by resident landlords in excess of five *cho* (1 *cho* = 2.45 acres), a measure that had originally been contemplated during the war. The debate in the Diet on the bill coincided with MacArthur's instructions to the government in December 1945 to remove obstacles to 'the revival and strengthening of democratic tendencies' in Japanese villages (SCAP felt that militarism and ultranationalism had taken root in the countryside because of exploitative landlord–tenant relations). Due to SCAP pressure a more radical Land Reform Bill was passed in October 1946. All tenanted land owned by resident landlords in excess of four *cho* in Hokkaido and one *cho* for the rest of Japan was to be purchased and resold to tenants, in addition to all land *cultivated* by landlords in excess of twelve *cho* (in Hokkaido) or three *cho* (for the rest of Japan). By 1950, when the transfer of land had been virtually completed, 2.8 million acres of riceland and 1.95 million acres of upland had been purchased from 2.34 million landowners and resold to 4.75 million tenants and farmers. Only 11 per cent of the land remained under tenancy and a mere 5 per cent of farmers still remained tenants (Dore 1959: 175; Hunter 1989: 99–101; Hane 1992: 348).

The process of land reform did not always go smoothly. One major problem was the attempt by some landlords to retrieve tenanted land (up to the allowed three *cho*) for their own cultivation; pressure was put on tenants to accept this, especially as landlords had equal representation with non-landlords on the land committees set up at the local level to oversee the transfers. In 1947, the government formally stipulated that farmers who were leasing land in November 1945 had the right to buy it even if they had been persuaded by their landlord to give up their tenancy. Landlords continued to protest the terms of the compulsory purchase, although the matter was formally laid to rest in December 1953 when the Supreme Court held that they had indeed received just compensation for their property. It should also be noted that the benefits of land reform were not distributed equally, with some tenants being able to purchase more land than others. In the immediate postwar years, too, curtailment of loans and investment, taxation, and compulsory rice deliveries at low prices led to a decline in the rural economy. Only when the Korean War (1950–2) stimulated economic recovery in Japan and the official price of rice was raised in 1951 did agricultural production regain its prewar levels.

Ultimately, land reform helped to buttress conservative support in the countryside. In 1947, an Agricultural Co-operatives Law had created politically independent co-operatives (*nokyo*) to replace the recently abolished agricultural associations (*nokai*), prewar institutions that had been dominated by local conservative elites. In time, however, these co-operatives became closely linked with the Agriculture Ministry, functioning as the sole collecting agent for rice as well as doubling up as the central village store and bank. They were to form a powerful pressure group ensuring the preservation of state rice subsidies (supplemented by government aid in the form of grants and low interest loans) with which conservative governments from the mid-1950s on guaranteed electoral success in the rural areas (van Wolferen 1989: 60–5). The Japan Farmers' Union, established in 1946 and inheriting the militant tradition of prewar tenant unions, in contrast became increasingly marginalized after 1949. The 1950s and 1960s were to bring growing material prosperity to the countryside, but were also to witness the decline in the number of rural households devoted to full-time farming (see chapter three).

Other reforms in the early occupation period included the decentralization of police powers, educational change and the legalization of trade union activity, all of which were to be reversed or modified in subsequent years. The powerful prewar Home Ministry, which had controlled the police and appointed prefectural governors, was abolished and its functions dispersed (prefectural governors were henceforth to be elected and made accountable to prefectural assemblies). The Police Reorganization Law (1947) empowered municipalities with populations over 5,000 to maintain their own forces, while a small national police force under the National Safety Public Commission (later to come under the control of the prime minister's office) was created for the less populated rural areas.

Educational change began almost immediately with the occupation as SCAP authorities screened textbooks and suspended the teaching of ethics and Japanese history in the schools. Teachers were also screened to investigate their pre-1945 activities; by the end of April 1949 over 942,000 had been investigated and just over 3,000 found unacceptable (Nishi 1982: 173). In accordance with SCAP's view that state-supported Shinto had fostered the fanatical loyalty to a divine Emperor and encouraged extreme chauvinism, the Shinto Directive of December 1945 ordered the deletion of all references to Shinto from school textbooks and forbade school trips to Shinto shrines. (Since, in fact, the constitution insisted on the separation of religion and state, as well as guaranteeing the freedom of religion, the Directive recognized Shinto as a religion like any other, none of which was to receive state patronage. (Woodward 1972; Hardacre 1989.)) The Meiji Emperor's 1890 Rescript on Education, calling for loyalty to the throne and the state, and which, along with the Emperor's portrait, had been displayed in every school (and before which teachers and pupils had to perform a daily bow) was abrogated in October 1946, although not formally rescinded by the Diet until June 1948. Following the visit of a US Educational Mission in 1946, the Fundamental Law of Education was passed in 1947, which stressed the development of the individual committed to a peaceful and democratic polity (Kawai 1960: 189–91; Cummings 1980: 32; Nishi 1982; Masami 1986). Compulsory education was extended to include six years of elementary and three years of junior high school; the school system itself was to be based on the American model. Over one hundred new universities were also created, although the former Tokyo Imperial University (now Tokyo University) was to remain the most prestigious institution of higher learning. Finally, the authority of the Education Ministry was curtailed, with elective boards of education gradually being established at prefectural, city and village levels. State authorized textbooks were banned and the choice of curricula and texts (in elementary and secondary schools) was assigned to the individual schools themselves. Education was to be a key battleground in the campaign by conservatives to overturn occupation reforms after 1952 (see chapter three).

Legislation guaranteeing workers' rights was embodied in the Trade Union Law (1945), which gave workers the right to organize, strike and engage in collective bargaining, and the Labour Standards Law (1947), which enacted minimum standards for working hours, safety and accident compensation. As in the case of land reform, these labour laws did not mark an entirely novel departure since they bore a resemblance to draft legislation proposed by social bureaucrats in the 1920s (Garon 1987; Dower 1993b: 22–3). Many of these prewar social bureaucrats helped draft the new labour laws and entered the newly organized Labour Ministry in 1947 (which now had a Women's and Minors' Bureau under the direction of Yamakawa Kikue, an activist in the prewar proletarian women's movement) (Pharr 1987). 'As in the 1920s', one historian notes, 'powerful officials within the government were determined to establish a liberal, yet supervised, framework within which unions would develop' (Garon 1987: 237). It is significant, for example, that although the new laws introduced the novel feature of tripartite commissions (comprising representatives of labour, management and the 'public interest') to mediate disputes, they also resurrected earlier provisions empowering the government to monitor union activities and finances. The trade union laws, nevertheless, had the enthusiastic support of New Dealers within SCAP such as T. A. Bisson in Government Section, and T. Cohen and J. Killen (himself a trade unionist) in SCAP's Labour Division.

The next few years witnessed a phenomenal increase in union membership. In September 1945 there were only two unions with a membership of just over 1,000. By February 1947 there were 18,929 unions with over 5 million members, representing 41 per cent of the workforce (Moore 1983: 42–5: see table 2.1). During the interwar period the highest rate of unionization had occurred in 1931, when 368,975 union workers comprised a mere 7.9 per cent of the work

Table 2.1 Growth of unions and union membership in Japan, August 1945–February 1947 (cumulative end-of-month totals)

Year	Month	Unions	Membership
1945	Aug.	0	0
	Sep.	2	1,177
	Oct.	9	5,072
	Nov.	75	68,530
	Dec.	509	380,677
1946	Jan.	1,517	902,751
	Feb.	3,243	1,537,606
	Mar.	6,538	2,568,513
	Apr.	8,531	3,023,979
	May	10,541	3,414,699
	Jun.	12,007	3,681,017
	Jul.	12,923	3,814,711
	Aug.	13,341	3,875,272
	Sep.	14,697	4,122,209
	Oct.	15,172	4,168,305
	Nov.	16,171	4,296,589
	Dec.	17,265	4,849,329
1947	Jan.	17,972	4,922,918
	Feb.	18,929	5,030,574[a]

Source: Moore (1983): Japan Prime Minister's Office, Cabinet Bureau of Statistics, *Japan Statistical Year-book* (Tokyo: Cabinet Bureau of Statistics, 1949), p. 717
[a] Membership first exceeded six million in December 1947

force (Large 1981: 134). Union membership was to peak in 1948 with just over 6.5 million, declining by one million in the next three years (Moore 1988: 19; Fukui 1988). At the same time two influential national federations emerged: the left-wing National Congress of Industrial Unions (*Sanbetsu*), formed in August 1946, and the Japan National Federation of Labour (*Sodomei*), which actually dated from 1919.

Organized workers, beginning with coal miners in Hokkaido, resorted to militant action in protest against low wages, forced redundancies and black market corruption. This labour militance took place against a background of stagnant industrial production (due to deliberate sabotage by management to slow down production in an attempt to weaken the union movement as well as to shortages of materials), inflation (partly fuelled by continued government payments to *zaibatsu* owners for wartime contracts), food shortages (with farmers often witholding crops or selling them on a black market) and massive unemployment (exacerbated by the return of Japanese soldiers from overseas), which totalled more than 13 million in 1946 (Dower 1979: 293). While one historian thinks the occupation created a 'Frankenstein monstrosity, in the form of an anti-capitalist, anti-American union movement of considerable strength' (Bronfenbrenner 1968: 23), another argues that the militance of these years represented a positive attempt by Japanese workers themselves to control their own destinies rather than merely being the passive recipients of rights conferred on them by occupation authorities (Moore 1988).

In some cases labour militance evolved into what was called 'production control' (*seisan kanri*), struggles in which workers took over the running of the enterprise themselves (as much as to revive production as anything else). Beginning with the 'occupation' of the *Yomiuri* newspaper in October 1945 by editorial staff in their dispute with the paper's right-wing owner, production control struggles took place in coal mines, factories and transport companies. Between April and May 1946 there were 110 such disputes involving 75,000 workers (Moore 1983: 101–3; 1988: 26). In some cases an integrated strategy was carried out; thus, for example, workers ran the Toyo Gosei chemical plant in Niigata (part of the Mitsui combine) between March and August 1946, selling its products and bartering with local farmers to obtain the required coal which the farmers had purchased from coalminers (Moore 1988). Interestingly, both the Socialist Party and the Communist Party were lukewarm in their support for production control, preferring to stress the role of unions and collective bargaining.

There were also massive anti-government demonstrations. In May 1946 up to 250,000 demonstrated in Tokyo (Gayn 1981: 226–31), which prompted MacArthur for the first time to denounce workers' 'abuse' of their civil rights. Emboldened by what he now saw as clear SCAP support for government and business, Prime Minister Yoshida openly condemned production control as subversive. As one historian has pointed out (Dower 1979: 336), just as Yoshida had always mistrusted radical elements within the army during the war for their proposals to enhance state control of the economy, so he now perceived organized labour as the greatest threat to the capitalist system. Militance continued, however, and in December 1946 Sanbetsu called for a nationwide strike on 1 February 1947. MacArthur's directive of 31 January 1947 prohibiting the strike signalled SCAP's support for a counter-offensive against labour.

The 'Reverse Course'

The term 'reverse course' (*gyakkosu*), used in the late 1960s and early 1970s by revisionist American historians critical of US foreign policy in Asia, was actually coined in the 1950s by Japanese left-wing scholars. It referred to the change of direction during the latter stages of the occupation, when the earlier reforms were modified or overturned by SCAP and the Japanese government amidst Cold War fears of communism. SCAP's obsession with transforming Japan into a bulwark against a perceived communist threat in East and Southeast Asia (especially after 1948, when the victory of the Chinese communists seemed ever closer), coupled with the Japanese conservative establishment's opposition to the democratizing reforms in the first place, meant that priority was now to be given to Japan's economic revival and the country's reintegration into the 'free world' as the loyal anti-communist ally of the United States. In the process labour militance was to be muted, the economic deconcentration programme ended, an anti-left wing purge carried out in the public sector (coinciding with the rehabilitation of those purged in 1945–6 for their wartime activities), the police and education recentralized, and tacit support given to Japan's rearmament. For Japanese left-wing intellectuals this reverse course was to continue beyond 1952, when the American occupation formally ended (see chapter three). Underlying the concept of the reverse course was the assumption that the occupation represented a betrayal in which the US and its Japanese conservative supporters, in the interests of the Cold War, halted the emergence of a genuine democracy and resurrected discredited features of Japan's pre-1945 past (Gluck 1983).

Recent research, however, has painted a more complex picture. Focusing on the social bureaucrats within Japan, for example, Garon (1987) has emphasized continuity in personnel and policies that spans the prewar and occupation periods. Thus, for the social bureaucrats who resurfaced in 1945 and helped draft the trade union laws in the early occupation period, the restrictions imposed on union activity after 1947 did not represent a reverse course but rather a second opportunity (the first one being in the 1920s and 1930s) to reshape the union movement along anti-communist lines. This view contrasts with that of Moore (1988), who sees MacArthur's denunciation of workers in May 1946 and ensuing SCAP support for the Japanese government's condemnation of production control as a key turning-point that *did* mark the beginnings of a reverse course, which had its origins in the fear of domestic unrest in Japan rather than of a communist threat from outside. Other historians, developing ideas first raised by 'revisionists' in the late 1960s and early 1970s (e.g. Dower 1971), have linked the reverse course more closely with global US strategic and economic concerns that were mutually reinforcing and which predate the onset of the Cold War in the late 1940s (Borden 1984; Schaller 1985; Dower 1993b: 155–207). It has even been argued (Borden 1984: 4; Cumings 1993: 36) that it was the *earlier* occupation period, with its stress on punitive economic measures, that represented an aberration, since the attempt after 1947 to revive the Japanese economy as a means of restoring multilateralism fitted in well with prewar American priorities.

It should also be noted, however, that US policy towards Japan during this period was not always monolithic. There were ongoing disagreements within the Washington administration (particularly between the Departments of State and Defense), as well as between Washington and MacArthur; American business interests, too, did not have a uniform view, with some (e.g. the textile industry) not as enthusiastic about the potential revival of the Japanese economy as those such as General Electric or Associated Oil which had invested heavily in prewar Japan (Halliday 1975; Borden 1984). With more attention now being focused on the Japanese input during the occupation (Ward and Sakamoto 1987), recent research has highlighted more clearly the differences (as well as the shared views) between Washington and Prime Minister Yoshida Shigeru over rearmament and perceptions of the communist threat in East Asia (Welfield 1988; Dower 1993b: 208–41). Finally, some historians do not accept the premise of a reverse course anyway, preferring to write of a shift in focus during the occupation period from political to economic aspects (Ward 1987b: 414), while a recent overview (Passin 1992) scarcely mentions a reverse course at all.

Whether one accepts the concept of a reverse course or not, there was clearly a gradual reorientation of US thinking concerning the Japanese economy and Japan's role internationally. For Schaller (1985: 72), this reorientation began with General Marshall's departure from China in January 1947, signalling the failure of American mediation attempts to prevent the onset of full-scale civil war between the nationalists and the communists. The fear of a communist victory on the Asian mainland was accompanied by increasing concern over both the parlous state of the Japanese economy and the spiralling costs of the occupation itself, which were to amount to $900 million by 1949 (ibid.: 82). A prominent State Department official, George Kennan, began referring in 1947 to the need for reviving the Japanese economy and in the same year Assistant Secretary of State Dean Acheson specifically described Japan as a potential 'workshop of Asia', the idea being that Japan would become a regional centre of production and trade based on the exchange of industrial products for raw materials from neighbouring regions. Ultimately, this was to mean Japan's reintegration with the economies of Southeast Asia, although up until 1950 the State Department did not preclude the prospect of Japanese economic links with north China and Manchuria (Cumings 1993: 41).

As Dower (1993b: 155–207) has pointed out, the primary concern of the US until mid-1949 was to prevent Japan's internal economic collapse and political subversion from within, which might push the country into the Soviet sphere. He characterizes mid-1947 to mid-1949 as a 'soft' Cold War period during which US planners were not as yet fully committed to the idea of an indefinite American military presence in Japan or to Japanese rearmament;

Washington at this time did not have a coherent vision of regional anti-communist integration in Asia. Nevertheless, it should be noted that some US planners already in the last year of the war were urging a more extensive American control of the Pacific (Iriye 1981), a notion that had more to do with expansionist ambitions from the turn of the century than with any perceived Soviet threat (Dower 1971).

Throughout 1948, US officials emphasized the importance of Japan's economic recovery. In January, for example, Army Secretary William Draper called for an end to the anti-*zaibatsu* campaign, echoing the growing criticism of the Japan Lobby that MacArthur's anti-monopoly measures were dangerously socialistic and contributing to Japan's economic collapse (Schonberger 1989), while in March Kennan visited Japan to impress upon MacArthur the reorientation of Washington's thinking. Such a visit should also be seen in the context of Washington's determination to regain closer control over the direction of occupation policy, hitherto almost the exclusive prerogative of MacArthur and the SCAP bureaucracy. As noted earlier, MacArthur, as much as to enhance his political ambitions back home as well as to resist this outside interference, continued to champion anti-monopoly legislation, and in early 1947 had even called for an international peace conference since, in his view, the occupation had been successfully concluded (Schonberger 1989). Washington, however, had different ideas.

In June 1948 a National Security Council document (NSC 13) submitted by Kennan and formally adopted in October stated that economic revival and political stability in Japan were to take priority over a quick peace settlement. The NSC document also reaffirmed long-term US military control over Okinawa (the main island in the Ryukyus which had been under *direct* American military control since the beginning of the occupation) and called for the expansion of a national police reserve; but a decision on whether to maintain long-term US military bases on the main islands of Japan after the conclusion of a peace treaty was left in abeyance. Interestingly, the Japanese government itself in 1947 had intimated to Washington that it was willing to accept Okinawa as a major US military bastion in return for an early end to the occupation (Dower 1993b: 171). By the summer of 1948, Congress for the first time had approved the use of funds ($180 million) specifically for reviving the Japanese economy; this appropriation was accompanied by the setting up of a National Fibres Revolving Fund, totalling $150 million, to be used for the export of American raw cotton to Japan (Dower 1993b: 174).

A nine-point stabilization programme was drawn up in December 1948 and a Detroit banker, Joseph Dodge, sent to Japan in January 1949 to oversee the economy. The 'Dodge Line', as it became known, aimed to bring about financial discipline in the country by imposing wage and price controls, balancing the budget and ensuring allocation of raw materials for export production with the aims of curbing inflation and dampening domestic consumption. Inflation, in particular, was seen as the main scourge, with prices having risen more than 700 per cent between September 1945 and August 1948 (Schonberger 1989: 198–235). The implementation of the Dodge Plan, which coincided with the termination of the anti-monopoly campaign, led to massive lay-offs: up to 1/4 million public service employees lost their jobs, with almost as many being affected in the private sector (Fukui 1988: 177).

Even after June 1948, however, differences still prevailed within the US administration. Whereas the State Department envisaged Japan as a political ally and was still unsure about Japanese rearmament, the Defense Department assumed the necessity of having US military bases in Japan, which would become virtually a permanent military enclave. Also, the State Department, until 1950, assumed that limited trade between China and Japan would continue (despite the advent of a communist government in China in October 1949), while the Defense Department pressed for a 'southern strategy', favouring Japan's integration with Southeast Asia – what some historians call in effect a new Co-Prosperity Sphere (Borden 1984; Schaller 1985; Welfield 1988). By the fall of 1949 the State Department had accepted the idea of an indefinite US military presence in the main islands of Japan and in early 1950 a consensus began to emerge in Washington over the need for limited Japanese rearmament, retention of US military bases in Japan after the peace treaty, and a bilateral defence agreement. This marked the stage, according to Dower (1993b: 162), of a 'hard' Cold War approach by Washington, when it was considered essential to incorporate Japan in a positive manner in US Cold War strategic planning. Globally, the American containment programme had begun well before the invasion of South Korea by communist North Korea in June 1950, when the US sent economic aid and an advisory team to Vietnam in early 1950 to assist the French-sponsored regime there in its struggle with the communist forces of Ho Chi Minh. On 22 June 1950 (three days before the outbreak of the Korean War) the US formally urged upon the Japanese government the need for rearmament. By November 1950, the question of continuing Japanese trade with communist China was more or less settled when the US, in line with its decision to halt its own trade with China, began to impose restrictions on Sino-Japanese trade that were to last until the early 1970s. Japan's integration with the economies of Southeast Asia became even more imperative, a prospect not entirely welcomed by the British government, which feared Japanese competition in the region (Buckley 1982; Borden 1984).

The domestic repercussions of this reorientation of US planning included the revision of trade union laws, the termination of the anti-*zaibatsu* campaign, the implementation of a more stringent and planning-based economic policy, an extensive left-wing purge and, finally, the beginnings of rearmament. Most of these developments occurred during the prime ministership of Yoshida Shigeru. Like the rest of the conservative establishment, Yoshida had never been enthusiastic about SCAP's earlier political and economic reforms and, as noted ealier, was able skilfully to exploit differences within SCAP itself by appealing to the anti-communist phobia prevalent amongst SCAP's Counter-Intelligence Section (particularly when arguing that SCAP's offensive against business smacked of socialism). At the same time, Yoshida's prewar career as a Foreign Ministry bureaucrat predisposed him to co-operate with the Anglo-American powers in Asia (while not precluding, of course, support for decisive action in China to protect Japan's interests there). It was Yoshida's championing of 'co-operative imperialism' (Dower 1979) that made him amenable after 1945 to the concept of tactical co-operation between Japan and the US (Welfield 1988) although, as will be seen later, Yoshida's ambivalent attitude towards the Japanese military, in addition to more pragmatic concerns with public opinion and the economy, prompted a far more cautious approach to rearmament than the US desired.

The beginnings of a shift in occupation policy towards labour from the summer of 1946, however, ironically coincided with the accession to power of a socialist-led government in April 1947, the only time in the postwar period (until 1993) that conservatives did not hold the reins of power. In the first elections held under the new constitution, which reintroduced the single-entry ballot, multi-member constituency system, the Socialist Party became the largest single party in the lower house, gaining 143 seats and 26.2 per cent of the vote (Scalapino and Masumi 1962: 37). Until February 1948, the socialist leader Katayama Tetsu led a coalition government comprising members of the JSP, the Democratic Party (which had gained 126 seats) and the smaller Japan Co-operative Party. During the period of this socialist-led government the Home Ministry was abolished, police administration decentralized, a Labour Ministry established and unemployment insurance introduced (Calder 1988: 76). Bedevilled by internal government wranglings, particularly over whether to nationalize the coal industry, and increasingly unable to halt the worsening economic situation, Katayama resigned in February 1948. The coalition limped on under Ashida Hitoshi, leader of the Democratic Party (with Nishio Suehiro, leader of the right-wing faction of the JSP as Deputy Prime Minister), until October 1948, when the government fell in the wake of a major corruption scandal, the first of many that were to rock postwar governments. Known as the Showa Denko scandal, government ministers (including Ashida and Nishio) were charged with accepting bribes from a fertilizer producer (Showa Denko) in return for securing low-interest government loans. All were eventually to be acquitted (Curtis 1988).

Yoshida took over as Prime Minister, a post he was to hold until 1954. In the lower house elections of January 1949 Yoshida's Liberals gained a plurality of seats (264 out of 466) and 43.8 per cent of the vote, while the JSP slumped to 48 seats (Stockwin 1982; Curtis 1988). Until the 1980s governments were to be dominated by the conservatives facing a weakened and divided opposition. After 1948 the offensive against labour accelerated. Breakaway unions known as 'democratization leagues' (*mindo*) were formed to rival communist-dominated unions and by 1950, with active SCAP and Japanese government support, a new trade union federation, the General Council of Trade Unions (*Sohyo*), was created to challenge *Sanbetsu*. Unexpectedly for SCAP and the Japanese government, however, *Sohyo* was to come under the influence of left-wing socialists and became increasingly radical in its condemnation of the Dodge Plan.

Reductions in the bureaucracy and in the state sector (in line with the Dodge Plan) were also aimed at reducing the power of the unions, which had been particularly evident amongst blue collar workers in the railways, postal services and telecommunications. By the spring of 1949, for example, 126,000 railway employees (20 per cent of the work force) had been dismissed. This led to a number of sabotage incidents, the most notorious of which was the derailing of a train near Matsukawa (north of Tokyo) in August 1949 resulting in three deaths. The incident was blamed on the communists; 20 people, most of whom were JCP members and former railway employees, were indicted, but all were eventually judged innocent in 1963 (Johnson 1972).

Legislation was passed in July 1948 to prohibit public sector employees from striking, while a National Public Service Law in December 1948 denied civil servants the right to strike and engage in collective bargaining, a ban that was extended to workers employed in local government-owned enterprises in 1952. Additional government control was imposed over the certification and internal procedures of unions in 1949 and in July 1952 government intervention in critical strikes that remained unsettled after 50 days was sanctioned. Employers also went on the offensive after 1948, organizing the Japan Federation of Employers'Associations (*Nikkeiren*); it promptly set about renegotiating early postwar contracts and limiting the scope of union activities (Garon and Mochizuki 1993: 157; Gordon 1993: 379–80), one consequence of which was to reduce the influence of management–labour councils to that of simple advisory bodies.

The defeat of the radical labour movement after 1947 was to result in the emergence of enterprise unions (comprising both white and blue collar workers, as well as employers and employees), that bore uncanny similarities with the wartime Patriotic Industrial Unions (*Sanpo*) in which the head of the union had also been the head of the enterprise and workers were indoctrinated with corporatist ideals (Moore 1983; Dower 1993b: 20). Membership of *Sanbetsu* declined dramatically from nearly 1.5 million in 1948 to under 50,000 in 1951 (Scalapino 1967: 69; Halliday 1975: 218; Garon 1987: 241) and was to be dissolved in 1958.

The offensive against labour was accompanied by an extensive 'anti-Red' purge that began in 1949. Thousands of left-wing sympathizers were sacked or barred from public service. Significantly, the purge was directed by Attorney-General Ohashi Takeo, a social bureaucrat in the wartime Home and Welfare Ministries (Garon 1987: 240). It was preceded by staff changes within SCAP itself as prominent New Dealers either resigned (in the case of T. Bisson and J. Killen) in protest against the new shift in labour policy or were dismissed. The atmosphere of recrimination and suspicion that pervaded SCAP at this time (Schonberger 1989) is illustrated by the memoirs of T. Cohen. Cohen, head of SCAP's Labour Division and a vocal supporter of SCAP's internal purge, was himself apparently accused of being a communist (Cohen 1987: 111). The anti-Red purge of 1949–50 was soon followed by the rehabilitation of those originally purged in 1945–6 for their association with, or support for, Japan's wartime regime. In the 1952 elections, for example, 139 such 'depurgees' were elected to the lower house (Dower 1979: 333).

The change in US thinking during the latter stages of the occupation also prompted the Japanese government to emphasize planned industrial policy and foreign trade controls, symbolized by the creation of the Ministry of International Trade and Industry (MITI) in 1949. Originating as the Ministry of Commerce and Industry established in 1925 (and briefly renamed the Ministry of Munitions during the last two years of the war), MITI not only drew on personnel from the former ministry – until the mid-1970s all top officials in MITI came from the pre-1945 bureaucracy – but also, ironically, was to attain more extensive controls over the economy than had ever been envisaged by militarists and renovationist bureaucrats before 1945 (Johnson 1982: 41; Dower 1993b: 24). MITI had two important legacies on which to draw. First, during the 1930s emphasis had increasingly been placed on industrial 'rationalization' (i.e. competition to be replaced by co-operation). In 1931, for example, the Important Industries Control Law sanctioned government-supervised cartel agreements to fix levels of production and prices, while in 1937 a law authorized the government to restrict or prohibit imports or exports of any commodity and to control the manufacture, distribution and consumption of imported raw materials (Johnson 1982: 136). Such measures were important precedents for MITI's 'administrative guidance' of the economy after 1949.

Second, MITI took over the controls originally exercised by SCAP after 1945 (Hollerman 1979). Until 1949, SCAP controlled all foreign trade and exchange. On the Japanese side a Board of Trade, set up in December 1945, accounted for and distributed goods SCAP imported as well as receiving and then transferring to SCAP all products manufactured in Japan for export. MITI, in fact, was formed from the merger of the Ministry of Commerce and

Industry and the Board of Trade. Through such measures as the Foreign Exchange and Foreign Trade Control Law (December 1949) MITI's controls over foreign exchange, exports and import licensing were formalized. MITI also took over the role of the Economic Stabilization Board (set up in 1946) in supervising all technology imports and joint ventures. The pre-eminence of economic bureaucrats in industrial policy-making in subsequent years was thus a direct result of SCAP's concern with restoring economic efficiency in the wake of the spiralling costs of the occupation and Washington's fear that Japan might become permanently dependent on American aid, as well as of SCAP's selective purge of 1945–6, which had left the economic bureaucracy virtually intact (Calder 1988). Ironically, it was SCAP that also finally fixed the exchange rate of the Japanese yen to the US dollar in order to bring about stability in Japan's foreign trade. The rate had varied from 13.6 (August 1945) to 231 (March 1948) before SCAP fixed it generously at 360 (Cohen 1987: 465). By the late 1960s, with Japan beginning to run up a trade surplus with the US, complaints were to emanate from Washington that the yen was undervalued.

The most dramatic development arising from the shift in US priorities was rearmament. Already in 1948 US planners had called for an expansion of a national police reserve (see p. 46) and, as has been noted earlier, military and intelligence personnel within SCAP were planning future Japanese rearmament virtually from the beginning of the occupation (Welfield 1988). In 1948, the Maritime Safety Force was created, which was to become the basis of a navy in all but name, and in July 1950 Yoshida agreed to an American request that a National Police Reserve of 75,000 men be established and which would be commanded by former officers of the Japanese imperial army. Interestingly, however, both Yoshida and MacArthur initially viewed this police reserve as a useful tool to suppress internal dissent. The concern with internal subversion was already evident in 1949, when the Special Investigation Bureau was set up within the Attorney-General's Office (renamed the Ministry of Justice in 1952) to be exclusively concerned with the surveillance of communist activities. Many of its personnel were associated with the prewar Home Ministry and Special Higher Police (Dower 1979: 365). In his memoirs published in the 1960s, Yoshida (reflecting the views of the conservative establishment) was to paint a gloomy picture of the latter years of the occupation, a period known as *butsujo sozen no jidai* ('period of confused feelings') when strikes and sabotage appeared to be undermining the political and social order (Calder 1988: 78–80) and when the Left was obtaining electoral success – in April 1950, for example, the Left-sponsored candidate, Ninagawa Torazo, was elected Governor of Kyoto. In addition, the JCP, criticized by Moscow in January 1950 for its positive assessment of the American occupation, began to condemn 'US imperialism' after its Fifth National Congress in October 1951 and rejected the concept of 'peaceful revolution'. Such a policy change led in 1951–2 to a series of abortive attempts to create rural liberated areas as well as to a number of attacks on police stations. Not surprisingly, until the autumn of 1951 the expanded Police Reserve was concentrated in areas where support for the JCP was strongest.

Washington, however, continued to press for more large-scale rearmament, especially after MacArthur was replaced by General Ridgway in April 1951. Yet although Yoshida announced in January 1952 that the Police Reserve would be transformed into a Self Defence Force that would be supplied with artillery and tanks (Welfield 1988: 72–9) he remained ambivalent. Significantly, in May 1950 a secret Japanese government mission had been sent to Washington offering support for the presence of post-treaty US military bases in Japan while at the same time indicating unwillingness to undertake rearmament. Even when the Police Reserve was set up Yoshida moved slowly on its expansion. Such ambivalence was due to Yoshida's mistrust of the military (dating from the 1930s), his fear of a public backlash, his concern for the ailing economy and his suspicion that Japanese troops might be sent to Korea (Dower 1993b: 208–41). By the end of 1951 the Police Reserve had grown to 110,000 men even though US Secretary of State John Foster Dulles insisted upon a force of 350,000. In 1954 the numbers had increased to 180,000. It was Yoshida's success in resisting American demands for massive rearmament that has led one historian to reject the view that Yoshida was an American puppet and instead to portray him as a 'nationalist of a very subtle sort' (Duus 1976: 252)

The Peace Treaty (text in Cortazzi 1993: 199–210) formally ending the occupation was finally signed in San Francisco in September 1951 (to come into effect in April 1952). The treaty was signed by 49 countries; the Soviet Union declined to sign, while China was not represented at the peace conference because the United States and Britain could not agree on which government to invite – that of

Mao Zedong's communist regime (the People's Republic of China) which now ruled the mainland, or Chiang Kai-shek's Nationalist regime (the Republic of China) on the offshore island of Taiwan, to where the defeated nationalists had fled in 1949. The treaty itself was lenient; no insistence on the payment of reparations was made and no requirement stipulated that the occupation reforms be maintained. At the same time the Japanese government surrendered the right to demand compensation for the survivors of the atomic bombings (Article 19 of the treaty). It should be noted in this context, however, that the Japanese government itself did little for such victims. Limited medical aid laws were passed in 1957 and 1968 but these did not extend either to second and third generation sufferers or to the more than 10,000 Korean survivors (most of whom were in Japan at the time as conscript labour) who had returned to South Korea after 1945 (Kamata and Salaff 1988).

On the same day the Peace Treaty was signed the US and Japan signed a Security Treaty, the details of which had been kept secret until then. It firmly tied Japan to the imperatives of American foreign policy and allowed for the presence of US military bases in Japan to deter any foreign military threat (Okinawa was to remain under American military control until 1972). Some 260,000 American troops were stationed in 2,824 bases and had the authority to suppress internal disturbances. Furthermore, under the treaty the US could use its bases in Japan for actions in Asia without consulting the Japanese government. An Administrative Agreement in February 1952 gave the US the authority to garrison specified areas, remove buildings, acquire rights of way and even to arrest Japanese citizens committing disturbances outside base areas. The US also had jurisdiction over all American personnel who committed crimes in Japan (Welfield 1988; Schonberger 1989: 236–78). No provisions were made for termination of the treaty except for mutual consent.

Yoshida was also compelled to fall into line with American policy on China (confirmed by a letter he sent to Secretary of State Dulles in December 1951), despite his previous assumptions that the new Chinese communist regime did not pose a threat to Japan and that China would remain Japan's natural market. He formally agreed to abide with the trade boycott of the Chinese mainland and in April 1952 signed a treaty with Chiang Kai-shek's regime in Taiwan (recognizing it as the Republic of China), thus bringing Japan into line with the 'two China' policy of the United States

(Livingston, Moore and Oldfather 1973: 248–50). Such developments have led some historians (e.g. Dower 1979) to refer to
Japan's 'subordinate independence' after 1951 (the term itself,
juzokuteki dokuritsu, was first used by the Japanese Left in the
1950s). It is ironic, however, that doubts persisted on the American
side concerning Japan's trustworthiness (the presence of American
troops in Japan, for example, was perceived in some circles just as
much as a means to keep Japan under American supervision as to
deter any armed attack on Japan), doubts that were to re-emerge in
the 1980s and early 1990s when Japan's trade superiority *vis-à-vis*
the United States was seen as the product of deviousness and a lack
of ethical sense (Dower 1986; 1993b: 257–85).

The Security Treaty also had divisive consequences for Japan's
domestic politics. Yoshida had to confront bitter criticism from
both the Right (on nationalist grounds) and from the Left, who
warned of the dangers of remilitarization and condemned the
country's association with American hardline Cold War policies.
Japanese public opinion itself was ambivalent on the question of a
continued American military presence in Japan, although polls at
the time indicated a general enthusiasm for the US and the American way of life (Welfield 1988: 56–9).

Historical Interpretations of the Occupation

How has the occupation been viewed by historians? In the 1950s
and 1960s American scholars took a benign view, referring to the
occupation as a positive example of 'planned political change' that
built on prewar developments (e.g. the liberalism of the Taisho era)
to produce a democratic society (Ward 1968b). This view was
recently reiterated enthusiastically by a former US ambassador to
Japan and himself an eminent Japan scholar (Reischauer 1983;
1988), who argued that political, social and educational reforms of
some kind would have occurred anyway and that the occupation
merely set out the general parameters. Others (e.g. Kawai 1960)
preferred to emphasize the crucial role of the occupation in bringing about change that might not otherwise have occurred; the
explanation given for Japanese acceptance was psychological and
cultural – traumatic defeat had made the people disorientated and
open to new influences, while the traditional Japanese sense of

hierarchy made them susceptible to tutelage by what was seen as an all-powerful victor. As late as 1976 one historian referred to the occupation as an example of 'benevolent colonialism' (Duus 1976: 239). Accounts by those who worked for SCAP also highlighted the positive and far-sighted role played by MacArthur (Williams 1979; Cohen 1987), as the following observation illustrates:

> Converting a stern occupation of control and restraint into one of reconciliation and cooperation, MacArthur protected Japan from reparations assaults, insisted on disproportionate food imports and inspired the Japanese nation once more to believe in itself. (Cohen 1987: 457)

Another participant in the occupation (albeit minor), writing 40 years after the event, is convinced that the occupation made a substantial difference in the transformation of Japanese society (Passin 1992).

Revisionist historians in the early 1970s (e.g. Halliday and McCormack 1973; Dower 1975; Halliday 1975), dissatisfied with previous accounts that had treated the occupation simply as a phase in Japanese political development, emphasized the signifi-cance of the reverse course (in which Japanese conservatives were only too happy to participate) and linked this with American anti-communist and anti-populist policies throughout Asia (Schonberger 1989: 3–5). As a recent exponent of this view argues:

> In a very real sense Japan arose from the ashes of the Second World War largely on the crest of an expanded American military crusade in Asia. (Schaller 1985: 279)

In the final analysis, according to the revisionist view, the legacy of the occupation was a new conservative hegemony within Japan strongly supported by the United States.

Recent research has drawn out the continuities between war-time and postwar Japan, both in terms of personnel and a tradition of economic planning (Garon 1987; Dower 1993b: 9–32), the cru-cial strategic and economic concerns in US occupation policy (Borden 1984; Schaller 1984) and the Japanese input (both positive and negative) in the occupation reforms (Ward and Sakamoto 1987). MacArthur's role is also downplayed, with more attention being given to other SCAP officials (Schonberger 1989). The overall picture of the occupation that now emerges is a highly complex one, characterized by continuity as well as change, and by reactionary as well as progressive impulses.

One area of continuity, until recently very little explored, concerns state policy towards women. It is now argued (Uno 1993) that the prewar and wartime ideal of 'good wife, wise mother' (*ryosei kenbo*), which emphasized the importance of women's role in the home rather than in the public sphere, and the wartime government's pronatalist stance, continued to influence policy after 1945. Thus, the 1948 Eugenic Protection Law (which legalized contraception and abortion in cases where the mother's health was threatened) represented a continuing concern with the protection of mothers first evidenced in the Maternal and Infant Protection Law of 1938 (Buckley 1988). It is no coincidence either that the earliest postwar women's organizations such as the Housewives Association (established in September 1948) primarily focused on maternal and family concerns (Uno 1993: 294–308). Another recent study (Calder 1988) argues that the occupation *did* represent a fundamental break from the past, preferring to link it to political developments after 1952. Calder argues that the occupation reforms instilled in the minds of the conservative political establishment an acute sense of vulnerability that was to persist long after the occupation ended. Such an ongoing sense of vulnerability was to lead the ruling Liberal Democratic Party after the mid-1950s to adopt a systematic policy of compensating strategic interest groups (such as the small business and farming sectors) in times of political crisis as a way of maintaining the conservative hegemony. Perhaps the most significant long-term impact of the occupation, however, was that it forged amongst Japanese elites a unique and single-minded commitment to peaceful economic growth as *the* priority of national policy, which was to replace the discredited militaristic expansion of the past (Hein 1993).

3

The Creation of the Liberal Democratic Party and Political Conflict in the 1950s and 1960s

The 'San Francisco System', a term used by Japanese observers to describe Japan's alignment with US Cold War policy after the signing of the 1951 bilateral Treaty of Mutual Co-operation and Security (Dower 1993a: 4), ushered in a period of economic recovery for Japan. This recovery was initially fuelled by American military procurements during and after the Korean War, an ironical development since Washington had originally assumed in the late occupation period that Japan's economic revival would result from developing markets in, and close core–periphery links with, the countries of Southeast Asia (Cumings 1993: 50). Between 1951 and 1960 US procurements and expenditures in Japan were to pump $5.5 billion into the Japanese economy (Dower 1993b: 193). In 1952 alone the $800 million worth of US procurements in Japan represented 38 per cent of Japan's total foreign earnings (Johnson 1982: 200; Schonberger 1989: 234). Between 1951 and 1956 US military purchases in Japan paid for more than 25 per cent of Japanese imports (Hein 1993: 110) and even as late as 1958–9 such procurements were sufficient to pay for 14 per cent of Japan's imports (Halliday and McCormack 1973: 108).

It is important to note, however, that at the outset Japan faced a daunting task, not helped by the slow pace of economic recovery in Southeast Asia, the expected focus of Japan's export-led revival. Japan's trade deficit in 1953 (not including procurement income) was over $1.1 billion and even accounting for US procurements (which were declining anyway) the deficit was a hefty $400 million. US exports to Japan exceeded imports from Japan by $430 million in 1952 and $531 million in 1953 (Dower 1979: 475). In fact, throughout the nearly 20 years from 1946 to 1964 Japan's imports exceeded its exports (again excluding US procurements). Even with the benefit of US procurements Japan's current account balance was regularly in the red from 1952 to the late 1960s and on five occasions in the 1950s Japan had to borrow from the International Monetary Fund to finance basic imports (Calder 1988: 47). Nevertheless, by 1962 the London-based journal *The Economist* was referring to the Japanese economic 'miracle', characterized by high productivity, harmonious labour relations and a high rate of savings (Johnson 1982: 3). Throughout the 1960s Japan's real annual GNP growth averaged over 11 per cent and by 1965 the country had an export surplus. Japan's share of world export trade increased from 2.1 per cent in 1955 to over 7 per cent in the early 1970s (Welfield 1988: 171) and its GNP in 1970 was the third largest in the world (Hane 1992: 363). Industrial production between 1951 and 1973 grew fourteen-fold (Calder 1988: 173). This growth was spearheaded by shipbuilding, chemicals, steel and automobiles, although Japan still remained crucially dependent on imports of iron ore and oil. In 1950, for example, Japan produced 1,600 cars; by 1980 the total was 11 million, by which time Japanese car production exceeded that of the US (Horsley and Buckley 1990: 155). The economic recovery was accompanied by the increasing confidence of public opinion. Thus, in a newspaper poll in 1951 asking respondents whether they thought Japan was inferior to the US or Britain, 47 per cent answered in the affirmative and 23 per cent in the negative. In subsequent surveys those who replied that the Japanese were superior to Westerners increased from 20 per cent in 1953 to 47 per cent in 1968, while those who thought the Japanese were inferior to Westerners fell from 28 per cent to 11 per cent in the same period (Watanabe 1977: 119).

For the United States the 1951 Security Treaty not only represented a vehicle for controlling Japan by perpetuating its military subordination to Washington (Welfield 1988; Dower 1993b), but was also the cornerstone in the creation of an integrated Cold War policy that involved security treaties being signed with the Philippines, Australia and New Zealand shortly afterwards (as much as to quieten fears in those countries concerning a possible Japanese military resurgence) and later with South Korea (1953), Taiwan (1954) and various Southeast Asian nations (1954). The 1951 Security Treaty also made it clear that the Americans expected Japan in time to assume increasing responsibility for its own defence

(Stockwin 1982: 58). This was to be a continuing source of friction between the two countries in the 1950s and 1960s, as Washington's expectations collided with the reluctance of Japanese governments (evident since the late 1940s) to risk public opposition at home by moving too fast on rearmament or to divert funds needed for peaceful economic growth (Buckley 1992: 50). Close ties did develop, however, between Japan's Self Defence Forces, as they came to be called after 1954, and the American military services (Welfield 1988), as well as between the American and Japanese defence industries. Under American auspices also Japan joined the International Monetary Fund in 1952, became a member of GATT (General Agreement on Tariffs and Trade) in 1955 and entered the United Nations in 1956. International respectability was confirmed by the siting of the 1964 Olympic Games in Tokyo.

For domestic Japanese politics this period witnessed the transformation of the unstable multi-party system of the early postwar years into a quasi two-party system in the late 1950s when, in 1955, the two wings of the Socialist Party (which had formally split in 1951) were reunited and the two principal conservative parties merged to form the Liberal Democratic Party (*Jiminto*). An alternating two-party system, however, did not develop. The Liberal Democratic Party (LDP), which was more a coalition of conservative factions than a united political organization (Baerwald 1986; Curtis 1988), was to achieve majority party status in the Diet throughout the 1960s and 1970s, while the opposition fragmented as the Socialist Party again split in 1959 and a new party, the *Komeito* (Clean Government Party), emerged in 1964. Significantly, even though the LDP in its founding platform pledged to abolish Article 9 of the constitution (the Peace Clause) the party never achieved the hegemony necessary (i.e. a two-thirds majority in both houses of the Diet) for revising the constitution. Also, from the late 1960s on the LDP's share of the popular vote was never to exceed 50 per cent.

Although the LDP did not revise the constitution, the 1950s were marked by fierce political conflict as opposition parties in the Diet vigorously opposed government attempts to modify the occupation reforms and denounced Japan's continuing military alliance with the United States. These political conflicts were to culminate in the crisis over the revised Security Treaty in 1960 that sparked off the largest popular demonstrations in Japan up to that time. Political turmoil was to continue throughout the 1960s with the emergence of various citizens' movements that protested against the Vietnam War abroad and the effects of pollution and environmental damage at home. As a number of studies have shown (Upham 1987; Calder 1988; Pharr 1990), however, the LDP was able both to pre-empt the institutionalization of opposition by making concessions and to deflect political crisis by implementing redistributive policies which expanded its bases of support.

The End of the Yoshida Regime

Yoshida Shigeru, who in the years after his death in 1967 was to be hailed as the architect of Japan's postwar recovery with his espousal of economic nationalism, cautious remilitarization and close ties with the United States (referred to as the 'Yoshida Doctrine'), faced criticism from both the Right and Left in the wake of Japan's achievement of formal independence in April 1952 (Dower 1993b: 208–41). Paradoxically, whereas the nationalistic Right resented the American-imposed constitution with its limitations on the military and the diminution of the role of the Emperor while at the same time supporting hardline American Cold War policy, the Left condemned Japan's military alliance with the US and its alignment with Washington's foreign policy while staunchly defending the occupation reforms and the constitution as the principal bulwarks against the revival of militarism and undemocratic government.

Opposition to Japan's alignment with American Cold War policy had been evident before the outbreak of the Korean War in June 1950. In November 1948 the Peace Problems Symposium (*Heiwa Mondai Danwakai*), a loose grouping of academics, was formed to discuss the dangers Japan faced in becoming too closely associated with a hardline anti-communist stance. By 1950 the Symposium was drawing a clear connection between Japan's non-alignment abroad and the fate of democratic reforms at home (Koschmann 1993). In December 1949, the Japanese Socialist Party issued its Three Principles of Peace (a peace treaty to be signed with *all* former allied powers, permanent neutrality and no foreign military bases in Japan), to which a fourth – opposition to rearmament – was added in January 1951 (Stockwin 1968). Consensus began to break down once the Korean War broke out and with the signing of the Peace Treaty and the Security Treaty in 1951 the Socialist Party split at its eighth convention in October of that year (Cole, Totten and Uyehara 1966). The left wing of the party opposed both treaties, claiming that the Security Treaty did not represent deterrence and security but rather provocation that courted the danger of a pre-emptive nuclear strike by the Soviet Union, and upheld the principle of permanent neutrality. The right wing supported the Peace Treaty and although expressing ambivalence about the Security Treaty rejected neutralism and supported Japan's membership of the Western camp.

There was also division within the conservative camp, although mainly of a factional nature. Yoshida had taken advantage of the SCAP purge of party politicians to bring in his own supporters (mainly career bureaucrats like himself), two of whom – Ikeda Hayato (1899–1965) and Sato Eisaku (1901–75) – were to become prime minister themselves. After 1951, however, former party politicians now 'depurged' like Hatoyama Ichiro (whom Yoshida had replaced as head of the Liberal Party) returned to the fold to contest Yoshida's leadership, perceived by his opponents as unnecessarily high-handed and arbitrary (in the 1952 elections, 140 out of 466 lower house members elected were 'depurgees'). There was also some dissatisfaction both amongst Hatoyama's following and the rival conservative party (known originally as the Progressive Party, then the Democratic Party in 1947, and finally the Reform Party after 1952) with Yoshida's cautious approach to rearmament. In the two lower house elections of 1952 and 1953 Yoshida's Liberal Party fared badly, gaining only 240 (down from 264 previously) and 199 seats respectively; in the latter election the Hatoyama Liberals obtained 35 seats and the Reform Party 76 seats. When Hatoyama bolted the Liberal Party in November 1954 and joined with the Reform Party to form the Japan Democratic Party Yoshida's tenure as Prime Minister rapidly drew to a close. Following the passing of a no-confidence vote Yoshida resigned in December 1954, to be replaced as Prime Minister by Hatoyama. In further lower house elections in February 1955 the Democratic Party emerged as the largest single party (with 185 seats) and Yoshida's Liberals fell back further, gaining only 112 seats. Together, however, the two conservative parties held 64 per cent of the seats and obtained 63 per cent of the popular vote.

Dissatisfaction amongst some conservatives with Yoshida's go-slow policy on rearmament notwithstanding, it was during his tenure as prime minister that the first steps were taken to reverse or modify the occupation reforms, a development specifically encouraged by MacArthur's successor, General Ridgway, in May 1951, when he suggested that the Japanese government should evaluate the reforms with the intention of deciding which to retain or reverse. Shortly afterwards the government appointed a Committee for the Examination of Occupation Reform Policy (*Seirei kaisei shimon iinkai*), while in December 1953 Yoshida was to agree to the setting up of a Constitutional Revision Investigation Committee.

One of the first of the occupation reforms to be reversed was the organization of the police. By 1948, as part of SCAP's campaign to implement decentralization and disperse the powers of the prewar Home Ministry, over 1,300 local autonomous police forces at town and village level had been created. As a first step in recentralizing the police the government in June 1951 allowed communities to vote on whether to reject the continued maintenance of autonomous police forces and to opt for merging them with the National Rural Police; in the first wave of referenda carried out between June and September 1951 nearly 80 per cent of the communities concerned voted to merge, mainly for financial reasons (Livingston, Moore and Oldfather 1973: 340–6). By early 1954 only 129 towns and villages possessed their own forces (Dower 1979: 348). At the same time the government in 1952 introduced a Subversive Activities Prevention Bill, giving the police enhanced powers to target communists. Despite delaying tactics by the left-wing opposition in the Diet and a number of strikes organized by the Socialist Party's left wing and its ally *Sohyo*, the bill was enacted (Cole, Totten and Uyehara 1966). Finally, in June 1954 a new Police Law was enacted after a fierce struggle by the opposition to block its passage – a struggle that involved a riot staged in the chamber to prevent the chairman of the lower house from entering and which prompted the despatch of police forces to the Diet building to restore order, a phenomenon that was to occur on two more occasions in 1956 and 1960. The new law recentralized police administration with the National Public Safety Commission coming under the control of the prime minister's office and the creation of a National Police Agency with regional branches. Municipal police forces were abolished and local police administration was now concentrated at the prefectural level, headed by a chief of prefectural police appointed by the National Public Safety Commission. Significantly, the architect of police recentralization was

Nadao Hirokichi, a former senior official in the wartime Home Ministry.

Other changes occurring during Yoshida's last years as Prime Minister included the lifting of the ban (imposed during the occupation) on school visits to Shinto shrines and temples (Hardacre 1989), the imposition of further restrictions on organized labour in 1953 with the banning of strikes in the coal and electricity industries (Garon 1987: 241) and the curtailing of political activities amongst public school teachers (Duke 1973). This last measure was a product of the ongoing tussle between teachers and the government that has persisted throughout the postwar period (Rohlen 1984). The Japan Teachers' Union (*Nikkyoso*), created in 1947 from an amalgamation of three teachers' unions with over half a million members, had been a vigorous supporter of SCAP reforms that had decentralized education and diluted the powers of the *Mombusho* (Ministry of Education). Not surprisingly, the union had been in the forefront of radical activity during the occupation, campaigning for better working conditions and denouncing the pre-1945 system of nationalistic education; by the beginning of 1949 communist influence was pervasive amongst its leadership. The union suffered a serious setback later in 1949 during SCAP's anti-Left purge, which resulted in the dismissal of over 1,000 teachers, and as a result of laws passed in 1949 and 1950 *Nikkyoso* was deprived of its official status as a national union. Nevertheless, in the prefectural school board elections of 1950 (the first stage in the setting up of elective boards of education at the local level) one-third of the seats were gained by those affiliated with *Nikkyoso*. In the nationwide school board elections of 1952 for towns and villages as well as for prefectures *Nikkyoso* candidates gained 35 per cent of prefectural board seats and 30 per cent of board seats below the prefectural level (Duke 1973: 114).

Determined to curb the political influence of left-wing teachers, Yoshida's government in 1954 pushed through two bills in the Diet, again amidst fighting in the chamber. One measure subjected teachers in local schools to the same restrictions as those teaching in national schools; henceforth, they could not participate anywhere in political activities, except for voting, whereas previously the proscription had only applied to the district in which they worked. The other measure proscribed any teacher from inciting colleagues and students to support or oppose a political party or activity. Interestingly, the upper house replaced the criminal punishment stipulated for any infringement of this ruling with administrative punishment and insisted that intent had to be proved in the case of incitement or instigation, which ultimately made prosecution virtually impossible. As will be seen later, further conflict between teachers and government was to erupt after 1955 over the control of textbooks and the composition of school boards.

Finally, the last years of Yoshida's premiership witnessed important developments in the expanding role of MITI and the restructuring of Japan's defence forces. Because of MITI's crucial role in Japan's postwar recovery, Japan has been described as a 'developmental state' in contradistinction to the US, described as a 'regulatory state' (Johnson 1982). Whereas the latter is solely concerned with the forms and procedures of economic competition, the former is concerned with setting substantive social and economic goals. In other words, according to Johnson (ibid.: 19–24), the Japanese state had an industrial policy with a strategic or goal-oriented approach to the economy. This view has been modified recently with more emphasis being placed on the role of the private sector (particularly in consumer electronics, textiles and petrochemicals) in defining strategic long-term goals and on market competition as the motor of structural transformations (Calder 1993). Nevertheless, MITI's powers and influence were considerable in the 1950s. As was seen in chapter two, MITI inherited SCAP controls over foreign exchange after 1949, as well as powers to supervise technology imports and joint ventures. MITI, through its control of the Japan Development Bank (established in 1951), could now also implement an industrial policy via its screening of loan applications. A JDB loan, in effect, became MITI's seal of approval for a particular enterprise. Between 1953 and 1955, 83 per cent of JDB financing was funnelled into electric power, shipbuilding, coal and steel (Johnson 1982: 211). Significantly, funds that went to the JDB came under a separate budget (known as the Fiscal Investment and Loan Programme, or FILP). Funded by postal savings rather than government bonds, FILP (until 1973) was controlled by economic bureaucrats and not subject to public review or scrutiny in the Diet as was the case with the general account budget (Calder 1993: 58–61).

Also, through its Industrial Rationalization Council (comprising business executives and academics as well as bureaucrats), MITI involved itself with a variety of industrial issues such as management reform, lifetime employment and worker productivity. Interestingly, US influence was particularly prevalent in some of these areas in what has been called the 'politics of productivity', as American techniques of quality control and production management were imported into Japan (Gordon 1993: 376). MITI's labour sub-committee after 1951 produced standards for a wage promotion system and devised employee training programmes.

Through a process of 'informal advice' MITI also sought to rationalize production. It encouraged the recombining of former *zaibatsu* trading companies, allowing tax write-offs for the costs of opening foreign branches and for contingency funds against bad debt contracts. In 1952, MITI 'advised' the ten largest cotton spinning firms to reduce production and then assigned quotas to each individual firm; one form of leverage was to threaten to withhold foreign currency allocations for the supply of imported raw cotton. Similar advice was given to the rubber and steel industries (Johnson 1982: 224–5). The 1947 Anti-Monopoly Law was modified in 1953, allowing MITI to sanction 'co-operative behaviour' (*kyodo koi*) in order to limit production and sales for depressed industries and to lower costs and promote exports for industries undergoing rationalization.

In some ways the creation of MITI in 1949 launched the partnership between the bureaucracy and business that many have seen as the key factor in Japan's economic success (Yanaga 1968; Stockwin 1982; Johnson 1982). Many economic bureaucrats on retirement were to become corporate executives in what is known as *amakudari* ('descent from heaven') and there was thus plenty of scope for informal discussion between them and their incumbent juniors in the ministries they had formerly inhabited (known as *nemawashi*: 'digging around the roots'). Of the first five postwar presidents of *Keidanren* (Federation of Economic Organizations), three were former bureaucrats (Johnson 1982: 71). One observer, in pointing to the influence of the economic bureaucracy, even goes so far as to maintain that until the mid-1960s, MITI and the Ministry of Finance virtually ran Japan (van Wolferen 1989: 122). Quite apart from undermining his own thesis that Japan is not an orthodox state because it comprises a variety of overlapping hierarchies (the formal legislature, bureaucracy, big business) with no supreme institution having ultimate policy-making jurisdiction (ibid.: 5), such a description obscures the fact that MITI's informal advice on rationalization was not always accepted (see later) and that governments after the mid-1950s implemented redistributive policies not necessarily perceived as priorities by the economic bureaucrats or as in the interests of big business (Calder 1988).

Yoshida's premiership ended with the renaming of the National Police Reserve as the Self Defence Forces in July 1954 (Welfield 1988: 81–2). Defence laws passed in the Diet asserted that the SDF defended the 'peace and independence of the country' (rather than maintaining internal order) and thus entailed defence against direct or indirect aggression (Dower 1979: 438). By the time the occupation ended in 1952, the National Police Reserve was already equipped with mortars, artillery and tanks, and comprised 110,000 men. By 1954, its strength had increased to 180,000. With the addition of a newly established air force and the maritime safety force (created in 1948), the SDF (*jieitai*) formally came into existence. Unlike the prewar situation, however, civilian control over the military was firmly established (it has already been noted that Yoshida had always been wary of the military). The SDF came under the control of the Defence Agency, headed by a junior minister of state and attached to the prime minister's office. In 1956, the National Defence Council (*kokubo kaigi*) was to be created as a co-ordinating body. Headed by the prime minister, the council also comprised the foreign minister, finance minister and director-general of the Defence Agency (Dower 1979; Welfield 1988). In 1972, its membership was expanded to include the minister of MITI and the chief cabinet secretary (Stockwin 1982). Ironically, whereas Yoshida insisted on civilian and parliamentary control of the SDF in order to avoid the situation of an independent military that had prevailed in the 1930s, Washington was apprehensive that such control might paralyse the alliance at a time of crisis (Welfield 1988: 113).

Supporters of Yoshida's limited rearmament claimed that it was not unconstitutional since it did not constitute the kind of 'war potential' needed to wage modern war, a rather disingenuous argument since by the late 1960s the SDF were to possess a variety of sophisticated weapons (including antitank rockets) as well as diesel-powered submarines, destroyers and fighter aircraft (Bix 1970). Already an appeal made in 1952 by Suzuki Mosaburo, Chairman of the left-wing Socialist Party, to the Supreme Court to have the National Police Reserve declared unconstitutional under Article 9 had brought no success. The appeal was dismissed on the grounds that a judgement could only be sought in the courts when there existed a concrete legal dispute between specific parties

(Stockwin 1982: 182). The House of Councillors, however, *did* confirm in 1954 that both conscription and the despatch of forces overseas were unconstitutional. The defence laws, moreover, reflected Yoshida's more cautious approach rather than the more hawkish programme of the rival conservative Democratic Party, which in the 1952 elections had called for immediate large-scale rearmament, conscription and an independent foreign policy (Welfield 1988: 62–3).

The creation of the SDF in July 1954 was to some extent the product of American pressure. As a condition for US military aid as promised in the Mutual Security Assistance Agreement signed between the two countries in March 1954 (Washington agreed to supply $150 million worth of weapons and equipment as well as $100 million in the form of offshore procurements), Japan was expected to increase its own defence capabilities. In November 1953, on an official visit to Japan,Vice-president Nixon had even asserted that Article 9 of Japan's constitution was a mistake (Dower 1979: 464). Washington and Tokyo were still not on the same wavelength however. Negotiations for a Mutual Security Assistance agreement had begun in July 1953 but Yoshida was anxious that such an agreement would have as much economic as military significance. Not surprisingly it was Finance Minister Ikeda Hayato who led Japan's delegation to Washington to discuss the agreement in October 1953. Tokyo successfully rebuffed Washington's demands that Japan's military forces expand quickly and that they should play an active role overseas. The final agreement, while affirming that Japan would assume increasing responsibility, also recognized the importance of economic stability and that such increases in defence capability would be implemented in accordance with constitutional provisions (Dower 1979: 467; Welfield 1988: 106–7). Despite hopes expressed by Washington as early as 1952 that Japan's military forces would total 350,000 by 1955 (Dower 1979: 432), the overall strength of the SDF in 1954 was 180,000. On the other hand, the SDF obtained considerable US military assistance in subsequent years. Between 1954 and 1960 nearly 3,000 Japanese army, navy and airforce officers were trained in the United States, while in 1962 98 per cent of the weapons and 82 per cent of communications equipment had been obtained from the US (Welfield 1988: 111).

Furthermore, although Tokyo had to accept further restrictions on trade with the communist bloc as a result of the MSA agreement (although the provision had been relegated to an annex), Yoshida continued to believe that communist China remained Japan's natural market. Clearly he did not share Washington's Cold War hostility towards China, as his comments made in 1951 demonstrate:

> Red or white, China remains our next door neighbour. Geography and economic laws will, I believe, prevail in the long run over any ideological differences and artificial trade barriers. (Cited in Dower 1979: 395)

Such an approach would lead to the sanctioning of private and semi-official trade with China throughout the 1950s and 1960s.

The Creation of the LDP and the Security Treaty Crisis of 1960

The reuniting of the two wings of the Socialist Party in October 1955 – after their separate conventions the previous January had pledged to work together (Stockwin 1968) – prompted the two conservative parties to effect a similar arrangement. In the February 1955 elections the two wings of the Socialist Party had gained seats; the left wing increasing their representation from 72 to 89 seats and the right wing from 66 to 67. Together they had polled 29 per cent of the popular vote and with the merger the Socialist Party was now the second largest single party in the Diet. For the first time, too, the socialists possessed one-third of the lower house seats necessary to block constitutional revision. The newly united JSP now adopted the aim of 'self-reliant independence' to replace that of 'neutralism' espoused by the socialist left wing in the early 1950s; it also continued to oppose rearmament and called for the restoration of relations with communist China (a socialist delegation was to visit Beijing in April 1957).

In November 1955, barely one month after the socialist merger, the two principal conservative parties, actively encouraged by business interests behind the scenes, formed the Liberal Democratic Party. This helped to break the conservative deadlock since during the previous year Hatoyama and his Democratic Party government had faced constant criticism from Yoshida's Liberal Party and only remained in power at the suffrance of the socialists. For the first time the Japanese political structure seemed to be developing into a genuine two-party system; out of a total of 467 lower house seats the LDP had 297 and the JSP 156 seats. Conflict in the Diet was inevitable, especially as the LDP's founding platform committed the party to amending the constitution. Prime Minister Hatoyama Ichiro set up a cabinet commission to investigate the question in July 1956. Over the next few years, however, enthusiasm amongst conservatives for constitutional revision waned, partly a result of the LDP's lack of an overwhelming majority and partly because Article 9 was seen to have economic advantages. Although the LDP Constitution Investigation Committee proposed revising the 1948 Civil Code to allow for more importance to be attached to the *ie* (patriarchal household) this was effectively blocked by the opposition (Steiner 1987: 205). The LDP platform of 1962 was specifically to reject the idea of constitutional revision aimed at 'restoring the principles of imperial sovereignty or the prewar family system'. Not surprisingly, when the cabinet commission recommended revision in 1964 the recommendation was not acted upon (McNelly 1987; Dower 1993b).

The '1955 System', as it came to be called, seemed to many to mark a significant turning-point. In 1955, Japan's GNP surpassed the prewar peak for the first time, an event seen by one journal in 1956 as representing the end of the postwar period. MITI also announced at this time the inauguration of the 'citizen's car project' – the vehicle industry hitherto had concentrated on the manufacture of trucks and buses – which culminated in the appearance of the Datsun Bluebird in 1959. As one historian has noted (Dower 1993b: 17–18), the consolidation of conservative power thus coincided with economic recovery and the onset of a commercialized mass culture.

During Hatoyama's one year as Prime Minister after the creation of the LDP, relations with the Soviet Union were normalized while at home there was fierce opposition to the government's attempts to bring education under further centralized control. Hatoyama, in fact, had specifically announced his intention of normalizing relations with the Soviet Union after he succeeded Yoshida as Prime Minister in December 1954. After two years of negotiations (held in London) a joint declaration was signed in October 1956 normalizing diplomatic and economic ties between the two countries. Reparation claims were mutually renounced and former Japanese prisoners of war captured by Russian troops in the last weeks of the war and who had been detained in the Soviet Union since 1945 were repatriated. Normalization of relations with the Soviet Union facilitated Japan's entrance into the UN the same year. One issue, however, remained unresolved. At the end of the war the Russians had captured from Japan the four islands north of Hokkaido that make up the southern chain of the Kuriles (in Japan they are referred to as the Northern Territories). Hatoyama temporarily waived the demand for their return in favour of reaching an agreement (much to the chagrin of many within his party), but the issue was to remain a sore point in Soviet–Japanese relations, a problem that continues today even after the break-up of the Soviet Union, since the Russian Federation still refuses to negotiate the return of the islands to Japan.

As one study of the 1954–6 negotiations has shown (Hellmann 1969), there was considerable *intra-party* division over the question of normalization that paralleled similar divisions amongst the principal business organizations, all of which indicated that a consensus did not originally exist amongst conservative and business elites. The older and more conservative business leaders such as the heads of *Keidanren* (Federation of Economic Organizations) and *Nikkeiren* (Japan Federation of Employers' Associations), for example, advocated prudence, while those supporting a more flexible approach included the president of *Nissho* (Japan Chamber of Commerce), which represented small and medium enterprises, and younger executives affiliated with *Keizai Doyukai* (Economic Friends' Association), whose membership was limited to individuals who were generally critical of the prewar business establishment. Despite opposition from elements of big businesss Hatoyama pushed ahead with his policy of normalizing relations with the Soviet Union, demonstrating that business did not always have effective access to conservative decision-making. The view that the LDP was simply the political arm of big business (e.g. Yanaga 1968) needs to be modified. Interestingly, Hatoyama was also able to exploit differences amongst the JSP (like the LDP, a coalition of semi-autonomous factions whose origins dated from the ideological debates of the 1920s) to gain cross-party support for his policy.

Shortly after the normalization of relations with the Soviet Union was approved by the Diet in November 1956, Hatoyama resigned and was succeeded as Prime Minister by Ishibashi Tanzan, the Minister of Finance. As will be seen in the case of Kishi Nobusuke in 1960, Hatoyama's resignation was a concession to factional opponents within the LDP who had criticized his policy. Before his resignation, however, the government had confronted militant teachers over its proposed changes to the education system (Masami 1986). In April 1956 the School Boards Bill was passed in the lower house (with the opposition refusing to vote); elective school boards at the prefectural, municipal and village levels that had been set up in the wake of the occupation reforms were now to be appointed by prefectural and municipal governments and their membership was to be reduced in number. The following month a Textbook Bill was also passed in the lower house, enabling the appointed prefectural school boards to establish selection committees to make the final selections from an approved list of textbooks and to have one text used throughout the prefecture for a given subject at each grade level. In fact an elaborate system of textbook certification had evolved since the late 1940s. Postwar textbooks were produced privately with the Education Ministry providing course outlines for each age level and indicating what material should be covered. Each year publishers presented drafts to the Ministry, which were then submitted to a group of qualified educators to ascertain whether the drafts were in accordance with the educational aims as set out in the 1947 Fundamental Law of Education. Certification of textbooks (to ensure that texts did not legitimize ultranationalist and militarist ideals) had thus been an integral component of the occupation reforms. Once the manuscript was approved publishers could list their books and schools were free to choose from amongst them. In 1955, for example, 92 textbook publishers printed over 230 million texts and a sixth grade teacher had a choice of 173 books (Livingston, Moore and Oldfather 1973: 536). It was conservative condemnation of these textbooks as biased that prompted the passing of the Textbook Bill. Conservatives argued that with enhanced government control over certification and enforced uniformity of textbook use the Teachers' Union would be prevented from using texts that advanced its left-wing agenda.

Nikkyoso organized mass demonstrations in May 1956 and half a million teachers walked out of their classrooms. Joined by *Sohyo*, *Zengakuren* (All-Japan Federation of Student Self-Governing Bodies) and the Housewives Association, *Nikkyoso* also led demonstrations outside the Diet building. The government abandoned its Textbook Bill but persisted with the School Boards Bill. Fights broke out in the upper house in June 1956 and the police had to be called in to restore order before the bill was finally passed (Duke 1973: 133). Although the government did not succeed in changing the system of certification, subsequent administrative measures clearly demonstrated a conservative reversal of the occupation educational reforms. Beginning with junior high school level, for example, social science textbooks were again divided into history, geography and current affairs, whereas occupation reforms had eliminated history and geography as separate subjects. The Education Ministry's own review committee (expanded from 16 to 80), whose final approval of the decisions reached by the group of educators concerning the submitted textbook drafts had hitherto been a formality, began to take a more active role. One junior high school text was rejected on the grounds that it was overly partial to the new constitution and portrayed Japan's role in the Second World War in excessively negative terms (Livingston, Moore and Oldfather 1973: 536–7). The question of textbook revision was to have serious ramifications for Japan during the 1980s in its relations with China (see chapter four).

The conservative 'counter-offensive' against the occupation reforms came to a head during the premiership of Kishi Nobusuke (1957–60). From a former samurai family, Kishi was a graduate of the elite Tokyo University Law Faculty and while studying there had been a supporter of various right-wing student groups. He became one of the 'renovationist' bureaucrats in the 1930s serving in the Ministry of Commerce and Industry before working in Japanese-occupied Manchuria in the late 1930s. In 1941, Kishi became a member of Tojo's wartime cabinet as Minister of Commerce. After the war he was held in prison as a Class A war criminal, during which time he met and formed close ties with Kodama Yoshio, who was to become a key member of the ultranationalist underworld. Released in 1948 and 'depurged' in 1952, Kishi soon entered politics, eventually becoming Secretary-General of the LDP in 1955 and Deputy Prime Minister in Ishibashi's cabinet. When Ishibashi had to resign in early 1957 because of ill-health Kishi took over as Prime Minister. A vigorous supporter of constitutional revision, rearmament and patriotic education, Kishi also favoured close and active co-operation with the US (Welfield 1988: 116–25).

Kishi's approach was more confrontational than that of his predecessors. His government withdrew from certain categories of civil servants the right to maintain union membership, while the temporary law limiting the right of coalminers and electric power workers to strike was made permanent. Kishi also decided to confront *Nikkyoso* head on by instituting a teachers' rating system (based on 'efficiency') throughout the country, supposedly to determine salary increases. *Nikkyoso* perceived this measure as yet another government attempt to control teachers (in particular, it was feared that efficiency ratings would be used to penalize left-wing teachers) and called on its members to strike. In April 1958, 35,000 members of the union's Tokyo branch walked out of the classrooms in protest. Passions were further inflamed when the Ministry of Education (under Nadao Hirokichi, a pre-1945 Home Ministry bureaucrat) in August 1958 outlined a revised course of study that would standardize the curriculum and reintroduce moral education, or ethics (*shushin*), a subject previously proscribed during the occupation period. In one city, in August 1958, *Sohyo* sponsored a rally of thousands of workers and students to protest the rating plan, although an attempt to organize a nationwide boycott of classes in September failed. Prefectural boards of education proceeded to carry out the rating plan; during the turbulent process, which lasted until 1960, 112 teachers were dismissed, 1,018 demoted and over 52,000 had their salaries reduced (Duke 1973: 154).

Further evidence of Kishi's confrontational approach *vis-à-vis* the opposition was apparent after the May 1958 elections, the first to be held since the reunification of the Socialist Party and formation of the LDP. The LDP gained 287 seats (with 57.8 per cent of the vote), down ten seats compared to the combined strength of the previous Liberal and Democratic Parties in 1955, while the Socialist Party increased its number of seats from 156 to 166 (with 32.9 per cent of the vote). Nevertheless, the LDP voted itself the chairmanships of all the lower house committees, breaking with the previous tradition of sharing such chairmanships with the opposition. Kishi did not have everything his own way, however. In October 1958, after violent opposition in the Diet, he was forced to shelve a government bill (Police Duties Law Amendment Bill) that would have extended police powers to control demonstrations.

The most serious conflict during Kishi's premiership concerned the revised Security Treaty with the United States. Kishi's determined attempt to see the revised treaty ratified by the Diet was to result in the abuse of accepted norms of parliamentary procedure (Baerwald 1977). Japanese government attempts to revise the treaty had begun in early 1955 when Foreign Minister Shigemitsu Mamoru had visited Washington, during which time the American government had again pressed for a Japanese commitment to a more active overseas role for the Self Defence Force. A joint communiqué issued at the end of Shigemitsu's visit caused uproar in Japan because it seemed to suggest that Japan might undertake unspecified military commitments in the western Pacific in return for a revision of the treaty (Welfield 1988: 108).

Kishi had made it clear on becoming Prime Minister that he wished to renegotiate the treaty on more equal terms. For the Japanese government it was imperative that an agreement be reached given the importance of the US for the Japanese economy. By the end of the 1950s, for example, the US was Japan's most important trading partner, purchasing 27 per cent of Japan's exports and supplying 35 per cent of its imports (Welfield 1988: 90). Japan was also dependent on Washington's support in obtaining borrowing privileges from the World Bank (after India, Japan became the largest borrower in the 1950s) and the US Import–Export Bank to pay for its imports of food and raw materials (Halliday and McCormack 1973: 14).

The suspicion that Kishi's revised treaty would associate Japan even more with Washington's military and foreign policies fuelled growing domestic opposition. Incidents involving US military personnel in Japan also exacerbated the situation; a 1957 report, for example, noted that 150 Japanese had been killed or wounded by stray bullets or shells from US firing ranges (Packard 1966: 38). Already there had been several abortive legal attempts to have the Security Treaty declared unconstitutional. In March 1959, for example, the Tokyo District Court acquitted seven defendants who had been charged in 1957 with breaking into the US Air Force base at Tachikawa (west of Tokyo) after the runway had been extended onto agricultural land. Under the Administrative Agreement that accompanied the Security Treaty the demonstrators faced heavier penalties than those imposed for trespass on other kinds of property. The charges were quashed by the Tokyo District Court on the grounds that the Security Treaty (and hence the Administrative Agreement) was illegal under Article 9 of the constitution. In December 1959, however, the Supreme Court overturned the ruling, arguing that the Security Treaty was a 'political question' and could only be dealt with by the Diet and the government (Packard 1966: 131–3; Stockwin 1982: 208).

A more significant avenue of protest was the broad coalition that began to form in March 1959 to oppose the revised treaty.

Comprising socialists, communists and the student national federation (*Zengakuren*), this coalition called itself the People's Council for Preventing Revision of the Security Treaty (*Ampo joyaku kaitei soshi kokumin kaigi*). At its first meeting, opposition to nuclear weapons, foreign military bases and rearmament was confirmed as well as support for the constitution. A regional joint struggle council was formed in each prefecture and by August 1959 all 46 prefectures had such councils. By July 1960 there were also 1,686 district joint struggle councils (Packard 1966). Intellectuals also joined the protest movement when in December 1959 the Peace Problems Symposium issued a statement opposing treaty revision. The participation of the Communist Party in the protest movement was particularly noticeable, coming as it did after the party's modest electoral revival in 1955 and 1958. Driven underground after 1949 as the party resorted to an insurrectionary strategy (see chapter two) and wiped out electorally in the 1952 elections, the JCP at its 6th National Congress in July 1955 condemned the 'ultra-Left adventurism' of previous years and declared support for legal political activity within the system (Scalapino 1967). JCP leaders like Nosaka Sanzo appeared in public for the first time since 1950. In the 1955 elections the JCP won two seats (2 per cent of the vote) and in 1958 one seat (2.6 per cent of the vote). The party's electoral breakthrough, however, had to await the 1970s.

It should be noted, furthermore, that the coalition opposing the revised treaty was riven by internal tensions. The Socialist Party underwent another split in September 1959 when Nishio Suehiro, a veteran of the prewar moderate labour movement and leader of the party's right wing, bolted the party along with 53 followers in reaction to the growing influence of the Marxist Left within the party. In January 1960 he was to form the Democratic Socialist Party (DSP), which was to gain 17 seats in the November 1960 elections. The student national federation (*Zengakuren*), founded in 1948 (Krauss 1988), had initially been under communist influence, but by 1958 had become more assertively independent; it was to comprise a plethora of ideologically opposed factions, a feature that was to hamper the student movement in the late 1960s.

In January 1960 Kishi left for Washington (amidst huge demonstrations staged at Haneda airport) and signed the revised treaty; the following month it was introduced into the Diet. The treaty (text in Livingston, Moore and Oldfather 1973: 271–4) explicitly obliged the US to act 'to meet the common danger' in case of

armed attack on either party in the territories under Japan's jurisdiction, while a new administrative agreement relieved Tokyo of
the obligation to contribute to the maintenance of American military personnel in Japan. Kishi also pointed to the fact that two
objectionable features of the previous treaty had been removed:
the clause permitting US forces in Japan to quell internal disturbances at Tokyo's request, and the requirement for Japan to obtain
Washington's prior consent before granting military rights to a
third party. Furthermore, the revised treaty provided for joint government consultations in the event that the security of Japan or the
peace and security of the Far East were threatened (Buckley 1992:
92). In an exchange of notes accompanying the treaty, Washington
also agreed to consult with the Japanese government beforehand
on any major changes in the deployment of US military personnel
in Japan or in use of equipment, as well as in the event that US
bases in Japan were used for military combat operations outside
Japan. The treaty could be terminated after ten years if either party
gave one year's advance notice. A recent study argues that there
were few practical differences between the two treaties (Welfield
1988: 141–8), especially as neither treaty required direct Japanese
military participation in US Far Eastern strategy, while the article
on prior consultation did not operate if changes or operations were
undertaken to protect Japan itself or American bases from direct
external attack. Interestingly, while Kishi himself might have
wanted a firmer *bilateral* military alliance (involving a more active
role for Japanese forces), the certainty that such an alliance would
have met with fierce opposition from within the LDP prevented
him from pursuing the idea.

Kishi aimed to have the treaty ratified in the lower house by 19
May, the date when the Diet session ended (according to Japanese
parliamentary procedure legislation not completed by the time a
Diet session ended was automatically abandoned). Since a treaty
automatically came into effect 30 days after ratification by the
lower house if not approved of before that time by the upper house,
Kishi calculated that the matter would be resolved by the time US
President Eisenhower visited Japan in June. The political crisis
began when the government proposed a fifty-day extension of the
regular Diet session on May 19, since the socialist opposition had
been able to prevent formal ratification by that date (Baerwald
1977). Socialist Diet members thereupon staged a sit-down protest
outside the Speaker's office to prevent the Speaker from opening

the session. By the evening of 19 May the Diet building was also surrounded by up to 15,000 demonstrators. The police were ordered into the building (as they had been in 1956) with orders to remove physically the recalcitrant socialists, thus allowing the Speaker to open the plenary session approving the fifty-day extension (in the presence of LDP members only). With a new session opening the 'next day' (i.e. after midnight) the treaty was ratified shortly after midnight on 20 May, thereby ensuring that the treaty would go into effect 30 days later in time for President Eisenhower's visit. Significantly, not only were socialist members absent from the parliamentary session, but also a number of LDP members (not belonging to Kishi's faction) conspicuously absented themselves from the proceedings.

Tension was exacerbated in May with the collapse of the US–Soviet summit following the U-2 spyplane incident. The opposition charged that the American plane shot down over the Soviet Union was only one of many based in Japan that had been used for such purposes. Eisenhower's forthcoming visit to Japan, far from being perceived as a goodwill tour to cement American–Japanese cooperation, was increasingly denounced by the opposition as a provocative act designed to highlight the war preparedness of American military bases in Asia. This, together with Kishi's arbitrary methods in obtaining treaty ratification, sparked off the largest demonstrations to date. On 4 June, for example, a stoppage by communication workers involved over five million, while over 13 million people signed petitions urging new elections. On 10 June the US presidential secretary and the US ambassador (the son of General MacArthur) were surrounded by angry crowds as the former arrived at Tokyo airport to prepare for Eisenhower's visit. Clashes between demonstrators and police outside the Diet on 15 June resulted in 600 students being injured and one killed. Not surprisingly, Eisenhower's visit was formally cancelled on 16 June. Despite further demonstrations outside the Diet on 19 June (involving 300,000 people), the treaty was ratified by the upper house. In the wake of these protests (on 21 June another strike involving six million workers broke out), it appears that Kishi seriously considered mobilizing the ground Self Defence Force, only to be dissuaded from so doing by the director-general of the Defence Agency (Welfield 1988: 139).

Like Hatoyama before him, Kishi bowed to pressure from within the LDP and resigned shortly after the treaty was ratified by the upper house. Kishi's tactics had abused the norms of parliamentary procedure and the cancellation of Eisenhower's visit had resulted in an enormous loss of face for the government. Some factional leaders of the LDP had also opposed the revised treaty itself. By resigning, Kishi took responsibility for the crisis while also ensuring the maintenance of LDP rule. In July 1960 he was succeeded by another factional leader, Ikeda Hayato. Ikeda, a former finance minister and minister of MITI, had been elected LDP president a few days earlier and was known to have the support of the big business community (Yanaga 1968).

At the same time as the Kishi government was confronting opposition over the revised security treaty, a significant turning-point was occurring in the history of the postwar union movement. A bitter one-year strike (1959–60) at the Miike Coal Mine in Kyushu (owned by the Mitsui Mining Company) in response to lay-offs and technological change led to splits within the union movement and ultimately sealed the fate of the coal industry (Livingston, Moore and Oldfather 1973: 488–94; Gordon 1993: 381–2). The Mitsui Mining Company owned six of the country's largest collieries and its 35,000 employees constituted the Mitsui Coal Miners Federation (*Sankoren*). In August 1959, when the Federation accepted company proposals to encourage voluntary retirement (with severance allowances) for up to 5,000 employees the Miike local (the largest of the Federation's branches) fiercely opposed the plan, especially since 2,000 of the proposed redundancies were to occur at the Miike mine. A strike broke out in November 1959 when the company arbitrarily issued dismissal notices to 1,200 Miike employees (including 300 union activists).

The National Coal Union (*Tanro*) initially supported the strike while the Mitsui Coal Miners Federation remained distinctly cool. Splits soon occurred in the strike movement as the Mitsui White Collar Employees Federation, an affiliate of *Sankoren*, announced its intention to bargain separately with the company; by March 1960, also, a faction within the Miike local had organized a second union that seceded from the National Coal Union and was quickly recognized by the company. The National Coal Union thus failed to organize an industry-wide strike and was eventually forced to seek arbitration from the Central Labour Relations Commission. The resulting decision upheld the company's position (with severance pay increased); the National Coal Union rejected the decision while *Sankoren* accepted it. The strike lingered on until after the accession of Ikeda to the premiership and the drawing up of a revised mediation formula in August 1960. The 1,200 employees originally discharged the previous November, if they consented to resign 'voluntarily' within the ensuing month, were to receive an extra livelihood bonus, while retraining was promised for those made redundant. The National Coal Union accepted the formula in September 1960, thus bringing the strike to an end.

The outcome was a heavy defeat for one of the few national unions capable of organizing an industry-wide shutdown, as well as accelerating the rundown of the coal industry itself. Such a run-down took place against the background of a vigorous debate during the 1950s between those who emphasized natural resource development as an economic priority (implying support for the coal and hydroelectricity industries) and those who insisted that priority must be given to the growth of export industry (implying an in-crease in petroleum and coal imports). The second option won out since it was perceived as the quickest route to self-sufficiency (Hein 1993).

Economic Growth

Ikeda, on becoming Prime Minister, sought to avoid the politics of confrontation that had been so evident during Kishi's premiership. In particular, he promised to focus government attention on en-hancing economic growth and consumption, and the grandiose ambition was expressed to double people's incomes over the next few years. Hein (1994) points out, in fact, that strategies and goals of economic development were subjects of vigorous debate in the late 1950s and early 1960s. Disagreeing with a popularly held view that Japan is an apolitical society (e.g. van Wolferen 1989), Hein describes Japan as a "passionately political place" (Hein 1994: 759) during this period, since debate over economic growth always had a political agenda. For leftist critics, intellectuals and economists, economic growth was not promoted simply for its own sake but rather was invoked in the cause of peace and democracy. It was argued that the raising of living standards and equalization of in-comes would eliminate poverty (a cause of war). Furthermore, enhancement of civilian consumption rather than production of military goods was seen as the only way to ensure economic growth; it was therefore in Japan's interest to pursue a neutralist and non-nuclear foreign policy that would allow the country to trade as widely as possible within a stable global system. The LDP took on board the assumption that economic growth had to be linked with the improvement of people's living standards, although it remained committed to the military alliance with the US. As will be discussed later, the *political* dimension of economic policies implemented by LDP governments had more to do with preserving conservative hegemony.

The policy of pursuing rapid economic growth after 1960 entailed also the rationalization of agriculture (laws in 1961–2 encouraged larger holdings and relaxed restrictions on land transfers) and the phasing out of old industries. Priority was given to competitive heavy and chemical industries (steel, shipbuilding, oil refining, petrochemicals) as well as to the production of cost-effective and technology-intensive consumer durables (cars, electrical goods, synthetic fibres). Between 1958–65 the growth rate averaged 10 per cent annually (compared to 4.8 per cent in the US, 5.8 per cent in France and 3.4 per cent in the UK), while between 1965–70 it averaged 11 per cent annually (Fukui 1988: 188; Welfield 1988: 171). In 1960, Japan's GNP was already the fifth largest in the world and by the end of the decade was second only to that of the US. During this period, also, Japan began to reduce tariffs to a level below those of the US, as well as phasing out controls on currency transactions and easing restrictions on foreign investment. By 1970, for example, the American-owned IBM held 70 per cent of Japan's computer market through its subsidiary National Cash Register Company (Halliday and McCormack 1973: 5).

Industrial growth brought dramatic change to the Japanese countryside. Between 1955 and 1970 the number of farmer households declined by nearly one million (from 6.043 to 5.342 million), while the proportion of farmer household members actually engaged in agriculture decreased from 53 per cent to 39 per cent during the same period. Whereas, for example, the average farmer household in 1955 had 2.7 members engaged in full-time farming, by 1970 this had declined to one (Fukui 1988: 192–3). The proportion of farmers in the *total* workforce fell from 40 per cent to 19 per cent between 1955 and 1970. The number of part-time farming households increased, with male members often engaged, either full-time or part-time, in non-agricultural employment (one out of four farmers aged between 35 and 39 in 1955 had quit by 1970) and actual farming frequently being carried out by women and older male members. The importance of alternative employment for farmer households can be seen in the fact that while in 1955 the average farmer household derived 71 per cent of its income from farming, by 1970 only 37 per cent was derived from this source. Rural areas also witnessed enhanced material prosperity. The percentage of farmer households owning a washing machine increased from 5.2 per cent to 22.9 per cent between 1958 and 1962, while in the same period television ownership increased from 2.6 per cent to 48.9 per cent (Fukui 1988: 209–10).

A book published in 1970 captured the American sense of awe with Japan's industrial growth, a phenomenon described as a 'new Japonisme' in contrast to the 'old Japonisme' of the late nineteenth century when some Westerners, dismayed by Meiji Japan's modernization drive, extolled traditional Japan's artistic and cultural attributes (Lehmann 1984). Entitled *The Emerging Japanese Superstate: Challenge and Response* (Kahn 1970), it suggested that such growth was the result of workers' identification with, and loyalty to, the companies and enterprises for which they worked and of the assumption, shared by workers and employers alike, that increased production contributed to the national interest. The book cited a company song performed by workers of the Matsushita Electric Company to demonstrate this point:

> For the building of a new Japan,
> Let's put our strength and mind together
> Doing our best to promote production,
> Sending our goods to the people of the world.
> Endlessly and continuously,
> Like water gushing out of a fountain,
> Grow industry, grow! grow! grow!
> Harmony and sincerity,
> Matsushita Electric.
> (Cited in Kahn 1970: 110)

Two factors need to be considered, however. First, recent research (Garon 1987; Kinzley 1991) has emphasized that phenomena such as company loyalty and harmonious labour relations were not necessarily the product of innate Japanese cultural values as has often been claimed by both Western and Japanese commentators. In the late nineteenth century, despite appalling working conditions and labour unrest, Japanese employers frequently trumpeted the existence of a traditional paternalism that characterized their relationship to workers in order to distinguish Japan's labour relations from those prevailing in the West; hence, they argued, formal labour legislation (on the Western model) was unnecessary and unhelpful (Marshall 1967). Official propaganda and the initiatives of labour bureaucrats designed to promote consensus and co-operative labour relations during the 1920s and 1930s were the result of conscious *political* decisions to safeguard stability at a time of increasing labour turmoil. It is no coincidence that 'institutionalized paternalism', as one historian calls it (Smith 1984), began to emerge in the 1920s within larger firms whereby lifelong employment (*shushin koyo*), advancement based on seniority and various bonus schemes were introduced to secure the loyalty of workers. It is precisely this aspect of labour militance and the government response to it that is missing from Vogel's (1979) praise of the Japanese model, which simply notes that lifelong employment was introduced in order to ensure a highly skilled workforce.

Second, this 'institutionalized paternalism', which became more elaborate after 1945 as workers were encouraged to identify more closely with their companies (Ike 1973: 37, 40), only applied to larger enterprises, and even then only to regular employees of such companies, since many of them also employed temporary or day workers. Since the beginning of Japan's industrialization, in fact, a 'dual economy' had existed in which larger enterprises had been considerably outnumbered by smaller businesses and workshops (textiles, food processing, wholesale and retail trades) employing fewer workers. In 1965, for example, those working in businesses employing less than 100 workers accounted for 53 per cent of wage earners, while those in businesses employing less than 1,000 accounted for 83 per cent of the workforce. In 1981, 74.3 per cent of the workforce in manufacturing was employed in firms with fewer than 300 employees (Calder 1988: 314). These workers neither enjoyed the same privileges nor attained similar wage levels as their counterparts in the larger enterprises (Fukui 1988: 198; Buckley 1990: 44).

Furthermore, a recent study (Friedman 1988) argues that it was the expansion of *smaller* producers, who adopted flexible manufacturing strategies based on product modification or change to break up mass markets (rather than on price competition), that contributed to high-speed growth in the 1960s and 1970s. Between 1954 and 1977, for example, the contribution of small/medium firms employing less than 300 workers (which employed over 70 per cent of the workforce in 1977) to Japan's total manufacturing value rose from 49 per cent to 58 per cent (Friedman 1988: 10–11). Taking issue with both the bureaucratic regulation thesis espoused by Johnson (1982) and the market regulation thesis (the assumption that if economies were left to the market they would all move eventually towards larger units of mass production based on economies of scale), Friedman points out that Japanese manufacturing became increasingly decentralized amongst flexibly organized firms that were able to compete by offering new products. A system of small-firm support and regional co-operation amongst smaller enterprises, Friedman (1988: 34) continues, counteracted tendencies towards the institutionalization of the dual structure (in which small producers are preserved only for their ability to squeeze labour and provide cheap parts for larger firms) in the late 1950s and instead encouraged widespread flexible manufacturing by independent and technically efficient small firms. These flexible manufacturing techniques were carried out in the machine tool industry as well as in electronics and the automobile industry – industries usually thought of in the West as 'natural' mass markets.

Friedman's study is a much needed corrective to the conventional view that Japan's postwar economy was guided by the bureaucratic state as represented by MITI (Ike 1973; Johnson 1982). The case of the machinery industry, for example, demonstrates that despite MITI's desire to build up economies of scale through cartels, restrictions on market entry and consolidation, the market in fact fragmented: new entrants flooded the high-tech equipment sectors while existing firms refused to co-ordinate or consolidate production. During the 1960s, in other words, MITI may have referred to 'administrative guidance' and claimed to be speaking on behalf of the national interest (Johnson 1982: 266) but it did not always have the capacity to force private interests into compliance, nor was its advice always taken. It is now recognized, moreover, that such a situation even existed in the 1930s and during the war, when the military–bureaucratic regime's attempt to impose controls on the economy was frustrated by the continuing influence and competing interests of the private sector. The postwar situation was no different. In 1965, Sumitomo Metals refused to comply with MITI's guidelines on production quotas, although the government did promote a successful merger of the Yawata and Fuji steel companies in 1970. Significantly, in 1980 the Tokyo High Court ruled that MITI was not authorized to compel companies to restrict production. In the wake of capital liberalization measures carried out from the late 1950s onwards, MITI also planned for consolidation of the automobile industry to prepare for foreign competition. Yet its attempt to encourage a merger of Nissan and Toyota failed, while new entrants (Honda, Suzuki) further fragmented the industry (Johnson 1982: 299–300; Friedman 1988: 204–5). In 1969, against the express wishes of MITI, Mitsubishi Motors announced it was entering into a joint venture with the American-owned Chrysler. Even in the oil industry, which one might have expected to be closely supervised by the state because of Japan's acute dependence on outside sources of supply, private companies frustrated government initiatives. MITI's proposals to co-ordinate production through a state-owned company and to secure government influence in private firms through share ownership both came to nought. Its sole achievement was the creation of the Japan Development Corporation in 1967, permitted only to provide exploration and drilling support for private companies (Friedman 1988: 207–8).

Another important factor in Japan's economic recovery was the reparations agreements with Southeast Asian countries, which were frequently tied to economic aid and loan programmes (Halliday and McCormack 1973: 25–30). The first such agreement was reached with Burma in 1954; over the next 20 years Japan paid out $1,012 million in reparations and $490 million in economic aid to Burma, Indonesia, the Philippines, South Vietnam, Laos, Cambodia, Malaysia and South Korea. Since economic aid often involved the purchase of Japanese manufactures, these agreements considerably stimulated the steel, shipbuilding and electric goods industries (Hellmann 1972; Welfield 1988: 95). By 1969, Southeast Asia was receiving 83 per cent of Japan's bilateral aid flows and 79 per cent of the total transfer of private capital goods from Japan. The end of the 1960s, in fact, saw Japan as either the first or second trading partner of every country in the region. During the 1970s Japan was to become the major foreign investor in the region as well (see chapter four).

Japan's increasing economic clout in Southeast Asia did not preclude the country's dependence on outside sources for its raw materials, a situation that had existed since the beginnings of Japanese industrial expansion after the First World War. Just as then, Japan was still dependent on Southeast Asia for its mineral needs.

In 1960, for example, Japan imported 27.8 per cent of its iron ore needs from India and Portuguese Goa, and 43.2 per cent from other Asian countries (Welfield 1988: 96). By the end of the 1960s, 96 per cent of Japan's tin requirements and 45 per cent of its copper came from Southeast Asia; the region also supplied 98 per cent of Japan's natural rubber and 50 per cent of lumber requirements (ibid.: 214). Japan's dependence on the outside world for its energy needs was even more acute. In 1950, 60 per cent of Japan's energy requirements had been supplied by coal and only 7 per cent by oil. Once it was decided to concentrate on the growth of export industry (see earlier) oil imports became increasingly important. In 1960, oil was supplying 37.7 per cent of the country's energy needs and this had increased to 70.8 per cent by 1970. Most of this oil (95 per cent) was imported, principally from the Middle East (but distributed by US oil companies) and Southeast Asia (ibid.: 97). A Japanese government report in 1971 revealed that American capital controlled the supply of up to 80 per cent of the country's imports of crude oil (Halliday and McCormack 1973: 6).

Citizen Protest Movements

Economic growth notwithstanding, political turmoil continued to be the order of the day during the 1960s. The decade itself opened with the shocking assassination in October 1960 of Asanuma Inejiro, the recently elected chairman of the JSP, by a right-wing extremist during a televised political rally. Asanuma had been a member of a JSP delegation the previous year (in his capacity as Secretary-General of the party) that had visited Beijing. During the visit Asanuma had infuriated right-wingers at home when he advocated the restoration of diplomatic relations with the People's Republic and abrogation of Japan's 1952 treaty with Taiwan, as well as publicly declaring that US imperialism was the common enemy of the peoples of China and Japan (Stockwin 1968: 90).

In terms of party politics there was a change, in the words of a recent study (Hrebenar et al. 1986: 3), from a one-and-a-half party system in the 1950s to a multi-party system by the 1970s. Thus, in 1958 the LDP and JSP together polled 91 per cent of the popular vote and won 97 per cent of the lower house seats, but by the end of the 1960s there were two additional opposition parties, the JCP was attracting more electoral support, and both the LDP and JSP had slipped in the number of Diet seats gained and in the percentage of the popular vote obtained. In 1960, as noted previously, the right wing of the JSP formed its own party, the Democratic Socialist Party (DSP), which was to draw support from the more moderate trade union federation, the Japanese Confederation of Labour (*Domei*), formed in 1964 from amongst right-wing labour groupings that had split from the more radical *Sohyo*. In 1960 the DSP gained 17 Diet seats (with 8.7 per cent of the vote) and in 1969 31 seats (with 7.7 per cent of the vote).

In 1964 a new party – the *Komeito* (Clean Government Party) – was formed as the political arm of the *Soka Gakkai*, a lay Buddhist sect founded in 1930. The *Soka Gakkai*, like many new religions (Blacker 1969) that were founded before and after the war, appealed to the less privileged strata of the urban population (non-unionized workers, shop clerks, small businessmen, housewives) with their claims to heal illnesses, solve family problems and guarantee material prosperity; in the late 1980s membership of the new religions may have totalled up to 30 per cent of the country's population (Hardacre 1986: 3). Significantly, many of the founders were women and recruits were acquired by means of active proselytization and dramatic conversions. As early as 1955, 51 *Soka Gakkai* members running as independents were successful in local elections and in 1956 three *Soka Gakkai* members were elected to the House of Councillors. By the end of the 1960s *Soka Gakkai* membership comprised 6.5 million families (Curtis 1988: 25). The *Komeito* in 1964 advocated world peace, an end to corrupt politics and a humanitarian socialism. The party did well in the 1967 and 1969 lower house elections, winning 25 seats (5.4 per cent of the vote) and 47 seats (10.9 per cent of the vote) respectively, but its initial pacifist and anti-LDP stance was modified after 1970 when it formally severed its links with the *Soka Gakkai*. By 1981, for example, the party accepted the Japan–US Security Treaty. The JCP's electoral fortunes also revived by the end of the 1960s, with the party winning 14 seats in the 1969 elections (6.8 per cent of the vote). In fact JCP membership was higher than that of the JSP, recording 270,000 members in 1966 in addition to 326,000 subscribers to its newspaper *Akahata* (Red Flag) (Scalapino 1967: 292). Also, at its 10th Party Congress in October 1966 the JCP, which had hitherto veered from a pro-Moscow to a pro-Beijing stance during the Sino-Soviet dispute, finally affirmed its independence from both communist superpowers; henceforth, it would increasingly identify itself with the national interest. Despite the observation of one scholar in 1967 (Scalapino 1967: 354) that the JCP would become increasingly irrelevant, the party was to enjoy electoral success in the 1970s.

During the 1960s, therefore, the LDP and JSP lost ground electorally. In the elections for the lower house in November 1960 the LDP received 57.5 per cent of the popular vote and 63.3 per cent of the seats (296). In the 1967 elections the LDP's share of the popular vote dipped below 50 per cent for the first time (48.8 per cent) and the party dropped to 277 seats. By the time of the 1969 elections the party's popular support had again dropped to 47.6 per cent of the vote. Nevertheless, although the LDP ceased to be a majority party after 1967 in terms of its share of votes (in 1971 elections the party also lost its majority position in the House of Councillors), it continued to be the majority party in the lower house – in 1969 the LDP had 59.2 per cent of the seats – because of the retention of electoral boundaries that over-represented rural constituents (on whom the party relied) and because independents elected to the Diet were often co-opted by the LDP afterwards or at least supported LDP policies (see tables 3.1 and 3.2).

The JSP during this period declined more dramatically. In the 1960 elections it gained 145 seats with 27.5 per cent of the vote, but

Table 3.1 Party popularity, 1956–86 (in per cent)

	LDP	JSP	Komeito	DSP	JCP	NLC	SDL
1955–9	45.8	37.9	–	–	0.6	–	–
1960–3	46.0	30.3	–	5.0	0.7	–	–
1964–7	48.0	29.9	3.4	5.4	1.1	–	–
1968–71	46.5	25.8	5.8	7.5	3.8	–	–
1972–5	44.1	25.5	5.1	6.1	7.4	–	–
1976–9	45.8	20.2	5.2	5.3	4.8	6.6	1.0
1980–2	50.9	17.9	4.5	6.2	4.5	2.8	1.2
1983–4	52.8	17.0	5.0	5.6	4.4	2.4	1.2
1985–6	57.2	14.5	5.1	4.1	2.9	1.5	0.8

Note: The percentage figures represent the average percentages of all polls taken during the time periods indicated. The figure for 1985–6 includes polls taken through May 1986

Source: Curtis (1988): Compiled on the basis of opinion poll data provided by the *Asahi Shinbun*

Table 3.2 Party shares of the valid popular vote, lower house, 1958–86 (in per cent)

	LDP	JSP	Komeito	DSP	JCP	NLC	SDL	IND
1958	57.8	32.9	–	–	2.6	–	–	6.7
1960	57.6	27.6	–	8.8	2.9	–	–	3.2
1963	54.7	29.0	–	7.4	4.0	–	–	4.9
1967	48.8	27.9	5.4	7.4	4.8	–	–	5.8
1969	47.6	21.4	10.9	7.7	6.8	–	–	5.5
1972	46.9	21.9	8.5	7.0	10.5	–	–	5.3
1976	41.8	20.7	10.9	6.3	10.4	4.2	–	5.8
1979	44.6	19.7	9.8	6.8	10.4	3.0	0.7	5.0
1980	47.9	19.3	9.0	6.6	9.8	3.0	0.7	3.7
1983	45.8	19.5	10.1	7.3	9.3	2.4	0.7	5.0
1986	49.4	17.2	9.4	6.4	8.8	1.8	0.8	6.0

Source: Curtis (1988): Ministry of Home Affairs data

in 1969 it gained only 90 seats with 21.4 per cent of the vote. In some ways, as one scholar has noted (Stockwin 1968: 111), the JSP after 1961 became more akin to the LDP in that factional rivalry and advantage became more important than ideological differences within the party. Under Eda Saburo, Asanuma's successor as party chairman, the JSP toned down its radical Marxist rhetoric and advocated 'structural reform' (i.e. socialist revolution would come about slowly and gradually as a result of party and trade union pressure for better wages and working conditions). Although the Marxist Left within the party, centred on the Socialist Association (*Shakaishugi kyokai*), made a come-back in the mid-1960s under the chairmanship of Sasaki Kozo, Stockwin (ibid.: 142) argues that the LDP and JSP were not all that far apart in foreign policy either. In 1966, for example, some JSP members proposed sending unarmed elements of the previously condemned SDF to Southeast Asia on missions of peaceful economic construction.

For these reasons some scholars (Krauss 1984; Curtis 1988) argue that from the mid-1960s on a politics of compromise increasingly replaced the politics of confrontation so evident during the 1950s, as ideological polarization became less apparent and more opposition members were drafted onto Diet committees. In other words, the willingness of opposition parties to play by the rules of the parliamentary game (rather than resorting to dramatic boycotts of Diet sessions) and the LDP's increasing concern to seek consensus in the Diet led to the 'institutionalization of conflict management' (Krauss 1984). Another scholar (Calder 1988) refers to the years 1964–71 as an interlude of stability. Yet in many ways the 1960s, particularly the period of Sato Eisaku's premiership (1964–72), witnessed considerable controversy and popular discontent, in addition to continuing ambiguities in the Japan–US relationship.

Sato Eisaku (1901–75), one of Yoshida Shigeru's bureaucrat protégés and the brother of Kishi Nobusuke, had nearly been arrested in 1954 (when he was Secretary-General of the LDP) for his involvement in a bribery case and in the same year was indicted for violating an electoral funds law, although the case was dropped in 1956 (Curtis 1988: 160–1). During his premiership there occurred parliamentary and public opposition to the normalization of relations with South Korea in 1965, the emergence of a nationwide anti-Vietnam War movement, and the beginnings of various citizens' movements protesting against the negative consequences of rapid economic growth at a time when the parliamentary opposition was gaining electoral success at local government levels. Japanese domestic opposition to the Vietnam War strained relations between Tokyo and Washington, and although Sato managed to secure the renewal of the Security Treaty in 1970 and the return of Okinawa (hitherto under American military administration) to Japanese control in 1972, his premiership was marked by growing trade friction between the two countries.

The final normalization of relations with South Korea in 1965, after years of prodding by the US, sparked off huge public demonstrations as well as revealing the occasional unwillingness of even the LDP government to toe the American line. Washington had consistently encouraged an early rapprochement between Japan and South Korea, with whom the US had signed a security treaty in 1953 as part of its Cold War strategy of containing communism. American wishes notwithstanding, a number of disagreements between the two countries prevented such a rapprochement. Japan, for example, refused to accept South Korea's claim to be the only lawful government on the peninsula and declined to regard all Korean residents in Japan as citizens of South Korea (rather than communist North Korea). In fact, Tokyo concluded an agreement with North Korea in 1959 that permitted Koreans in Japan (whether they were originally from the north or the south) to be repatriated to the north under Red Cross supervision (Welfield 1988: 93). Other obstacles to rapprochement included Japan's rejection of the idea that it should compensate either North or South Korea for the consequences of Japan's colonial rule on the peninsula (1910–45), and its claim to a group of islands in the Sea of Japan that were also claimed by South Korea.

A basic treaty with South Korea, however, was finally signed in June 1965 and ratified by the Diet in December, with the government using the same tactics it had deployed in 1960 to achieve ratification of the Security Treaty (Baerwald 1977). Opponents of the treaty argued that it identified Japan even more with American Cold War policy and that it would help stabilize the repressive regime of Park Chung Hee, who had come to power in a military coup in 1961. Interestingly, although the treaty provided for Japanese loans and credits (described as 'economic co-operation' rather than 'compensation') it did not entail Tokyo's unequivocal recognition of the South Korean regime as the only legitimate government on the peninsula. Japanese trade with North Korea continued, as did Tokyo's refusal to recognize all Korean residents in Japan as citizens of South Korea (Welfield 1988: 200–8). Nevertheless, Japanese–South Korean trade became increasingly important after 1965; by 1969, for example, 40 per cent of South Korea's imports came from Japan (Halliday and McCormack 1973: 156) and Japanese investment in South Korea by 1976 accounted for 64 per cent of all foreign investment (Welfield 1988: 339).

The separation of politics and economics (*seikei bunri*) evident in Japan's approach to the two Koreas, was even more apparent in relations with the People's Republic of China (PRC) (Langdon 1973). As noted earlier, Yoshida Shigeru had never shared Washington's obsessive concern with isolating the PRC and although Japan officially went along with American policy an unofficial and private Japanese trade with the PRC had existed since 1953 (Whiting 1989: 39). From 1960 on, non-official exchanges between Beijing and Tokyo were a regular occurrence. In November 1962, just one year after the Japanese government co-sponsored an American resolution designed to prevent a decision on whether the PRC should join the UN (by making it an 'important question' that required a two-thirds vote by UN members), a trade memorandum was signed following the visit to Beijing of two unofficial Japanese delegations. Known as the Liao-Takasaki Memorandum, the agreement provided for a considerable expansion of commercial activity through private Japanese firms that accepted certain Chinese conditions (e.g. such firms were not to have business links with Taiwan or the US). In 1963 the largest ever Japanese trade fair was held in China (Welfield 1988: 182). During the 1960s Japan, in fact, became China's major trading partner (Hellmann 1972). It should also be noted that both the LDP and big business were internally divided over what attitude to take towards China, which inevitably involved attitudes towards American policy in Asia. The LDP, for example, polarized around two informal organizations: the Asian Problems Study Association, formed in December 1964, which supported US intervention in Asia, the continued exclusion of the PRC from the UN, and close association with South Korea, and the Afro-Asian Problems Study Association, formed in January 1965, which was opposed to an uncritical endorsement of US policy in Asia and which favoured more open relations with the PRC. Since the former drew support from members of the mainstream factions within the LDP (including that of Sato), Japan's relations with the PRC sharply deteriorated after Sato's accession to the premiership in October 1964, especially once Japan was perceived in Beijing to be fully supporting America's growing military involvement in Vietnam.

The Vietnam conflict placed Sato in an awkward position. On the one hand, Japan had formal relations with the American-backed regime of South Vietnam (to which, by 1965, Japan had extended $39 million in reparation payments for its occupation of Vietnam during the Second World War) and Sato was anxious to co-operate with Washington as much as possible in order to guarantee the speedy restoration of Okinawa to Japanese control. This meant that Japan was increasingly drawn into the Vietnam conflict. After the Gulf of Tonkin naval clash between North Vietnamese and American forces in August 1964, Tokyo acceded to US requests for permission to use American naval bases in Japan (at Sasebo and Yokosuka) as ports of call for American nuclear-powered submarines (Havens 1987: 22). From 1965, again in the wake of American pressure, Japan reduced the level of its unofficial trade with North Vietnam and stepped up its medical and financial assistance to South Vietnam. By 1967, also, over 1,000 Japanese were working for the US military sea transport service in Vietnam and other Pacific locations. US bases in Japan became vitally important for the war. In response to domestic critics, Sato's government argued that although Vietnam was outside the Far East the crisis there might still threaten Japan's peace and security; hence, US troops could use their bases in Japan for non-combat purposes without consulting the Japanese government beforehand (in accordance with the 1960 Security Treaty). American troops on Okinawa, however, *could* be used for direct combat without prior consultation; Okinawa, in fact, was the jumping off point for the first 15,000 US combat troops to enter the Vietnam War in 1965 , while in subsequent years it became a storage ground for poison chemicals and a training centre for military personnel from South Korea, South Vietnam and the Philippines. As Havens (ibid.: 27–9) points out, Washington never once resorted to the prior consultation clause of the Security Treaty throughout the duration of the war. Japan's involvement also brought economic dividends in the shape of American procurements. By 1970 such procurements may have totalled up to $467 million. There was also economic benefit from indirect procurements, as Japan increased its exports of materials and components to South Korea, Taiwan and various Southeast Asian countries, all of which had procurement contracts of their own to fill. Significantly, this period also witnessed a considerable increase in Japanese exports of television sets, auto parts, chemicals and machinery to the US in order to satisfy a consumer demand that American firms were unable to do, partly because of conversion to war-related production (Havens, ibid.: 94–5).

On the other hand, while Sato aimed to convince Washington of Japan's support for American policy in Vietnam, he had to confront opposition from within his own party and a growing anti-war movement that had the support of a number of local governors elected on an anti-government ticket. In January 1965 Sato's own Foreign Minister, Shiina Etsusaburo, compared American policy in Vietnam with that of the Japanese army in China during the 1930s (Welfield 1988: 211), while members of the anti-mainstream factions within the LDP associated with the Afro-Asian Problems Study Association consistently urged Sato to take the initiative and call for a truce and ceasefire in Vietnam. The anti-war movement, however, provided the biggest headache for Sato. The movement, which began to crystallise in 1965, drew inspiration and much of its constituency from the earlier anti-nuclear movement that had emerged in 1954 when radioactivity from an American H-Bomb test on Bikini atoll (in the Pacific) had showered a Japanese fishing boat (Havens 1987; Buckley 1992: 58–60). In 1955 the Japan Council Against Atomic and Hydrogen Bombs (*Gensuikyo*) was formed, enjoying support not only from socialists and communists but also, initially, from the LDP; it withdrew its support in 1958 once *Gensuikyo* began to condemn US bases in Japan. By the mid-1960s *Gensuikyo* itself had become hopelessly split between socialists and communists, who took divergent views of Soviet nuclear testing in the early 1960s. In 1965 the socialists bolted the organization and formed the Japan Congress Against Atomic and Hydrogen Bombs (*Gensuikin*).

The anti-Vietnam War movement that began in the wake of the first American bombing of North Vietnam in February 1965 was a less partisan and more widespread phenomenon. The first large nationwide rally against the war was held in June 1965, and attracted over 100,000 people. Joined by writers (including the novelist Oda Makoto), artists and scholars, the movement created in 1965 the Citizens' Federation for Peace in Vietnam (*Beheiren*). As a loosely structured organization not affiliated with any political party and based on self-supporting local constituent branches, *Beheiren* was to be a model for other citizens' movements that emerged in the late 1960s and early 1970s (McKean 1981: 7; Koschmann 1993: 414–16). Over the next few years *Beheiren* established links with anti-war movements abroad, inviting prominent Western radicals like Jean-Paul Sartre and Simone de Beauvoir to Japan, and introduced new styles of protest to Japanese politics such as teach-ins and folk-singing. More importantly, it sponsored huge peaceful demonstrations such as the one in June 1969 in which 70,000 people participated. The Tokyo branch of *Beheiren* held peaceful protests on the first Saturday of each month from September 1965 to October 1973 (Havens 1987: 63). For critics of the war Japan's peace and prosperity was being purchased at the cost of war and repression of democracy abroad. By 1969 *Beheiren* was calling for the termination of the Security Treaty and the return of Okinawa, as well as demonstrating solidarity with the opponents of the Narita airport extension (see later).

The anti-war movement was supported by unions (particularly *Sohyo*), although strikes often involved demands for a minimum wage and opposition to industrial rationalization, as well as by progressive local governors. In 1967, for example, both Ninagawa Torazo (elected governor of metropolitan Kyoto in 1950) and Minobe Ryokichi (elected governor of metropolitan Tokyo in

April 1967 on a united opposition ticket) called for a ceasefire in Vietnam.

In this tense atmosphere Prime Minister Sato was increasingly perceived as pro-American. The government's defence spending plans for 1967–71 strengthened the SDF (although not as much as Washington would have liked) and while on a tour of Southeast Asia in September–October 1967 Sato declared that an end to the American bombing would not bring peace. On the day of Sato's departure for a second tour of Southeast Asia (en route to visit American President Lyndon Johnson) in October 1967, massive student demonstrations took place at Haneda airport during which students wore helmets and carried staves for the first time. In the same month there were anti-war strikes involving over 250,000 workers (*Sohyo* estimated 1.5 million). Over the next two and a half years rallies and demonstrations involved nearly 19 million people (Havens 1987: 133). One of the largest occurred in January 1968 when the American nuclear-powered aircraft carrier, the *Enterprise*, arrived in Sasebo (Nagasaki prefecture). Significantly, soon after the *Enterprise* left, Sato proclaimed Japan's Three Non-Nuclear Principles (no manufacture, possession and introduction into Japan of nuclear weapons) for which he was later to be awarded the Nobel Peace Prize.

To some extent Sato was able to mollify opposition when he returned from Washington in November 1969 with a commitment from President Nixon that Okinawa would revert to Japan in 1972 (an earlier visit with President Johnson in November 1967 had not resulted in a specific timetable for Okinawa's return). In return, however, Sato had to agree to the renewal of the Security Treaty. The text of the Sato–Nixon communiqué of November 1969 (Livingston, Moore and Oldfather 1973: 279–80) also recognized the regional scope of the alliance since for the first time the two governments acknowledged that the security of South Korea and Taiwan were important to Japan's own security. At a press conference in Washington the following month Sato even proclaimed the beginning of a new 'Pacific Age' underpinned by a close US–Japan alliance. Such rhetoric, however, belied the continuing tensions in the relationship. Already in the early 1960s, even though American ambassador Reischauer in 1961 could suggest that Japan's development might serve as a model for capitalist modernization in Asia (Koschmann 1993: 413), American politicians were for the first time criticizing Japan for its 'free ride' in security affairs (Cumings 1993: 53). In his talks with President Nixon, Sato also had secretly to agree to 'restrain' Japanese exports of synthetic fibres to the US. Such pressure had been used before in 1956 and 1968 with regard to Japanese exports of cotton textiles and crude steel respectively.

In the lower house elections of December 1969 the LDP gained 288 seats (up from 277 in 1967), although with only 47.6 per cent of the popular vote. Despite huge demonstrations in 416 cities involving 3/4 million people on 23 June 1970 to denounce the automatic renewal of the Security Treaty, Sato escaped unscathed. The anti-Vietnam War movement began to wind down after 1970 and in 1973–4 *Beheiren* itself wrapped up its activities. One intriguing footnote to the movement occurred in May 1972 when the Tokyo High Court ruled that public employees *could* wear anti-war badges without violating rules banning political activity on the job, on the grounds that wishing for peace in Vietnam was not a political act but instead showed 'the general opinion of the people and thus does not violate the political neutrality' of the government agency concerned (Havens 1987: 226). In many of the pollution lawsuits (see later) the courts were to demonstrate a similar independent outlook *vis-à-vis* the establishment.

The anti-Vietnam War peace movement occurred at a time when other protest movements symbolizing public dissatisfaction with the negative consequences of economic growth began to assume nationwide importance. These 'citizens' movements' (*shimin undo*) have been defined as grassroots movements that were independently organized by members themselves and which engaged in protest against established authority in connection with local issues (McKean 1981). Another scholar (Fukui 1988: 190–1) has described them as politically conservative because they were concerned with the protection or promotion of particular local interests; such an assessment obscures their significance. Not only did these movements foster a wider political activism (McKean 1981: 230), but they also demonstrated the willingness of ordinary citizens to confront powerful economic interests in the courts and even to oppose state policy itself. By 1973 there were to be around 3,000 such groups, involving 60,000–90,000 activists and more than one million rank and file participants (ibid.: 8). An extensive network of community and associational organizations ensured the rapid spread of these protest movements (Krauss and Simcock 1980: 207).

The context within which these protests took place was an increasing disillusionment with the government's 'GNP-first' policy of rapid economic growth that brought in its wake widespread pollution, spiralling land costs, environmental damage, rising consumer prices, poor welfare facilities and bad housing. For growing numbers of people official appeals to the ethos of sacrifice were beginning to ring hollow (Taira 1993: 170–1). Even within the government concern was being shown; in 1969, for example, three government white papers discussed environmental issues and referred to the poor quality of life as the price paid for obsession with GNP as the sole indicator of progress. Thus, although in terms of *aggregate* GNP Japan overtook West Germany to become number two in 1969, the country was 22nd among capitalist economies in terms of *per capita* GNP. Statistics also indicated that in the late 1960s the numbers of people below the poverty line were considerable (ibid.: 174, 178–9).

The most significant of the citizens' movements were those that denounced industrial pollution and demanded apologies and compensation for the victims. Whereas anti-pollution protest earlier in the century had relied on the support of local elites and Diet representatives (McKean 1981: 35–41), the protests of the 1960s and early 1970s were organized by the victims and their families themselves, bypassing local elites as intermediaries and directly confronting the corporations held responsible. The first group to organize comprised victims of organic mercury poisoning in Minamata (Kumamoto prefecture). In the early 1950s residents in the fishing villages along Minamata Bay began suffering from physical and mental disorders as a result of consuming fish that had been infected by the industrial waste of a nearby chemical fertilizer plant (Chisso Corporation). Inhibited initially by a sense of shame and shunned by their more affluent neighbours who assumed the disease was caused by poor hygiene, the victims were reluctant to publicize their plight (Upham 1987: 1993). Interestingly, the novel *Black Rain* (Ibuse 1979) depicts a similar situation in which survivors of the atomic bombing at Hiroshima suffer local discrimination. In 1959, however, the Minamata victims organized a Mutual Assistance Society, which negotiated an informal settlement with Chisso after members had descended on the plant and locked in the management. Monetary compensation paid to the victims was referred to as *mimaikin* (sympathetic payments), thus leaving open the question of actual responsibility for the disease. The govern-

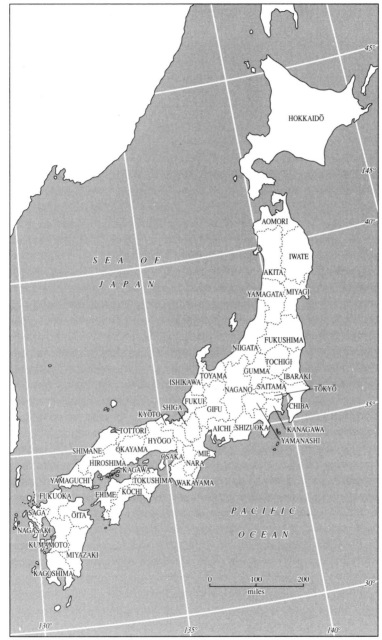

Map 3.1 Japanese prefectures
Source: Hane (1992)

ment, in fact, resorted to a cover-up, since it did not formally agree that organic mercury from Chisso was the causative agent until 1968. Yet the government's own research findings (within the Ministry of Health and Welfare) had pointed to Chisso in 1958, as had a government-funded research team at the Kumamoto University Medical School in 1959 (the research team was disbanded shortly afterwards).

Meanwhile, in 1965, similar symptons of Minamata disease came to light in Niigata prefecture, where a company using the same processes as Chisso was located. In June 1967, 13 victims filed suit against the company, the first pollution lawsuit. Later in the same year nine plaintiffs filed suit against six enterprises (some of which were owned by Mitsubishi) in Yokkaichi city (Mie prefecture), claiming that they had suffered from chronic bronchial asthma as a result of sulphurous fumes emanating from the industrial plants. In July 1968 over 500 victims of long-term cadmium poisoning in Toyama prefecture filed suit against the Kamioka plant of Mitsui Mining and Smelting, claiming that industrial waste (cadmium, zinc, lead) released upstream by the plant had contaminated the water used to irrigate rice paddies. Finally, in June 1969, over 100 of the original Minamata victims decided to sue Chisso in the courts. These 'four big pollution lawsuits', as they became known, were of enormous significance. In a society that supposedly valued harmony and consensus, and thus avoided formal litigation, ordinary citizens now demonstrated their willingness and determination to utilize fully their legal rights in order to seek moral justice (Upham 1987: 38–40).

The district courts overwhelmingly found in the plaintiffs' favour. In 1971, the victims of cadmium poisoning in Toyama and organic mercury poisoning in Niigata won their cases; Mitsui's appeal to a higher court in the cadmium poisoning case was rejected and the company was ordered to pay additional compensation to other victims who had not originally filed suit. The Yokkaichi asthma victims won their case in 1972, while in 1973 the Minamata victims were awarded the largest settlement to date in a pollution case. By June 1976 Chisso had paid out nearly 23 million yen in compensation and pollution prevention programmes; in 1979 the president of Chisso and the manager of the Minamata plant were each to be imprisoned for two years on charges of professional negligence.

Litigation was not the only weapon in the anti-pollution movement. Sometimes citizen groups were able to pressure particular firms to draw up 'pollution prevention' contracts, while more confrontational tactics included individuals purchasing single shares in a polluting firm so as to gain admission to annual shareholder meetings and the opportunity thereby to denounce the management directly (McKean 1981: 149–53). Citizens also made use of the direct demand initiative (i.e. signatures from 2 per cent of eligible voters in a prefecture would require assembly action on a particular question within 20 days). In 1970 Toyama citizens gathered 21,400 signatures demanding from the prefectural assembly a stricter anti-pollution ordnance (ibid.: 45–50). Although the assembly defeated the measure it had been shown once again that ordinary citizens were willing to become politically involved.

As a recent study notes, however, the government responded to the anti-pollution movement by passing pre-emptive legislation and instituting compensation and mediation procedures designed to prevent litigation from becoming an ongoing vehicle for social change (Upham 1987: 18–19, 65). Such concessions were also aimed at neutralizing opposition and ensuring that localized conflicts would not be transformed into generalized national ones. In 1970 the Diet passed a number of laws to regulate certain types of pollution (including one that designated as a crime an act of pollution that damaged human health). A bureaucratically administered system of identifying and mediating pollution disputes was also created, as well as a compensation scheme in 1973 administered by the government but financed by polluters themselves through additional taxes on industry and car owners. By 1979 over 73,000 people had been officially recognized as pollution victims and they were all entitled to compensation (McKean 1981: 20). In 1980 a total of 85 billion yen was paid out in compensation to over 80,000 certified pollution victims (Upham 1993: 343). In time, Japan came to spend more of its GNP on anti-pollution measures than any other developed country.

Other citizens' movements involved resistance of rural communities to incoming industrial development (McKean 1981: 83–92) and urban opposition to high-rise construction that threatened 'sunshine rights' (*nisshoken*). Protests took the form of demonstrations, lobbying of officials and litigation. In some cases citizen groups were able to gain the support of progressive mayors and prefectural governors. Thus, after a housewives group had lobbied the socialist mayor of Musashino city (western Tokyo prefecture) public guidelines were issued in 1971 requiring anyone erecting a building over ten metres high to obtain the permission of surrounding residents. In 1972 the Supreme Court declared that Article 25 of the constitution, guaranteeing minimum standards of wholesome and cultured living, included the right to sunshine. Sometimes citizens sued local officials, as in 1965 when residents of Tsu city (Mie prefecture) sued the mayor for violating the constitution (which prohibited state patronage of religion) when he paid local shrine priests to conduct a Shinto purification ceremony (*jichinsai*) prior to the construction of a municipal gymnasium (Hardacre 1989: 149). The case dragged on until 1977 when the Supreme Court finally ruled in the mayor's favour, arguing that the ceremony had become thoroughly secularized.

The most dramatic of the citizens' movements concerned farmers' opposition to the construction of Narita airport (Apter and Sawa 1984). The original decision to build a new airport had been taken in 1960, but it was not until 1965 that the site (at Sanrizuka) was finally chosen. Farmers on whose land the airport would be built formed the Sanrizuka-Shibayama Farmers' League Against the New Tokyo International Airport (*Rengo kuko hantai domei*), presided over by a Christian, Tomura Issaku, an artist and businessman who had inherited a farm machinery shop. The League welcomed the support of outside groups as long as they did not dominate the movement. *Beheiren* soon lent its support to the farmers' protest, as it linked the building of the new airport with the increasing demands of the Vietnam War. After 1967 the farmers were also joined by representatives of the national student federation (*Zengakuren*) and of a number of splinter New Left groups. Protest then became more confrontational as demonstrators frequently clashed with police and a series of fortified encampments were constructed around the site. The airport was finally opened in 1978 (seven years behind schedule) but it was restricted to only one runway.

Student involvement in violent demonstrations at the site of Narita airport reflected the widespread turbulence on university campuses. Student struggles began in 1968 at Tokyo University when students protested against working conditions (Livingston, Moore and Oldfather 1973: 552–6); unrest spread to other campuses and soon deteriorated into bitter factional disputes within the student movement. *Zengakuren* spawned at least 32 separately named factions, some of which were to become involved in left-wing terrorism in the early 1970s (see chapter four). By the late 1960s, a 29,000 strong elite police force (*Kidotai*), originally founded in 1952, was devoting most of its time to controlling student riots and gathering intelligence on student organizations. Between 1968 and 1975 there were 1,776 student factional disputes that came to the authorities' attention because of the violence involved. Such disputes resulted in nearly 5,000 injuries, 44 deaths and nearly 3,500 arrests (Steinhoff 1984: 182).

Finally, the activities of certain women's groups and the Buraku Liberation League (representing the interests of *burakumin*, descendants of former outcaste groups) constituted an important element of citizen protest at this time. Although one of the first women's organizations, *Shufuren* (Housewives Association, founded in 1948), was primarily concerned with protecting family budgets at a time of rationing and food shortages (see chapter two), those in the 1950s and 1960s concerned themselves with a wide variety of public issues (Uno 1993). As early as 1954, housewives in a Tokyo suburb participated in the peace movement, collecting signatures for an anti-nuclear petition. Some women's organizations (calling for equal rights) affiliated with labour unions, such as the Housewives Council of the Japan Coal Miners Union (1952), and opposition parties, such as the Japan Women's Council (1962), which affiliated with the JSP, and the New Japan Women's Association (1962), which affiliated with the JCP. The National Coordinating Council of Regional Women's Associations (*Chifuren*), established in 1952, campaigned on a wide variety of issues that included calling for an end to legalized prostitution (which was enacted in 1956), opposition to above-ground nuclear testing, blocking the legal reinstatement of the prewar family system, and demanding cleaner elections. Women were also involved in the consumer protection movement, which helped put pressure on the government to pass a consumer protection law in 1968 that provided for proper standards and labelling.

Throughout the postwar period, however, discrimination against women (in politics, education and employment) was rife. Although from the mid-1960s more women than men went to the polls, there were only seven women in the 1963 Diet. Before the 1990s only two women served as cabinet ministers, both appointed during Ikeda Hayato's premiership: Nakayama Masa became Minister of Health and Welfare in 1960, and Kondo Tsuruyo Director of the Science and Technology Agency in 1962. In education, although the percentage of girls advancing to senior high school exceeded that of boys in 1970 (Robins-Mowry 1983: 138) most women tended to end up in the inferior two-year colleges rather than the regular four-year universities. The official adherence to rigid gender roles was clearly demonstrated in 1969 when the Ministry of Education made homemaking courses mandatory for high school girls, a measure that remained in force until 1989 (Uno 1993: 306).

In employment women had to confront both the prejudices of employers and the ambivalent attitude of the state towards women working outside the home. As recent studies have pointed out (Molony 1993; Buckley 1993), the Labour Standards Law of 1947 guaranteeing equal access to employment opportunities and equal pay for equal work was undermined to some extent by additional protective clauses that secured maternal and menstrual leave and prohibited women from having to perform night work and other 'strenuous labour'. Employers could henceforth justify discriminatory employment practices on the grounds that women could not perform the same jobs. In the 1950s and 1960s the state encouraged mostly young unmarried women to take up full-time work outside the home (in the manufacturing and service sectors), although it was expected they would leave work permanently on marriage (or on the birth of their first child); married women whose children had grown up often returned to outside part-time employment. Thus, although the number of salaried female employees increased dramatically from the 1950s on (from 4 million in 1953 to 13.5 million in 1980) (Buckley 1993: 349), a clear gender division of labour emerged in which women were disadvantaged in terms of pay and advancement. Since companies structured their wage and promotion systems so as to emphasize continuity and duration of tenure, as well as making a clear distinction between permanent and temporary employees, they were able to pay women less and avoid the gender-based wage discrimination prohibited by the Labour Standards Law (Upham 1993: 333). At the same time, while the state encouraged women's participation in the labour force (one advantage of which was that it helped keep the levels of welfare spending down), by the early 1960s some government officials were expressing concern about the reduced level of the nation's birthrate, assumed to be a consequence of more women working outside the home. Prime Minister Sato in 1964 appealed to women to bear more children (Buckley 1993: 351).

As with the anti-pollution movement, the courts became involved in gender discrimination at the workplace. A female worker, Suzuki Setsuko, took her employer (Sumitomo Cement) to court after she was dismissed in 1964 for refusing to retire after she got married the year previously (in 1958 Sumitomo Cement had introduced employment policies requiring female employees to resign on marriage or, if unmarried, when they reached 30 years of age). In 1966 the Tokyo District Court found in the plaintiff's favour, and in subsequent years the courts struck down numerous early retirement systems in accordance with Article 90 of the Civil Code, which prohibited acts in violation of 'public order and good morals' (Upham 1993). Unfortunately, employers then began only to hire women who were likely to retire voluntarily and stopped hiring female university graduates. Nevertheless, the fact that individuals like Suzuki Setsuko were willing to demand their rights in the courts makes a nonsense of the claim put forward by van Wolferen (1989: 22) that the Japanese have never understood the concept of 'citizen' as opposed to that of 'subject'.

Burakumin (comprising about 1.3 per cent of the population) also faced social discrimination in the postwar period despite the constitutional ban on discrimination based on 'race, creed, sex, social status or family origin'. Although a government report in 1965 called attention to the problem of continuing discrimination (Upham 1987: 84–5) and a Special Measures Law for Assimilation Projects (*dowa*) was passed in 1969 to provide local governments with financial incentives to assist *burakumin*, the government had no legal duties to enforce fair treatment nor was there a law banning private discrimination against *burakumin*. Until the mid-1970s, for example, private detectives were often hired by employers or prospective parents-in-law to check an individual's family register to ascertain whether the person was a *burakumin*. When access to family registers was limited from the mid-1970s on, commercially published books known as Buraku Lists became widely available. They gave the place names of buraku ghettos, thus indicating a person's identity by the address (Upham 1987: 114–15; Pharr 1990: 78). The Buraku Liberation League (BLL), founded just after the war, became more militant in the 1960s. Resorting to the tactics of denunciation (*kyudan toso*), which involved confronting those deemed to have practised discrimination and threatening the possible use of limited physical force if a change of attitude was not forthcoming, the BLL was able to intimidate employers and teachers who opposed assimilation. The BLL also frequently lobbied the government, persuading MITI to persist with import restrictions in sectors (leather, beef) that still employed large numbers of *burakumin*. As one study notes, the government preferred the BLL strategy of denunciation rather than formal litigation since, by keeping the whole issue of discrimination out of the courts, it could prevent 'the crystallisation of the BLL's grievances into questions of equality, discrimination, and social structure that have universal normative appeal' (Upham 1987: 121).

The Nature of LDP Rule

Before proceeding to discuss the changes in Japan's domestic politics and foreign policy in the 1970s and 1980s and the growing problem of political corruption that was ultimately to lead to the demise of LDP rule in 1993, it is first necessary to explain how the LDP was able to retain its dominance after 1955 given the political turmoil of the 1950s and 1960s.

It has already been noted earlier that the LDP was more a coalition of conservative factions than a unified political party. At the time of its formation in 1955, the LDP comprised eight principal factions, based on a mixture of personal, regional and historical ties rather than on identification with a particular policy issue or ideological viewpoint; in fact, not all members of a particular faction would necessarily share the same view on certain issues. These factions in subsequent years sometimes split (as did Kishi Nobusuke's faction), merged or disappeared altogether on the death of a factional leader. By the mid-1960s there were at least eleven factions although in the early 1980s the number had stabilized to around five (Baerwald 1986: 18–28). The allocation of party and cabinet posts was often a long drawn-out process of bargaining amongst factional leaders. Thus, even the LDP president, who was elected every two years (in 1971 a maximum limit of two terms was imposed) and who automatically became prime minister (since the prime minister was elected by the lower house of the Diet and the LDP retained the majority of seats from 1955 to 1993), had to perform a skilful balancing act to ensure the support of factions other than his own. LDP leadership itself was often rotated amongst factional leaders; sometimes, as in the 1970s (see chapter four), rivalry for the leadership could spill over into open conflict within the party. The electoral system itself prolonged and accentuated the factional nature of the LDP since the single-vote multi-member constituency usually resulted in LDP candidates (from different factions) competing against each other as much as against opposition candidates. In time individual LDP members attached themselves to a particular faction for the advantages it might bring in terms of election to the Diet and advancement within the party (Stockwin 1988a: 32–3).

As a recent study argues (Calder 1988), factional competition within the LDP, mutual suspicions amongst conservative ranks that dated from the late 1940s (some LDP factional leaders, such as Miki Takeo, had served in Katayama's socialist cabinet in 1948), the legacy of the occupation reforms, which had loosened conservative controls in the countryside, in education and over labour, and Japan's precarious economic situation in the late 1940s and 1950s (in 1955, for example, raw material, fuel and food imports totalled $2.17 billion, $160 million more than Japan's entire export income) (ibid.: 47) inculcated a pervasive sense of vulnerability amongst the conservative establishment. This made the LDP, at times of perceived political crisis, particularly receptive to 'distributive' or 'compensation' politics to expand its network of support and ensure the continuation of conservative hegemony. The view that LDP dominance was due to the support of big business, whom it benefited with a favourable tax structure (Ike 1973), is therefore insufficient. Certainly, big business (fearful of a newly united socialist party) was a key player in promoting the formation of the LDP in 1955. Referred to as *keiretsu* (enterprise groups), big business was comprised of two horizontal groups of companies: those organized around the former *zaibatsu* (Mitsui, Mitsubishi, Sumitomo) and those held together by large banks (Fuji, Dai-ichi Kangyo, Sanwa). Such enterprise groups were important contributors to LDP funds, but it should be noted that the interests of big business and LDP policy did not always coincide; this was particularly so in the case of agricultural policy, as will be shown later. Of equal, if not more, importance in explaining LDP electoral success was its cultivation of support amongst farmers and small business, as well as its implementation of welfare and regional policies.

Conservative support for agriculture began during the last years of Yoshida Shigeru's premiership. The militance of the newly established Japan Farmers' Union and the proliferation of politically independent agricultural co-operatives in the early occupation period, as well as the JSP's electoral success in 1946 and 1947 (when it gained 20 per cent of the rural vote), bred fears that the countryside was slipping away from conservative control. Yoshida's government doubled the producer price of rice between 1949 and 1953, increased public works spending in rural areas, extended more privileges to the co-operatives, and implemented a system of subsidies for land reclamation and rice production. By 1953 agricultural subsidies comprised 28.1 per cent of the general account budget (Calder 1988: 262). It was not until after 1960, however, that long-term support for agriculture became established government policy. In the mid-1950s, for example, agricultural subsidies and the domestic producer rice price had been reduced; interestingly, at this time agriculture support levels were *lower* than those in Western Europe. The political crisis of 1959–60 and growing rural discontent engendered by falling agricultural incomes in relation to industrial wages, prompted the LDP to consolidate its rural support (ibid.). The Basic Agricultural Law of 1961 promised to increase agricultural incomes on a par with those in industry, and in subsequent years the producer rice price was again doubled. Price support was also extended to livestock products, vegetables and soybeans. By 1965 Japan had the highest quantitative levels of support for agriculture in the industrialized world (ibid.: 268).

Other policies favourable to the rural population included low taxation on agricultural land, tariff protection against agricultural imports and increased public works spending in rural areas that provided enhanced employment opportunities. Such support facilitated the survival of small-scale, spare-time farming (with farm members able to find outside employment), but also resulted in high rice prices for consumers. Not surprisingly, from 1960 on LDP electoral support in the countryside began to exceed its support nationally (ibid.: 255), a situation that was greatly helped by the gross overweighting of rural constituencies in relation to the more populated urban areas, as well as by the interesting phenomenon between the late 1950s and early 1970s of a higher voter turnout in rural areas (Fukui 1988: 209). Although metropolitan areas were allocated extra Diet seats in the mid-1960s and mid-1970s this did not seriously threaten LDP dominance, as it was able in the 1960s to take advantage of the fragmentation of the opposition, which often competed amongst itself for the urban vote.

The LDP's cultivation of the rural vote was not necessarily in the interests of big business (Bernier 1988), which favoured liberalization of agricultural imports, low consumer prices and more 'efficient' large-scale farming (through the consolidation of farms), but

Calder (1988) argues that in the interests of preserving the conservative hegemony it fell into line with LDP policy. By the late 1970s, however, with slower rates of economic growth and the ballooning expenditures required to subsidize rice production, the LDP began to cut back on its support for agriculture (see chapter four).

Another constituency that the LDP cultivated was small business (including the retail and wholesale distribution sector). As noted earlier, small business was a major employer of the labour force – in 1981 more than 50 per cent of the total labour force worked in enterprises employing less than 30 workers (ibid.: 315). It was ironically the socialist coalition government of 1947–8 that pioneered support for small business (which was particularly hard hit by the Dodge Plan) when it set up the Small and Medium Enterprises Agency within the Ministry of Commerce and Industry. Its first head was Ninagawa Torazo, who went on to become the JSP–JCP backed governor of Kyoto prefecture from 1950 to 1978 (Krauss 1980). Conservative governments after 1948 co-opted the small business interest by providing credits and loans (through the People's Finance Corporation set up in 1949 and the Small Business Finance Corporation set up in 1953), allowing small firms to pay lower rates of taxation than large corporations, and, in 1956, checking the expansion of large department stores. The government also sanctioned selective exemptions from the Anti-Monopoly Law when it allowed cartels to be organized by small business to prevent both damaging competition within the sector and infiltration by larger firms. In 1960 the LDP strengthened its ties to small business with the creation of a business policy liaison council; the participating organizations formed the Federation of Small and Medium Enterprise Organizations (*Sorengo*) in 1961 and it became an influential pressure group as well as a vocal supporter of the LDP.

In addition to incorporating small business the LDP also to some extent incorporated labour into the policy-making process in the 1950s and 1960s through the Labour Ministry's deliberative and advisory councils (first set up in 1947) and the presence of four labour representatives on MITI's Industrial Council, which was created in 1964 (Garon and Mochizuki 1993). In 1970 the Labour Ministry sponsored the Industry and Labour Conference (*Sangyo rodo konwakai*), which became a central forum for tripartite (government, business, labour) consultation on wages. The LDP also benefited from the emergence of a centrist labour movement after 1954, when the All-Japan Labour Union Congress (*Zenro kaigi*) broke away from the more radical *Sohyo*.

It expanded into the heavy industrial sector and its share of organized labour rose from 9.8 per cent to 13.3 per cent between 1954 and 1961 (ibid.: 138). In 1964 it merged with *Sodomei* to form *Domei* (Japan Confederation of Labour), whose membership amongst private sector workers exceeded that of *Sohyo* after 1967. Furthermore, after the trauma of the Miike strike in 1960 the LDP embarked on a more active role in maintaining employment, providing financial support for technical training, subsidized housing to encourage workers to move to new jobs, and expanded retraining programmes for redundant workers aged 45 and over.

LDP regional policy was also designed to provide more employment opportunities as well as to encourage new industries to locate in areas outside the principal urban conurbations. In 1962 the government designated 15 new industrial cities as centres of economic growth to counterbalance the Tokaido area (the urban sprawl between Tokyo and Osaka). In the same year a Coal Mine Area Rehabilitation Corporation was created to promote the construction of industrial parks in former coal-mining areas and to encourage non-mining industries to move there. Between 1962 and 1982 over 100 such industrial parks were built (Calder 1988: 305).

Finally, welfare policy was another example of 'compensation politics'. While government spending on social welfare had been low in the 1950s the Kishi government in 1958 legislated for universal healthcare benefits (implemented in 1961) and passed a number of major welfare measures in 1958–9 (e.g. a National Pension Law). Prime Minister Ikeda Hayato in 1960 even committed Japan to building a 'welfare state' (*fukushi kokka*), although pensions ultimately failed to keep up with the cost of living and inflation. In many cases it was local governments supported by the opposition parties (which became a feature of the political landscape in the late 1960s and 1970s) that took the lead in welfare provision, particularly with regard to child allowances and free medical care for the aged. As will be seen in chapter four, however, the LDP government co-opted many of these measures in the 1970s.

The LDP's financial support for agriculture and small business, and its increasing expenditures on welfare and public works after 1960, were accompanied by a corresponding decline in defence expenditures. After an actual *increase* in defence spending in the mid-1950s (in 1954 it totalled nearly 14 per cent of the general account budget), subsequent years witnessed a steady decline both in terms of relation to GNP and as a share of the national budget (Calder 1988: 414). As a percentage of the general account budget, defence spending declined from 12.6 per cent in 1957 to 7.2 per cent in 1970; by 1981 it was 5.1 per cent. Whereas in 1944 defence spending represented 68 per cent of GNP, by 1970 it represented 0.79 per cent of GNP (ibid.: 413–15, 436). One study points out, however, that the annual rate of increase in Japan's *actual* military expenditures was the highest in the world (Welfield 1988: 364). Thus, in 1955 total military expenditures amounted to $368 million; by 1969 the total was $1,344 million, equalling the combined defence budgets of Burma, Thailand, Malaysia, Indonesia, Laos, Cambodia, South Vietnam, South Korea, the Philippines and Taiwan!

The LDP's 'compensation politics', therefore, ensured continued conservative dominance until well into the 1980s. In contrast to those who underline transwar continuities, such as the contribution of economic planning during the war to postwar economic growth (Hein 1993; Dower 1993a), Calder (1988) views the compensation politics pursued by conservatives after 1949 as marking a fundamental break from the pre-1945 period. Conservative dominance was also facilitated by a divided opposition and an electoral system that favoured rural constituencies. The very nature of the LDP itself encouraged flexibility and the accommodation of different interests. Even when local governments backed by the Left (at prefectural and municipal levels) emerged in the late 1960s and 1970s (see chapter four) the LDP proved skilfully adept at co-opting progressive policies, a phenomenon that has been termed 'creative conservatism' (Pempel 1982).

4

The Emergence of an Economic Superpower

As with the previous decade the 1970s opened with a dramatic act of violence when the celebrated novelist Mishima Yukio committed ritual suicide on 25 November 1970 in protest against the constitution and what he perceived as its delegitimization of the Japanese military (Horsley and Buckley 1990: 100–1). Mishima had organized a small private army, the *Tate no kai* (Shield Society), which made use of SDF facilities and participated in SDF training exercises. When he and four followers occupied the Eastern Regional Headquarters of the SDF in Tokyo on 25 November Mishima expected that his emotional appeal to the assembled SDF personnel calling for a revision of the constitution would meet with enthusiastic acclaim. Instead, his words were greeted with bewilderment and derisory amusement, whereupon Mishima decided to stage the ultimate protest.

Mishima's death was regarded by conservative politicians (including Sato Eisaku) as the act of a madman, while the Left viewed it as a possible harbinger of a revival of militarism within the country. In many ways Mishima and his views were an anachronism in a country that had forsaken its militarist past and was now embarked on high-speed growth and the attainment of material prosperity. Yet his dissatisfaction with the course of postwar developments might very well have struck a chord amongst both extreme right-wing and left-wing elements. In a written appeal compiled just before his death (but only published three weeks after the event) Mishima praised the SDF as the only vigorous institution in a Japan that was politically and spiritually bankrupt, concerned solely with national economic growth at the expense of everything else (Mishima 1971: 73–7). He condemned Japan's sub-servience to foreign powers (i.e. the US), the country's inability to efface its wartime humiliation and guilt, and the desecration of Japanese traditions. One of those traditions – absolute loyalty to the Emperor – was highlighted one year later in 1972 when a Japanese soldier, Yokoi Shoichi, was 'discovered' in the jungles of Guam, the Pacific island occupied by Japan during the war (Ike 1973). Yokoi had been hiding there since 1944, refusing to surren-der out of the single-minded desire not to besmirch the imperial honour. Public reaction on Yokoi's return to Japan, as in the case of Mishima's suicide, was one of embarrassed puzzlement.

This is not to say that there was no extreme right-wing constitu-ency in Japan. In the late 1960s ultranationalist organizations ex-panded their membership so that by 1973 there were 500 such organizations with a total membership of 120,000 (Welfield 1988: 428). They demanded constitutional revision, an independent mili-tary, changes in education and the implementation of hardline anti-communist policies. There was an extraordinary continuity of personnel amongst some of these organizations; thus the Chairman of the National Council of Patriotic Associations (*Zenkoku aikokusha*) until his death in 1972, Sagoya Yoshiaki, was the ultra-nationalist assassin of a Japanese prime minister in 1930. Unlike the extreme left-wing organizations, however, these ultranational-ist groups had links with both the criminal underworld and the LDP establishment; they operated within the system rather than against it. Some underworld figures like Yotsumoto Yoshitaki and Kodama Yoshio had been prominent ultranationalists before the war. In the postwar period they became confidants of several prime ministers, including Yoshida Shigeru, Hatoyama Ichiro, Kishi Nobusuke, Sato Eisaku and Nakasone Yasuhiro (ibid.: 431–2). In 1973 one ultranationalist organization, the Young Storm Associa-tion (*Seiran kai*) – of which the LDP politician Ishihara Shintaro (see introduction) was a member – was actually established within the LDP itself.

At the other end of the political spectrum, left-wing terrorist groups in the early 1970s also sought an end to the postwar system. Known generically as the Red Army (*Sekigun*), these terrorist groups comprised the original Red Army Faction, which began in 1968 as a branch of a major student organization before becoming independent in 1969; the United Red Army (*Rengo sekigun*), which was active in 1971–2; and a group that developed abroad in

Lebanon and which split from the Red Army Faction in 1972 to form the Japanese Red Army (*Nihon sekigun*). The Japanese Red Army developed close ties with the Palestinian Popular Front for The Liberation of Palestine and remained active throughout the 1970s. The original Red Army attracted elite university students and placed itself beyond the pale when it began to resort to violence against the state in the form of bombings, post office and bank robberies, and highjackings. These Red Army groups perceived themselves very much in an *international* context, claiming to be a part of the international vanguard of a global revolution. Terrorist acts carried out by these groups included the highjacking of a domestic plane to North Korea in November 1970 and the 1972 attack by the Japanese Red Army on Lod airport in Israel, which resulted in the killing of 24 people. Subsequent terrorist acts by the Japanese Red Army, such as the occupation of the American and Swedish embassies in Kuala Lumpur in 1975 and the highjacking of a JAL plane in Bombay in 1977, were aimed at securing the release of their imprisoned comrades in Japan. The Red Army's domestic network was essentially smashed in 1972 when a group was besieged in a mountain lodge near Karuizawa (100 miles north of Tokyo) and forced to surrender to the authorities.

A recent study of the Red Army (Steinhoff 1989) shows how it replicated certain features of the Japanese managerial style (delegation of activities to relatively autonomous work groups operating under general direction from above, precision planning, and fastidious self-evaluation in the wake of setbacks), as well as making the intriguing suggestion that the Red Army's organizational methods drew on *both* the culture of the postwar elementary school, where SCAP-instigated reforms had encouraged children to work together in decision-making groups, and Japan's traditional style of decision-making by consensus. This hybrid was then subsequently assumed by American observers to be a distinctive characteristic of Japanese culture.

Notwithstanding the anguish of the extreme Right as symbolized by Mishima's dramatic suicide and the highly visible acts of opposition to the state by the extreme Left, Japan's onward march to economic superpower status seemed unstoppable. Despite the revaluation of the yen in 1971, 1977 and 1985–7 (308 yen to the US dollar in 1971 had become 120 yen to the dollar in early 1988), which made Japanese exports more expensive, dramatic increases in oil prices in 1973 and 1979, and growing trade friction with the

US in the 1970s and 1980s, which resulted in restraints on a number of Japanese exports, Japan's growth rate still attained higher levels than the rest of the developed world (see table 4.1). By 1986–7 Japan's global current account surplus had soared to over $80 billion, while the US global deficit had increased to over $160 billion, more than $59 billion of which accrued from trade with Japan (Calder 1988: 120). In 1987 Japan's per capita GNP was $19,600, exceeding that of the US (Beasley 1990: 259). Also, from the early 1970s on, with the relaxing of MITI controls and financial liberalization, Japanese corporations began to invest abroad as the revaluation of the yen made costs higher at home. In the process Japan became increasingly integrated with the global economy. Thus, while in 1970 foreign trade constituted 16 per cent of Japan's GNP, by 1985 it constituted 22 per cent; in 1970 Japanese direct overseas investments were negligible, yet by the end of 1986 cumulative overseas investments totalled $108 billion. By this time, also, Japanese security houses had become the primary dealers in US treasury bonds (Calder 1988: 121). Japanese firms after 1980 began to establish plants and subsidiaries not only in Western Europe and the US (where, by 1987, there were 900 Japanese-owned factories) (Beasley 1990: 252) but also in Southeast Asia, South Korea and Taiwan. By 1976 Japanese investment in South Korea accounted for 64 per cent of all foreign investment there (Welfield 1988: 339).

Table 4.1 Comparative real GNP growth in the industrialized world, 1971–86 (in percentages)

Country	1971–5	1976–80	1981–6
Japan	4.7	5.0	3.7
Canada	5.0	3.0	2.7
United States	2.6	3.7	2.4
United Kingdom	2.0	1.4	2.2
West Germany	2.1	3.6	1.5
France	4.0	3.3	1.3
Italy	4.1	3.8	1.2

Note: Real GNP for 1971–80 is in 1970 prices, and for 1981–6 in 1980 prices
Source: Calder (1988): Bank of Japan Research and Statistics Department (Nihon Ginko Chosa Tokei Kyoku), *Kokusai Hikaku Tokei (International Comparative Statistics)* (Tokyo: Nihon Ginko, 1982), p. 26; *Kokusai Hikaku Tokei*, 1987 edn, pp. 7–8

A recent study, focusing on direct Japanese investments and joint ventures in Southeast Asia, has referred to this phenomenon as Japan's 'new imperialism' (Steven 1990).

Yet despite economic superpower status, popular perceptions of Japan's economic vulnerability persisted. This is clearly demonstrated in a recent translation of a Japanese comic book, *Manga Nihon keizai nyumon* ('An Introduction to Japanese Economics – the Comic Book'), which became a bestseller in 1986 (Ishinomori 1988). The comic book magazine (*manga*) since 1945 has been popular reading material for both adults and children. In addition to the *gekiga* (dramatic picture story), there are two other genres of comic book: the *benkyo manga* (study comic) and the *jitsumu manga* (practical comic). Ishinomori, well known for his educational comic strips, portrayed a Japan continually buffeted by economic uncertainty as a result of ongoing trade disputes with the US, the rapid appreciation of the yen and rising oil prices.

With increasing economic wealth Japan not only became highly urbanized – in 1975 already the urban population had risen to 76 per cent of the total, while in 1981 farmers comprised a mere 9 per cent of the working population (Beasley 1990: 255) – but had also been transformed into a truly mass consumption society (Ivy 1993; Horioka 1993) in which by the 1970s most people referred to themselves as 'middle class' and educational levels were the highest in the world (Fukui 1988: 205). By 1980, for example, 37.9 per cent of the relevant age population were attending some form of tertiary education, while 94.3 per cent of junior high school graduates (i.e. 15-year-olds) were proceeding to senior high school (Buckley 1990). Declining birthrates (the population grew from 83 million in 1950 to 120 million in the mid-1980s) were matched by the highest life expectancy rates in the world; in the 1980s they were 80 for women and nearly 75 for men, compared to 54 and 50 respectively in 1947. Whereas only 5.7 per cent of the population were over 65 in 1960, it has been estimated that by 2020 the proportion will be 21.8 per cent, higher than anywhere else except Sweden (Tasker 1987: 106).

Politically, the LDP's dominance was contested in the 1970s at both national and local levels as the LDP's share of the popular vote in Diet elections continued slowly to decline and as progressives (those representing, or supported by, the leftist opposition parties) headed a number of prefectural and municipal governments. The political landscape became more fluid as opposition parties increased their representation on Diet committees and the LDP in 1976 experienced its first split since its formation. In the 1980s, following a period of bitter factional rivalry, the LDP achieved some electoral success during the premiership of Nakasone Yasuhiro (1982–7). Nakasone's premiership was marked by a reassertion of national pride and an attempt to enhance Japan's profile on the international stage. Although seeking to align Japan more closely with US strategic thinking and increasing defence spending for the first time since the 1950s, however, Nakasone could not stem the ongoing bitter trade friction with Washington. Nearer home, Japan's growing economic ties with the People's Republic of China did not preclude tensions between the two countries arising from the nature of that economic relationship and controversial history textbook revisions sanctioned by the Japanese Ministry of Education that whitewashed Japan's aggressive actions in China during the Second World War.

Domestically, the 1980s witnessed a reorientation of LDP policy as Nakasone's government embarked on administrative reform that included cutbacks in welfare spending and agricultural subsidies, the privatization of major public utilities and services, and tentative proposals to change the tax system. By the end of the decade growing public disillusionment with official corruption, which had first attained nationwide significance during the premiership of Tanaka Kakuei (1972–4), threatened to undermine the LDP hegemony. In the early 1990s the LDP began to disintegrate and new political alliances were forged that would finally bring an end to the LDP's uninterrupted rule since 1955.

The Nixon Shocks of 1971 and the Premiership of Tanaka Kakuei

The end of Sato Eisaku's premiership was marked by dramatic changes in American foreign and domestic policy that took the Japanese government unawares (Barnhart 1995: 174–5). Barely one year after Sato had ironed out details concerning Okinawa's return to Japanese jurisdiction in October 1970, US President Nixon, anxious to secure Beijing's co-operation in an orderly American withdrawal from Vietnam and perhaps also to exploit the Sino-Soviet split for Washington's advantage, announced in July 1971 that he would shortly visit the People's Republic of

China, thus signifying an end to American Cold War policy laid down since 1950 of isolating communist China and recognizing Chiang Kai-shek's regime on Taiwan as the sole legitimate government of China (normalization of relations was announced in February 1972 at the end of Nixon's visit). This *démarche* proved especially embarrassing to Sato, not only because he had not been informed beforehand but also because he had publicly supported both American hardline anti-communist policies in Asia and the Taiwan regime (Buckley 1992: 130–1). Further shocks were to follow in August 1971 when Nixon, in an attempt to rectify a worsening economic situation at home principally brought about by the country's disastrous involvement in Vietnam, arbitrarily imposed a 10 per cent surcharge on all imports and abandoned fixed exchange rates (established at Bretton Woods in 1944). This latter measure soon forced a nearly 17 per cent upward revaluation of the yen, which eventually stabilized at 308 to the US dollar.

At the same time (in October 1971) Washington finally compelled Sato to accept voluntary restraints on Japanese synthetic textile exports to the US after two years of wrangling between Japanese and American negotiators (ibid.: 123–9). As noted in chapter three, Tokyo had already imposed restrictions on its exports of cotton textiles and steel in order to pre-empt American protectionist legislation. Thus, the American share of Japan's total steel exports declined from 53 per cent in the mid-1960s to 28 per cent in 1971. The dispute over textile exports was somewhat ironical, given the fact that before the 1971 arrangement Japanese textile exports to the US had been declining. Between 1966 and 1970, for example, Japan's share of the American market for synthetic fibre goods had fallen from 66.8 per cent to 34.9 per cent, and for cotton goods from 22.6 per cent to 21.6 per cent (Welfield 1988: 286). This did not prevent hostile talk amongst American businessmen of a possible trade war and of Japan's plan to become the world's leading power; *Time* magazine in May 1971 saw the US locked into a struggle with 'a mighty industrial economy that has been shaped by Oriental history and psychology' (ibid.: 287). Such hyperbole conveniently overlooked the fact that in 1970 American investment in Japan was 6.5 times more than Japanese investment in the US (Halliday and McCormack 1973: 211) or that Japan took 34 per cent of its imports from the US while the latter took only 10.8 per cent of its imports from Japan. For example, Japan was particularly dependent on American agricultural imports; in 1971,

85 per cent of wheat consumed in Japan, as well as 93 per cent of soybeans, were imported from the US (Halliday 1975: 195).

The 'Nixon shocks' seriously damaged Sato's credibility and he faced much criticism from within his own party. In July 1972, two months after Okinawa was returned, he resigned and was succeeded as Prime Minister by Tanaka Kakuei. Tanaka, a self-made grassroots politician, was one of the few postwar prime ministers who had not attended the elite Tokyo University and, unlike his arch-rival for the LDP leadership, Fukuda Takeo, he had not risen through the bureaucracy. President of his own construction company at the age of 19, Tanaka saw brief military service in Manchuria during the war and was elected to the Diet in 1947. In 1948, at the age of 30, he became a vice-minister in Yoshida Shigeru's second cabinet. He went on to become Minister of Posts (1957), Minister of Finance (1962) and Minister of MITI (1971) before gaining the LDP leadership in 1972. Tanaka and Nakasone Yasuhiro have been regarded by Western observers as the only postwar prime ministers to have stamped their own personalities on Japanese politics and to have asserted more initiative in a policy-making process that generally tended to favour consensus (Tasker 1987). Although originally a member of Sato's faction, Tanaka after 1972 steadily built up his own faction (through the adept and widespread use of personal support networks) that was eventually to become the largest and most influential within the LDP. As will be seen later, Tanaka's faction continued to grow and exercise influence even after Tanaka's own resignation as Prime Minister in 1974.

The major foreign policy success of Tanaka's premiership was the normalization of relations with China, which was to lead to more extensive economic ties between the two countries. Japan's growing economic clout in Southeast Asia, however, fuelled resentment that was to be dramatically manifested during Tanaka's tour of the region in early 1974. At home, Tanaka's premiership was marked by an abortive attempt at political reform and the failure to implement an ambitious plan to reshape regional development; at the same time, Tanaka's government proved skilful in co-opting progressive welfare policies first pioneered by Left-supported local governments. Finally, increased public works spending (often connected with pork-barrel politics) at a time of slower economic growth led to growing government deficits. The ominous prevalence of 'money politics', fuelled by Tanaka himself in his attempts to cement his personal support networks, was to result in more blatant forms of corruption.

One of Tanaka's first acts on becoming Prime Minister in July 1972 was to begin negotiations with China. Interestingly, relations with China had been one of the few political issues that had polarized factions within the LDP, as well as even transcending factional and party lines. Sato's rigid pro-US policy had been continually criticized from within the LDP and in October 1970 pro-China members of the party joined with opposition parties to form the Parliamentarians' League for the Restoration of Ties with China (*Nichu kokko kaifuku sokushin giin renmei*). By December 1970, 50 per cent of lower house members and just over half the upper house membership had joined the League (Welfield 1988: 292). Business interests also took a lead in pressing for a change in policy. As noted in chapter three, unofficial trade with China had been growing since the 1950s; trade between the two countries totalled $822 million in 1970 (compared to $150 million in 1956), by which time Japan had become China's primary trading partner, accounting for 20 per cent of China's trade (Ogata 1977: 178–80). Tanaka was thus assured of broad support when he visited China in September 1972 and signed an agreement with Chinese Premier Zhou Enlai that finally normalized relations. A formal treaty of peace and friendship was to be signed six years later. The question of Japan's war guilt and the nature of Japanese actions in China during the war, however, were not fully discussed or resolved; during his visit Tanaka merely apologized for the 'great inconvenience' Japan had caused China (Barnhart 1995: 176). This was to be an issue that would haunt Sino-Japanese relations in the 1980s.

Tanaka's tour of Southeast Asia in early 1974 was not so successful, since it brought to the fore growing public resentment in the region toward Japan's economic influence. In fact, during the 1970s, Japan became the leading economic power in the region. In 1971 Japanese investment in Indonesia totalled more than that of all other foreign countries combined; in the same year Japan overtook the US as the main foreign investor in Thailand. By 1975 Japan had become the largest single foreign investor in Malaysia, Singapore and the Philippines. In that year every country in the region (except Laos, South Vietnam and Burma) received more aid and private investment from Japan than from the US (Havens 1987: 247). Overall, while 15.62 per cent of Japan's overseas investments in 1971 were concentrated in ASEAN (the Association of Southeast Asian Nations formed in 1967 comprising Indonesia, Malaysia, Singapore, Thailand and the Philippines), by 1976 this proportion had increased to 36.44 per cent (Borden 1984: 219; Welfield 1988: 346). A graphic illustration of Japan's presence in the region was the country's participation in joint naval exercises with Australia and Malaysia in 1969, during which a Japanese naval squadron cruised through the Malacca Straits for the first time since the war (Halliday and McCormack 1973: 105). When Tanaka visited Thailand, Indonesia and the Philippines he was met with hostile demonstrations and accusations of Japanese business arrogance. Clearly, such concerns were also exacerbated by lingering suspicions that dated from the Second World War.

At home, the political landscape changed at both national and local levels. In the December 1972 elections for the lower house the LDP dropped from 288 to 271 seats (its share of the popular vote again falling to 46.9 per cent), while the socialists and communists made gains; the JSP won 118 seats (with 21.9 per cent of the vote) and the JCP 38 seats (with 10.5 per cent of the vote). For the first time since 1955 the LDP gave up the chairmanships of many special Diet committees to the opposition, a phenomenon that became more pronounced after 1976. The upper house elections of July 1974 left the LDP with only a majority of seven over the opposition as a whole. At the local level, by the early 1970s a large number of prefectural and municipal administrations were controlled by progressives, that is to say those who were associated with one or more of the opposition parties (Steiner 1980b), thus breaking the conservative monopoly of local government that had existed since 1947. A combination of three trends contributed to the emergence of progressive local governments.

First, the government's campaign since the early 1960s to encourage local governments to set up new industries had siphoned off workers from the primary sector as well as bringing in workers from outside. This resulted in expanded urbanization and the consequent shrinkage of the LDP's traditionally secure rural electoral base (Steiner 1980a: 5–6). Second, after an initial period of neglect, the opposition parties began to focus more on local politics in the 1960s. This was illustrated by the election in 1963 of a former JSP Diet member, Asukata Ichio, as mayor of Yokohama; he remained mayor until 1977, when he took up the chairmanship of the JSP. Third, as noted in chapter three, there was growing public dissatisfaction with the damaging effects of pollution on local communities as a result of the government's high-speed economic growth policy.

It has been estimated that in 1974 nearly 41 per cent of the Japanese population lived in prefectures and cities in which prefectural governors or municipal mayors were backed by opposition parties (Flanagan 1980: 41–2; Curtis 1988: 261). By 1975 there were nine progressive prefectural governors (including those of Kyoto, Tokyo and Osaka) and 130 progressive city mayors (out of a total of 643). Furthermore, in seven of the 47 prefectures the LDP and conservative independents no longer held a majority of seats in the prefectural assembly. Not surprisingly, those prefectures that experienced the most rapid rates of population growth and urbanization witnessed the sharpest rise in opposition support (Flanagan 1980: 38–9). In the western suburbs of Tokyo metropolitan prefecture, for example, which had seen considerable numbers of in-migrating workers to take up employment in new industries, nine of the 26 municipalities had progressive mayors (Allinson 1980: 95).

The most celebrated of progressive local chief executives (who, unlike the prime minister, are directly elected) was Ninagawa Torazo. Ninagawa, a former economics professor, was elected seven times as prefectural governor of metropolitan Kyoto between 1950 and 1978. He was able to create a broad base of support (including conservative and independent voters) attracted by his championing of local autonomy *vis-à-vis* central government and promotion of small business interests; 84 per cent of Kyoto's industrial and commercial facilities, after all, employed less than four people (Krauss 1980: 387). Ninagawa's administration became the first local government to institute a no-collateral loan programme for small and medium enterprises. Minobe Ryokichi, the progressive governor of metropolitan Tokyo between 1967 and 1979 (interestingly another former economics professor), implemented free medical care for those over 70 in 1969. By early 1972, 44 prefectures had adopted free medical care for the elderly programmes (Calder 1988: 372). Also, in 1969, Minobe legislated for the provision of children's allowances, itself a measure that had been adopted two years earlier by the socialist mayor of Musashino city (western Tokyo prefecture). Asukata Ichio, as mayor of Yokohama, emphasized direct democracy by encouraging consultation and the public airing of views. He also pioneered voluntary pollution control agreements between local government and industry in 1964. By the end of 1970, 30 prefectures and 100 cities, towns and villages had entered into such agreements with over 500 companies (Steiner 1980b: 329).

The LDP government in the early 1970s appropriated many of these progressive policies. This has been described as a 'preemptive concessions strategy', which allowed the authorities to introduce social change on their own terms rather than respond to organized pressure from society (Pharr 1990: 219), although it might be argued that the government's appropriation of progressive policies pioneered at the local level was itself a response to grassroots pressure. It endorsed the no-collateral loan programme for the benefit of small business when, in 1973, funds from the Fiscal Investment and Loan Programme (FILP) were channelled via the government-run People's Finance Corporation to local chambers of commerce for low-interest no-collateral loans; in 1977 the scheme was extended to small retail and service industries. Also, in 1973, as a further demonstration of its support for small business, the government passed the Large-scale Retail Law, which controlled the expansion of chain stores. In 1973 Tanaka's government instituted free medical care for the elderly, a benefit that was to last until 1983 when cutbacks in welfare services to deal with growing deficits necessitated those over 70 having to contribute a share of their medical costs. Other welfare measures adopted by the central government included the provision of children's allowances in 1972 and the indexing of pensions to the inflation rate in 1973. One study (Curtis 1988) has noted that the government deficits of the 1980s were a direct consequence of Tanaka's premiership, when these increased expenditures on welfare occurred. The 1974 budget, for example, allowed for the first time more government spending on social welfare than on public works, although expenditures on the latter, which also became significant during Tanaka's premiership, sharply increased subsequently, by 21.2 per cent in 1976 and 22.5 per cent in 1979. In 1981 government spending accounted for 34.1 per cent of GNP, compared to 21.7 per cent in 1971 (ibid.: 66, 69, 71).

Under Tanaka, public works spending became increasingly associated with the cultivation of local constituency support, as was demonstrated by the benefits that accrued to his own electoral district in Niigata (a predominantly rural prefecture on the Japan Sea coast). It was in fact a measure of Tanaka's continuing influence after his resignation that Niigata in the early and mid-1980s received three times as much in public works spending as it paid in taxes. By 1982 Niigata had a direct train link to Tokyo (with high-speed trains stopping at small rural stations in the constituency) and was connected to other parts of the country via two major highways. Other leading LDP politicians followed in Tanaka's wake. Thus, the home prefecture of Takeshita Noboru (Finance Minister 1981–6 and Prime Minister 1987–9) was the largest recipient of public construction projects in 1984 (Calder 1988: 275, 281).

While Tanaka achieved some success abroad with the agreement signed in Beijing normalizing Sino-Japanese relations, his two domestic initiatives came to nought. First, Tanaka's proposal to replace multi-member constituencies with single-member ones for elections to the lower house of the Diet had to be quickly dropped as a result of fierce criticism by the opposition parties. Tanaka's ostensible aim had been to put an end to the virtually institutionalized factionalism within the LDP that the multi-member constituency system produced, but the opposition feared that such a change would squeeze out the smaller parties and allow the LDP to gain larger electoral majorities. The second initiative fell foul of the worsening economic situation in the wake of the 1973 oil crisis. On becoming Prime Minister in 1972, Tanaka outlined an ambitious plan for regional development, published under the title *Building a New Japan: The Remodelling of the Japanese Archipelago*. The plan envisioned the rebuilding of decaying regional centres, the development of industry in outlying areas in order to reverse migration to the overpopulated metropolitan centres, the expansion of the road and railway network throughout Japan, and the construction of bridges linking the main island of Honshu to Shikoku in the south and an underwater tunnel linking Honshu to Hokkaido in the north (Horsley and Buckley 1990: 111). Almost immediately there was increased speculation and spiralling land prices.

The situation was exacerbated after the Middle East War of October 1973 when OAPEC (Organization of Arab Petroleum-Exporting Countries) imposed an oil embargo on the US for its pro-Israel stance and threatened Japan and other oil-importing countries with a similar measure unless they demonstrated support for the Arab cause. In Japan this led to panic buying and hoarding of goods by manufacturers and wholesalers, further driving up prices. On the eve of the war Japan was the world's second largest consumer of petroleum and, as noted in chapter three, was dependent on outside sources for 99.7 per cent of its oil (80 per cent of which came from the Middle East). Even before the war, therefore, the government was looking into the possibilities of other sources of supply and in 1971 sanctioned negotiations between the quasi-official Japan–Soviet Economic Committee (formed in 1965) and the Soviet authorities concerning possible Japanese participation in the development of oil resources in Siberia. This was another example of the separation of politics and economics in Japanese foreign policy, since the question of the disputed Northern Territories (Shikotan, Habomai, Etorofu, Kunashiri) held by the Soviet Union was still unresolved (this did not prevent them from appearing on Japanese maps as Japanese territory after 1969). The project was ultimately stalled, however, because of Tokyo's reluctance to go ahead without US involvement (Curtis 1977).

The threat of an oil embargo thus posed an acute problem for Japan. By December 1973, much to Washington's chagrin, the Japanese government was calling for Israeli withdrawal from the occupied territories acquired during the 1967 Middle East War and was expressing support for Palestinian self-determination. Although such statements prompted OAPEC to exempt Japan from any cuts in oil imports, the sharp rise in the price of crude oil in 1973 slowed down economic growth. In 1974 Japan's industrial output fell by 9 per cent and in 1974–5 the growth rate registered its first negative figure in the postwar period, -0.2 per cent compared to 5.3 per cent in 1973–4 (Stockwin 1982: 79; Horsley and Buckley 1990: 117). Japan's balance of payments moved from a surplus of \$4.6 billion in 1971 to a deficit of \$10 billion in 1973 (Beasley 1990: 264). In order to stabilize the economic situation the government imposed an energy-saving programme on industry and implemented rationing and price controls. It also sought to lessen the country's dependence on oil by using or developing alternative sources for its energy needs. During the 1970s, for example, liquefied natural gas replaced oil as the main fuel in electric power generation and the nuclear energy programme was speeded up. By 1982 there were 24 nuclear reactors supplying up to 30 per cent of the country's electricity (Horsley and Buckley 1990: 122). Overall, the general dependence on oil for energy needs was brought down from 80 per cent in 1972 to 61 per cent in 1983 (Hane 1992: 379); by the early 1990s nuclear power provided Japan's single most important source of electricity (Donnelly 1993). Finally, Tanaka's grandiose blueprint for a new Japan had to be put on hold, although some projects were completed many years after his premiership; thus, in

1988 the tunnel between Honshu and Hokkaido was opened and by 1990 five of the originally planned 12 bullet-train lines were in operation (Horsley and Buckley 1990: 121).

Tanaka's premiership came to an abrupt end in December 1974, just a few weeks after US President Ford visited Japan (the first American head of state to do so). Amidst newspaper reports of financial wrongdoings that included laundering of campaign funds, the bribery of LDP politicians to secure the party's presidency, and the failure to report earnings and donations to the tax authorities, Tanaka resigned. Interestingly, years before when he was a junior minister, Tanaka had been charged with accepting bribes in 1948 from local coalmine owners (in return for his help to guarantee their continued ownership); found guilty by a lower court he had subsequently been cleared by a higher court. By February 1976 Tanaka's name was also being linked to another financial scandal when the US Senate began an investigation of US multinationals and their lobbying of foreign officials. One such corporation, the Lockheed Corporation, claimed to have paid Tanaka (amongst others) 500 million yen to ensure that its own Tristar jets would be purchased by a domestic Japanese airline rather than the jets of its rival, the McDonnell Douglas Corporation. It was also revealed that one of Lockheed's secret consultants in Japan during the late 1960s was the underworld boss Kodama Yoshio, an intriguing parallel to the way in which SCAP had made use of former Japanese imperial army officers and thought police during the occupation (Welfield 1988: 431–2).

Tanaka was arrested in July 1976 but it was not until October 1983 that judgement was finally passed. Although sentenced to four years of imprisonment he was freed on bail pending appeal. Until 1986, when he suffered a stroke, Tanaka and his faction continued to exercise enormous influence within the LDP even though he himself formally quit the party in 1976. By 1986 Tanaka's faction was the largest in the party and he had played a part in the fall of two prime ministers (Miki Takeo and Fukuda Takeo), as well as nominating three subsequent ones (Ohira Masayoshi, Suzuki Zenko and Nakasone Yasuhiro). His local constituents, regarding him as a hero for the benefits he had bestowed on their region, continued to elect him to the Diet. In the December 1983 elections, for example, just three months after being sentenced to imprisonment, Tanaka recorded the highest vote of his career in Niigata.

Internecine Strife Within the LDP

In order to stabilize the political situation and avoid open factional conflict, LDP leaders decided to choose a compromise candidate to succeed Tanaka as prime minister. Miki Takeo, the leader of one of the party's smaller factions and unblemished by the revelations of financial corruption within the LDP, was an ideal choice. First elected to the Diet in 1937, Miki had led one of the smaller reform-minded conservative parties during the occupation period, during which he had been a member of the socialist coalition government of 1947–8. In the two years of his premiership, perhaps to the surprise of many of his colleagues, he attempted to tackle head-on the question of political corruption. In 1975 Miki's sponsored reform bills attempted to both reassert the party, rather than factions, as the focus of electioneering and to regularize contributions of funds to political parties and individuals (Curtis 1988: 164).

In the 1950s a blanket prohibition had been imposed on party activity during the electoral campaign period, although this was modified in 1962 when parties were allowed to convene up to four meetings for each of their candidates and could display up to 500 posters per meeting, without mentioning any of their candidates. Miki now sought to permit more party activity by allowing 1,500 posters per election district (although candidates' names again were not to be mentioned). Parties would also be able to issue an unlimited number of officially registered handbills and no limits were to be set on the number of meetings in any one district. Candidates, who could now be named and endorsed by party leaders, would be permitted to make speeches during the campaign period as long as party leaders were present to demonstrate clearly that the purpose of such meetings was to publicize party policies. To further emphasize the party-centred nature of the campaign political parties were allowed after 1975 to advertise in the media, but only to publicize party policies. At the same time the restrictions on individual campaign activities (dating from the 1920s) were still to prevail. These included no pre-election campaigning, house-to-house canvassing, use of unauthorized written materials (such as name cards), and distribution of monetary payments, food and drink amongst supporters (Stockwin 1982: 104; Curtis 1988: 170). Such activities, particularly the bestowal of gifts and the holding of banquets for potential supporters, had been a feature of election politics at the very beginning of Japan's constitutional system in the 1890s (Mason 1969: 155). The line between formal election campaigning and the activities sponsored by a candidate's personal support group (*koenkai*) throughout the year was a very thin one, however, and continued to be crossed in subsequent years.

Likewise, although Miki's government in 1975 set ceilings on corporate and trade union contributions to parties, factions and individuals – contributions to parties were to be calculated according to a firm's capitalization, while contributions to factions and individuals were not to exceed 1.5 million yen – this did not prevent LDP members from creating multiple organizations through which funds were channelled. Illegal political contributions continued to be funnelled to LDP leaders in what Curtis (1988: 185) refers to as an 'underground political economy'. Also, as the *Keidanren* (Federation of Economic Organizations) became less significant as a source of political funds for the LDP after the mid-1970s, faction leaders obtained increasing financial support from the consumer electronics industry, insurance companies and the construction industry, reflecting the growing importance of high-tech and service industries in the Japanese economy after the 1973 oil crisis. In 1979, for example, the 46 major construction companies contributed 760 million yen to the LDP (ibid.: 184). Miki's reforms, in the end, neither reduced the importance of factions within the LDP nor stemmed the tide of money politics. Miki himself was eased out of the LDP presidency (and hence the premiership) by a temporary alliance between two powerful factional leaders, Fukuda Takeo and Ohira Masayoshi (associated with Tanaka's faction). Fukuda became Prime Minister in December 1976 with the understanding that Ohira would take over after his two-year term.

A more dramatic consequence of the financial scandals surrounding the Tanaka premiership was the first split within the LDP since its formation in 1955. In June 1976 six members of the party, led by Kono Yohei, announced their defection from the LDP and the creation of a new party, the New Liberal Club (NLC). Although the defectors clearly wanted to distance themselves from the LDP in the wake of the Lockheed Scandal, a recent study (Pharr 1990: 51–3) has argued that Kono and his colleagues (all in their 30s and 40s) were also engaging in 'status politics', expressing their dissatisfaction with the age-based hierarchy of the party that left little promise of rapid advancement for younger generations such as themselves. By the 1970s promotion within the party (based on age and the number of times one had been elected to the Diet) had become more institutionalized and rigid. The creation of the NLC was thus just as much to do with the thwarted ambitions of a younger generation of LDP members as it was with demonstrating condemnation of LDP corruption. Interestingly, too, Kono was the son of Kono Ichiro, an important LDP factional leader in the 1950s and 1960s, who had failed in an attempt to form a new party in 1960 when his faction failed to obtain a cabinet post. Kono Yohei (like two of the other founding members of the NLC) was therefore a *nisei*, a second-generation politician having a famous political father or close relatives in the LDP. As Pharr (1990) points out, *nisei* generally inherited safe seats, thereby obviating the need for LDP endorsement, and had less to lose by engaging in status politics.

In the December 1976 elections the NLC gained 17 seats, while the LDP for the first time since 1958 obtained less than 50 per cent of the lower house seats (with only 41.8 per cent of the vote) and had to rely on conservative independents to enjoy a slim majority in the house. Although the NLC in its ten year existence (it dissolved in 1986) was never again to be so successful, gaining only four seats in 1979, 12 in 1980 and eight in 1983, it formed a coalition with the LDP between 1983 and 1986 (when again the LDP held less than 50 per cent of lower house seats), thus guaranteeing the party a cabinet post. What the NLC did, however, was to prevent the opposition from fully exploiting public disillusionment with the LDP after the scandals of 1974–6 by siphoning off part of the protest vote (Curtis 1988: 34).

Nevertheless, within the Diet during the 1976–80 period (when the LDP held less than 50 per cent of the seats) the opposition was able to enhance its representation on Diet committees. Until the elections of 1976 the LDP had provided all the chairmen and majority of members of all Diet committees, yet by 1978 only nine of the 25 lower house committees had both an LDP chairman and a majority of LDP members (Krauss 1984). In January 1980 the LDP provided 261 and the opposition 257 of the members of all lower house standing committees (Stockwin 1982: 95). The fierce political struggles of the 1950s and 1960s, which were often underpinned by clear ideological differences between the LDP and the JSP, gave way to consultation and accommodation as both government and opposition grappled with the problems arising from economic growth. After 1976 Ohira Masayoshi, the Secretary-general of the LDP, began referring to a new strategy of 'partial coalition' with the opposition, by which he meant that the cabinet would henceforth negotiate with individual opposition parties on each piece of legislation (Krauss 1984: 263). The seemingly strange political alliances that emerged in the early 1990s after the LDP's hegemony was ended (see next chapter) thus had a precedent in the cross-party consultation that occurred in the late 1970s between the LDP and the opposition.

The accession of Fukuda Takeo to the premiership in December 1976, however, brought out into the open the bitter rivalry *within* the LDP between Fukuda and Tanaka that dated from 1972, when both men had competed for the party leadership (Baerwald 1986: 125–39). Although one study (van Wolferen 1989: 142) notes that the rivalry represented the persistent division within the party between grassroots politicians such as Tanaka and career bureaucrats turned politician such as Fukuda, it should be noted that the dominance of career bureaucrats within the LDP so evident during the 1950s and 1960s was gradually withering away as specialized career politicians began to exert more influence in the 1970s (Allinson 1993a). Many of these career politicians became expert members of Diet committees, often being identified with particular policy issues; in Japanese they were referred to as 'policy tribes' (*seisaku zoku*). The omnipotence of the bureaucracy (which had traditionally drafted most legislation) was also being dented by the LDP's own legislative organ, the Policy Affairs Research Council (*seimu chosakai*), which began to take a more active role in the 1970s researching policy and drafting legislation (Stockwin 1982). Of the nine prime ministers who served between 1972 and 1990, seven were career politicians and by the late 1980s 45 per cent of all LDP Diet members were second-generation politicians (Allinson 1993a: 137).

The temporary agreement reached between Fukuda and Ohira Masayoshi (allied with Tanaka) in order to oust Miki from the leadership gave way to bitter recriminations when Ohira successfully ran against Fukuda as party leader in 1978 with the help of Tanaka's faction. The choice of party leader in 1978 was significant because for the first time a system of primaries was used in which the party rank and file voted for candidates (i.e. those who had the support of at least 20 Diet members), with the party convention, comprising all LDP Diet members and representatives from prefectural branches, then choosing from amongst the top two contenders. Although designed to allow the party as a whole to have a say in the choice of leader, the primary system in practice simply accentuated factional rivalry within the party. Fukuda had confidently expected to be reconfirmed as party leader in 1978. As Minister of Finance during the last year of Tanaka's premiership he had played a significant part in restoring stability to the economy after the 1973 oil crisis. As Prime Minister he had helped to smooth relations with the countries of Southeast Asia, whose suspicions of Japan had been so clearly demonstrated during Tanaka's tour of the region in 1974. In August 1977 Fukuda attended ASEAN summit meetings in Malaysia; shortly afterwards, in Manila, in what became known as the 'Fukuda Doctrine', he insisted that Japan would not become a military power or produce nuclear weapons. Fukuda also committed Japan to fostering relations with the countries of Southeast Asia on an equal basis, as well as to contributing to peace in the region (Havens 1987: 247–8). Neighbouring countries in Asia would have also noted with approval a ruling laid down by Prime Minister Miki in 1976 that no more than 1 per cent of Japan's GNP was to be spent on defence, a ruling adhered to until 1987.

Fukuda's resentment at being replaced in 1978 was to edge the LDP to the brink of an irreversible split. When Ohira refused to step down as Prime Minister in the wake of the party's poor showing in the October 1979 lower house elections (gaining only 48.5 per cent of the seats) Fukuda took the extraordinary step of presenting himself to the Diet as a candidate for prime minister, thus providing the spectacle of two LDP leaders vying for the premiership. Although Fukuda had the support of the Miki faction, Ohira won on the second round (with the opposition abstaining), again with the help of Tanaka's faction. The Fukuda and Miki factions achieved their revenge in May 1980 when they abstained during the vote on a JSP no-confidence motion. When the motion passed Ohira was compelled to call new elections in June 1980. During the campaign Ohira died of a heart attack, which helped to give the LDP a huge sympathy vote. For the first time since the 1972 elections the LDP gained a majority of seats (increasing its representation from 248 to 286 seats). Suzuki Zenko, the leader of the Ohira faction and Party President, took over as Prime Minister, although the 1980s were to be dominated by Nakasone Yasuhiro, whose five-year tenure as Prime Minister (1982–7) was the longest since that of Sato Eisaku.

The 1980 elections seemed to herald a return of LDP primacy. The party regained control of all Diet standing committees, while at the local level only four out of the 47 prefectural governorships remained in opposition hands (Ninagawa and Minobe had retired in 1978 and 1979 respectively). Interestingly, however, the political landscape in 1980 at the local level did not indicate a return to the former conservative monopoly. Many local administrations were headed by centre-right coalitions, with the DSP, Komeito and even the JSP allied with the LDP as a result of joint campaigns against the JCP (Flanagan, Steiner and Krauss 1980: 469). By the end of the 1980s, too, the LDP would once again be rocked by scandal and corruption that threatened its hegemony.

Nakasone and the 'Final Settlement of Postwar Politics'

With the support of Tanaka's faction Nakasone Yasuhiro was chosen LDP leader in November 1982 after a primary election in which four candidates took part (in 1981 the original 1977 regulations on party primaries were amended to stipulate that there had to be at least four candidates for a primary to take place); shortly afterwards he was voted prime minister in the Diet. A graduate of the prestigious Law Faculty of Tokyo Imperial University, Nakasone had been a junior naval officer during the war and was first elected to the Diet in 1947 after a brief spell as an official in the Home Ministry. He entered politics very much as a nationalist, castigating Yoshida's cautious policy of deference to the US and condemning the American-imposed 1947 constitution. This did not prevent him from joining the cabinet of the pro-American Sato Eisaku (by which time he headed a faction of his own within the LDP), becoming Minister of Transport in 1967 and then Director of the Defence Agency in 1969, during which time he had allowed Mishima Yukio and his private army to use SDF facilities. Nakasone supported Tanaka for leader in 1972 and was appointed Minister of MITI. During Suzuki Zenko's premiership Nakasone first became associated with the programme of financial retrenchment that was to be a feature of his own premiership when, as Minister of the Administrative Management Agency, he supervised a government commission on administrative reform set up in 1981 and chaired by a former president of *Keidanren*, Doko Toshio.

On becoming Prime Minister, Nakasone referred to the 'final settlement of postwar politics' (*sengo seiji no sokessan*), making it clear that he wished Japan to assert more responsibility in international affairs and to end its dependence on the US (Horsley and

Buckley 1990: 176). For Nakasone this also meant a reassertion of Japanese pride, an end to lingering feelings of war guilt and a definitive reassessment of the occupation reforms that would include a revision of the constitution. His energetic leadership both at home and abroad (which some Western commentators likened to a presidential-style leadership) brought him popularity amongst the Japanese public and the LDP was prompted in 1986 to extend his term as leader beyond the normal two term maximum (four years) for another year. At the same time Nakasone's attempt to enhance Japan's strategic role as an equal partner of the US aroused fears amongst the Left opposition parties that the country was on the verge of becoming a military power. At home, Nakasone's initiatives to end the country's sense of war guilt were not only fiercely denounced by the Left opposition but also by China and other Asian countries that had suffered from Japanese aggression during the war.

Nakasone made clear his intent to change Japan's image as both economic giant and 'political dwarf' (Barnhart 1995: 180) at his first press conference after becoming Prime Minister, when he noted that Japan had obtained its defence on the cheap and compared the country's defence efforts unfavourably with those of the West (Buckley 1992: 143). In January 1983 he visited Washington and in talks with President Reagan sought to demonstrate Japan's new sense of international responsibility. To some extent Nakasone was responding to increasing American criticism from the late 1970s that focused on both Japan's trade surplus with the US and its low defence spending at a time when the collapse of American–Soviet detente in 1978–9 had led to growing tension between the two superpowers.

Washington's alarm at the growing trade imbalance with Japan, which increased from $1.69 billion in 1974 to nearly $10.5 billion by the end of the 1970s, had already resulted in pressure on Tokyo to restrain its exports of specialty steel (1974) and colour television sets (1977) to the US. The Carter administration (1976–80) also increased import duties on Japanese light trucks and insisted that Japan accept more American imports of agricultural products and enriched uranium (Welfield 1988: 330–1). This growing trade friction was not helped by further American displeasure with Japan in the wake of the second oil crisis of 1978–9, when Tokyo initially hesitated to join in a concerted response by the Western industrialized countries to the oil price hike imposed by the oil producing countries (which would have involved cutting back on oil imports). Also, following the sharp deterioration in American–Iranian relations after the Islamic Revolution of 1979, Tokyo again prevaricated when Washington called on its allies to embargo Iranian oil in 1980 (Iran ultimately cut off oil supplies to Japan in April 1980 when Tokyo refused to pay higher prices). Crucially dependent on Middle Eastern oil, Japan's economy was affected more by the crises of 1978–9 and 1980 than most of its Western partners, but by the early 1980s recovery had sufficiently occurred to make Japan the world's largest manufacturer of motor vehicles as well as the dominant producer of consumer electronics, video recorders and computer chips (which were now Japan's major export items rather than textiles and steel). Further American pressure on Tokyo led to the acceptance by the Japanese car industry of a 'voluntary' arrangement in April 1981 restricting the volume of annual exports to the US, an arrangement that was to remain in force throughout the decade. Unfortunately, this concession failed to quieten criticism of Japan within the US, nor did it effectively reduce the American trade deficit.

American criticism of Japan's defence spending added fuel to the trade friction. Although Prime Minister Ohira had co-operated with Washington in boycotting the Moscow Olympic Games and imposing economic sanctions on the Soviet Union in 1980 to protest the Soviet invasion of Afghanistan at the end of 1979, the American Secretary of Defence in December 1980 publicly reproached Tokyo for its low defence expenditures in the wake of what was perceived in Washington as a renewed Soviet military threat (Buckley 1992: 136–7). A meeting between Prime Minister Suzuki and President Reagan in May 1981 produced an official communiqué that stated Japan would make greater efforts in improving its defence capabilities in and around Japan (including eventual assumption of responsibility for the defence of sea lanes up to 1,000 miles to the south of Japan). Aware of the likely public *furore* at home such a commitment would cause, however, Suzuki was compelled later to deny much of what had been agreed to in the official communiqué (ibid.: 142).

Nakasone's talks with Reagan in January 1983, therefore, seemed to represent a major turning-point in Japanese foreign policy (Barnhart 1995: 181). Pledging Japan's determination to stand shoulder to shoulder with the US in containing the Soviet threat in the Far East, Nakasone portrayed his country as 'an unsinkable aircraft carrier putting up a tremendous bulwark of defence against infiltration of the [Soviet] backfire bomber' (Welfield 1988: 446). He committed Japan to defending the sea lanes up to 1,000 miles from all the home islands, promised to extend the range and strike power of the airforce, and agreed to future joint exercises between the SDF and American forces designed to prevent Soviet access to the Pacific. Nakasone was also prepared to break with former Japanese government practice. First, by sanctioning the export of dual-use technology (i.e. civilian and military) and the exchange of military technology between Japan and the US, Nakasone undermined the general ban on all arms exports (including military technology) that had been implemented since 1976 (in 1967 Prime Minister Sato had endorsed a ban on arms exports to communist states and to countries either involved in international disputes or subject to UN sanctions) (Barnhart 1995: 181–2). Second, Nakasone promised during his meeting with Reagan that he would seek to abandon the 1 per cent of GNP ceiling for military spending, again first laid down in 1976.

While the American press hailed the new US–Japan understanding symbolized by the 'Ron–Yasu' relationship, opposition parties and the press in Japan denounced Nakasone's rhetoric as warmongering. In fact, very little changed during his premiership. The 1 per cent of GNP ceiling for defence spending was only just exceeded in 1987 (see figure 4.1). Overall, between 1982 and 1987, defence spending increased from 5.2 per cent to 6.5 per cent of the general account budget (in 1954 it had been 14 per cent) (Calder 1988: 417) and the SDF ground forces remained at 180,000 in total as they had been in 1953. In 1990, 0.997 per cent of Japan's GNP was committed to defence (Pharr 1993: 249). At the same time Japan's trade surplus with the US continued to mushroom. Ironically, also, Japan increasingly financed the US domestic deficit; in 1986, for example, Japanese investors purchased up to 40 per cent of US government bonds (Welfield 1988: 447).

During the 1980s, US congressional criticism of Japan became more vociferous, while the ugly phenomenon of inflammatory 'Japan bashing' was prevalent in the media and written publications. In July 1985 an article in the *New York Times Magazine* predicted a trade war between the two countries and warned Japan that the American response would be as forthright as that demonstrated after Pearl Harbour (Johnson 1988: 36). Lee Iacocca, Chief

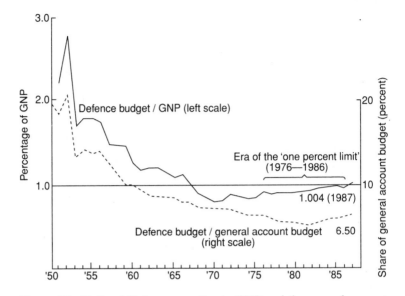

Figure 4.1   Ratio of Defence spending to GNP and the general account budget
Source: Calder (1988): Asagumo Shimbun Sha Henshu So kyoku (ed.) *Boei Handbook (Defence Handbook)* (Tokyo: Asagumo Shimbun Sha, 1987), pp. 221–3

Executive Officer of the Chrysler car company, likewise noted in his 1985 autobiography that the US was currently engaged in a major trade war with Japan (ibid.: 122). Japanese exports were subject to restraint and sanctions throughout this period. In 1984 Japan agreed to limit its share of the American steel market to 5.85 per cent from the following year, while in 1986 Tokyo again agreed to impose limits on exports of IC chips to the US. In 1985 Reagan himself sanctioned the use of penalties against Japanese imports on the grounds that Japan had restricted imports of American goods. In June 1987, shortly after Washington had imposed sanctions on imports of Japanese electrical goods (claiming that Tokyo had broken an agreement to 'restrain' exports of machine tools and semi-conductors), the US House of Representatives approved an extraordinary resolution requiring the US Secretary of State to discuss with Tokyo the possibility of Japan increasing its military spending to at least 3 per cent of its GNP or providing the US with an equivalent amount of cash as a security fee. When it was later discovered in the summer of 1987 that Toshiba had sold computer software and machine-tool manufacturing equipment to the Soviet Union in violation of COCOM (Coordinating Committee for East–West Trade Policy, founded in 1950 to regulate trade with Warsaw Pact countries), the US Senate voted to ban imports of Toshiba products for two to five years (Welfield 1988: 445). It was estimated in 1987 that one-third of all Japan's exports to the US in that year were subject to some kind of restriction (Tasker 1987). Japan's attempts to accommodate American complaints, which ranged from the tokenism of Nakasone's appeal to the Japanese people to buy $100 worth of imports to the more substantial if often over-looked programme of increased overseas aid – in 1987 Japan's overseas aid totalled $7.5 billion, the second highest in the world – did little to ease the situation.

Not surprisingly, hostile criticism from the US was to prompt reaction amongst some Japanese politicians in the late 1980s and early 1990s; they argued that Japan was simply being used as a scapegoat to mask long-term weaknesses within the US economy itself and that in any case Japan, as an economic power in its own right, need no longer automatically and deferentially take on board American criticisms. Perhaps a more dramatic illustration of the impact American criticism had within Japan was the result of a newspaper survey of junior high school students in August 1987, 49 per cent of whom declared that if Japan went to war again the enemy would be the US (Welfield 1988: 448). The vision espoused by the former American Secretary of State, Zbigniew Brzezinski, in 1987, when he referred to the imminent formation of 'Amerippon' – a North Pacific superstate characterized by 'overlapping elites, corporate structures, and, increasingly, joint political planning' (ibid.: 447) – seemed far off the mark. Welfield (ibid.: 448), in his study of the US–Japan alliance 'system' since the 1950s, predicted on the contrary that it would divide into eastern and western wings rather like the Roman Empire after the death of Theodosius in the fourth century, with each wing 'politically autonomous, economi-cally self-sustaining, and culturally distinct, evolving in accordance with their own traditions and requirements'.

Domestically, also, Nakasone attempted to effect a change in government direction. Like Hatoyama Ichiro in the mid-1950s, he had to quickly abandon his call for constitutional revision (and in particular for the abrogation of the Peace Clause) because it was clear that political and public opposition would have been substan-tial, but he became a vigorous advocate of what he referred to as 'structural (or administrative) reform' of the economy. This structural reform aimed to reduce the public-sector deficit by cutting back on agricultural price support and social welfare payments, to privatize public utilities and services, and to encourage domestic consumption through tax reform and greater expenditures on housing and public works. Other aims were to liberalize the financial markets and provide greater market access for foreign goods and investment. For Nakasone, administrative reform (*gyosei kaikaku*) was not just about reducing deficits, privatizing public corporations and opening up Japan to the outside world, but was also a design, as one scholar has put it, for a 'radically new Japan' (McCormack 1986: 52). Implicit in this design was the idea of a spiritual renewal in which notions of patriotism and pride in Japanese achievements would provide the building blocks of social integration rather than the concern with economic growth and productivity *per se*. It is this very important aspect of administrative reform that a recent study overlooks when it simply notes that Nakasone decisively took Japan into the Western camp, and championed both the dismantling of bureaucratic controls and the conversion of Japan into a 'more open pluralistic society' (Horsley and Buckley 1990: 171).

Financial retrenchment had begun in 1980 when the government adopted the 'zero ceiling' formula for the following year's budget, whereby ministries were not to spend more than they received the previous year (defence and official overseas aid were exempted). As noted earlier, Nakasone himself first became identified with structural reform when he oversaw the setting up of the Provisional Commission on Administrative Reform (*Rincho*) in 1981. During its two year existence the commission submitted five reports calling for reduction of public expenditures (particularly in the areas of medical and healthcare insurance, pensions and social welfare) and the privatization of public corporations (Allinson 1993b: 41). Such measures were necessary, it was argued, within the context of Japan's increasing international role, moderate economic growth (compared to the 1960s) and an ageing society (Ito 1988). The latter was a particular source of concern; the phrase 'ageing society' (*koreika shakai*) had, in fact, become commonplace by 1978. It was estimated that whereas the dependent age group (those aged 65 and over) comprised only 5 per cent of the population in 1960 and 9 per cent in 1980, it would comprise 14 per cent by the year 2000 and nearly 19 per cent by 2020. With the continuing low birthrates the numbers of those aged 15 to 65 able to support this ageing population would inevitably decline. Thus, while in the mid-1970s there had been over seven people of productive age per one dependent person, the ratio was predicted to fall to 4:1 by 2000 and to less than 3:1 in 2015 (Collick 1988: 217). Not surprisingly, free medical care for the elderly, a legacy of the early 1970s, was one of the first 'casualties' of administrative reform when a 1982 law was passed imposing patient fees. Responsibility for social welfare in general was now to be shifted from the state to the family and/or the private sector. In Nakasone's view, the encouragement of traditional values of group solidarity, frugality and hard work (*hangurii seishin*: literally, 'a lean and hungry attitude') would be required to fill the welfare gap.

Ironically, while a persistent Western stereotype of the Japanese was one of a work-obsessive people – in 1979 an EEC report described the Japanese as 'workaholics living in rabbit hutches' (Burks 1981: 178) – Nakasone and growing conservative opinion within the LDP saw things differently. At its General Assembly in 1981 the party proclaimed:

> The time when politics could pander to or stir up excessive demands among the people is past. Now what is demanded both of politics and of people alike is the spirit of self-help grounded in the understanding of a stormy new age. While striving to foster such a spirit, we call upon the various strata of the people to put an end to softness and indolence and wake up to their responsibility and role in this new age. (Cited in McCormack 1986: 53)

This statement itself, of course, was a disingenuous justification for the cutbacks in public welfare spending that were soon to be implemented. Substantial welfare provision in any case was only a recent phenomenon, while the view of a work-shy populace was clearly belied by the report of yet another government committee in 1988 which recommended the compulsory imposition of a five-day working week so as to provide more leisure time and hence boost domestic consumption.

During his premiership Nakasone frequently made use of advisory councils (or commissions) of experts and societal representatives (*shingikai*) to discuss and promote policy issues, hoping thereby to bypass vested interests such as the bureaucracy and the party (Allinson 1993b: 42). One such advisory commission was the Study Group on Economic Structural Adjustment for International

Harmony, chaired by Maekawa Haruo, a former governor of the Bank of Japan. It looked into previously taboo subjects such as the subsidized and protected agricultural market (Frost 1987: 50) and its report in April 1986 proposed to increase domestic demand through tax reform and increased public works expenditures (measures that were being called for by Washington in order to increase Japan's imports while reducing its exports), as well as recommending reduced levels of government agricultural price support.

The fate of Nakasone's tax reform package in 1987, however, revealed that powerful pressure groups within Japanese society could influence policy. In an attempt to appeal to an urban middle-class constituency, Nakasone proposed to reduce levels of income tax while imposing a 5 per cent sales tax to make up the revenue deficit. Fierce opposition from organized labour, small business and consumers forced Nakasone to withdraw the proposals and it was left to his successor, Takeshita Noboru, in 1988, to push through a modified tax reform bill that made concessions to small business (whose influence had already been demonstrated in 1978 when it joined with opposition and LDP Diet members to ensure the strengthening of the 1973 Large-scale Retail Stores Law, which had restricted expansion of supermarkets and other large retailers). Lower levels of income tax and a slightly reduced corporation tax were now accompanied by a new capital gains tax and a 3 per cent consumption tax based solely on a firm's accounting records, thus allowing for continued tax avoidance by small business. Furthermore, enterprises with annual revenues of less than 30 million yen were exempted from the consumption tax (Garon and Mochizuki 1993: 154). It is government accommodation of demands originating from such organizations as small business, which has been described in terms of a 'social contract' (ibid.), that has led some scholars to argue that a 'pluralist' perspective (which empasizes the political influence of organized societal interests and the subsequent 'pluralization of participation'), rather than one that simply focuses on a ruling triad (of government, business and bureaucracy) or a dominant bureaucracy, is more meaningful in explaining Japanese politics during the 1970s and 1980s (Allinson 1993a: 144; McKean 1993: 83–5).

While Nakasone had difficulty in implementing one of the proposals (tax reform) in the Maekawa Report, he was able to act on three recommendations submitted by the Provisional Commission on Administrative Reform and the Maekawa Commission: to roll back government agricultural price support, privatize public corporations and liberalize the financial market. As was noted in chapter three, farmers had benefited from LDP support of agriculture. In the words of one study, government subsidies and low taxation had made the farmers and agricultural co-operatives virtual 'political wards of the state' (Donnelly 1984: 336). In 1982 only 14.6 per cent of farmers paid any tax (compared to 88.4 per cent of urban workers) and the average tax for those farmers who *did* pay was 20 per cent of the national average. It has been estimated that by 1984 the average farm household in Japan earned 19 per cent more than the average American farming family (Calder 1988: 242–3). As a recent study points out, however, it had never been the intention of the LDP to prevent the decline of agriculture *per se*, but rather to maintain farmer income at high levels for those who did remain in agriculture (Curtis 1988: 53). Despite government calls for rationalization and its hopes that part-time farmers might sell their land to those engaged in full-time farming, small farmer households remained the norm in the postwar period. Part-time farming persisted precisely because it benefited the most from rice price support. In 1982 only 13 per cent of farm households engaged in full-time farming, compared to 35 per cent in 1955 (ibid.: 55–6). As noted earlier, most farming came to be undertaken by elderly grandparents and women, a phenomenon referred to as *san-chan nogyo* (mama-grandma-grandpa agriculture).

Overall, agriculture's importance in the national economy gradually declined. Its contribution to the net national product fell from 17.4 per cent in 1955 to 5 per cent in 1975, and then to 3.1 per cent in 1984 (Donnelly 1984: 339; Hunter 1989: 105). While 50 per cent of the workforce had been employed in the primary sector (agriculture, fisheries, forestry) in 1950, by 1980 the proportion had fallen to 12 per cent (Pempel 1982: 65). Japan by the 1970s, in fact, was already a 'post-industrial' society, characterized by the predominance of employment in the tertiary (or service) sector as well as by high levels of production, per capita income and personal savings (Burks 1981: 173; Buckley 1990: 45). Even for those engaged in farming, non-agricultural income assumed greater significance. In 1977, for example, nearly 70 per cent of all farmer households earned over half their total income from non-agricultural employment (Calder 1988: 270–2). It has also been noted (Stockwin 1988b: 160; Curtis 1988: 43, 50) that politically the LDP during the 1970s and 1980s found increasing support amongst a growing urban population – in the early 1980s 65 per cent of the population lived in towns with populations over 50,000 (Hunter 1989: 102–3). Furthermore, by the 1980s the overweighting of rural districts in the electoral system increasingly came to be perceived as an anomaly. Following a Supreme Court ruling in July 1985, which declared the existing distribution of lower house seats unconstitutional, the Diet passed a bill in early 1986 increasing representation in eight urban districts by one seat each and reducing it by one seat in each of seven rural districts.

It is within this context that changing LDP policy towards rice price support needs to be viewed. Anxious to reduce growing public-sector deficits, the government sought from the late 1970s on to reduce the gap between the producer price (the amount the government paid to the farmers) and the consumer price, which fell from 3,365 yen per 60 kilos of rice in 1975 to 341 yen in 1985 (Curtis 1988: 57). In 1987, after several years in which the producer price had not risen even in nominal terms, Nakasone's government for the first time actually cut the producer price by 5.9 per cent. Ironically, it was now the JSP, no longer predominantly an urban-based party (in the 1976 elections the JSP won 60 per cent of its seats in semi-urban and rural districts), that championed the interests of rice farmers. Certain agricultural products (rice, beef), however, continued to be protected from foreign competition. It is significant that although by 1983 average tariff levels had been reduced from 6.9 per cent to 4.9 per cent, and then to 2.5 per cent by the early 1990s, comparing favourably with average tariff levels of 2.7 per cent for the EEC and 3.5 per cent for the US, and that residual import restrictions were gradually reduced – by 1975 there were restrictions on 29 product categories compared to 490 in the 1960s – in the 1980s most of the import restrictions that remained in place affected agricultural products (Pempel 1993). While this may have been a contentious issue in US–Japan trade negotiations it should not be forgotten that Japan continued to be heavily dependent on the US for its supply of grain and soybeans; in 1986, 20 per cent of American agricultural exports (worth $6 billion) went to Japan (Frost 1987: 28). Finally, the government cutback in rice price support did not affect high public works spending in rural areas. In 1985 the 15 mostly rural prefectures in Hokkaido, Shikoku and along the Japan Sea coast, comprising 17.4 per cent of the total population, accounted for 23 per cent of public works spending (Calder 1988: 240).

Privatization also became a feature of Nakasone's premiership when the state-run Nippon Telephone and Telegraph (NTT) and Japan National Railways (JNR) were returned to the private sector in 1985 and 1987 respectively. This inevitably led to the 'emasculation' (McCormack 1986) of public sector labour unions, which had tended to be the most politically radical during the postwar period. Such a consequence, however, was the culmination of a longer process. One study notes that the government in the 1980s saw privatization and administrative reform as the means to destroy the last vestiges of a particular 'workplace culture' championed by the public sector unions since the late 1940s (Gordon 1993). This 'workplace culture' emphasized safety, equality of opportunity and result (at least for regular male workers), job security and substantial worker participation in management decisions, in contradistinction to the version propounded by management and co-operative enterprise unions that stressed productivity, profit, technological innovation and management control of the workforce through the distribution of rewards according to merit and loyalty. With the defeat of the Miike coalminers' strike in 1960 (see chapter three) a 'union-dominated workplace culture' increasingly gave way to a 'management culture' (ibid.: 383) that recognized workers' entitlement to a share of the economic pie (as productivity increased) in exchange for employer freedom to introduce new technology, rearrange work and implement pay and promotion systems based on merit (rather than uniquely on seniority). Such a management culture also sought to encourage worker identification with the enterprise through the use of small group workplace activities (in which all workers were expected to participate) designed to improve efficiency and productivity.

Although *Sohyo* continued to launch its 'spring offensive' (*shunto*), a once-yearly campaign first introduced in 1955 designed to mobilize workers for its wage negotiations with employers at the national level, such activity became increasingly ritualistic. Except for seamen, teachers and other public workers who belonged to nationwide federations, most workers belonged to management-supported enterprise unions; bargaining and negotiation of contracts with employers were generally carried out at the plant level regardless of affiliation with a national federation (Garon 1987: 242–3). An unsuccessful one-week stoppage by public workers in late 1975 (calling for the right to strike, which had been denied them since 1948) heralded the decline of public sector unions and the deradicalization of labour. After peaking in 1975 at around 3,400 disputes per year, the number of strikes and lockouts (of more than one day's duration) dropped to only 10 per cent of that level by the late 1980s (Allinson 1993b: 47). The number of workers involved in such disputes fell from nearly 3 million in 1975 to less than 100,000 in 1989, while days lost to work fell from 8 million to 220,000 during the same period. Some scholars (Garon and Mochizuki 1993: 163) have argued that after 1976 a 'social contract' existed between labour and government whereby the latter implicitly promised to maintain employment and institute welfare programmes in return for the former keeping wage demands down.

Quite apart from the increasing moderation of labour and the declining influence of public sector unions after 1975, it should be noted that throughout the postwar period union membership steadily declined. Total union membership fell from 55.8 per cent of the labour force in 1947 to 28.9 per cent at the end of 1985 (falling below 30 per cent for the first time in 1984). By June 1992 only 24 per cent of the labour force were in unions (Curtis 1988: 212; Garon and Mochizuki 1993: 164). A major reason for this was the continued predominance of small firms. These firms (employing less than 100 workers) comprised 99.2 per cent of all private business establishments by the end of the 1960s and employed 71 per cent of the private sector labour force. Most new jobs in the 1970s and 1980s were created by small firms so that by the end of the 1980s these figures had even increased, to 99.3 per cent and 77 per cent respectively. Since union membership had always been prevalent in large firms – in 1970, for example, 58 per cent of workers in large firms (employing over 1,000 workers) joined unions, whereas fewer than 5 per cent of those employed in small firms did – the decline in the unionization rate was inevitable (Allinson 1993b: 23–4). Even membership in the public sector unions declined in the 1980s; one of the major JNR unions, *Kokuro*, for example, saw its membership fall from 245,000 in 1982 to 85,000 on the eve of privatization in 1987 (Calder 1988: 114).

The labour movement itself in the 1980s underwent a significant change. Private sector unions began to strengthen their ties with each other, culminating in the formation of the National Council of Private Sector Trade Unions (*Zenminrokyo*) in 1982. By 1985 its membership comprised 55 unions, accounting for 54.6 per cent of unionized workers in the private sector (Curtis 1988: 218). Private sector unions affiliated with *Sohyo* also began to join, and in November 1987 the organization was transformed into the National Federation of Private Sector Trade Unions (*Rengo*) with the aim of unifying a politically neutral labour movement. *Sohyo*, weakened by the defection of its private sector union members and the diminished influence of public sector unions in the wake of the NTT and JNR privatizations, ceased to exist in 1989 when public sector unions affiliated with *Rengo*. For the first time in Japan the bulk of the labour movement was now unified, with *Rengo* comprising 65 per cent of all unionized workers. It embraced 78 industrial federations with 12,000 enterprise union affiliates; *Rengo*, in fact, was a 'confederation of confederations' (Tsujinaka 1993). Developments in the 1980s have been described as 'the incorporation of labour' (Garon 1987) or 'corporatism with labour' (Gordon 1993) as labour representatives, although not sitting on government advisory councils or exercising influence in LDP parliamentary committees, were able to advance policies in direct negotiation with the bureaucracy and the LDP. However, as one study has noted (Mochizuki 1993), labour had little influence over the government's decisions to privatize NTT and JNR, and the JNR's major union, *Kokuro*, opposed privatization to the bitter end. Nevertheless, in contrast to Thatcher's Britain, privatization was more sensitive to workers' interests with few employees being laid off abruptly, voluntary retirees receiving sizeable allowances, and retraining and job placement being provided for those not hired by the new railway companies (ibid.: 196–7).

Finally, during Nakasone's premiership the financial markets were further liberalized and foreign participation in the Tokyo Stock Exchange was allowed. Already in 1980 the Foreign Exchange and Control Law (dating from the occupation period) had been scrapped, thus facilitating the movement of foreign capital into Japan. Direct foreign investment in Japan increased from $299 million in 1980 to $2.6 billion in 1988 (Pempel 1993: 117). The loosening of MITI controls and the appreciation of the yen, however, also meant that Japanese manufacturers increasingly transferred their operations to low wage sites in East and Southeast Asia in addition to building plants in North America and Western Europe to pre-empt potential protectionist legislation (Hein 1993: 118–19). By 1986 12 per cent of Japanese car firms' output was being produced in factories abroad (Horsley and Buckley 1990: 160) and during the Nakasone years Japan became the largest direct foreign investor in the US, with Japanese companies having 2,000 subsidiaries there (Frost 1987: 56).

Nakasone and Japanese Nationalism

Perhaps the most controversial aspect of Nakasone's premiership was his championing of the conservative cause through educational reform, textbook revision and his public association with the worship of Japan's war dead at the Yasukuni Shrine in Tokyo (McCormack 1986). For Nakasone, such issues were central in his attempt to reinvigorate Japanese pride that had been badly dented both by feelings of guilt about the war and assumptions of inferiority as a result of the country's dependent relationship with the US since 1945. One study makes the equally valid point, however, that Nakasone also sought to appease the LDP's conservative constituency in the wake of economic liberalization that ended the party's protectionist policies for domestic markets (Hardacre 1989: 153).

Neo-conservative thought did not begin with Nakasone's premiership. As early as 1974 the then Prime Minister, Tanaka Kakuei, had suggested reviving the 1890 Imperial Rescript on Education for use in schools because of its universal moral principles (Masami 1986: 98), while in 1978 the prewar anthem (*Kimi ga yo*) was officially designated the national anthem. Under Nakasone, however, a more concerted campaign was carried out to promote traditional values. In early 1984 Nakasone insisted that the inculcation of patriotism and filial piety had to be major goals of education (ibid.: 111); in the same year a special Education Council was set up under government auspices to explore educational reform. In 1985 the Ministry of Education caused uproar amongst teachers when it instructed all school heads to ensure that the national flag was hoisted and the anthem sung at school ceremonies (van Wolferen 1989: 290–2). Conservative talk of curbing excessive individualism (often blamed on the occupation reforms) and encouraging patriotism at school hardly addressed more concrete problems in education. While conservatives might bewail the breakdown of discipline by pointing to the fact that incidents of violent attacks on teachers at school increased from 191 to 929 between 1978 and 1983 (Beauchamp 1989: 248), the 1980s also brought to light organized bullying within the schools and violence committed by teachers against their pupils (van Wolferen 1989: 91). The education system itself, with its single-minded emphasis on the passing of competitive examinations for entry to elite universities that alone guaranteed the top jobs, placed enormous pressures on students (not least from parents). Failure in this 'examination hell' (*shiken jigoku*), as the system was described, sometimes resulted in suicide.

Nakasone's call for the promotion of traditional values in education and a reassertion of Japanese pride was accompanied by an increasing emphasis amongst writers, scholars and conservative politicians on Japan's unique cultural heritage. While in the 1950s indigenous values and practices had been condemned as 'feudal' and 'backward', by the 1970s there was more emphasis on the positive virtues of Japanese culture, which was now perceived as highly compatible with modern industrial life. Significantly, the book that rose to the top of the bestseller list in the late 1970s was the Japanese translation of E. Vogel's *Japan as Number One*, the book that had compared Japanese values and practices favourably with those of the West (Curtis 1988: 231). Nakasone himself suggested in 1987 that Japanese culture should be exported as well as its products (Koschmann 1993: 419–20), but most discussion focused on what made Japan unique. This phenomenon, known as *Nihonjinron* (discussions of Japanese identity), has been described as the 'commercialized expression of modern Japanese nationalism' (Dale 1986: 14). A bibliography in 1978 listed nearly 700 titles connected with *Nihonjinron* published since 1946 (25 per cent of which were published between 1976 and 1978), making it a mass phenomenon in contrast to earlier periods in Japanese history (in the eighteenth and nineteenth centuries), when some scholars had first emphasized the clear distinction between Japanese ethics and Western material civilization (Befu 1993: 108–9, 123). *Nihonjin* writers, drawing on the work of earlier Japanese scholars in the 1920s and 1930s (who themselves drew on the geographical determinism of earlier Western thinkers such as Montesquieu), argued that geo-ecological factors explained important features of Japanese cultural, social and economic life as well as the national character. These features included wet-rice cultivation, community-oriented village life, an emphasis on harmonious social relationships, and respect for nature. Even the language was cited as proof of Japan's uniqueness.

A policy report submitted to Prime Minister Ohira in 1980 by a committee of *Nihonjinron* advocates lauded Japanese culture for the value it placed on harmonious human relations rather than on self-centred individualism as practised in the West. The government's approval of the report meant that *Nihonjinron* was now an officially sanctioned ideology, but as one study points out, *Nihonjinron* had more to do with prescriptions for behaviour rather than with the description of an actual state of affairs (ibid.: 118). Official endorsement of the supposedly eternal Japanese values of harmony and consensus, for example, could be used to mask social conflict. Paradoxically, as references to 'internationalization' (i.e. the need for Japan to interact more with the world) became more frequent during Nakasone's premiership, so *Nihonjinron* became ever more pervasive as its advocates felt the need to define the Japanese people and their culture in a growing global economy; the idea of Japanese uniqueness also became more pronounced whenever international criticisms were made of Japan (Dale 1986).

Nakasone's own contribution to *Nihonjinron* ranged from his initiative in setting up an International Research Centre for Japanese Studies (opened in 1988) to promote co-operative international research on Japanese culture, to his outrageous remarks in August 1986 claiming that the Japanese were more intelligent than the Americans because Japan was more racially homogeneous and had fewer immigrants (Horsley and Buckley 1990: 189–90). The assumption that Japan is unique because of its homogeneity is an important theme of *Nihonjinron*, and clearly ignores the presence of, and discrimination against, the Ainu (descendants of the earliest inhabitants of Japan who now reside in Hokkaido and number about 24,000) and the nearly 700,000 Korean residents in Japan, most of whom were born in Japan but who, until the early 1990s, were still regarded as resident aliens (e.g. they had to carry ID cards and undergo regular fingerprinting). During the 1980s and early 1990s, also, an increasing number of immigrant workers (both legal and illegal) began arriving in the country, mostly to perform menial and unskilled work. These immigrant workers included Asian women who were promised attractive jobs but who were often forced into prostitution after their arrival (Mackie 1988; Hane 1992: 412–14). Mention has already been made (see chapter three) of the continued discrimination against the two to three million *burakumin*.

Textbook revisions and Nakasone's approval of official worship at the Yasukuni Shrine aroused the most heated opposition both at home and abroad. Controversy had always surrounded the writing of history texts since it provided the opportunity for the expression of competing interpretations of Japanese history and, in particular, Japan's role in the Second World War. In 1965, for example, the publication of Hayashi Fusao's *Dai Toa Sensei Kotei Ron* ('An Affirmation of the Greater East Asian War') caused consternation amongst left-wing critics because of its depiction of the war as the culmination of Japan's 100-year struggle against Western imperialism (Ienaga 1979). Also, the fact that history texts had to be formally approved by the Ministry of Education could be a source of contention. In 1966 Ienaga Saburo, a Tokyo University professor, successfully sued the Ministry (on constitutional grounds) after it had rejected his text on Japanese history in its original form, insisting that references to the important role of labouring people in history and the fabrication of myths to legitimize imperial rule be deleted (Livingston, Moore and Oldfather 1973: 538–45; Duke 1973: 178). The first textbook controversy occurred in the last months of Suzuki Zenko's premiership when Tokyo newspapers in June 1982 charged the Ministry of Education with approving textbook revisions that toned down the language on Japan's aggression in Asia (Whiting 1989: 46–51). Japan's invasion of China in 1937, for example, was described as an 'all round advance into China', while the Nanjing Massacre in 1938 (when occupying Japanese troops killed thousands of civilians) was attributed to the 'stubborn resistance of the Chinese troops' (Dirlik 1993: 54). This led to angry official protests from the Chinese government and a mass media campaign within China that denounced the attempt by Japanese 'reactionaries' to distort historical truth. The Chinese authorities also claimed that the revisions betrayed the spirit of the Sino-Japanese Treaty of Peace and Friendship signed in 1978 (formalizing the 1972 rapprochement), in which it was stated that 'the Japanese side is keenly aware of Japan's responsibility for causing enormous damage in the past to the Chinese people through war and deeply reproaches itself' (ibid.: 52). Only when the Japanese publishers agreed to withdraw the revisions in September 1982 did the controversy end and Prime Minister Suzuki's official visit to China allowed to proceed.

Another textbook controversy broke out in 1986, but this time it was exacerbated by Nakasone's official attendance at the Yasukuni Shrine the year before on 15 August, the anniversary of Japan's surrender in 1945. The Yasukuni Shrine, the second most important Shinto shrine after the Ise Shrine, which was dedicated to the Sun Goddess (Amaterasu), had been established as a shrine to Japan's war dead in 1869. The names of all Japanese soldiers killed in the Second World War were thus enshrined at Yasukuni. The occupation reforms separating state and religion had deprived the Yasukuni Shrine (along with all other Shinto shrines) of public patronage, as well as affirming the principle that no Japanese government official should attend ceremonies there commemorating the war dead; in SCAP's view such action could be construed as approval for Japan's militaristic past. During the postwar period the political opposition successfully blocked five attempts (in 1969, 1970, 1971, 1972 and 1974) by conservative Diet members to introduce legislation that would have restored state support for the Yasukuni Shrine (Hardacre 1989: 146–7). Nevertheless, despite charges of unconstitutional practice by the Left, most LDP prime ministers continued to attend spring and autumn festivals at Yasukuni, while in 1975 Prime Minister Miki Takeo inaugurated the custom of government leaders (strictly in a private capacity) visiting the shrine on the anniversary of Japan's surrender. Nakasone thus broke precedent when he (accompanied by his entire cabinet) attended the 15 August ceremony in his official capacity as Prime Minister. While clearly a deeply symbolic act on Nakasone's part to restore Japanese pride and end lingering war guilt, it was perceived by the political opposition and by Japan's Asian neighbours (occupied by Japan during the Second World War) as insensitive and a blatant encouragement to those Japanese conservatives who wished to reinterpret Japan's actions prior to, and during, the Second World War in Asia. Matters were not helped by the fact that in 1978 the names of 14 convicted Class A war criminals (including that of Japan's wartime leader, Tojo Hideki) had been enshrined at Yasukuni and designated as 'martyrs of the Showa era' (ibid.: 148).

In addition to protests from Asian governments, there were anti-Japanese student demonstrations in China during September 1985. Sparked off by Nakasone's attendance at Yasukuni, these demonstrations also reflected growing dissatisfaction with the state of Sino-Japanese economic relations. Following a trade agreement in 1978, Chinese exports of crude oil and coal went to Japan in exchange for Japanese industrial technology and low-interest loans for the purchase of construction machinery. By the 1980s, according to official Chinese sources, China had a huge trading imbalance with Japan, with deficits totalling $5.22 billion in 1985 and $5.13 billion in 1986 (Whiting 1989: 165). The situation was to worsen with the appreciation of the yen in 1985–7 and the fall in the price of oil, China's principal export. It was increasingly felt in China that while Japan was happy to export its manufactured goods it was unwilling to share its technology. During the student demonstrations references were made to a 'second Japanese invasion', while a big character poster at Beijing University reportedly depicted a Japanese declaring 'I used to be a Japanese imperialist, decapitating fifty people in Shenyang [during the war], but now I am selling you colour televisions' (Dirlik 1993: 63–4).

In June 1986 a new Japanese text stoked up further controversy by claiming that it was Chinese government provocation that led to the Sino-Japanese War in 1937 and describing the war in Asia as a crusade by Japan to liberate Asian peoples from Western imperialism. In late July and August 1986 Nakasone's Education Minister, Fujio Masayuki, insisted that the Allied Tribunal's condemnation of Tojo as a war criminal could not be considered correct and that the Nanjing Massacre was simply the product of war. He also angered the governments of the two Koreas by suggesting that Japan's annexation of Korea in 1910 had been agreed to by Korea's rulers. Given the fact that Nakasone, in an attempt to smooth relations with South Korea, had been the first Japanese premier since the end of the war to visit the country in January 1983 (when he had pledged $4 billion in official economic aid), these comments were highly inappropriate. The situation was finally eased when Nakasone cancelled his scheduled visit to the Yasukuni Shrine, sacked his education minister and promised that no textbook changes would be implemented.

A recent study of the textbook controversy has argued that suggestions within Japan to revise history texts should be seen in terms of the contemporary situation rather than as simply the resurgence of right-wing attitudes. At a time when Nakasone was insisting that the Japanese people openly recognize the country's growing economic power in the 1980s and that Japan should play a more active role in the world, the context was provided in which some felt the need to portray the history of the Second World War in Asia more in keeping with Japan's current place in the world (ibid.: 75). For Beijing, on the other hand, a 'correct' interpretation of the war, which had to include explicit Japanese acknowledgement of their country's aggression in China, would help balance

China's current economic dependence on Japan. The question of how Japan was to come to terms with its recent past remained an important political issue even after Nakasone left office in 1987. Although more controversial statements were made – in 1988, for example, the Director-General of the National Land Agency, Okuno Seisuki, had to resign after he denied that Japan was the aggressor prior to and during the Pacific War (Whiting 1989: 200) – successive Japanese governments from the late 1980s on were more prepared to acknowledge the seamier aspects of Japan's imperialist role in Asia.

Japanese Women and the Economic Miracle

As noted earlier, an important theme in discussions of administrative reform during the 1980s had been the need to shift welfare responsibility from the state to individual families. In order to bring about a 'Japanese-style welfare state', as it was termed, conservative politicians called for a 'return' to traditional family values, an ideal that took on special meaning against a background of growing neotraditionalism (Buckley 1993: 369). Clearly, such sentiments had implications for women, but what *were* women's roles in the economy and how had their position in society evolved since the 1960s?

Women entered the labour force in much larger numbers after 1970, gaining new positions as salaried employees in manufacturing firms, service establishments and retail stores (before then most women were in unpaid employment on the family farm or in the family shop). However, as a recent study argues, high levels of female labour force participation did not necessarily enhance women's socio-economic status or alter sex-segregated roles (Brinton 1993). Thus, while finding that the female participation rate in Japan was comparable to a number of Western countries, Brinton (ibid.: 3–4) concludes that Japanese women were more likely to be piecework or part-time workers, blue collar employees and employees in family-run enterprises (where wages and benefits were considerably less than those in larger firms); the male–female wage gap was also greater. As noted in chapter three, young unmarried women were expected to leave full-time employment on marriage or when they had children. When they returned to the workforce after child-rearing duties had lessened, a phenomenon that became more common after the 1970s, women tended to go into low-status part-time work since they had lost both seniority and status as 'regular' or 'permanent' workers. In 1960, for example, 43 per cent of all part-time workers were women; by 1986 the proportion had increased to 70 per cent (ibid.: 10). By the late 1970s Japan was the only advanced country where women's employment opportunities and wages relative to men were declining (Upham 1993: 336). Thus, whereas women received 53.8 per cent of men's wages in 1980, this had declined to 52.8 per cent by 1982 (Upham 1987: 125). During the 1970–90 period as a whole, women were generally paid 60 per cent of the wages of men with a comparable education (Allinson 1993b: 25).

Sex-segregated roles were also clearly delineated in the education system. Most female high school graduates continued to enter two year junior colleges (where home economics, education and the humanities dominated the curriculum) rather than regular four year universities (Brinton 1993: 201), even though by 1989 the proportion of female high school graduates entering post-second-ary education slightly exceeded that of male graduates (36.8 per cent to 36.6 per cent). In 1980 only 12 per cent of female high school graduates entered university compared to 39 per cent of male graduates (Robins-Mowry 1983: 138). Over the next decade there was a slight improvement, although in 1990 there was still twice as many males (33.4 per cent) going on to regular university than females (15.2 per cent) (Brinton 1993: 70). Even female university graduates faced discrimination. It has been estimated that in the mid-1980s, 70–80 per cent of Japanese companies refused to hire female graduates. The reasons given by employers were that women would soon leave to get married and have children (but it was assumed that this was what women *should* do anyway!), that more opportunities for career women would result in male unemployment, and that career women would not fit in with the corporate family (Upham 1987: 128).

Whereas the immediate postwar period had witnessed a continuation of the close relationship between women's groups and the state that had marked the prewar period, with organizations such as the Housewives Association (*Shufuren*) assisting the authorities during the late 1940s with stamping out black marketeering or serving on local councils to promote savings during the 1950s (Garon 1993), a women's liberation movement (*uman ribu*) emerged after 1970 that *did* challenge traditional gender roles.

Groups such as the Fighting Women's Group (*Gurupu tatakau onna*) rejected the new interpretations of the *ryosai kenbo* ('good wife, wise mother') ideal that had legitimized women's activism in the public sphere as caring mothers, and insisted that women should be free *not* to become wives and mothers (Uno 1993: 313). Such groups helped block attempts to tighten the abortion law in 1973 and 1982 (in 1949 abortion was made permissable if the mother's health might be endangered for 'economic reasons') and lobbied successfully to have home economics removed as a compulsory course for high school girls in 1989 (ibid.: 317).

Most women's organizations (in 1978 there were 37,000, of which 75 were national in scope) (Robins-Mowry 1983: 151), whether strictly feminist or not, continued to be involved in a wide variety of issues (e.g. campaigning against nuclear weapons and political corruption), one of the most significant of which was consumer protection. In 1970–1, for example, the National Co-ordinating Council of Regional Women's Associations (*Chifuren*) and the Housewives Association organized a boycott of Matsushita colour television sets; the company eventually conceded, announcing retail price reductions of 15 per cent and admitting that it had carried out illegal retail price fixing practices (ibid.: 202–3). 'Consumer' (*shohisha*), in fact, became a widely used term during the 1970s, reflecting a growing public awareness of citizens's rights. By 1977 there were more than 2,600 consumer organizations with ten million members (most of whom were women).

Although feminist activism did not bring about equality in the workplace there were some signs of change during the 1980s. The number of women in professional and technical occupations rose from 1 million in 1970 to nearly 3 million in 1989, while the number of women in managerial positions rose from 50,000 to 190,000 in the same period (although the latter figure represented only 8 per cent of the total) (Allinson 1993b: 26). In 1982 Takashimaya Department Stores announced they would begin hiring male and female management trainees on a one-to-one basis, and in 1983 the Law Department of Tokyo University hired its first female faculty member (Upham 1987: 146). The Women and Minors' Bureau within the Labour Ministry lobbied vigorously against separate retirement systems; as of 1983, 90 per cent of firms previously maintaining them had discontinued their practice of requiring women to retire on marriage or pregnancy (ibid.: 147).

The enactment of an Equal Employment Opportunity Law in May 1985, the result of the government's signing up to the UN Convention on the Elimination of All Forms of Discrimination Against Women in 1980, was potentially beneficial for women, but in practice may have produced an opposite result (Buckley and Mackie 1986; Allinson 1993b). There had been a furious debate surrounding the passage of the law, with critics (men and women) claiming that it would destroy the housewife's privileged position (by undermining traditional gender roles), threaten the low male unemployment rate and break up families. Interestingly, some women remained ambivalent about the law since they felt that the working life of men (focused entirely on their place of work with little outside interests) was not the ideal to which women should aspire (Brinton 1993: 230–2). Employers, in fact, used the law as a pretext to relax or eliminate statutory protections for female workers (laid down in the 1947 Labour Standards Law) such as restrictions on overtime, shift work and night work; guaranteed menstrual leave was also abolished. Furthermore, the law was rather toothless, simply requiring that employers 'strive' to treat female workers equally and to refrain from all discriminatory practices; no sanctions or penalties were imposed for violations.

In any event, conservative political opinion now favoured women remaining at home and bringing up families. There was much anguish expressed at the declining birth rate (from 34 births per 1,000 population in the immediate postwar period, to 13.7 in 1980 and 1.57 in 1990), which was attributed to women marrying later and working full time. In 1990 the Director-General of the Economic Planning Agency suggested that women place racial and national interests above the personal gratification of embarking upon a career:

> There is now a mood [in Japan] to enjoy life, rather than giving birth and suffering. . . . Many Japanese women have entered university and taken a job that will lead them to marry late and have a shorter time for having babies. . . . At every wedding reception that I have attended . . . I speak out and say that if this excellent Japanese tribe is on its way to becoming extinct, then I cannot die easily. (Cited in Uno 1993: 321)

With an increasing proportion of elderly amongst the population, women were also urged to stay at home to look after aged parents and thus help to revitalize the ideal three-generational family. Such blandishments, however, could not mask a significant change in Japanese society. By 1987, 60.5 per cent of all households were nuclear households (Buckley 1993: 348), while in 1985 one out of four Japanese aged 65 or over was living alone or only with a spouse. By the 1980s the number of elderly living alone had doubled (since 1960) and the number of elderly couples living alone had tripled (ibid.: 356). Many women, ironically, were forced to re-enter the workforce in their middle age in order to accumulate savings for their old age.

Conservative hankering for traditional family values notwithstanding, it has also been suggested that with the declining birth rates and the consequent reduction in the numbers of young people entering the workforce, employers in the future may be compelled to utilize female labour in other than low wage and marginal jobs (Brinton 1993: 234). In recent years some women's junior colleges have closed because of dwindling numbers, while others are teaching more technical subjects. Significantly also, women's age at marriage began to rise during the 1980s; 31 per cent of women aged 25–9 remained unmarried in 1985, compared to 21 per cent in 1980 (ibid.: 235). The 1990s may therefore bring substantial changes to the pattern of female employment.

5

A New Imperial Era and the End of the LDP Hegemony

The end of the 1980s witnessed the most serious crisis for the LDP since its founding in 1955. It was to make more urgent calls for political reform and would eventually lead to the unravelling of LDP rule. A new coalition government (from which the LDP was excluded) took power in 1993; committed to political reform, the new government seemed to herald the beginning of a new era in Japanese politics and perhaps even to suggest that Japan was now in a post-postwar period, especially as the ending of the LDP hegemony coincided with the death in 1989 of Emperor Hirohito, a powerful symbol of continuity with pre-1945 Japan. Others have argued that the postwar period ended earlier. Hein (1993) thinks that postwar Japan came to a close with the ending of high-speed growth in 1973–4; Dower (1993a) suggests that the postwar period ended during the 1980s, when debates contrasting the benefits of cosmopolitanism with the need to stress Japanese uniqueness replaced the earlier ideological discourse focusing on peace and democracy (the Japanese government itself maintained that 1956 marked the end of the postwar period, since that year saw both GNP and national income attain prewar levels). It may be premature to come to a firm conclusion about this, however. By the mid-1990s two questions still remained unanswered that would make it difficult to envisage Japan in a post-postwar phase: would Japan's enormous economic power be accompanied by enhanced international responsibilities, and would a domestic consensus emerge on how to assess Japan's colonial and wartime past?

The Recruit Scandal

The mid-1980s began well for the LDP. In the July 1986 double elections for both houses of the Diet the LDP, riding on the crest of Nakasone's popularity, had achieved its best election results since 1963. After failing to achieve an overall majority of lower house seats in 1976, 1979 and 1983, the LDP gained 300 seats (58.6 per cent of the total) with nearly 50 per cent of the vote (Curtis 1988: 192–3). In the upper house the LDP gained 140 seats, compared to 131 previously. Shortly afterwards the New Liberal Club (NLC) dissolved itself and its six elected members rejoined the ranks of the LDP. All the other opposition parties lost ground, particularly the JSP whose lower house representation was reduced from 112 to 85 seats (Hrebenar et al. 1986: 295). The JSP had been hampered by continuing internal divisions and the public perception that it was backward looking and associated with outmoded ideas and policies (e.g. outright opposition to the SDF). As noted in chapter three, the party had been bitterly divided between those like Eda Saburo, who pioneered 'structural reform' (an emphasis on evolutionary change) and the members of the Socialist Association, who adopted a more orthodox Marxist viewpoint. By the time of the JSP's 38th Congress in 1974 the Socialist Association had the support of the majority of delegates (although only three of the party's Diet representatives were members); the party platform strongly supported the Soviet Union and referred to a future revolutionary socialist government as the 'dictatorship of the proletariat'. Eda Saburo left the party in 1977 to form a splinter group, the Social Citizen's League. By 1979 it had been transformed into the Social Democratic League and in the 1986 elections it won four seats. Although the influence of the Socialist Association within the JSP began to wane after 1977, first under the chairmanship of Asukata Ichio (1977–83) and then under that of Ishibashi Masashi (1983–6), who declared that he presided over a post-Marxist JSP, public suspicion of the party persisted. After the heavy electoral defeat in 1986 Ishibashi was replaced as party leader by Japan's first woman political leader, Doi Takako, a constitutional lawyer who had been elected to the Diet seven times. In the next three years she was able to revive the party's fortunes, skilfully exploiting public dissatisfaction with LDP policies and political corruption.

Within less than a year of Takeshita Noboru taking over the premiership from Nakasone, a political and financial scandal broke out that threatened to engulf the ruling party. In September 1988 it became known that the Recruit Group, a growing business empire involved in publishing, telecommunications and property development, had distributed shares at low face value to scores of prominent politicians before its subsidiary property company (Recruit Cosmos) had been officially listed on the Tokyo Stock Exchange in October 1986. These shares had then subsequently quadrupled in value (Horsley and Buckley 1990: 244–6). Given the fact that property development was nearly always dependent on the approval of politicians and bureaucrats this represented bribery on a massive scale. After police raids on Recruit offices in October 1988 it soon became evident that most members of the previous Nakasone cabinet had profited from the share dealings, while most of Takeshita's cabinet (including Takeshita himself) had received huge sums in the form of donations from the company.

The first casualty of the Recruit Scandal was Takeshita's Finance Minister, Miyazawa Kiichi, who resigned in November 1988 after admitting he had dealt in Recruit Cosmos shares. In February 1989 charges were brought against members of the Recruit management, a former Nakasone cabinet member, several bureaucrats and the manager of NTT, accused of accepting shares in return for selling Recruit some of its privileged data lines. Pressure mounted on Takeshita to declare his involvement; in April 1989 he finally admitted to receiving $1.2 million from Recruit and announced he would step down as prime minister once a successor was found. Significantly, however, by May 1989, when investigations into the scandal were formally brought to a close, only two Diet members had been charged. At least 11 national politicians known to have been involved were not indicted. Miyazawa, who had earlier resigned from the cabinet, was to return as prime minister in 1991. Altogether only 15 people were tried in November 1989; apart from a suspended jail sentence for a Recruit Cosmos executive, no one was imprisoned. Nakasone himself was questioned in the Diet about his possible association with Recruit; although no further action was taken Nakasone later resigned from the LDP, his political reputation considerably undermined.

The Accession of a New Emperor

At the height of the scandal an era ended in January 1989 with the death of Emperor Hirohito, who had reigned since 1926. His reign name, Showa ('Illustrious Peace'), had been a deeply ironic one since he had presided over militarist rule in the 1930s and the carnage of the Second World War in Asia as well as over peaceful economic reconstruction after 1945. Hirohito himself had been transformed from a 'god-emperor' to whom the nation owed absolute loyalty and obedience before 1945 to the constitutional monarch of a parliamentary democracy after 1947 in which sovereignty lay with the people. As such Hirohito paradoxically had represented both continuity and change, and it is for this reason that the precise nature of the Emperor's symbolic role was always contested in the postwar period (Large 1992: 164–79). Thus, while the mass media sought to popularize the Emperor as the supporter of the constitution and of democratic values, portaying him as a model family man devoted to peace and science (he was a keen marine biologist), various LDP governments (particularly that of Nakasone Yasuhiro) attempted to reconvert him into a 'neo-nationalist icon' (ibid.: 177), often to buttress and legitimize continued conservative rule.

Yet although conservative governments were successful in some of their attempts to restore imperial 'sub-symbols' of the past – in 1966, for example, *Kigensetsu* (Empire Day), the national holiday on 11 February prescribed by the Meiji government after 1868 to commemorate the accession of Japan's mythological first Emperor in 660 BC (and which had been abolished during the occupation) was revived as National Founding Day (*Kenkoku Kinenbi*) – increasing numbers of the public remained non-committal. National opinion polls exploring attitudes towards the Emperor revealed that 30 per cent of respondents in 1961 and 33 per cent in 1965 expressed 'indifference' (*mukanshin*); further polls in 1978 and 1988 (after it was publicly known that the Emperor was seriously ill) indicated that 44.1 per cent and 47 per cent of respondents respectively were indifferent about the Emperor and the imperial institution (ibid.: 166, 193, 198). It should be noted, however, that there were always minority elements who either vigorously denounced the imperial institution (the far Left) or fanatically upheld its primacy (the far Right). On the day of Hirohito's funeral in February 1989 (at which 164 countries and 28 international organizations were represented), 100,000 people participated in rallies denouncing the Emperor as a fascist war criminal (ibid.: 201). Those thought to be committing *lèse-majesté*, on the other hand, might be the target of extreme right-wing violence; in 1990 the mayor of Nagasaki, well known for his criticisms of the Emperor, was shot and seriously wounded.

The accession of Hirohito's son, Akihito (reign name Heisei: 'Achieving Peace'), in many ways marked a real break from the past. Only four years old when Japan embarked on its disastrous invasion of China in 1937, Akihito was untainted by the militaristic aggression of the 1930s and 1940s. As Crown Prince during the postwar period he had been portrayed in the Japanese press as a popular symbol, especially after his marriage in 1959 to Shoda Michiko, the 'commoner' daughter of a flour milling company president. In contrast to his father, Akihito had also travelled abroad extensively, having visited 37 countries by 1989. Critics at home, nevertheless, cast some doubts on Akihito's modern image on the occasion of his enthronement. There were, in fact, two enthronement ceremonies in November 1990, the first attended by representatives of over 150 countries and which adopted the features of Western coronation ceremonies and the second, known as the Great Food Offering Rite (*Daijosai*), which was an exclusively Japanese affair. This latter ceremony had its origins in the seventh century as a Shinto ritual in which the new Emperor partook of the first crops of the harvest in communion with the *kami* (divinities). From the Meiji period on the *Daijosai* was imbued with a new meaning; after undergoing the ritual the Emperor was supposedly transformed into a living god able to communicate with the imperial ancestors and the gods of the land. The government controversially sanctioned the performance of the ritual and even provided public funding, thus undermining legislation in 1969 that had defined religious ceremonies performed by the court as 'private functions' of the court (Bowring and Kornicki 1993: 156; Titus 1993).

The start of Akihito's reign also witnessed a more outspoken 'imperial household diplomacy' (ibid.) than that of his father. In the 1970s, LDP governments had taken steps to promote Hirohito abroad as a symbol of Japanese democracy and goodwill (Large 1992: 182); thus, in September–October 1971, the Emperor visited a number of countries in Western Europe and four years later he visited the US. While Hirohito made no references to the war on his European tour, in the US he expressed gratitude for American assistance after 'that most unfortunate war, which I deeply deplore' (ibid.: 188). This was the only public apology Hirohito made after 1945; vague statements of regret such as those made to visiting

South Korean President Chun Doo Hwan in September 1984 ('It is indeed regrettable that there was an unfortunate past between us for a period in this country and I believe that it should not be repeated again') (Titus 1993: 67; Ahn 1993: 265) were not considered satisfactory in Korea. Akihito, on the other hand, in April 1989 personally apologized to the visiting Chinese premier, Li Peng, for Japan's wartime role in China and in May 1990 he expressed his 'deepest regret' over Japan's colonial rule in Korea on the occasion of a state visit to Japan by South Korean President, Roh Tae Woo. On a historic visit to China in October 1992 (the first of its kind by a Japanese Emperor) to mark the twentieth anniversary of the normalization of relations between the two countries, Akihito in an official speech 'deplored' the 'unfortunate period' in which Japan 'inflicted great sufferings on the people of China'. As will be discussed later, Akihito's statements reflected a growing government sensitivity to the feelings of Japan's Asian neighbours.

The End of the *Ancien Régime*

The sense of a new beginning with the accession of Akihito did not help the LDP. In June 1989 Takeshita's Foreign Minister, Uno Sosuke, took over as Prime Minister. Public disgust with the ramifications of the Recruit Scandal was exacerbated by public discontent with the 3 per cent consumption tax. To make matters worse, Uno became involved in a sex scandal (interestingly the first of its kind in postwar Japan) when a former *geisha* claimed she had been the Prime Minister's mistress 20 years earlier. In the elections for the upper house in July 1989 the LDP fared badly, declining from 142 to 109 seats (out of 252) and gaining only 27 per cent of the vote. For the first time the opposition took control of the upper house (White 1993: 431–2). Significantly, a large number of female candidates had run for election, campaigning against corruption, the consumption tax and the ineffectiveness of the Equal Employment Opportunity Law. Twenty-two women (out of 148 candidates) were elected (Buckley 1993: 371). By way of contrast, in the double elections of 1980 only nine women had been elected to the lower house and nine to the upper house (Stockwin 1982: 107).

Shortly after the July elections Uno resigned and, after a leadership election, was replaced as prime minister by a former education minister, Kaifu Toshiki. As a member of a minor faction within the LDP who was relatively untainted by Recruit, Kaifu was seen by the party bosses as a convenient stopgap leader. In the run up to elections for the lower house in February 1990 Kaifu sought to placate public dissatisfaction with the LDP by implementing revisions to the consumption tax (exempting childbirth costs, education and food at the retail level) and by pledging to carry out political reform. He also appealed to the female vote by appointing two women to his cabinet (although they were not reappointed after the February elections). In the 1990 lower house elections the LDP did not perform as badly as some of their supporters had feared. Nevertheless, the number of seats the party gained fell from 300 to 275 (with its share of the vote falling from 49 per cent to 46 per cent). Many conservatives had run as independents to avoid association with the Recruit Scandal, although key LDP leaders who had been directly implicated in the scandal such as Takeshita Noboru and Miyazawa Kiichi were re-elected. The JSP, having failed to reach a common agreement with the other opposition parties, was not able to capitalize on its success the previous December and could only increase its Diet representation from 85 to 136 seats (with 27 per cent of the vote) (Allinson 1993b: 33–4).

Kaifu's premiership was dominated by the Gulf Crisis (August 1990 to February 1991) and the debate within Japan concerning the role of the SDF. During the first half of 1990 Kaifu had adopted a high diplomatic profile that suggested Japan might embark on a more active international role now the Cold War was winding down. In January he visited Europe, pledging a nearly $2 billion aid programme for Poland and Hungary; at a summit meeting with US President Bush in March he talked of a 'global partnership'; and in May, on a tour of five South Asian nations (during which $645 million in low interest loans were extended to India), Kaifu referred to a new order for the global economy which would tackle the problems of the environment, drugs, terrorism and population growth (Calder 1991). Yet following the despatch of multilateral forces (led by the US though under UN auspices) to Saudi Arabia and the Persian Gulf in August 1990 following Iraq's invasion of Kuwait, the US criticized the insignificance of Japan's aid package. Within weeks of the Iraqi invasion, in fact, Japan had pledged $1 billion, which was increased to $4 billion by September. It was argued in the US that Japan should contribute more given the fact that the multilateral forces were confronting the threat to continued oil supplies posed by Iraq's occupation of Kuwait. In January 1991, soon after hostilities against Iraq began, Kaifu pledged a further $9 billion. Together with the earlier $4 billion Japan's financial contribution to the multilateral forces was to represent 20 per cent of the entire cost of operations before and during the war (Calder 1992: 33; Pharr 1993: 252–3).

Washington's criticisms of Japan, nevertheless, did not subside. There were complaints about the slowness of payments and delays in support initiatives (such as the despatch of medical personnel), while Washington remained unimpressed with Kaifu's attempt (ultimately unsuccessful) to secure Diet approval for the use of SDF aircraft to evacuate refugees from the Gulf. After the war, in April 1991, however, Kaifu *did* secure Diet approval to send SDF minesweepers and supply ships to the Middle East in order to help clear the Gulf of mines. Although little remarked upon in the Western press this was the first formal offshore deployment of Japanese military forces since 1945 (Calder 1992: 35). Tokyo's response to the Gulf Crisis confirmed American assumptions that Japan was unwilling to undertake more responsibility in world affairs (Barnhart 1995: 185–7), a view subscribed to by a recent study (Buckley 1992), which argues that Japan in 1990 did not fulfil the hopes at the beginning of the 1980s that the country would begin to act as a major power. In Buckley's words (ibid.: 139), 'Japan by 1990 was most certainly recognized as a global player but rarely behaved as a global player'. Such an observation perhaps overlooks the significance of the domestic debate within Japan during the Gulf Crisis; for the first time the peaceful deployment of SDF personnel overseas was seriously considered.

Kaifu tackled another sensitive issue during his premiership, that of political reform. When he indicated his determination to press ahead with proposals to implement clearer guidelines on financial contributions to political parties and individual politicians and to change the electoral system so as to reduce the importance of factions, he had to confront opposition from within his own party. Many incumbent Diet members (not just LDP members) were wary of the consequences of electoral reform, which might threaten their secure bailiwicks. Of the 512 successful candidates in the lower house election of 1990, for example, 125 were elected from constituencies that had previously sent their fathers or other close relatives to the Diet (Christensen 1994: 592). Furthermore, amongst the formally endorsed LDP candidates who ran during the 1990 election, 130 were second, third or even fourth-generation politicians who had 'inherited' their *jiban* (electoral base of support) from a father or close relative (Donnelly 1990: 311). The JSP also remained sceptical about any proposal to replace a multi-member with a single-member constituency system, fearing that this might entrench LDP rule.

When the leader of the LDP's most powerful faction, Kanemaru Shin, withdrew his support in October 1991 Kaifu decided not to seek re-election as LDP leader. Kanemaru now backed Miyazawa Kiichi, a member of the LDP 'old guard', who duly became party leader and prime minister in November 1991. The elevation of Miyazawa contributed further to the growing public disillusionment with political life (the upper house elections in July 1992 were to have a very low voter turnout of 50.7 per cent). A graduate of Todai (Tokyo University) who had served in all the top cabinet posts, Miyazawa had been directly implicated in the Recruit Scandal and had resigned in disgrace as Finance Minister in 1988. Yet on becoming Prime Minister he appointed to his cabinet three politicians who had also been implicated in the scandal. As if this was not enough, Miyazawa's tenure as Prime Minister was marked by continuing scandals within the LDP. In February 1992 Abe Fumio (a former minister in Kaifu's cabinet and a leading member of Miyazawa's faction) was indicted for accepting bribes from the Kyowa Corporation, a bankrupted steel-frame manufacturer; two other members of Miyazawa's faction were implicated. Then in August 1992 Kanemaru Shin admitted that he had accepted 500 million yen ($4 million) in illegal campaign contributions from Tokyo Sagawa Kyubin, a parcel delivery company that allegedly had close links with the criminal underworld (*yakuza*). Although he resigned his post as party vice-president, he insisted on retaining his Diet seat. The public was further outraged when it became known that Kanemaru had arranged not to appear in court and instead had been fined a token 200,000 yen ($1,500). In October 1992, with vociferous protests emanating from a number of prefectural assemblies, Kanemaru finally resigned his Diet seat (he was to be indicted in March 1993 on tax evasion charges), but the damage had been done. There were now groups *within* the LDP who demanded substantial electoral reform; as will be seen later, this led to a partial disintegration of the LDP and a realignment of political parties.

The most significant event of Miyazawa's premiership was the passing of a Peacekeeping Operations Bill (PKO), which authorized deployment of SDF units abroad for non-combatant peacekeeping operations under UN auspices (although not those with any military component such as monitoring ceasefires). Introduced into the lower house in November 1991, the bill finally passed both houses in June 1992; by the end of the year SDF units were in Cambodia helping to monitor elections. The passage of the bill had been greatly facilitated by a more pragmatic stance on the part of the JSP. Following the party's poor performance in 1991 local elections, Doi Takako resigned as leader and was replaced by Tanabe Makoto, a member of the party's right wing who insisted that the JSP (its English name now rendered as the Social Democratic Party of Japan) recognize the legitimacy of the SDF.

As a recent article has noted, although the introduction of the PKO Bill seemed to confirm Japan's 'reactive' diplomacy (i.e. responding to US pressure during the Gulf Crisis) it nevertheless was a precedent-breaking decision, since for the first time SDF forces will be able to conduct operations on foreign soil (George 1993). The PKO Bill also represented a departure from Japan's usual reliance on financial power as its primary instrument in international affairs ('chequebook diplomacy') since peacekeeping (as in Cambodia) will not necessarily bring Japan any direct commercial benefits. George (ibid.: 570) concludes that Japan may be moving 'beyond the politics of the trading state' and acquiring a more balanced set of foreign policy instruments. More generally, despite a recent assessment of Japanese foreign policy since the late 1980s which insists that Japan's basic diplomatic strategy of the Cold War era (continued alliance with the US, closer ties with neighbours in Southeast and East Asia, and greater influence in multilateral forums) will not change in the 1990s (Curtis 1993: xxvi), there has been a fascinating debate over the direction of Japanese foreign policy (Brown 1993). Just as during the 1880s and 1890s Meiji leaders debated whether Japan should join with the West and become an imperialist power in East Asia or join with China in a common front against Western imperialism, so in the early 1990s there was a debate between those who believed Japan should focus on the bilateral axis with the US in a global partnership and those who favoured a more active regional role that would link Japan with the rest of Asia.

Concerning this latter option, for example, it is significant that in 1992 Prime Minister Miyazawa supported an Australian proposal that the 15 members of APEC (Asia–Pacific Economic Cooperation Forum, set up in 1989 on Australia's initiative) hold regular summit meetings to discuss regional and security matters, while in early 1993 on a visit to Thailand he pledged Japan's active participation in discussions concerning the long-term security interests of the Asia–Pacific Region. It should also be noted that a strand of opinion within the LDP was increasingly critical of Japan's 'subservience' to the US. Sometimes reactions against the wave of 'Japan bashing' in the US could be equally inflammatory, such as the comments made by the LDP Speaker of the lower house, Yoshio Sakurauchi, who blamed the trade imbalance between Japan and the US on 'inferior American workers'. Perhaps the most outspoken critic of the US was Ishihara Shintaro, a novelist and right-wing LDP Diet member, whose 1989 book *No to ieru Nihon* ('The Japan That Can Say No') appeared in an authorized English-language edition in 1991. (The original edition was co-authored with Morita Akio, the Chairman of Sony, but he requested that his portions of the book, which contained references to American economic inefficiency and the poor quality of American products, be withdrawn in the English-language edition.) Ishihara maintained that American criticisms of Japan (particularly in the wake of ongoing trade disputes between the two countries) were unfounded and that they were the product of a deeply ingrained racism. Pointing to Japan's creativity and achievements in the sciences and arts, Ishihara insisted that Japan should not feel guilty in standing up to Washington when its interests warranted and he condemned previous Japanese leaders (particularly Nakasone) who had meekly followed in Washington's path:

> Today, the worldwide attention focused on Japan is due to our prosperity and wealth. Of course, money counts, but we also have tradition and culture, wellsprings of creativity and high technology that neither Moscow nor Washington can ignore. To be fully appreciated, we must, when matters of crucial national interest warrant, articulate our position and say no to the US. (Ishihara 1991: 62)

Unfortunately, Ishihara, in seeking to explain white racism, unwittingly revealed a certain condescension towards other Asian peoples:

There is a *certain historical justification* for Caucasian attitudes towards other races. Europeans created most of the modern era and they feel superior to Africans and Orientals, who *were unable to modernize rapidly* and became colonies. Although the Japanese were the only non-white people to avoid western domination, *it is not surprising* that Europeans and Americans look down on us, too. (Ibid.: 80, emphasis added)

For Ishihara, Japan had to be treated equally and with respect by the US precisely because (unlike other Asian countries) it had modernized successfully and was now a more dynamic economic power than the US.

Political Realignment and the Debate over War Guilt

The final crisis for the LDP occurred in June 1993, when Miyazawa lost a parliamentary vote of confidence after failing to get a political reform bill passed in the Diet and was forced to call for new elections. The LDP soon began to disintegrate. Already in the previous year Hosokawa Morihiro, who had started his political career as an LDP member of the upper house in the 1970s and served as governor of Kumamoto prefecture in the 1980s, had founded the Japan New Party (*Nihon Shinto*), which won four seats in the 1992 upper house elections. Following the no-confidence vote, 50 LDP members led by former Finance Minister Hata Tsutomu and former LDP Secretary-general Ozawa Ichiro bolted the party and formed the Renewal Party (*Shinseito*). Yet another small LDP splinter group formed the Harbinger Party (*Sakigake*), which allied with Hosokawa's Japan New Party. In the elections for the lower house in July the LDP was unable to obtain a majority, gaining 223 seats with only 36.6 per cent of the vote. The Renewal Party (55 seats), Japan New Party (35 seats) and Harbinger Party (13 seats) all performed well, as did Komeito (51 seats). The JSP, the principal opposition party throughout the postwar period, slumped from 134 to 70 seats. For the first time since 1955 the LDP was excluded from power as Hosokawa became the leader of a seven-party coalition government (from which the LDP, JCP and a few minor parties were excluded), although most of the cabinet posts were held by members of the JSP and Hata's Renewal Party.

With its commitment to political reform the new Hosokawa government raised hopes that a new style of politics would emerge. The profile of the new government also suggested change with the appointment of three women to the cabinet (14 women had been elected to the lower house in 1993, the highest total since the immediate postwar period). Nevertheless, the extent of the change should not be exaggerated. There was still a whiff of the *ancien régime* pervading the new government – Hosokawa's maternal grandfather was Konoe Fumimaro, who had served as prime minister in 1937–9 and 1940–1, and two of the parties in the coalition were LDP splinter groups – while a UN survey of women's participation in elected legislatures ranked Japan 110th among 130 countries investigated (FEER, 5 August 1993). Furthermore, the end of the LDP hegemony was to usher in a further period of political instability and shifting alliances that was to culminate in the formation of a JSP–LDP coalition government in 1994.

Uncertainty over the political situation was exacerbated by a slowdown in economic growth during the early 1990s. The economic growth rate fell to 1.5 per cent in 1992 and was estimated to rise by only 2.8 per cent in 1995 (Noble 1994; Blaker 1995). The appreciation of the yen (by the spring of 1995 the exchange rate was 83 yen to the US dollar) made Japanese exports expensive, not only accelerating the shift to overseas production on the part of Japanese manufacturers but also for the first time allowing cheaper foreign imports (particularly from South Korea and Taiwan) to compete successfully with Japanese products. Japanese semiconductor manufacturers, for example, faced stiff competition from Samsung and other lower-cost Korean producers of memory chips. Lack of business confidence led to a stock market collapse in 1992, while a number of firms, hampered by the high cost of capital at a time of weak demand, found themselves increasingly vulnerable. In 1993 Nissan shut down one of its plants near Tokyo, the first closure of an auto assembly plant in the postwar period (Noble 1994).

Although Hosokawa's government did not last long – in April 1994 Hosokawa was forced to resign amidst charges of financial corruption – it did manage to present an electoral reform bill to the Diet in November 1993, which was passed the following January (and to take effect in 1995). The new law abolished the multi-member constituency system used for elections to the lower house, seen by many as the root cause for the factionalized nature of politics. Henceforth, the lower house (currently comprising 511 members from 129 multi-member districts) would have 500 members, 300 of whom would be elected from single-seat constituencies and 200 to be selected according to the parties' proportional share of the vote in 11 regional blocs (voters would cast two ballots, one for an individual representative and the other for a political party). The law also provided for government subsidy of political parties (allocated according to the number of seats held and the number of votes received in the previous election), insisted that politicians report contributions exceeding $500, and imposed a maximum of $5,000 yearly that corporations could contribute to any one candidate (interestingly, the original bill had restricted corporate contributions to political parties only).

Hosokawa's government also took the initiative on two other important and controversial issues. First, at the end of 1993, Hosokawa secured approval from his coalition partners for his proposal to open up Japan's rice market to foreign competition. At GATT (General Agreement on Tariffs and Trade) talks Tokyo agreed to allow rice imports equivalent to 4–8 per cent of domestic consumption for the next six years, after which import controls would be replaced with tariffs. The LDP policy of protecting Japan's rice farmers had thus finally been overturned (although, as mentioned earlier, LDP governments in the 1980s had gradually reduced the government subsidy for domestic rice production). Such a change of policy, however, may not have dramatic effects for domestic rice growers because of the 'westernization of consumption patterns' (Horioka 1993). Thus, the share of rice and *mochi* (rice cakes) in total cereal consumption fell from 96 per cent in 1926 to 59.1 per cent in 1989. The quantity of rice consumed has also fallen: the average annual consumption per household of non-glutinous rice in 1989 was only 30 per cent of what it was in 1960, although there has been a slowdown in the shift to Western cereal products in recent years (ibid.: 273).

Second, Hosokawa confronted the issue of Japan's war past. On 10 August 1993 he publicly stated that Japan had fought a war of 'aggression' and 'wrongdoings' in Asia. In his first major policy speech in the Diet on 23 August 1993 he formally apologized to Asian countries (FEER, 26 August 1993); later, while meeting South Korean President Kim Young Sam, Hosokawa apologized for Japan's colonization of Korea. Hosokawa's immediate predecessors, in fact, had tentatively begun the process of coming to terms with Japan's colonial and wartime past. In May 1990 Prime Minister Kaifu expressed remorse and apologies for Japanese actions in Korea and in January 1991, while visiting the South Korean capital of Seoul, he laid a wreath at the place where, in March 1919, a peaceful demonstration by Koreans calling for independence had been violently suppressed by Japanese troops. In the last days of Miyazawa Kiichi's government in 1993 it was finally admitted that thousands of Korean and other Asian women (insultingly described as 'comfort women') had been brutally forced into prostitution to serve the Japanese Imperial Army during the war (the question of compensation, however, was not addressed). Within Japan there was also a gradual change of policy towards Korean residents. During the war over one million Koreans had been forcibly conscripted as slave labourers in Japan, so that by the end of the war (taking into account those who had been recruited to work in Japan in the 1920s and 1930s) there were nearly 2.5 million Koreans in the country. Many returned to the Korean peninsula in 1945 but those who remained (and their descendants) had to endure persistent discrimination as second class citizens. Although 20,000 Koreans died in the atomic bombing of Hiroshima on 6 August 1945, for example, there was no monument for them at the Hiroshima Peace Park (Koreans held their own separate commemoration on the anniversary of the atomic bomb blast in another part of the city) (Hane 1992: 412–13). Korean residents were subject to fingerprinting every five years and had to renew their alien registration cards annually. In April 1990, however, the government agreed to abolish fingerprinting requirements for third-generation Korean residents, and in January 1991 it finally agreed to end fingerprinting for all Korean residents by the end of 1992 (Ahn 1993). It remains to be seen whether the considerable discrimination that still exists (particularly in employment and education) will be seriously tackled in the future.

Following Hosokawa's resignation in April 1994, Hata Tsutomu took over as Prime Minister but his government was fatally weakened from the start when the JSP refused to join the coalition. Facing a no-confidence vote in the Diet, Hata resigned in June. An extraordinary realignment of parties then took place as Murayama Tomiichi, a septugenarian socialist, was elected Prime Minister of a three-party coalition government comprising the JSP, LDP and the Harbinger Party (Blaker 1995). Together the three parties in the Diet had 294 seats (LDP: 200; JSP: 73; Harbinger Party: 21). As the largest party in the coalition the LDP held 13 cabinet posts, compared to five for the JSP and two for the Harbinger Party. The JSP and LDP, bitter ideological enemies during the 1950s and 1960s, were now allied in government. The arrangement was not entirely unprecedented since (as noted in chapter four) the LDP had joined with the JSP, DSP and Komeito at the local level during the 1980s. The JSP had also adopted a more pragmatic stance over the preceding four years, ending its opposition to the despatch of SDF personnel abroad, electoral reform and the opening up of Japan's domestic rice market (in November 1994, while reducing income taxes, the Murayama government even raised the consumption tax to 5 per cent, to take effect in April 1997).

The formation of a JSP–LDP coalition government prompted a merger of opposition parties in December 1994, the largest since the formation of the LDP itself in 1955. Politicians from nine noncommunist opposition parties (including the New Life Party, the Japan New Party, DSP, Komeito and LDP dissidents) formed the New Frontier Party (*Shinshinto*), headed by former prime minister Kaifu Toshiki with Hata Tsutomu as Vice-president and Ozawa Ichiro as Secretary-general (all three were former LDP members). The incentive for the merger was provided by the electoral law, which allowed parties with more than five members in the lower house to receive state subsidies in proportion to their parliamentary strength.

By 1995, therefore, Japan's political landscape had dramatically changed. A JSP–LDP coalition government now faced a large opposition bloc led by LDP defectors, leading some to hypothesize that a two-party system might emerge. Electoral reform held out the possibility that the factional and money politics of the past might finally come to an end. Public disillusionment with the established political parties, however, continued to prevail; in April 1995 gubernatorial elections, voters chose independents as governors of Tokyo and Osaka (the newly elected governor of Tokyo, Aoshima Yukio, is a transvestite actor). Natural and man-made disasters in 1995 contributed to a sense of malaise in society. In January an earthquake in Kobe killed over 5,000 people and the government was bitterly criticized for the way it handled relief operations; in March a nerve gas (sarin) attack on the Tokyo subway left 12 people dead and was believed to be the work of the followers of *Aum Shinrikyo* ('Way of Supreme Truth'), one of thousands of 'new religions' legally registered in Japan. Founded by a former acupuncturist and herbalist, Asahara Shoko (original name: Matsumoto Chizuo), in 1987, *Aum Shinrikyo* predicts armageddon by the end of the century in which only *Aum* believers will survive. Following police raids on the sect's compounds near Mount Fuji, stockpiles of chemicals, equipment to manufacture automatic rifles and technology for biological warfare were discovered. Arrested in May 1995, Asahara is currently awaiting trial.

In the international arena three issues remain to be resolved. First, there is the ongoing trade dispute with the US. Believing that much of Japan's $66 billion trade surplus with the US (out of a world-wide trade surplus of $145 billion) was due to Japanese car exports, Washington announced in May 1995 that it would impose punitive sanctions on Japanese luxury car exports unless Tokyo agreed to open its own car market to American products (ironically, Japanese auto parts were not targeted because many of them were needed for American models). Although a compromise was reached by the time of the 28 June deadline, American suspicions that Japan is not playing by the rules of the game will continue to hamper relations between the two countries. It may be, however, that Japan's economic ties with the US will become less important as Japan's influence in Asia grows. A recent article notes that Japan's two-way trade with Asia now exceeds that with the US, while nearly two-thirds of its total developmental aid is now directed at Asian countries (Blaker 1995).

Second, there is the debate over whether Japan should become a permanent member of the UN Security Council. When Japan entered the UN Security Council for a two-year term as an ordinary member in 1992, Tokyo requested that it be considered as a candidate for permanent membership, especially given the fact that Japan is currently the second largest contributor to the UN budget. Opponents argued that Japan's pacifist constitution (which, it should be remembered, had been imposed on the Japanese during the American occupation) prevented it from adopting the role of a major power willing to assume global responsibilities, and could point to the country's low defence costs; budgeted defence expenditures for 1994–5 will mean that defence related costs will fall to .855 per cent of GNP (ibid.), well below the 1 per cent Nakasone had promised at the start of his premiership. At the same time, however, Japan has gradually become more involved in UN peace-keeping operations, with 50 SDF personnel being sent to Mozambique in 1993 and a contingent of air and ground force personnel being sent to Rwanda in 1994. Clearly, a consensus has yet to emerge, both within Japan and amongst the international community, concerning the precise nature of Japan's future role in the world. Whatever the case, Japanese governments in the future, while anxious to enhance Japan's role in the world, will have to accommodate a public opinion that is still deeply pacifist (not unsurprising when one considers that Japan is the only country to have experienced atomic bomb destruction) as well as the views of its neighbours in East and Southeast Asia, who still have painful memories of the Japanese military.

Third, in the year (1995) that commemorated the 50th anniversary of Japan's surrender at the end of the Second World War, it was evident that no consensus existed either within the country on the nature of its colonial and wartime past. While Prime Minister Murayama was anxious that the Diet pass a resolution in time for the 50th anniversary (on 15 August) that would unequivocally acknowledge, and apologize for, Japan's aggression, he had to take into account the views of some of his LDP partners who argued that the war had been justified and hence no apology was required. There were also individual conservative politicians who continued to justify Japan's colonial rule in Asia. In early June, for example, a former foreign minister, Watanabe Michio, publicly claimed that Japanese rule in Korea was the result of peaceful negotiations with Korean rulers; this led to angry demonstrations in the South Korean capital and the Japanese cultural centre there was attacked. The war-apology resolution that was finally passed in the lower house on 9 June, while expressing remorse for the suffering inflicted upon the people of other nations as a result of Japanese aggression, placed Japanese actions within the wider context of 'countless instances of colonial domination and aggression in modern world history'. The opposition New Frontier Party boycotted the vote, insisting that the resolution should have been more strongly worded (although some of its own members continue to claim that the war was justified).

Although public opinion in general was known to favour a frank expression of Japan's guilt – a view supported by the mayor of Hiroshima on the eve of the 6 August commemoration, when he criticized Japanese politicians for failing to apologize fully for Japanese wartime atrocities – there were still those amongst veteran groups and surviving relatives of the war dead who felt this would be a betrayal of the soldiers who died during the war. On

29 May up to 10,000 relatives of Japanese war victims (including 40 Diet politicians) demonstrated in Tokyo to vent their opposition to a war-apology resolution. It should be noted, however, that Japanese veteran groups were not the only ones trapped in the past. As a result of political pressure emanating from American veteran organizations, the Smithsonian Institution in Washington was obliged to cancel an atomic bomb exhibit (on loan from the Atomic Bomb Museum in Hiroshima) to coincide with the 6 August anniversary. It was felt that dwelling on the horrific consequences of the atomic bombing of Hiroshima would detract from the celebration of America's victory over Japan (as well as questioning the morality of the act itself). Instead, the *Enola Gay* (the plane that dropped the atomic bomb on Hiroshima) became the centre of the exhibition, not as a sober reminder of the awesome destruction of a city and its civilian inhabitants, but as a symbol of American perseverance and heroism. Such a mean-spirited attitude would only confirm assumptions amongst Japanese conservatives that American (and Western) insistence on monopolizing the high moral ground betrayed double standards.

On the 50th anniversary of Japan's surrender (15 August 1995) Prime Minister Murayama in a television broadcast apologized for the sufferings inflicted by Japan on Asian peoples and allied prisoners of war. It still remained unclear, however, whether Murayama was formally speaking on behalf of the government; and the campaign by both the surviving Korean women who were forced into prostitution during the war and by former Allied prisoners of war to seek Japanese government compensation continues to be unsuccessful. Perhaps the almost obsessive Western attention on Japan's 'failure' in 1995 to fully acknowledge its war guilt smacks of one-sidedness and hypocrisy; after all, it could be asked, will the US government ever formally 'apologize' for the destruction wrought on Vietnam during the American intervention? Nevertheless, there remained the feeling, as much within Japan as amongst the international community, that an opportunity had been missed to finally bring the curtain down on a disastrous period in recent Japanese history, both for Japan itself as well as for its Asian neighbours. Only when this happens can Japan's 'postwar' period be said to have ended.

Guide to Further Reading

For overviews of Japanese history since the mid-nineteenth century M. Hane, *Modern Japan: A Historical Survey* (2nd edn) and J. Hunter, *The Emergence of Modern Japan* are the most useful. The former is arranged chronologically and provides detailed information on politics, the economy and society up to the end of the 1980s; the latter adopts a thematic approach, focusing on such themes as rural and urban development, gender relations, religion, popular protest, militarism and the role of the Emperor. An accessible introduction to contemporary Japan is R. Buckley, *Japan Today* (2nd edn). Most general studies of contemporary Japan, however, have tended to be rather anecdotal and unhistorical; an important new collection of essays – A. Gordon (ed.), *Postwar Japan as History* – seeks to locate political, social and cultural developments within the context of modern Japanese history. Oral history is providing intriguing insights into modern Japan; one of the best examples of this genre is T. Morris-Suzuki, *Showa: An Inside History of Hirohito's Japan*, which charts the changes experienced by ordinary Japanese through the lives and words of four people born in the 1920s. Emperor Hirohito himself is the subject of a useful biography – S. Large, *Emperor Hirohito and Showa Japan*; it is particularly useful on the ways the imperial institution was manipulated by conservative elites after 1945.

On Japan during the Second World War, the best account is Ben-Ami Shillony, *Politics and Culture in Wartime Japan*, which convincingly modifies the conventional image of wartime Japan as a unified polity under the firm control of the military. Two other important studies of the war period which have relevance for postwar developments are I. Iriye, *Power and Culture: The Japanese–American War 1941–1945*, which traces parallels between American and Japanese geopolitical thinking in the last stages of the war, and J. Dower, *War Without Mercy: Race and Power in the Pacific War*, which analyses American–Japanese mutual images and how such images were adapted in different ways after 1945, a subject that is also explored in J. Dower, *Japan in War and Peace*.

Availability of archival sources in recent years has allowed for a more nuanced understanding of the American Occupation period. R. Ward and Y. Sakamoto (eds), *Democratizing Japan: The Allied Occupation* represents the most up-to-date research on Japanese–American interaction during this period. The life and thought of Yoshida Shigeru, the most significant Japanese politician during the Occupation, is the subject of J. Dower, *Empire and Aftermath*; this work also contains useful chapters on the reversal of occupation policies during the early 1950s. The role of Japanese labour during the occupation, a subject frequently overlooked in earlier accounts, is discussed in J. Moore, *Japanese Workers and the Struggle for Power 1945–1947*. Many of the essays in A. Gordon (ed.), *Postwar Japan as History* (noted above) deal with the impact of the occupation period on post-1952 developments, for example in the realms of gender and labour policies. Two studies that place the occupation in its international context are M. Schaller, *The American Occupation of Japan* and W. Borden, *The Pacific Alliance*; both link US policy towards Japan with its overall political and economic strategy in East and Southeast Asia.

The crucial role of the bureaucracy in Japan's economic recovery after 1945 is the subject of C. Johnson, *MITI and the Japanese Miracle*; quite a different view on the reasons for rapid economic growth in the postwar period is presented in D. Friedman, *The Misunderstood Miracle: Industrial Development and Political Change in Japan*, which focuses on the continuing importance of small business. One of the most important studies of postwar Japan to emerge in recent years is K. Calder, *Crisis and Compensation: Public Policy and Political Stability in Japan 1949–1986*; it seeks to locate the making of economic and social policy within a political context by demonstrating that official support for agriculture, small business and social welfare emerged from the ruling conservative party's need to maintain its hegemony at times of political crisis. For analyses of the Japanese political system after 1945, the two most useful works are C. Stockwin, *Japan: Divided Politics in a Growth Economy* (2nd edn) and G. Curtis, *The Japanese Way of Politics*. The changing nature of the Japanese–American alliance and how it affected Japan's foreign policy after 1952 is exhaustively discussed in J. Welfield, *An Empire in Eclipse*; Welfield's study is particularly useful on the origin of Japan's Self Defence Forces.

More attention is now being focused on conflict (and how it is managed) in Japanese society and politics as a way of modifying a common Western stereotype of Japan as a harmonious polity. Two earlier studies of protest in Japan are G. Packard, *Protest in Tokyo: The Security Treaty Crisis of 1960*, which analyses the political and public opposition to the revision of the 1952 US–Japan Security Treaty, and B. Duke, *Japan's Militant Teachers*, which discusses the conflict between the government and the radical Japan Teachers Union. More recent studies include K.

Steiner, E. Krauss and S. Flanagan (eds), *Political Opposition and Local Politics in Japan*, a useful reminder of the ways in which opposition parties were able to contest the hegemony of the ruling conservative party at local government level; T. Havens, *Fire Across the Sea* is a study of the anti-Vietnam War movement in Japan; D. Apter and N. Sawa, *Against the State: Politics and Social Protest in Japan* is an intriguing case study of the long struggle by Japanese farmers to protest against the building of Tokyo's new international airport; M. McKean, *Environmental Protest and Citizen Politics in Japan* discusses the widespread anti-pollution movements of the 1960s and 1970s; and E. Krauss, T. Rohlen and P. Steinhoff (eds), *Conflict in Japan*, which focuses on conflict at all levels of Japanese society, from the village and individual enterprise to the national Diet. Two important analyses of the ways in which the ruling conservative party were able to co-opt opposition and 'manage' conflict are F. Upham, *Law and Social Change in Postwar Japan* and S. Pharr, *Losing Face: Status Politics in Japan*. Of course, the idea of Japan as a uniquely homogeneous and conflict-free society is one championed by certain Japanese politicians and scholars themselves. For illuminating discussions of this phenomenon – known as *Nihonjinron* (theories of Japaneseness) – see P. Dale, *The Myth of Japanese Uniqueness* and H. Befu, 'Nationalism and Nihonjinron', in H. Befu (ed.), *Cultural Nationalism in East Asia*.

A gender history of postwar Japan has yet to be written. M. Brinton, *Women and the Economic Miracle* is a sociological study of how women are disadvantaged in education and employment in contemporary Japan. Individual essays on gender policy during the occupation, the evolution of women's roles in the economy and the debates over equal rights legislation can be found in A. Gordon (ed.), *Postwar Japan as History* (chapters by S. Buckley and K. Uno), G. McCormack and Y. Sugimoto (eds), *Democracy in Contemporary Japan* (chapter by S. Buckley and V. Mackie), and G. McCormack and Y. Sugimoto (eds), *The Japanese Trajectory* (chapter by S. Buckley).

For discussions of social and cultural change, see R. Smith, *Japanese Society: Tradition, Self and the Social Order* (Cambridge: Cambridge University Press, 1984), which argues that Japan is a complex society based on 'premises fundamentally different from our own' (p. 6), and J. Hendry, *Understanding Japanese Society* (London: Croom Helm, 1987), which provides a stimulating analysis of the family system, communal relations, education and employment patterns, religious beliefs, and the arts. The latter book also has useful suggestions for further reading at the end of each chapter.

Bibliography

Ahn, Byung-joon 1993: 'Japanese policy toward Korea'. In G. Curtis (ed.) *Japan's foreign policy after the Cold War: coping with change.* New York: M. E. Sharpe, 263–73.

Allinson, G. 1980: 'Opposition in the suburbs'. In K. Steiner, E. Krauss and S. Flanagan (eds) *Political opposition and local politics in Japan.* Princeton: Princeton University Press, 95–130.

Allinson, G. 1993a: 'The structure and transformation of conservative rule'. In A. Gordon (ed.) *Postwar Japan as history.* Berkeley: University of California Press, 123–44.

Allinson, G. 1993b: 'Citizenship, fragmentation, and the negotiated polity'. In G. Allinson and Yasunori Sone (eds) *Political dynamics in contemporary Japan.* Ithaca: Cornell University Press, 17–49.

Anderson, J. and Richie, D. 1982: *The Japanese film: art and industry.* Princeton: Princeton University Press.

Apter, D. and Sawa, N. 1984: *Against the state: politics and social protest in Japan.* Cambridge, Mass.: Harvard University Press.

Baerwald, H. 1977: 'The Diet and foreign policy'. In R. Scalapino (ed.) *The foreign policy of modern Japan.* Berkeley: University of California Press, 37–54.

Baerwald, H. 1986: *Party politics in Japan.* Berkeley: University of California Press.

Baerwald, H. 1987: 'Early SCAP policy and the rehabilitation of the Diet'. In R. Ward and Sakamoto Yoshikazu (eds) *Democratizing Japan: the allied occupation.* Honolulu: University of Hawaii Press, 133–56.

Barnhart, M. 1995: *Japan and the world since 1868.* London: Edward Arnold.

Beasley, W. 1972: *The Meiji restoration.* Stanford: Stanford University Press.

Beasley, W. 1987: *Japanese imperialism 1894–1945*. Oxford: Clarendon Press.

Beasley, W. 1989a: 'The foreign threat and the opening of the ports'. In M. Jansen (ed.) *The Cambridge history of Japan, vol. 5: the nineteenth century*. Cambridge: Cambridge University Press, 259–307.

Beasley, W. 1989b: 'Meiji political institutions'. In M. Jansen (ed.) *The Cambridge history of Japan, vol. 5: the nineteenth century*, 618–73.

Beasley, W. 1990: *The rise of modern Japan*. New York: St. Martin's Press.

Beauchamp, E. 1989: 'Education'. In T. Ishida and E. Krauss (eds) *Democracy in Japan*. Pittsburgh: University of Pittsburgh Press, 225–51.

Befu, H. 1993: 'Nationalism and Nihonjinron'. In H. Befu (ed.) *Cultural nationalism in East Asia: representation and identity*. Berkeley: University of California Press, 107–35.

Benda, H. 1967: 'The Japanese interregnum in Southeast Asia'. In G. Goodman (ed.) *Imperial Japan and Asia*. New York: Columbia University Press, 65–79.

Bernier, B. 1988: 'The Japanese peasantry and economic growth since the land reform of 1946–1947'. In E. Patricia Tsurumi (ed.) *The other Japan: postwar realities*. New York: M. E. Sharpe, 78–90.

Bix, H. 1970: 'The Security Treaty system and the Japanese military–industrial complex'. *Bulletin of Concerned Asian Scholars*, 2, 30–53.

Bix, H. 1988: *Peasant protest in Japan 1590–1884*. New Haven: Yale University Press.

Bix, H. 1995: 'Inventing the "Symbol Monarchy" in Japan 1945–1952'. *Journal of Japanese Studies*, 2, 319–63.

Blacker, C. 1969: 'Millenarian aspects of the new religions in Japan'. In D. Shively (ed.) *Tradition and modernization in Japanese culture*. Princeton: Princeton University Press, 563–600.

Blaker, M. 1995: 'Japan in 1994: out with the old, in with the new?' *Asian Survey*, 1, 1–12.

Borden, W. 1984: *The Pacific alliance: United States foreign economic policy and Japanese trade recovery 1947–1955*. Madison: University of Wisconsin Press.

Bowen, R. 1980: *Rebellion and democracy in Meiji Japan: a study of commoners in the popular rights movement*. Berkeley: University of California Press.

Bowring, R. and Kornicki, P. (eds) 1993: *The Cambridge encyclopedia of Japan*. Cambridge: Cambridge University Press.

Boyle, J. 1972: *China and Japan at war 1937–1945: the politics of collaboration*. Stanford: Stanford University Press.

Brackman, A. 1989: *The other Nuremberg: the untold story of the Tokyo war crimes trials*. London: Collins.

Braw, M. 1991: *The atomic bomb suppressed: American censorship in occupied Japan*. New York: M. E. Sharpe.

Brinton, M. 1993: *Women and the economic miracle: gender and work in postwar Japan*. Berkeley: University of California Press.

Bronfenbrenner, M. 1968: 'The American occupation of Japan: economic retrospect'. In G. Goodman (ed.) *The American occupation of Japan: a retrospective view*. Lawrence: Center for East Asian Studies, University of Kansas, 11–25.

Brown, E. 1993: 'The debate over Japan's strategic future'. *Asian Survey*, 6, 560–75.

Buckley, R. 1982: *Occupation diplomacy: Britain, the United States and Japan 1945–1952*. Cambridge: Cambridge University Press.

Buckley, R. 1990: *Japan today* (2nd edn). Cambridge: Cambridge University Press.

Buckley, R. 1992: *U.S.–Japan alliance diplomacy 1945–1990*. Cambridge: Cambridge University Press.

Buckley, S. 1988: 'Body politics: abortion law reform'. In G. McCormack and Yoshio Sugimoto (eds) *The Japanese trajectory: modernization and beyond*. Cambridge: Cambridge University Press, 205–17.

Buckley, S. 1993: 'Altered states: the body politics of "Being-Woman"'. In A. Gordon (ed.) *Postwar Japan as history*. Berkeley: University of California Press, 347–72.

Buckley, S. and Mackie, V. 1986: 'Women in the new Japanese state'. In G. McCormack and Yoshio Sugimoto (eds) *Democracy in contemporary Japan*. New York: M. E. Sharpe, 173–85.

Bunker, G. 1971: *The peace conspiracy: Wang Ching-wei and the China War 1937–1941*. Cambridge, Mass.: Harvard University Press.

Burks, A. 1981: *Japan: profile of a postindustrial power*. Boulder: Westview Press.

Buruma, I. 1985: *Behind the mask: on sexual demons, sacred mothers, transvestites, gangsters and other Japanese cultural heroes*. New York: New American Library.

Calder, K. 1988: *Crisis and compensation: public policy and political stability in Japan 1949–1986*. Princeton: Princeton University Press.

Calder, K. 1991: 'Japan in 1990'. *Asian Survey*, 1, 21–35.

Calder, K. 1992: 'Japan in 1991'. *Asian Survey*, 1, 32–41.

Calder, K. 1993: *Strategic capitalism: private business and public purpose in Japanese industrial finance*. Princeton: Princeton University Press.

Carlberg, E. 1976: 'Women in the political system'. In J. Lebra, J. Paulson and E. Powers (eds) *Women in changing Japan*. Boulder: Westview Press, 233–53.

Christensen, R. 1994: 'Electoral reform in Japan: how it was enacted and changes it may bring'. *Asian Survey*, 7, 589–605.

Cohen, T. 1987: *Remaking Japan: the American occupation as New Deal*. New York: Free Press.

Cole, A., Totten, G. and Uyehara, C. 1966: *Socialist parties in postwar Japan*. New Haven: Yale University Press.

Collick, M. 1988: 'Social policy: pressures and responses'. In J. Stockwin et al. *Dynamic and immobilist politics in Japan*. Basingstoke: Macmillan, 205–36.

Coox, A. 1988: 'The Pacific war'. In P. Duus (ed.) *The Cambridge history of Japan, vol. 6: the twentieth century*. Cambridge: Cambridge University Press, 315–82.

Cortazzi, H. 1993: *Modern Japan: a concise survey*. Basingstoke: Macmillan.

Crawcour, E. 1989: 'Economic change in the nineteenth century'. In M. Jansen (ed.) *The Cambridge history of Japan, vol. 5: the nineteenth century*. Cambridge: Cambridge University Press, 569–617.

Crowley, J. 1966: *Japan's quest for autonomy: national security and foreign policy 1930–1938*. Princeton: Princeton University Press.

Cumings, B. 1993: 'Japan's position in the world system'. In A. Gordon (ed.) *Postwar Japan as history*. Berkeley: University of California Press, 34–63.

Cummings, W. 1980: *Education and equality in Japan*. Princeton: Princeton University Press.

Curtis, G. 1977: 'The Tyumen oil development project and Japanese foreign policy'. In R. Scalapino (ed.) *The foreign policy of modern Japan*. Berkeley: University of California Press, 147–73.

Curtis, G. 1988: *The Japanese way of politics*. New York: Columbia University Press.

Curtis, G. (ed.) 1993: *Japan's foreign policy after the Cold War: coping with change*. New York: M. E. Sharpe.

Dale, P. 1986: *The myth of Japanese uniqueness*. London: Croom Helm.

Dirlik, A. 1993: '"Past experience, if not forgotten, is a guide to the future"; or what is in a text? the politics of history in Chinese–Japanese relations'. In Masao Miyoshi and H. Harootunian (eds) *Japan in the world*. Durham, NC: Duke University Press, 49–78.

Donnelly, M. 1984: 'Conflict over government authority and markets: Japan's rice economy'. In E. Krauss, T. Rohlen and P. Steinhoff (eds) *Conflict in Japan*. Honolulu: University of Hawaii Press, 353–74.

Donnelly, M. 1990: 'No great reversal in Japan: elections for the House of Representatives in 1990'. *Pacific Affairs*, 3, 303–20.

Donnelly, M. 1993: 'Japan's nuclear energy quest'. In G. Curtis (ed.) *Japan's foreign policy after the Cold War: coping with change*. New York: M. E. Sharpe, 179–201.

Dore, R. 1959: *Land reform in Japan*. London: Oxford University Press.

Dower, J. 1971: 'Occupied Japan and the American lake 1945–1950'. In E. Friedman and M. Selden (eds) *America's Asia: dissenting essays on Asian–American relations*. New York: Vintage Books, 146–206.

Dower, J. 1975: 'Occupied Japan as history and occupation history as politics'. *Journal of Asian Studies*, 2, 485–504.

Dower, J. 1979: *Empire and aftermath: Yoshida Shigeru and the Japanese experience 1878–1954*. Cambridge, Mass.: Harvard University Press.

Dower, J. 1986: *War without mercy: race and power in the Pacific war*. London: Faber.

Dower, J. 1988: 'Art, children and the bomb'. In E. Patricia Tsurumi (ed.) *The other Japan: postwar realities*. New York: M. E. Sharpe, 39–45.

Dower, J. 1993a: 'Peace and democracy in two systems: external policy and internal conflict.' In A. Gordon (ed.) *Postwar Japan as history*. Berkeley: University of California Press, 3–33.

Dower, J. 1993b: *Japan in war and peace: selected essays*. New York: Free Press.

Duke, B. 1973: *Japan's militant teachers: a history of the left-wing teachers' movement*. Honolulu: University of Hawaii Press.

Duus, P. 1968: *Party rivalry and political change in Taisho Japan*. Cambridge, Mass.: Harvard University Press.

Duus, P. 1976: *The rise of modern Japan*. Boston: Houghton Mifflin.

Duus, P. 1989: 'Japan's informal empire in China 1895–1937: an overview'. In P. Duus, R. Myers and M. Peattie (eds) *The Japanese informal empire in China 1895–1937*. Princeton: Princeton University Press.

Flanagan, S. 1980: 'Electoral change: an overview'. In K. Steiner, E. Krauss and S. Flanagan (eds) *Political opposition and local politics in Japan*. Princeton: Princeton University Press, 35–54.

Flanagan, S., Steiner, K. and Krauss, E. 1980: 'The partisan politicization of local government: causes and consequences'. In K. Steiner, E. Krauss and S. Flanagan (eds) *Political opposition and local politics in Japan*. Princeton: Princeton University Press, 427–69.

Friedman, D. 1988: *The misunderstood miracle: industrial development and political change in Japan*. Ithaca: Cornell University Press.

Frost, E. 1987: *For richer, for poorer: the new U.S.–Japan relationship*. New York: Council on Foreign Relations.

Fukui, H. 1988: 'Postwar politics 1945–1973'. In P. Duus (ed.) *The Cambridge history of Japan, vol. 6: the twentieth century*. Cambridge: Cambridge University Press, 154–213.

Garon, S. 1984: 'The imperial bureaucracy and labor policy in postwar Japan'. *Journal of Asian Studies*, 3, 441–57.

Garon, S. 1987: *The state and labor in modern Japan*. Berkeley: University of California Press.

Garon, S. 1993: 'Women's groups and the Japanese state: contending approaches to political integration 1890–1945'. *Journal of Japanese Studies*, 1, 5–41.

Garon, S. and Mochizuki, M. 1993: 'Negotiating social contracts'. In A. Gordon (ed.) *Postwar Japan as history*. Berkeley: University of California Press, 145–66.

Gayn, M. 1981: *Japan diary*. Tokyo: Kodansha.

George, A. 1993: 'Japan's participation in U.N. peacekeeping operations'. *Asian Survey*, 6, 560–75.

Glazer, N. 1975: 'From Ruth Benedict to Herman Kahn: the postwar Japanese image in the American mind'. In A. Iriye (ed.) *Mutual images: essays in American–Japanese relations*. Cambridge, Mass.: Harvard University Press, 138–68.

Gluck, C. 1983: 'Entangling illusions: Japanese and American views of the occupation'. In W. Cohen (ed.) *New frontiers in American–East Asian relations*. New York: Columbia University Press, 145–66.

Gluck, C. 1985: *Japan's modern myths: ideology in the late Meiji period*. Princeton: Princeton University Press.

Gordon, A. 1991: *Labor and imperial democracy in prewar Japan*. Berkeley: University of California Press.

Gordon, A. 1993: 'Contests for the workplace'. In A. Gordon (ed.) *Postwar Japan as history*. Berkeley: University of California Press, 373–94.

Halliday, J. 1975: *A political history of Japanese capitalism*. New York: Pantheon Books.

Halliday, J. and McCormack, G. 1973: *Japanese imperialism today: coprosperity in greater East Asia*. Harmondsworth: Penguin.

Hane, M. 1982: *Peasants, rebels, and outcastes: the underside of modern Japan*. New York: Pantheon.

Hane, M. 1992: *Modern Japan: a historical survey* (2nd edn). Boulder: Westview Press.

Hardacre, H. 1986: *Kurozumikyo and the new religions of Japan*. Princeton: Princeton University Press.

Hardacre, H. 1989: *Shinto and the state 1868–1988*. Princeton: Princeton University Press.

Hauser, W. 1991: 'Women and war: the Japanese film image'. In G. Lee Bernstein (ed.) *Recreating Japanese women 1600–1945*. Berkeley: University of California Press, 296–313.

Havens, T. 1978: *Valley of darkness: the Japanese people and World War Two*. New York: Norton.

Havens, T. 1987: *Fire across the sea: the Vietnam War and Japan 1965–1975*. Princeton: Princeton University Press.

Hein, L. 1993: 'Growth versus success: Japan's economic policy in historical perspective'. In A. Gordon (ed.) *Postwar Japan as history*. Berkeley: University of California Press, 99–122.

Hein, L. 1994: 'In search of peace and democracy: postwar Japanese economic debate in political context'. *Journal of Asian Studies*, 3, 752–78.

Hellmann, D. 1969: *Japanese foreign policy and domestic politics*. Berkeley: University of California Press.

Hellmann, D. 1972: *Japan and East Asia*. New York: Columbia University Press.

Hollerman, L. 1979: 'International economic controls in occupied Japan'. *Journal of Asian Studies*, 4, 707–19.

Horioka, C. 1993: 'Consuming and saving'. In A. Gordon (ed.) *Postwar Japan as history*. Berkeley: University of California Press, 259–92.

Horsley, W. and Buckley, R. 1990: *Nippon new superpower: Japan since 1945*. London: BBC Books.

Hrebenar, R. et al. 1986: *The Japanese party system: from one party rule to coalition government*. Boulder: Westview Press.

Huber, T. 1981: *The revolutionary origins of modern Japan*. Stanford: Stanford University Press.

Hunter, J. 1989: *The emergence of modern Japan: an introductory history since 1853*. London: Longman.

Ibuse, Masuji 1979: *Black rain* (trans. J. Bester). New York: Kodansha International.

Ienaga, Saburo 1979: *Japan's last war: World War Two and the Japanese 1931–1945*. Oxford: Blackwell.

Ike, N. 1973: *Japan: the new superstate*. Stanford: Stanford Alumni Association.

Iriye, A. 1967: *Across the Pacific: an inner history of American–East Asian relations*. New York: Harcourt, Brace and World.

Iriye, A. 1972: *Pacific estrangement: Japanese and American expansion 1897–1911*. Cambridge, Mass.: Harvard University Press.

Iriye, A. 1975: 'Japan as competitor 1895–1917'. In A. Iriye (ed.) *Mutual images: essays in American–Japanese relations*. Cambridge, Mass.: Harvard University Press, 73–99.

Iriye, A. 1981: *Power and culture: the Japanese–American war 1941–1945*. Cambridge, Mass.: Harvard University Press.

Iriye, A. 1987: *The origins of the Second World War in Asia and the Pacific*. London: Longman.

Iriye, A. 1989: 'Japan's drive to great power status'. In M. Jansen (ed.) *The Cambridge history of Japan, vol. 5: the nineteenth century*. Cambridge: Cambridge University Press, 721–82.

Ishida, T. and Krauss, E. (eds) 1989: *Democracy in Japan*. Pittsburgh: University of Pittsburgh Press.

Ishihara, Shintaro 1991: *The Japan that can say no*. New York: Simon and Schuster.

Ishinomori, S. 1988: *Japan Inc: an introduction to Japanese economics: the comic book*. Berkeley: University of California Press.

Ito, Daiichi 1988: 'Policy implications of administrative reform'. In J. Stockwin et al. *Dynamic and immobilist politics in Japan*. Basingstoke: Macmillan, 77–105.

Ivy, M. 1993: 'Formations of mass culture'. In A. Gordon (ed.) *Postwar Japan as history*. Berkeley: University of California Press, 239–58.

Jansen, M. (ed.) 1965: *Changing Japanese attitudes towards modernization.* Princeton: Princeton University Press.

Jansen, M. 1984: 'Japanese imperialism: late Meiji perspectives'. In R. Myers and M. Peattie (eds) *The Japanese colonial empire 1895–1945.* Princeton: Princeton University Press, 61–79.

Jansen, M. 1989: 'The Meiji restoration'. In M. Jansen (ed.) *The Cambridge history of Japan, vol. 5: the nineteenth century.* Cambridge: Cambridge University Press, 308–66.

Johnson, C. 1972: *Conspiracy at Matsukawa.* Berkeley: University of California Press.

Johnson, C. 1982: *MITI and the Japanese miracle: the growth of industrial policy.* Stanford: Stanford University Press.

Johnson, S. 1988: *The Japanese through American eyes.* Stanford: Stanford University Press.

Jones, H. 1980: *Live machines: hired foreigners and Meiji Japan.* Vancouver: University of British Columbia Press.

Kahn, H. 1970: *The emerging Japanese superstate: challenge and response.* Englewood Cliffs, NJ: Prentice-Hall.

Kamata, S. and Salaff, S. 1988: 'The atomic bomb and the citizens of Nagasaki'. In E. Patricia Tsurumi (ed.) *The other Japan: postwar realities.* New York: M. E. Sharpe, 60–71.

Kanda, M. (ed.) 1989: *Widows of Hiroshima: the life stories of nineteen peasant wives.* Basingstoke: Macmillan.

Kawai, K. 1960: *Japan's American interlude.* Chicago: University of Chicago Press.

Kinzley, W. 1991: *Industrial harmony in modern Japan: the invention of a tradition.* London: Routledge.

Koschmann, V. 1993: 'Intellectuals and politics'. In A. Gordon (ed.) *Postwar Japan as history.* Berkeley: University of California Press, 395–423.

Krauss, E. 1980: 'Opposition in power: the development and maintenance of leftist government in Kyoto prefecture'. In K. Steiner, E. Krauss and S. Flanagan (eds) *Political opposition and local politics in Japan.* Princeton: Princeton University Press, 383–424.

Krauss, E. 1984: 'Conflict in the Diet: toward conflict management in parliamentary politics'. In E. Krauss, T. Rohlen and P. Steinhoff (eds) *Conflict in Japan.* Honolulu: University of Hawaii Press, 243–93.

Krauss, E. 1988: 'The 1960s Japanese student movement in retrospect'. In G. Bernstein and H. Fukui (eds) *Japan and the world: essays on Japanese history and politics in honour of Ishida Takeshi.* Basingstoke: Macmillan, 95–115.

Krauss, E. and Simcock, B. 1980: 'Citizens' movements: the growth and impact of environmental protest in Japan'. In K. Steiner, E. Krauss and S. Flanagan (eds) *Political opposition and local politics in Japan.* Princeton: Princeton University Press, 187–227.

Krauss, E., Rohlen, T. and Steinhoff, P. (eds) 1984: *Conflict in Japan*. Honolulu: University of Hawaii Press.

Langdon, F. 1973: *Japan's foreign policy*. Vancouver: University of British Columbia Press.

Large, S. 1981: *Organized workers and socialist politics in interwar Japan*. Cambridge: Cambridge University Press.

Large, S. 1992: *Emperor Hirohito and Showa Japan: a political biography*. London: Routledge.

Lebra, J. (ed.) 1975: *Japan's Greater East Asia Co-Prosperity Sphere in World War Two: selected readings and documents*. Kuala Lumpur: Oxford University Press.

Lebra, J. 1977: *Japanese trained armies in Southeast Asia*. New York: Columbia University Press.

Lehmann, J.-P. 1978: *The image of Japan: from feudal isolation to world power 1850–1905*. London: Allen and Unwin.

Lehmann, J.-P. 1982: *The roots of modern Japan*. London: Macmillan.

Lehmann, J.-P. 1984: 'Old and new Japonisme: the Tokugawa legacy and modern European images of Japan'. *Modern Asian Studies*, 4, 757–68.

Lehmann, J.-P. 1988: 'Japan as a commercial power: implications for the world economy'. In S. Henny and J.-P. Lehmann (eds) *Themes and theories in modern Japanese history: essays in memory of Richard Storry*. London: Athlone, 245–70.

Livingston, J., Moore, J. and Oldfather F. (eds) 1973: *The Japanese reader 2: postwar Japan 1945 to the present*. New York: Pantheon Books.

McCormack, G. 1986: 'Beyond economism: Japan in a state of transition'. In G. McCormack and Yoshio Sugimoto (eds) *Democracy in contemporary Japan*. New York: M. E. Sharpe, 39–64.

McCormack, G. and Yoshio Sugimoto (eds) 1986: *Democracy in contemporary Japan*. New York: M. E. Sharpe.

McCoy, A. (ed.) 1980: *Southeast Asia under Japanese occupation*. New Haven: Yale University Press.

McNelly, T. 1987: ' "Induced revolution": the policy and process of constitutional reform in occupied Japan'. In R. Ward and Sakamoto Yoshikazu (eds) *Democratizing Japan: the allied occupation*. Honolulu: University of Hawaii Press, 76–106.

McKean, M. 1981: *Environmental protest and citizen politics in Japan*. Berkeley: University of California Press.

McKean, M. 1993: 'State strength and the public interest'. In G. Allinson and Yasunori Sone (eds) *Political dynamics in contemporary Japan*. Ithaca: Cornell University Press, 72–104.

Mackie, V. 1988: 'Division of labour: multinational sex in Asia'. In G. McCormack and Yoshio Sugimoto (eds) *The Japanese trajectory: modernization and beyond*. Cambridge: Cambridge University Press, 218–32.

Marshall, B. 1967: *Capitalism and nationalism in prewar Japan: the ideology of the business elite 1868–1941*. Stanford: Stanford University Press.

Maruyama, Masao 1963: *Thought and behaviour in modern Japanese politics*. London: Oxford University Press.

Masami, Yamazumi 1986: 'Educational democracy versus state control'. In G. McCormack and Yoshio Sugimoto (eds) *Democracy in contemporary Japan*. New York: M. E. Sharpe, 90–113.

Mason, R. 1969: *Japan's first general election 1890*. London: Cambridge University Press.

Minear, R. 1971: *Victor's justice: the Tokyo war crimes trial*. Princeton: Princeton University Press.

Mishima, Yukio 1971: 'An appeal'. *Japan Interpreter*, 1, 73–7.

Mitani, T. 1988: 'The establishment of party cabinets 1898–1932'. In P. Duus (ed.) *The Cambridge history of Japan, vol. 6: the twentieth century*. Cambridge: Cambridge University Press, 55–96.

Miyoshi, M. 1991: *Off center: power and culture relations between Japan and the U.S.* Cambridge, Mass.: Harvard University Press.

Mochizuki, M. 1993: 'Public sector labor and the privatisation challenge: the railway and telecommunication unions'. In G. Allinson and Yasunori Sone (eds) *Political dynamics in contemporary Japan*. Ithaca: Cornell University Press, 181–99.

Molony, B. 1993: 'Equality versus difference: the Japanese debate over "motherhood protection" 1915–1950'. In J. Hunter (ed.) *Japanese women working*. London: Routledge, 122–48.

Moore, J. 1983: *Japanese workers and the struggle for power 1945–1947*. Madison: University of Wisconsin Press.

Moore, J. 1988: 'Production control: workers' control in early postwar Japan'. In E. Patricia Tsurumi (ed.) *The other Japan: postwar realities*. New York: M. E. Sharpe, 14–35.

Moore, R. 1979: 'Reflections on the occupation of Japan'. *Journal of Asian Studies*, 4, 721–34.

Morris-Suzuki, T. 1984: *Showa: an inside history of Hirohito's Japan*. London: Athlone.

Najita, T. 1967: *Hara Kei in the politics of compromise 1905–1915*. Cambridge Mass.: Harvard University Press.

Nishi, T. 1982: *Unconditional democracy: education and politics in occupied Japan 1945–1952*. Stanford: Hoover Institution Press.

Noble, G. 1994: 'Japan in 1993: Humpty Dumpty had a great fall'. *Asian Survey* 1, 19–29.

Ogata, S. 1977: 'The business community and Japanese foreign policy'. In R. Scalapino (ed.) *The foreign policy of modern Japan*. Berkeley: University of California Press, 175–203.

Packard, G. 1966: *Protest in Tokyo: the Security Treaty crisis of 1960*. Princeton: Princeton University Press.

Passin, H. 1992: 'The Occupation – some reflections'. In C. Gluck and S. Graubard (eds) *Showa: the Japan of Hirohito*. New York: Norton, 107–29.

Paulson, J. 1976: 'Evolution of the feminine ideal'. In J. Lebra, J. Paulson and E. Powers (eds) *Women in changing Japan*. Boulder: Westview Press, 1–23.

Peattie, M. 1988: 'The Japanese colonial empire 1895–1945'. In P. Duus (ed.) *The Cambridge history of Japan, vol. 6: the twentieth century*. Cambridge: Cambridge University Press, 217–70.

Pempel, T. 1982: *Policy and politics in Japan: creative conservatism*. Philadelphia: Temple University Press.

Pempel, T. 1987: 'The Tar Baby target: "reform" of the Japanese bureaucracy'. In R. Ward and Sakamoto Yoshikazu (eds) *Democratizing Japan: the allied occupation*. Honolulu: University of Hawaii Press, 157–87.

Pempel, T. 1993: 'From exporter to investor: Japanese foreign economic policy'. In G. Curtis (ed.) *Japan's foreign policy after the Cold War: coping with change*. New York: M. E. Sharpe, 105–36.

Pharr, S. 1987: 'The politics of women's rights'. In R. Ward and Sakamoto Yoshikazu (eds) *Democratizing Japan: the allied occupation*. Honolulu: University of Hawaii Press, 221–52.

Pharr, S. 1990: *Losing face: status politics in Japan*. Berkeley: University of California Press.

Pharr, S. 1993: 'Japan's defensive foreign policy and the politics of burden sharing'. In G. Curtis (ed.) *Japan's foreign policy after the Cold War: coping with change*. New York: M. E. Sharpe, 235–62.

Powell, J. 1980: 'Japan's germ warfare: the U.S. cover-up of a war crime'. *Bulletin of Concerned Asian Scholars*, 4, 2–17.

Pyle, K. 1989: 'Meiji conservatism'. In M. Jansen (ed.) *The Cambridge history of Japan, vol. 5: the nineteenth century*. Cambridge: Cambridge University Press, 674–720.

Reischauer, E. 1983: 'The allied occupation: catalyst not creator'. In H. Wray and H. Conroy (eds) *Japan examined: perspectives on modern Japanese history*. Honolulu: University of Hawaii Press, 335–42.

Reischauer, E. 1988: *The Japanese today: change and continuity*. London: Belknap Press.

Robins-Mowry, R. 1983: *The hidden sun: women of modern Japan*. Boulder: Westview Press.

Rohlen, T. 1984: 'Conflict in institutional environments: politics in education'. In E. Krauss, T. Rohlen and P. Steinhoff (eds) *Conflict in Japan*. Honolulu: University of Hawaii Press, 136–73.

Scalapino, R. 1967: *The Japanese communist movement 1920–1966*. Berkeley: University of California Press.

Scalapino, R. 1989: *The politics of development: perspectives on twentieth century Asia*. Cambridge, Mass.: Harvard University Press.

Scalapino, R. and Masumi, Junnosuke 1962: *Parties and politics in contemporary Japan*. Berkeley: University of California Press.

Schaller, M. 1984: 'Japan, China and South-East Asia: regional integration and containment 1947–1950'. In T. Burkman (ed.) *The occupation of Japan: the international context*. Norfolk, Va.: MacArthur Memorial Foundation, 164–84.

Schaller, M. 1985: *The American occupation of Japan: the origins of the Cold War in Asia*. New York: Oxford University Press.

Schonberger, H. 1975: 'Zaibatsu dissolution and the American restoration of Japan'. *Bulletin of Concerned Asian Scholars*, 2, 16–31.

Schonberger, H. 1989: *Aftermath of war: Americans and the remaking of Japan 1945–1952*. Kent Ohio: Kent State University Press.

Shillony, Ben-Ami 1981: *Politics and culture in wartime Japan*. Oxford: Clarendon Press.

Smith, T. 1955: *Political change and industrial development in Japan: government enterprise 1868–1880*. Stanford: Stanford University Press.

Smith, T. 1984: 'The right to benevolence: dignity and Japanese workers 1890–1920'. *Comparative Studies in Society and History*, vol. 26, 587–613.

Smith, T. 1988: *Native sources of Japanese industrialization 1750–1920*. Berkeley: University of California Press.

Steiner, K. 1980a: 'Toward a framework for the study of local opposition'. In K. Steiner, E. Krauss and S. Flanagan (eds) *Political opposition and local politics in Japan*. Princeton: Princeton University Press, 3–32.

Steiner, K. 1980b: 'Progressive local administrations: local public policy and local–national relations'. In K. Steiner, E. Krauss and S. Flanagan (eds) *political opposition and local politics in Japan*. Princeton: Princeton University Press, 317–52.

Steiner, K. 1987: 'The occupation and the Reform of the Japanese civil code'. In R. Ward and Sakamoto Yoshikazu (eds) *Democratizing Japan: the allied occupation*. Honolulu: University of Hawaii Press, 188–220.

Steiner, K., Krauss, E. and Flanagan, S. (eds) 1980: *Political opposition and local politics in Japan*. Princeton: Princeton University Press.

Steinhoff, P. 1984: 'Student conflict'. In E. Krauss, T. Rohlen and P. Steinhoff (eds) *Conflict in Japan*. Honolulu: University of Hawaii Press, 174–213.

Steinhoff, P. 1988: 'Tenko ideology and thought control'. In G. Bernstein and H. Fukui (eds) *Japan and the world: essays on Japanese history and politics in honour of Ishida Takeshi*. Basingstoke: Macmillan, 78–94.

Steinhoff, P. 1989: 'Highjackers, bombers and bank robbers: managerial style in the Japanese Red Army'. *Journal of Asian Studies*, 4, 724–40.

Steven, R. 1990: *Japan's new imperialism*. New York: M. E. Sharpe.

Stockwin, J. 1968: *The Japanese Socialist Party and neutralism: a study of a political party and its foreign policy*. Carlton: Melbourne University Press.

Stockwin, J. 1982: *Japan: divided politics in a growth economy* (2nd edn). London: Weidenfeld and Nicolson.

Stockwin, J. 1988a: 'Parties, politicians and the political system'. In J. Stockwin et al. *Dynamic and immobilist politics in Japan*. Basingstoke: Macmillan, 22–53.

Stockwin, J. 1988b: 'Japanese politics: good or bad?' In G. Bernstein and H. Fukui (eds) *Japan and the world: essays on Japanese history and politics in honour of Ishida Takeshi*. Basingstoke: Macmillan, 158–75.

Stockwin, J. et al. 1988: *Dynamic and immobilist politics in Japan*. Basingstoke: Macmillan.

Taira, K. 1993: 'Dialectics of economic growth, national power, and distributive struggles'. In A. Gordon (ed.) *Postwar Japan as history*. Berkeley: University of California Press, 167–86.

Tasker, P. 1987: *Inside Japan: wealth, work and power in the new Japanese empire*. London: Sidgwick and Jackson.

Thomas, R. 1989: *Japan: the blighted blossom*. London: Tauris.

Thorne, C. 1978: *Allies of a kind: the United States, Britain and the war against Japan 1941–1945*. New York: Oxford University Press.

Titus, D. 1993: 'Accessing the world: palace and foreign policy in post-occupation Japan'. In G. Curtis (ed.) *Japan's foreign policy after the Cold War: coping with change*. New York: M. E. Sharpe, 62–89.

Tsujinaka, Yutaka 1993: 'Rengo and its osmotic networks'. In G. Allinson and Yasunori Sone (eds) *Political dynamics in contemporary Japan*. Ithaca: Cornell University Press, 200–13.

Tsurumi, E. Patricia (ed) 1988: *The other Japan: postwar realities*. New York: M. E. Sharpe.

Tsurumi, E. Patricia 1990: *Factory girls: women in the thread mills of Meiji Japan*. Princeton: Princeton University Press.

Uno, K. 1993: 'The death of "Good Wife, Wise Mother"?' In A. Gordon (ed.) *Postwar Japan as history*. Berkeley: University of California Press, 293–322.

Upham, F. 1987: *Law and social change in postwar Japan*. Cambridge, Mass.: Harvard University Press.

Upham, F. 1993: 'Unplaced persons and movements for place'. In A. Gordon (ed.) *Postwar Japan as history*. Berkeley: University of California Press, 325–46.

van Wolferen K. 1989: *The enigma of Japanese power: people and politics in a stateless nation*. London: Macmillan.

Vlastos, S. 1989: 'Opposition movements in early Meiji 1868–1885'. In M. Jansen (ed.) *The Cambridge history of Japan, vol. 5: the nineteenth century*. Cambridge: Cambridge University Press, 367–431.

Vogel, E. 1979: *Japan as number one*. Cambridge, Mass.: Harvard University, Press.

Ward, R. (ed.) 1968a: *Political development in modern Japan*. Princeton: Princeton University Press.

Ward, R. 1968b: 'The American occupation of Japan: political retrospect'. In G. Goodman (ed.) *The American occupation of Japan*. Lawrence: Center for East Asian Studies, University of Kansas, 1–9.

Ward, R. 1987a: 'Pre-surrender planning: treatment of the emperor and constitutional changes'. In R. Ward and Sakamoto Yoshikazu (eds) *Democratizing Japan: the allied occupation*. Honolulu: University of Hawaii Press, 1–41.

Ward, R. 1987b: 'Conclusion'. In R. Ward and Sakamoto Yoshikazu (eds) *Democratizing Japan: the allied occupation*. Honolulu: University of Hawaii Press, 392–436.

Ward, R. and Yoshikazu, Sakamoto (eds) 1987: *Democratizing Japan: the allied occupation*. Honolulu: University of Hawaii Press.

Watanabe, A. 1977: 'Japanese public opinion and foreign affairs 1964–1973'. In R. Scalapino (ed.) *The foreign policy of modern Japan*. Berkeley: University of California Press, 105–45.

Welfield, J. 1988: *An empire in eclipse: Japan in the postwar American alliance system*. London: Athlone.

White, J. 1993: 'The dynamics of political opposition'. In A. Gordon (ed.) *Postwar Japan as history*. Berkeley: University of California Press, 424–47.

Whiting, A. 1989: *China eyes Japan*. Berkeley: University of California Press.

Williams, J. 1979: *Japan's political revolution under MacArthur*. Athens, Ga.: University of Georgia Press.

Woodward, W. 1972: *The allied occupation of Japan 1945–1952 and Japanese religions*. Leiden: E. J. Brill.

Yanaga, C. 1968: *Big business in Japanese politics*. New Haven: Yale University Press.

Glossary of Japanese Words

Amakudari 'Descent from heaven'; the process whereby bureaucrats on retirement are employed by business

Ampo joyaku kaitei soshi kokumin kaigi People's Council for Preventing Revision of the Security Treaty, formed in 1959 to protest against revision of the 1951 US–Japan Security Treaty

Beheiren Citizen's Federation for Peace in Vietnam

Benkyo manga Study comic book

Burakumin Former outcasts

Butsujo sozen no jidai 'Period of confused feelings'; a term used by Japanese conservatives referring to the popular unrest, strikes and sabotage during the years 1949–50

Chifuren National Co-ordinating Council of Regional Women's Associations, established in 1952

Cho Unit of land measurement, equivalent to 2.45 acres

Daijosai Great Food Offering Rite, a Shinto ceremony performed by newly enthroned Emperor

Daimyo Feudal lord

Domei Japan Confederation of Labour, formed in 1964

Dowa Assimilation; used in reference to government policies towards the *burakumin*

Fukushi kokka Welfare state

Gekiga Dramatic picture story

Genro   Senior statesmen who controlled the levers of political power in the wake of the 1868 Meiji restoration

Gensuikin   Japan Congress Against Atomic and Hydrogen Bombs, formed in 1965

Gensuikyo   Japan Council Against Atomic and Hydrogen Bombs, formed in 1955

Gurupu tatakau onna   Fighting Women's Group

Gyakkosu   'Reverse Course'; refers to the change in American occupation policy after 1947

Gyosei kaikaku   'Administrative reform', a term used by Nakasone's government (1981–7) to refer to privatization, reduction of public spending and the widening of Japan's international ties

Han   Feudal domain

Hangurii seishin   'A lean and hungry attitude'; the spirit of hard work

Ie   Household

Jiban   Politician's electoral base

Jichinsai   Shinto purification ceremony

Jidaigeki   Film genre focusing on samurai exploits

Jieitai   Self Defence Forces

Jiminto   Liberal Democratic Party

Jitsumu manga   Practical comic book

Juzokuteki dokuritsu   'Subordinate independence', a term used by the Japanese Left to describe Japan's international position after 1952

Kami   Shinto divinity

Keidanren   Federation of Economic Organizations

Keiretsu   Enterprise groups, often centred around a particular bank and tied together by interlocking directorates and mutual shareholding

Kenkoku kinenbi   National Founding Day, a national holiday prescribed in 1966 as a replacement for Empire Day

Kidotai   Riot police force formed in 1952

Kigensetsu   Empire Day (11 February), a national holiday inaugurated in 1868 to commemorate the accession of Japan's mythological first Emperor in 660 BC

Kimi ga yo   Prewar national anthem revived in 1978

Koenkai   Politician's personal support group

Kokubo kaigi   National Defence Council, created in 1956

Komeito   Clean Government Party, founded in 1964

Koreika shakai   'Ageing society'

Manga   Japanese comic book

Mimaikin   'Sympathy payments', a term used to describe financial compensation to pollution victims

Mindo   'Democratization Leagues', breakaway anti-communist trade unions formed during the occupation period

Minseito   Prewar conservative political party

Mombusho   Ministry of Education

Nemawashi   'Digging around the roots'; refers to informal discussions within government ministries before policy is formulated

Nichu kokko kaifuku sokushin giin renmei   Parliamentarians' League for the Restoration of Ties with China, formed in 1970

Nihon jiyuto   Japanese Liberal Party

Nihon sekigun   Japanese Red Army

Nihon shakaito   Japanese Socialist Party

Nihon shimpoto   Japanese Progressive Party

Nihon shinto   Japan New Party, formed in 1992

Nihonjinron   General term referring to discussions of Japanese identity or Japaneseness

Nikkeiren   Japan Federation of Employers' Associations

Nikkyoso   Japan Teachers' Union

Ningen sengen   Declaration of Humanity, Emperor Hirohito's public renunciation of his divine status broadcast in January 1946

Nisei   Second-generation politician having a well-known political father or close relatives in the ruling Liberal Democratic Party

Nisshoken   'Sunshine rights', advocated by environmentalist movement in the 1960s to protest against high-rise building construction

Nokyo   Agricultural co-operative

Rengo   National Federation of Private Sector Trade Unions, formed in 1987

Rengo kuko hantai domei   Sanrizuka-Shibayama Farmers' League Against the New Tokyo International Airport

Rengo sekigun   United Red Army

Rincho   Provisional Commission on Administrative Reform, created in 1981

Ryosei kenbo   'Good wife, wise mother'

Sakigake   Harbinger Party, formed in 1994

Sanbetsu   National Congress of Industrial Unions, formed in 1946

San-chan nogyo   'Mama-grandma-grandpa agriculture', a reference to the increasingly dominant role of elderly grandparents and married women in farming activity

Sangyo rodo konwakai   Industry and Labour Conference

Sankoren   Mitsui Coal Miners' Federation

Sanpo   Patriotic Industrial Unions, formed during the Second World War

Seikei bunri   'Separation of politics and economics', a reference to Japan's foreign policy approach to communist China and North Korea

Seimu chosakai   Policy Affairs Research Council, an organ of the Liberal Democratic Party

Seiran kai   Young Storm Association, an ultranationalist organization

Seisan kanri   'Production control'; refers to worker takeover of enterprise management during the occupation period

Seiyukai   Prewar conservative political party

Sekigun   Red Army

Sengo seiji no sokkesan   'Final settlement of postwar politics', a term used by Prime Minister Nakasone in the early 1980s to highlight the need for Japanese autonomy in international affairs

Shakaishugi kyokai   Socialist Association, a Marxist faction within the Japanese Socialist Party

Shiken jigoku   'Examination hell', a reference to Japan's education system

Shimin undo   Citizens' movements

Shingikai   Advisory council or commission

Shinseito   Renewal Party, formed in 1993

Shinshinto   New Frontier Party, formed in 1994

Shohisha   Consumer

Showa   'Brilliant Peace', the reign title of Emperor Hirohito (r.1926–89)

Shufuren   Housewives Association, formed in 1948

Shunto   Spring labour offensive

Shushin   Ethics

Shushin koyo   Lifelong employment

Sodomei   Japan National Federation of Labour, founded in 1919

Sohyo   General Council of Trade Unions, formed in 1950

Soka gakkai   Lay Buddhist sect founded in 1930

Sorengo   Federation of Small and Medium Enterprises, created in 1961

Taishu engeki   Small-scale itinerant popular theatre

Tanro   National Coal Union

Tate no kai   Shield Society, the private army formed by the novelist Mishima Yukio

Tenko   Apostasy

Tokko   Special Police Section, a bureau within the prewar Home Ministry

Uman ribu   Women's Liberation Movement

Yakuza   Gangster; general term for criminal underworld

Zaibatsu   Prewar corporate groupings centred on a holding company

Zengakuren   National Federation of Students

Zenkoku aikokusha   National Council of Patriotic Associations

Zenminrokyo   National Council of Private Sector Trade Unions, formed in 1982

Zenro kaigi   All-Japan Labour Congress

Index

SECOND EDITION

DEVELOPING EFFECTIVE RESEARCH PROPOSALS

KEITH F PUNCH

SAGE Publications
London ● Thousand Oaks ● New Delhi

First published 2000. Reprinted 2001, 2002, 2003, 2004, 2005 (twice)

SAGE Publications Ltd
1 Oliver's Yard
55 City Road
London EC1Y 1SP

SAGE Publications Inc.
2455 Teller Road
Thousand Oaks, California 91320

SAGE Publications India Pvt Ltd
B-42, Panchsheel Enclave
Post Box 4109
New Delhi 110 017

British Library Cataloguing in Publication data

A catalogue record for this book is available
from the British Library

ISBN10 1 4129 2125 2   ISBN13 978 1 4129 2125 1
ISBN10 1 4129 2126 0 (pbk) ISBN13 978 1 4129 2126 8 (pbk)

Library of Congress Control Number: 2006924245

Typeset by C&M Digitals (P) Ltd., Chennai, India
Printed and bound in Great Britain by The Cromwell Press, Trowbridge, Wiltshire
Printed on paper from sustainable resources

SECOND EDITION

DEVELOPING EFFECTIVE RESEARCH PROPOSALS

KEITH F PUNCH

Summary of Contents

Contents

Preface to Second edition

The second edition of *Developing Effective Reserarch Proposals* builds on the first edition in several ways:

- A section on reviewing literature has been added in Chapter 4
- An expanded consideration of ethical issues is included in Chapters 5 and 6
- A Section on academic writing has been added in Chapter 6
- An expanded discussion of getting started in proposals development now appears in Chapter 7

In addition, a glossary has been added, the number of examples of proposals has been increased from two to five in Chapter 8, and review concepts and questions at the end of chapters have been modified to reflect changes in the text. I want to thank Myra Taylor for her assistance in re-doing the index for the new edition, Robyn Wilson for first class secretarial and clerical assistance, and Claire Chinnery, Tim Mazzarol and Kay Price for permission to include their proposals, alongside those of Nola Purdie and Ron Chalmers, as exemplars. One again, it has been a pleasure to work with Patrick Brindle and the editorial team at Sage Publications.

Keith F Punch
Professor
Graduate School of Education
The University of Western Australia
Email: keith.punch@uwa.edu.au

1

Introduction

1.1 Research proposals: purpose and use of this book

The research proposal is a central feature of the research world. Typically, the presentation and approval of a formal proposal are required before a piece of research can proceed.

This applies to the graduate student in a university, for whom the research dissertation (or thesis) lies ahead, and for whom the approval of a research proposal is required in order to proceed with the dissertation. It applies also to the application for funds to support research, where the proposal is the vehicle by which the proposed research is assessed, and decisions are made about its funding.

This book is mainly written for the graduate student in the university, but I hope it will also be useful for other situations where proposals are required. *Its central purpose is to help students develop research proposals, assuming that the research involved is empirical research in some area of social science.* The idea of empirical research is discussed in Section 1.2.1. The ideas of social science, and of different social science areas which use empirical research, are discussed in Section 1.2.4.

To achieve its purpose, the book is organized around three central themes:

- What is a research proposal, who reads proposals and why (Chapter 2)?
- How can we go about developing a proposal? What general guidelines and strategies are there to help students, while recognizing, at the same time, that the wide variety of social science research implies that we should not try to be too prescriptive or restrictive about this? This theme is subdivided into a general framework for developing proposals (Chapter 3), theory and literature (Chapter 4), methods (Chapter 5) and tactics (Chapter 7).
- What might a finished proposal look like (Chapter 6)?

By way of introduction, I suggest a '4 Ps' view of the proposal: Phase, Process, Product, Plan.[1] Thus:

- The research proposal is a *phase* of the overall research process – the phase which launches the project, and therefore a very important first phase.
- Developing a research proposal is a *process* of planning, designing and setting up the research, including placing it in context and connecting it to relevant literature.
- The finished proposal is a *product*, where the proposal is formally presented as a document.
- That document contains the proposed *plan* for the execution of the research.

This description of the proposal suggests different ways you might read this book, choosing the chapters according to your interests and needs. For example, if your main interest is in the process of developing a proposal (How is it done?), I suggest you concentrate first on Chapters 2 and 7, then on Chapter 3, and then fit the other chapters in around these. If your main interest is in the proposal as a finished product (What does it look like?), you might start with Chapter 6, then read Chapter 2 and then the other chapters as required. If you want to focus on the plan for the research (How will the research be done?), I suggest starting with Chapter 3, then proceeding to Chapters 5 and 6. If you want an overview of all of this, you might read the chapters in the order presented.

Section 1.4 gives more detail about the chapter plan for the book. The remainder of this chapter now gives some background to it.

1.2 Background to this book

1.2.1 Empirical research: data

Our subject is empirical social science research, and developing proposals for doing such research. *Empiricism* is a philosophical term to describe the epistemological theory that regards experience as the foundation or source of knowledge (Aspin, 1995: 21). Since experience refers here to what is received through the senses, to sense-data or to what can be observed, I will use the general term 'observation' alongside the term 'experience'. Thus 'empirical' means based on direct experience or observation of the world. To say that a question is an empirical question is to say that we will answer it – or try to answer it – by obtaining direct, observable information from the world, rather than, for example, by theorizing, or by reasoning, or by arguing from first principles. The key concept is 'observable information about (some aspect of) the world'. The term used in research for this 'observable information about the world', or 'direct experience of the world', is *data*. The essential idea in empirical research is to use observable data as the way of answering questions, and of developing and testing ideas.

Empirical research is the main type of research in present day social science, but it is not the only type. Examples of other types of research are theoretical research, analytical research, conceptual-philosophical research and historical research. This book concentrates on empirical research. At the same time, I believe many of the points it makes about proposal development have applicability to other types of research.

1.2.2 Quantitative and qualitative data

'Data' is obviously a very broad term, so we subdivide data for empirical research into two main types:

- *quantitative data* – which are data in the form of numbers (or measurements);
- *qualitative data* – which are data not in the form of numbers (most of the time, but not always, this means they are in the form of words).

This leads to two simplifying definitions:

- *Quantitative research is empirical research where the data are in the form of numbers.*
- *Qualitative research is empirical research where the data are not in the form of numbers.*

These simplified definitions are useful for getting started in research, but they do not give the full picture of the quantitative–qualitative distinction. The term 'quantitative research' means more than just research which uses quantitative or numerical data. It refers to a whole way of thinking, or an approach, which involves a collection or cluster of methods, as well as data in numerical form. Similarly, qualitative research is much more than just research which uses non-numerical data. It too is a way of thinking,[2] or an approach, which similarly involves a collection or cluster of methods, as well as data in non-numerical or qualitative form.

Thus full definitions of the terms 'quantitative research' and 'qualitative research' would include:

- the way of thinking about the social reality being studied, the way of approaching it and conceptualizing it;[3]
- the designs and methods used to represent that way of thinking, and to collect data;
- the data themselves – numbers for quantitative research, not-numbers (mostly words) for qualitative research.

In teaching about research, I find it useful initially to approach the quantitative–qualitative distinction primarily through the third of these points, the nature of the data. Later, the distinction can be broadened to include the first two points – the ways of conceptualizing the reality being studied, and the methods. Also, I find that in the practical business of planning and doing research, dissertation students very often focus on such questions as: will the data be numerical or not? Am I going to measure variables in this research, or not? Or, in other words, will my research be quantitative or qualitative?

For these reasons, I think that the nature of the data is at the heart of the distinction between quantitative and qualitative research, and that is why I start with the simplified definitions shown above. But we need also to remember that there is more to the distinction than this, as shown in the other two points above, and that qualitative research is much more diverse than quantitative research, in its ways of thinking, in its methods and in its data.

1.2.3 Relaxing the quantitative–qualitative distinction

The quantitative–qualitative distinction has been of major significance in social science research, and a basic organizing principle for the research methods literature, up until now. Despite that, we should note that the value of this sharp distinction has been questioned in the literature (see, for example, Hammersley, 1992: 41–3), and that there are important similarities between the approaches.

Therefore, once understood, this distinction can be relaxed. This book deals with research proposals for both quantitative and qualitative studies, and is based on the view that neither approach is better than the other, that both are needed, that both have their strengths and weaknesses, and that they can and should be combined as appropriate.

Rather than either–or thinking about this distinction, or tired arguments about the superiority of one approach over the other, the viewpoint here is that the methods and data used (quantitative, qualitative or both) should follow from, and fit in with, the question(s) being asked. In particular, quantitative questions require quantitative methods and data to answer them, and qualitative questions require qualitative methods and data to answer them.

These statements are examples of the principle that questions and methods need to be matched with each other in a piece of research. In general, I believe that the best way to do that is to focus first on what we are trying to find out (the questions) before we focus on how we will do the research (the methods). This matter of question–method connections is discussed in Section 3.7.2.

1.2.4 Social science and social science areas

To call our research 'scientific', as in 'empirical social science research', requires that we have a conception of science as a method of inquiry and of building knowledge. There are different conceptions of science, but the one I suggest here is very general and widely applicable, has been prominent in the social sciences, and has great value in teaching research students.[4]

In this conception, the essence of science as a method is in two parts. One part concerns the central role of data. Science accepts the authority of empirical data; its questions are answered and its ideas are tested using data. The other part is the role of theory, particularly theory which explains (or explanatory theory). The aim is to explain the data, not just to collect the data and not just to use the data to describe things. The two essential parts to science are therefore *data* and *theory*. Put simply, it is scientific to collect data about the world guided by research questions, to build theories to explain the data, and then to test those theories against further data. Whether data come before theory, or theory comes before data, is irrelevant. It only matters that both are present. There is nothing in this view of science about the nature of the empirical data, and certainly nothing about whether the data are quantitative or qualitative. In other words, it is not a requirement of science that it involve numerical data, or measurements. It may well do so, but it is not necessary that it does so.

The general term 'social science' refers to the scientific study of human behaviour. 'Social' refers to people and their behaviour, and to the fact that so much of that behaviour occurs in a social context. 'Science' refers to the way that people and their behaviour are studied. If the aim of (all) science is to build explanatory theory about its data, the aim of social science is to build explanatory theory about people and their behaviour. This theory about human behaviour is to be based on, and tested against, real world data.

Together the social sciences cover a very wide domain, and we can distinguish between them in several ways. One distinction is between the basic social sciences (for example, sociology, psychology, anthropology) and the applied social sciences (for example, education, management, nursing). Behind this distinction is the idea that there are different perspectives (for example, individual or group) applied to different areas or settings. Despite the differences, however, one thing that unifies the social sciences is their focus on human behaviour, and the important role of empirical research in the way they are studied. Because of this central role of empirical research, a premise of this book is that there is a great deal of similarity in research methods across the various social science areas.

1.2.5 Relationship of this book to Introduction to Social Research

Developments in the last 35 years or so have greatly broadened the field of research methods in the social sciences. The main development has been the growth of interest in, and the rapid development of, qualitative research methods, in virtually all basic and applied social science areas. As a result, qualitative methods have moved much more into the mainstream of social science research, compared with their marginalized position of 35 years ago. They now sit alongside quantitative methods on a much more equal basis.

In my opinion, therefore, researchers today need to understand the basic logic, characteristics and applicability of both quantitative and qualitative methods. For beginning researchers, I believe a firm foundation of understanding in both approaches is desirable, before any subsequent methodological specialization. It is also desirable that we reinforce the recent trends to move past the either–or thinking which characterized the quantitative–qualitative debate, and towards making full use of the two approaches.

Introduction to Social Research (Punch, 2005) aims to provide that foundation of understanding in both approaches. Its goal is to provide an overview of the essentials of both quantitative and qualitative methods, set within a view of research which stresses the central role of research questions, and the logical priority of questions over methods. In this view, questions come before methods. We concentrate first on what we are trying to find out, and second on how we will do it. I see this view of research as pragmatic and robust. By 'pragmatic' I mean that it works, both in getting research started and in getting it finished. By 'robust', I mean it works in a wide variety of situations and across many different areas.

Because *Introduction to Social Research* aims to be comprehensive, covering the essentials of both approaches for many social science areas, it does not go into details on some topics. The present book deals with the proposal development stage of research in much greater detail and in a much more hands-on way than was possible in *Introduction to Social Research*. It operates with the same model of research, and with the same view of quantitative and qualitative methods as is described in *Introduction to Social Research*, but it elaborates and develops issues and points about proposal development much further than was possible in that book.

1.3 A view of research

Faced with the many definitions, descriptions and conceptions of research in the methodological literature, I think it is sufficient for our present purposes to see research as an organized, systematic and logical process of inquiry, using empirical information to answer questions (or test hypotheses). Seen this way, it has much in common with how we find things out in everyday life; thus, the description of scientific research as 'organized common sense' is useful. Perhaps the main difference is the emphasis in research on being organized, systematic and logical.

This view of research, which I use as a teaching device, is shown in diagram form as Figure 2.1. It stresses the central role of research questions, and of systematically using empirical data to answer those questions. It has four main features:

- framing the research in terms of research questions;
- determining what data are necessary to answer those questions;
- designing research to collect and analyse those data;
- using the data to answer the questions.

A modification of this model, to include hypothesis-testing research, is shown as Figure 3.1.

As well as capturing essential elements of the research process, I think this view also takes much of the mystery out of research, and enables students immediately to get started in planning research. It focuses on research questions, whereas some other writers focus on research problems. Whether to define the research in terms of questions or problems is a matter of choice for the researcher. The question–problem distinction in approaching research is discussed in Section 2.6.

1.4 Chapter outline

After this introductory chapter, Chapter 2 describes the proposal and its functions, and discusses who reads proposals and with what expectations. It then takes up the question–problem distinction, and presents the model of research referred to above. Chapter 3 provides a general framework for developing proposals, using this model of research and focusing on the central role of research questions. Chapter 4 discusses four issues the researcher may need to consider, which arise because of the complexity of contemporary social science research methodology. Chapter 5 then moves on to consider the methods for the research, and Chapter 6 deals with the proposal as a finished product. Chapter 7 is concerned with the process of developing a research proposal and describes some tactics I have found useful when working with students in proposal development. Chapter 8 includes five full proposals and points to other examples of proposals in the literature.

At the end of Chapters 1 to 5 the main concepts discussed, and the questions which can help in proposal development, are brought together for review.

Two appendices and a glossary complete the book. The first appendix suggests a way of disentangling the overlapping terms 'perspective', 'strategy' and 'design' in research, and gives some examples of quantitative and qualitative strategies. The second brings together in consolidated form the various questions guiding proposal development which are discussed in different chapters. In this way they constitute a checklist of questions to help in developing a proposal. The glossary focuses on terms which are prominent in this book, and which often have specialized meanings.

1.5 Review concepts

concepts

empiricism – empirical research
quantitative data
qualitative data
quantitative research
qualitative research
science – scientific research – social science
research questions

2

The Proposal: Readers, Expectations and Functions

2.1 What is a research proposal?

In one sense, the answer to the question 'What is a research proposal?' is obvious. The proposal for a piece of research is a document which deals with

- what the proposed research is about;
- what it is trying to find out or achieve;
- how it will go about doing that;
- what we will learn from it and why that is worth learning.

After it is approved, the proposal leads to the project itself.

In another sense, the dividing line between the research proposal and the research project itself is not so obvious. The proposal describes what will be done, and the research itself is carried out after approval of the proposal. But preparing the proposal may also involve considerable research.

This is because the completed proposal is the *product* of a sustained *process* of planning and designing the research. And both the planning of the research and the proposal for the research are just as important as the phases of research which come after the proposal – those of executing and reporting the research. Indeed, in some types of research, especially those which are tightly pre-planned (see Section 2.4), the planning of the research can be seen as the most critical phase of the process. In this sort of research, the plan which is developed forms the basis for the rest of the research.

Thus the research proposal is a document which is the product of a process of planning and designing. As I will stress throughout this book, it is also an argument which needs to have a coherent line of reasoning and internal consistency.

Two other less obvious, but important, characteristics of the proposal are:

- The proposal is often the first time a researcher (especially a dissertation student) presents his/her work to some wider audience.
- As a finished product, the proposal needs to be a 'stand-alone' document. This means that, at certain points in the approval process, it will be read by people who have not discussed the work with the researcher.

I return to these points later. To finish this section, I quote Krathwohl's comprehensive definition of a research proposal:

> What is a proposal? It is an opportunity for you to present your idea and proposed actions for consideration in a shared decision-making situation. You, with all the integrity at your command, are helping those responsible for approving your proposal to see how you view the situation, how the idea fills a need, how it builds on what has been done before, how it will proceed, how you will avoid pitfalls, why pitfalls you have not avoided are not a serious threat, what the study's consequences are likely to be, and what significance they are likely to have. It is not a sales job but a carefully prepared, enthusiastic, interestingly written, skilled presentation. Your presentation displays your ability to assemble the foregoing materials into an internally consistent chain of reasoning. (1998: 65)

2.2 Readers and expectations

There are two main situations where research proposals are required: the university context, where the issue is approval of the dissertation proposal for the research to proceed to enable the graduate student to complete the honours, masters or doctoral degree; and the research grant or funding context, where the issue is the competitive application for (usually scarce) research funds. Some of this goes on inside universities but much of it happens outside universities.

As noted in Chapter 1, this book is written mainly with the graduate student in mind, who is preparing a research dissertation. As well as being a convenient way to organize and present the material about proposals, this is perhaps an area of greater need, because several books already exist to guide proposal writers in the research grant context (for example, Lauffer, 1983; 1984; Lefferts, 1982; Meador, 1991; Miner and Griffith, 1993; Schumacher, 1992). But, while written mainly with the dissertation student in mind, much of what is said in this book applies to proposals in both contexts. And, as Kelly (1998: 111) points out, the two contexts come together in the sense that social science graduates will have to apply their knowledge and earn their living in an increasingly competitive marketplace, so that practical skills such as proposal writing become important.

In the dissertation context, readers of the proposal (and members of dissertation committees or proposal review committees in particular) are required to make two sorts of judgements. First, there are judgements on a general level, which are concerned with the overall viability of the proposed study as a dissertation. Second, there are judgements on a more detailed and technical level – such as, for example, those concerned with the appropriateness of the research design, or quality control issues in data collection, or the proposed methods of data analysis. This section concerns judgements on the more general level.

These more general judgements centre on such questions as:

- Is the proposed research feasible and 'doable'?
- Is the research worth doing?
- Can the candidate do it?
- If done, will it produce a successful dissertation, at whatever level is involved?

In other words, review committees use the proposal to judge both the viability of the proposed research, and the ability of the candidate to carry it out. It is therefore a pivotal document in the dissertation student's journey. As Locke et al. point out:

> In the context of graduate education the research proposal plays a role that reaches beyond its simple significance as a plan of action. In most instances the decision to permit the student to embark on a thesis or dissertation is made solely on the basis of that first formal document. The quality of writing in the proposal is likely to be used by advisors as a basis for judging the clarity of thought that has preceded the document, the degree of facility with which the study will be implemented if approved, and the adequacy of expository skills the student will bring to reporting the results. In sum, the proposal is the instrument through which faculty must judge whether there is a reasonable hope that the student can conduct any research project at all. (1993: xii)

The four general questions shown above give a sense of the expectations readers are likely to have when they read the proposal, and of the general criteria they will use for judging it. Some implications for the proposal writer follow immediately from those questions. For example:

- The reader needs to have sufficient information in the proposal to make the judgements shown above; the proposal needs to be thorough, and to address all necessary headings.
- The proposal needs to be clear, especially on what the research is trying to find out (or achieve), on how it will do that, on why it is worth doing, and on the context for the research.

- The proposal should show evidence of thorough and careful preparation, even when the research is of the less preplanned, more emerging kind. Research itself demands a systematic, thorough and careful approach, with attention to detail. The proposal should demonstrate, in its content and its presentation, that the student is aware of this.
- As noted already, the proposal needs to be a stand-alone document. This means that it needs to make sense to a reader, often non-expert, who has not discussed the work with the student, and who may not even know the student. The proposal should not need the student's presence to interpret or make clear what is being said.[1]

2.3 Functions and purpose of the proposal

Locke et al. (1993: 3–5) list three functions of the research proposal: communication, plan and contract. This section notes their comments on the communication and contract aspects of the proposal. Section 2.5 deals with the research proposal as a plan.

Communication

The proposal communicates the investigator's intentions and research plans to those who give approval, or allocate funds. The document is the primary resource on which the graduate student's review panel (or dissertation committee) must base the functions of review, consultation and approval of the research project. It also serves a similar function for persons holding the purse strings of foundations or governmental funding agencies. The quality of assistance, the economy of consultation, and the probability of approval (or financial support) will all depend directly on the clarity and thoroughness of the proposal.

Contract

In the research funding context, an approved grant proposal results in a contract between the investigator (and often the university) and a funding source. In the higher degree context, an approved proposal constitutes a bond of agreement between the student and the advisers/supervisors, department or university. The approved proposal describes a study that, if conducted competently and completely, should provide the basis for a dissertation that would meet all standards for acceptability – a dissertation which should itself be approved. Accordingly, once the contract has been made, all but minor changes should occur only when arguments can be made for absolute necessity or compelling desirability (Locke et al., 1993: 5). This idea of the proposal as contract is valuable, but this last statement needs modification for research which is more unfolding than prespecified. The distinction between prespecified and unfolding research is dealt with in Section 2.4 and again in Section 4.3.

Maxwell stresses that the form and structure of the proposal are tied to its purpose: 'to explain and justify your proposed study to an audience of non-experts on your topic' (1996: 100–1). *Explain* means that your readers can clearly understand what you want to do. *Justify* means that they not only understand what you plan to do, but why. *Your proposed study* means that the proposal should be mainly about your study, not mainly about the literature, your research topic in general or research methods in general. *Non-experts* means that researchers will often have readers reviewing their proposals who are not experts in the specific area.

2.4 Prestructured versus unfolding research

At this point, it is necessary to distinguish between research which is prestructured (or preplanned or prefigured or predetermined) and research which is unfolding (or emerging or open-ended). The distinction is about the amount of structure and specificity which is planned into the research.

More accurately, it is about the timing of such structure. The structure can be introduced in the planning or pre-empirical stage, as the proposal is being developed. Or it can emerge in the execution stage of the research, as the study is being carried out. Across the whole field of empirical social science research, studies may vary from tightly preplanned and prestructured to almost totally unfolding, with many positions between. This is therefore a central issue to be clear about in planning the research, and in communicating that plan through the proposal. The distinction applies to the research questions, the design and the data, and it may also include the conceptual framework.

Research which is highly prestructured typically has clear and specific research questions, a clear conceptual framework, a preplanned design and precoded data. The clearest examples of prestructured studies come from quantitative research: experimental studies, and non-experimental quantitative studies with well developed conceptual frameworks. On the other hand, research which is not prestructured typically does not have specific research questions which are clear in advance. A general approach is described rather than a tightly prefigured design, and data are not prestructured. These things will emerge or unfold as the study progresses. The clearest examples here are from qualitative research: an unfolding case study, an ethnography, or a life history.

These two descriptions represent the ends of a continuum. It is not a case of either/or, and varying degrees of prestructuring or unfolding are possible. Figure 4.1 shows the continuum. When it comes to presentation of the proposal, it is likely that projects towards the left hand end of this continuum will be easier to describe: by definition, such research is highly preplanned, and the proposal describes that plan. Towards the right hand end, the proposal writer has a different (and sometimes more difficult) problem: by definition, the proposal now cannot contain a detailed, highly specific plan. This is noted in the next section, and is discussed again in Sections 4.3 and 6.3.

2.5 The research proposal as a plan

The proposal also serves as the action plan for carrying out the research. However, as noted above, how tightly preplanned the research is, and therefore how specific the plan in the proposal is, will vary across different research styles.

Much of the literature on proposals is relevant to research at the left hand end of the structure continuum just described, and shown in Figure 4.1. Thus Locke et al. describe tightly preplanned research when they write that empirical research

> consists of careful, systematic, and pre-planned observations of some restricted set of phenomena. The acceptability of results is judged exclusively in terms of the adequacy of the methods employed in making, recording, and interpreting the planned observations. Accordingly, the plan for observation, with its supporting arguments and explications, is the basis on which the thesis, dissertation or research report will be judged.
>
> The research report can be no better than the plan of investigation. Hence, an adequate proposal sets forth the plan in step-by-step detail. The existence of a detailed plan that incorporates the most careful anticipation of problems to be confronted and contingent courses of action is the most powerful insurance against oversight or ill-considered choices during the execution phase of the investigation. The hallmark of a good proposal is a level of thoroughness and detail sufficient to permit the same planned observations with results not substantially different from those the author might obtain. (1993: 4)

Similarly, Brink and Wood (1994: 236–7) are writing about highly prestructured research when they say that the plan is all-important, forming the basis for the remainder of the research process, and that developing the plan may well be the most critical part of the whole process. In this type of research, figuring out what you are going to do and how you are going to do it (that is, figuring out the plan) is the difficult part. Once that is done, all that is left to do is to 'do it' – to execute the preplanned steps.

These comments describe research which falls towards the left hand end of the continuum shown in Figure 4.1. They need modification for those types of research which fall towards the right hand end of the continuum. Proposals for unfolding studies are discussed in Sections 4.3 and 6.3.

2.6 Research questions or research problems?

Based on my experience in supervising, I prefer to focus on the concept of research questions, as a generally useful way of helping students to get their research planning and proposal under way. When a student is having trouble getting started or making progress with the proposal, or is confused, over-loaded or just stuck in developing it, one of the most helpful questions I can raise is 'What are we trying to find out here?' It is a short step from this to 'What questions is this research trying to answer?', or 'What are the research questions?' This approach makes *research questions* central.

By contrast, some writers tend to focus more on the 'problem behind the research', or on research problems, rather than on research questions. Thus for Coley and Scheinberg, writing about proposal development in the human services context: 'Proposal writing includes the entire process of assessing the nature of the problem, developing solutions or programs to solve or contribute to solving the problem, and translating those into proposal format' (1990: 13). This approach makes the *research problem* central.

Other writers draw a sharp distinction between question and problem. Locke et al. (1993: 45–51), for example, arguing for 'semantic and conceptual hygiene', distinguish sharply between problem and question, and recommend a logical sequence of problem, question, purpose and hypothesis as the way forward in research planning and proposal development. Similarly, Brink and Wood (1994: 45) see proposal development as building or constructing the research problem, and see research question(s) as one of the central components of that. I think both of these frameworks are useful for highly preplanned research, and especially for intervention studies, but are less useful for more unfolding studies. In those cases, the distinction between problem and question is not so sharp.

Sometimes social research is concerned with interventions, and assessing their outcomes. Some areas of nursing research are a good example, especially those concerned with nursing in the clinical setting. Behind this focus on inter-ventions lies the idea of a problem which needs a solution, and it is the inter-vention which is proposed as a solution. This is the logic of the approach to proposal development described by Brink and Wood (1994) and by Tornquist (1993). Writing also about nursing, Tornquist describes research as intervention and action followed by evaluation and assessment. Similarly, programmes and interventions in education or management might be driven by the same logic: a problem requiring a solution, which takes the form of an intervention. The research then becomes an evaluation or assessment of the effects of the intervention.

This line of thinking concentrates on the identification of a problem – something requiring a solution – followed by an intervention or activity designed to solve it, and the research becomes the assessment or evaluation of that intervention. Another, more general, line of thinking concentrates on the identification of question(s) – something requiring an answer – followed by an investigation designed to collect the data to answer the question(s).

In intervention research, the intervention is designed to solve or change some unsatisfactory situation. This unsatisfactory situation is the problem. On the other hand, thinking about research in terms of research questions is a more general approach, which can be used in naturalistic[2] research as well as in intervention research (the effects of an intervention can always be assessed through a series of research questions), and in basic research as well as applied research. I use the focus on research questions as a way both of getting started in research, and of organizing the subsequent project. I think it also has the benefits of reinforcing the 'question first, methods later' advice of Section 3.7.2, and of flexibility, in the sense that students often find it easier to generate research questions than to focus on a problem. But if it helps to think in terms of identifying a research problem, rather than identifying research questions, there is no reason at all not to do so. Nor is there any reason not to use both concepts – problems and questions – and to switch between them as appropriate, in developing and presenting the proposal. In any case, there is interchangeability between the two concepts. Thus a problem, as something requiring a solution, can always be phrased as questions. Likewise a question, as something requiring an answer, can always be phrased as a problem.

2.7 A simplified model of research

My focus on research questions, as a useful tool and strategy for developing proposals, leads to a simple but effective model of the research process. When the research is organized around research questions, and when each question conforms to the empirical criterion described in Section 3.6, we have the model of research shown in Figure 2.1.

This simplified model of research stresses:

- framing the research in terms of research questions;
- determining what data are necessary to answer those questions;
- designing research to collect and analyse those data;
- using the data (and the results of the data analysis) to answer the questions.

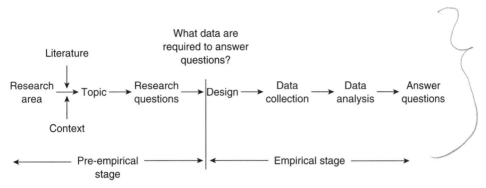

Figure 2.1   *Simplified model of research (without hypotheses)*

This version of the model shows research questions without hypotheses. In Chapter 3, we consider the issue of hypotheses in the proposal. Where hypotheses are appropriate, this model can easily be modified to include them. The expanded model is shown as Figure 3.1.

Based on this model of research, we can see that two overall questions guide the research planning process. They are also the questions around which the research proposal can be written, and, later and with some additions, the dissertation (or research report). The questions are the straightforward ones of *what* (What questions is the research trying to answer?) and *how* (How will the research answer these questions?). Chapter 3 deals with ways of answering the 'what' question. Chapter 5 concentrates on the 'how' question, the question of methods. There is also a third question, the *why* question (Why are these questions worth answering? Why is this research worth doing?). This concerns the justification for doing the research, and is discussed in Chapter 6.

This model of research helps to organize the research proposal. During planning, it also helps to counter overload and possible confusion. It is effective with quantitative, qualitative and mixed-method research. It needs modification where prespecified research questions are not possible or desirable, and where the plan for the research is that they will be developed as the early empirical work provides focus. In those cases, it is still worth keeping this model in mind, in order to see where and why it is not appropriate. When research questions are developed as the research becomes focused, the analytic process is delayed. It comes during and after some empirical work, not before. When that happens, development of the research questions will be influenced by insights and trends emerging from the initial data. Otherwise, it is much the same process, and just as important for ensuring the fit between the parts of the research. This model is also effective with research conceptualized in terms of problems rather than questions. If the research is the assessment of an intervention designed as a solution to some problem, the assessment or evaluation can easily be structured as a series of research questions.

2.8 Review concepts and questions

Concepts
research proposal the proposal as: *plan* *product* *process* *phase* prestructured research unfolding research research questions research problems

Questions
• Who will read my proposal? • What will their expectations be? • What is the process for approval of my proposal? • What departmental and/or university guidelines are there for my proposal and its presentation?

3
A General Framework for Developing Proposals

This chapter describes a general framework for developing and organizing research proposals, focusing on the central role of research questions. While this description has organization and structure, this does not mean that developing a proposal does (or should) proceed in the tidy, organized, deductive way that might be inferred from this description. It is possible for a proposal to develop in this way. But it is more likely that its development will be a messy, cyclical process, with hesitations and frustrations, where the researcher cycles backwards and forwards between different issues and different sections, iterating towards a final version. This echoes the process–product distinction noted in Chapter 2. The process is untidy, but the product is (expected to be) neat, well structured and easy to follow.

3.1 An overall framework

Chapter 2 suggested that the proposal must deal with these main themes:

- what the proposed research is about;
- what it is trying to find out or achieve;

- how it will go about doing that;
- what we will learn from that and why it is worth learning.

We can now represent these themes in three general but central questions, which the proposal needs to answer:

- What?
- How?
- Why?

Irrespective of the position a researcher takes on the issues raised in the next chapter, these three general questions are at the heart of the proposal. Together they form an overall framework for its development.

- *What* means what this research is trying to find out (or do, or achieve). Phrased this way, it points directly to research questions, first general and then specific.
- *How* means how the research proposes to answer its questions. Answering the 'how' question means dealing with the methods of the research. Methods are seen here as dependent on research questions.
- *Why* means why this research is worth doing. This points to the justification (or significance, or importance, or contribution, or expected outcomes) of the research. It acknowledges that all research requires the investment of considerable time, energy and other resources, and it asks for justification of that investment. It also involves the idea of the proposal (and research) as a coherent argument. To some extent, the argument presented in the proposal should itself answer the question of why the research is worth doing. In addition, as suggested in Chapter 6, there may well be another section in the proposal which addresses explicitly the justification or contribution of the proposed research.

Generally speaking, a good way to proceed in developing a proposal is to work on 'what' before 'how' (see Section 3.72). Therefore, this chapter concentrates on research questions. Putting the 'what' before the 'how' means putting questions before methods. Methods are dealt with in Chapter 5.

3.2 A hierarchy of concepts

One advantage of planning research in terms of research questions is that it makes explicit the idea of levels of abstraction in research. We can distinguish five levels of concepts and questions, which vary in levels of abstraction, forming an inductive-deductive hierarchy:

- research area;
- research topic;
- general research questions;
- specific research questions;
- data collection questions.

To say these five things form a hierarchy is to say that they vary systematically in levels of abstraction and generality, and that they need to be connected to each other logically, by induction and deduction, across those levels. The top level is the most general and the most abstract. The bottom level is the most specific and the most concrete.

Thus, from the top down, the research area is more general than the research topic, which itself is more general than the general research question(s), which are more general than the specific research questions, which in turn are more general than the data collection questions.

Another way of saying this, and now moving from the bottom up, is that the data collection questions follow on from (or are implied by, or are included in), the specific research questions, which in turn follow on from (or are implied by or are included in) the general research questions, and so on up the hierarchy.

A benefit of thinking this way, and of organizing research this way, is that it exposes and highlights the links between these different levels of abstraction. It is necessary to have tight logical links between these levels for the research to have internal consistency, coherence and validity. This is what is meant by 'follow on from' in the paragraph above. The technical concepts or processes involved here are deduction and induction. We move downwards in the hierarchy by deduction, and upwards by induction. Both processes are governed by logic.

Not all research projects can be organized or planned this way. In particular, those which have a more unfolding design would not fit easily with this well prestructured approach. There are also issues about 'generalizing' versus 'particularizing' research questions (Maxwell, 1996: 54–5),[1] and the intended emphasis on one of these types of question or the other in a particular study. At the same time, however, many projects do fit well into this approach, and, in any case, this hierarchy of concepts is useful both pedagogically and practically. Not only does thinking in these terms help to organize the developing proposal; it also helps you to communicate clearly about your research, and to write the proposal (and, later on, the dissertation). And if a study emphasizes particularizing question(s), working through these levels of abstraction helps to sharpen its logic and to strengthen its internal validity.

3.3 Research areas and topics

Research areas are usually stated in a few words, and sometimes just one word. Topics similarly are a few words, but usually more than those describing the

Table 3.1 *From research area to research topics*

Research area
Youth suicide.

Four possible research topics
1   Suicide rates among different groups.
2   Factors associated with the incidence of youth suicide.
3   Managing suicide behaviour among teenagers.
4   Youth culture and the meaning of suicide.

Note
Topics 1 and 2 imply a predominantly quantitative approach.
Topics 3 and 4 imply a predominantly qualitative approach.

research area. The topic falls within the area. It is an aspect, or a part, of the area – a step towards making the general area more specific. It is included in the area, but it is, of course, not the only topic within the area.

Examples of research areas are absenteeism at work, youth culture in high schools, living with Tourette's syndrome, academic success and failure at university, membership of voluntary organizations, and youth suicide. Four possible research topics within the research area of youth suicide are shown in Table 3.1.

Identifying first the research area, and then the topic within the area, immediately gives a first level of focus to the research, a first narrowing of the possibilities. Of course, any research area includes many topics, so two decisions are involved here: the first is the selection of an area, the second is the selection of a topic within the area. Many times, students have not so much difficulty with the first decision, the area. They know generally what research area they are interested in. Often, they have rather more difficulty with the second decision: with all these possible topics within this area, which should I choose?

A valuable consequence of identifying the research area is that it enables you as the researcher immediately to connect your work to the literature. It defines a body of literature as relevant to this piece of research. Identifying a topic within an area gives still more specific direction to the literature. It enables a more specific body of literature to be identified as centrally relevant to the research.

3.4 General and specific research questions

General and specific research questions bring things down to the next level of specificity, further narrowing the focus of the proposed research. The distinction between them is in terms of specificity. General research questions are more general, more abstract, and (usually) are not themselves directly answerable because they are too general. Specific research questions are more specific, detailed and concrete. They are directly answerable because they point directly at the data needed to answer them. This point is elaborated in Section 3.6.

Just as there are many research topics within a research area, so there are many possible general research questions within a research topic. Specific

Table 3.2 *From research topic to general research questions*

Research topic:
Factors associated with the incidence of youth suicide.

General research question 1
What is the relationship between family background
factors and the incidence of youth suicide?

General research question
What is the relationship between school experience
factors and the incidence of youth suicide?

Note
More general research questions are possible. These are only two examples. As noted in
Table 3.1, this topic and these general questions have a quantitative bias.

Table 3.3 *From general research question to specific research questions*

General research question
What is the relationship between family background factors and the incidence of
youth suicide?

Specific research question 1
What is the relationship between family income and the incidence of youth suicide?
  or
Do youth suicide rates differ between families of different income levels?

Specific research question 2
What is the relationship between parental break-up and the incidence of youth suicide?
  or
Do youth suicide rates differ between families where parents are divorced or separated, and
families where they are not?

Note
More specific research questions are possible. These are only two examples.

research questions take the deductive process further, subdividing a general
question into the specific questions which follow from it.

A general question is normally too broad to be answered directly, too broad
to satisfy the empirical criterion (see Section 3.6). Its concepts are too general. It
therefore requires logical subdivision into several specific research questions.
The general research question is answered indirectly by accumulating and integrating the answers to the corresponding specific research questions. A study
may well have more than one general research question. In that case, each will
require analysis and subdivision into appropriate specific research questions.
Tables 3.2 and 3.3 illustrate this process with the research area of youth suicide.

This distinction is really a matter of common sense, and, in the practical business of planning research, is not difficult to make. And, as already noted, while the
description here is presented deductively, it is by no means necessary for things to
proceed that way. They may also proceed inductively, and, as is probably most
common, by some cyclical and iterative mixture of induction and deduction.

In formal terms, a good way to distinguish general from specific research questions is to apply the empirical criterion (Section 3.6) to each question, as it is developed: is it clear what data will be required to answer this question? If the answer for each question is yes, we can proceed from questions to methods. If the answer is no, one thing probably needed is further specificity. This criterion is also a good check on deciding whether we have reached a set of researchable questions.

At the heart of this discussion is the process of making a general concept more specific by showing its dimensions, aspects, factors, components or indicators. In effect, you are defining a general concept 'downwards' towards its data indicators. Of the several terms given (dimensions, aspects, factors, components, indicators), I prefer the term *indicators* because of its wide applicability across different types of research. It applies in quantitative and qualitative contexts, whereas the terms 'dimensions', 'factors' and 'components' have more quantitative connotations.

A proviso, more likely to be needed in qualitative studies, is that the research may proceed upwards in abstraction from indicators to general concepts, rather than downwards in abstraction from general concepts to indicators. To repeat, the important thing is not which way the research proceeds. You can proceed downwards, using deduction, from general concept to specific concept to indicators, or you can proceed upwards, using induction, from indicators to specific and general concepts. Or deduction and induction can both be used. The important thing is that the finished product as a proposal (and, ultimately, as a piece of research) shows logical connections across the different levels of abstraction.

3.5 Data collection questions

At the lowest level in this hierarchy come data collection questions. They are questions at the most specific level.

The reason for separating out data collection questions here is that students sometimes confuse research questions with data collection questions. A research question is a question the research itself is trying to answer. A data collection question is a question which is asked in order to collect data in order to help answer the research question. In that sense, it is more specific still than the research question. In that sense too, more than one data collection question, sometimes several and sometimes many, will be involved in assembling the data necessary to answer one research question.[2]

What does this hierarchy of concepts mean for proposal development? I have gone into this detailed analysis because it is often a central aspect of the pre-empirical, setting-up stage of the research, and because it shows clearly the differing levels of abstraction. Understanding this hierarchy of concepts is important, but it is unlikely to be applicable, formula-like, in proposal development. As already noted, the question development stage is likely to be messy, iterative and cyclical, and it can proceed any way at all.[3] But if you are aware of this hierarchy, you can use it to help disentangle and organize the many questions which serious consideration of almost any research area and topic will produce.

3.6 Research questions and data: the empirical criterion

In empirical research, it is necessary that data be linked to concepts, and concepts to data, and that the links between concepts and data be tight, logical and consistent. This idea needs to be applied to our research questions.

Concepts are embedded in research questions. General questions use general concepts, and specific questions use specific concepts. General concepts are typically too general and abstract to be linked directly to data indicators. Rather, they are linked indirectly to data through specific concepts. Translating general concepts down to specific concepts means specifying what the researcher will take to be indicators, in the empirical data, of these concepts.

The idea of the empirical criterion for research questions is that a well developed and well stated research question indicates what data will be necessary to answer it. It is the idea behind the expression that 'a question well asked is a question half answered'. Ultimately, each research question needs to be phrased at such a level of specificity that we can see what data we will require in order to answer it.

We can routinely apply this empirical criterion to research questions as they are developed. For each question, is it clear what data will be required to answer the question? If the research questions do not give clear indications of the data needed to answer them, we will not know how to proceed in the research when it comes to the data collection and analysis stages.

One common example of this concerns 'should' questions, which arise frequently when students are first planning research. It is worth looking at this in some detail, both because it illustrates the point being made in this section, and because it arises frequently. By 'should' questions, I mean such questions as:

- Should teachers assess students? Should teachers know the IQ of students? Should teachers use corporal punishment?
- Should nurses wear white uniforms? Should nurses allow patients to participate in care planning (Brink and Wood, 1994: 8)?
- Should managers use democratic or authoritarian leadership styles? Should organizations have a flat structure or a hierarchical structure?

Such questions are complex, not least because they involve (or appear to involve) a value judgement. But, for our purposes in this section, these questions fail the test of the empirical criterion. Thus, for any of these 'should' questions, it is not clear what data would be required to answer them. Therefore, they are not researchable or answerable with data, as stated. They are not empirical questions, as they stand, and they need rephrasing if they are to be answered by empirical research.

I am not saying that these value questions are unimportant questions. On the contrary, a strong argument can be made that 'should' questions are among the most important type of questions that we need to answer. I am only saying that they are not empirical questions, as phrased, and therefore they need either to be answered using methods which are not empirical, or to be rephrased to make them empirical.

Usually such questions can be rephrased, to make them answerable empirically. There are different ways this can be done. One simple way, which is often helpful, is to rephrase using 'Does X think that. . .' (where X needs to be defined). Thus 'Should nurses wear white uniforms?' might become:

- Do nurses think they should wear white uniforms?
   or
- Do hospital administrators think nurses should wear white uniforms?
   or
- Do patients think nurses should wear white uniforms?

And so on. These rephrased questions now start to meet the empirical criterion. Thus the first rephrasing clearly indicates that we will need data from nurses about their views on the wearing of white uniforms.[4] The second shows we will need similar data from hospital administrators; and so on.

To sum up, as you develop your research questions, you should ask, for each question, 'What data are needed to answer this question?'

3.7 Three tactical issues

Chapter 7 deals with some general and specific tactics in developing a proposal. In addition to that discussion, three tactical issues are noted here, because they fit in well with the content of this chapter. They are:

- the importance of the pre-empirical stage of research;
- questions before methods;
- Whether you need hypotheses.

3.7.1 The importance of the pre-empirical stage

The pre-empirical stage of research refers to the issues discussed in this chapter, and also in Chapter 4 . I use the term 'question development' to describe this stage of the analysis and development of the research questions. In my opinion, it is just as important as the empirical or methods stage of the research. It is really where things are set up, and it therefore has an important determining influence on what is done later – although, naturally, that influence is more important in prestructured than in unfolding studies. But its importance is not very often stressed in the research methods literature. I think that has been partly because of the preoccupation in the field with methodological issues. Of course, I do not say that these methodological issues are unimportant. Rather, I want to counterbalance them by stressing the importance of the question development and conceptual analysis work required in the pre-empirical stage. A crucial step in this pre-empirical work is the selection and identification of research area and topic. Once these decisions are clear in the research student's mind, a great deal has been achieved.

3.7.2 Questions before methods

Questions and methods need to be aligned with each other in a piece of research. This is part of the internal validity of a piece of research, and is more important than ever in social science research today, where quantitative and qualitative methods sit alongside each other, and may be combined in the one study.

In general, the best way to achieve this alignment is to focus first on developing the research questions, and second on methods to answer those questions. 'In general' in this sentence means that there are exceptions to this order of events, and that it is not mandatory. But I recommend it because I have found that a common difficulty for research students is to worry about issues of method in advance of getting a clear view of the research questions. Too often, a student wants to ask, too early, 'How will I do this?' or 'Can I use such and such a method?' Those questions of course have their place. But that place is not so early in the process of planning the research that they come before the substantive issues dealing with what the research is trying to find out.

3.7.3 Do I need hypotheses in my proposal?

On a much more specific level, I single out the question 'Do I need hypotheses?' because I find it comes up frequently, and causes confusion. In a nutshell, I believe that hypotheses should be used in research as and when appropriate, rather than in some mandatory or automatic way. This belief is based on the view that hypotheses have an important function in research when they can be deduced from a theory, or when they are explained by a theory, so that the research, in testing the hypotheses, is really testing the theory behind the hypotheses.

This is the 'classical' or traditional hypothetico-deductive model of research, and it has its place and its importance. But not all social research does or should align itself with this model. There are two straightforward questions which can help in determining whether hypotheses are appropriate in a particular study:

- For each specific research question, can I predict (in advance of the empirical research – that is, in advance of getting and analysing the data) what I am likely to find?
- If so, is the basis for that prediction a rationale, some set of propositions, a 'theory' from which the hypotheses follow, and which 'explains' the hypotheses?

If the answer to these two questions is 'yes', I should by all means formulate and test hypotheses in the research, and, in so doing, test the theory. If not, I suggest we leave the matter at the level of research questions. I can see no logical difference between answering research questions and testing hypotheses, when it comes to what data we will get and how we will analyse them. The same operations are required.

This question (Hypotheses or no hypotheses?) does not have to be a strict either–or matter. The idea of the 'guiding hypothesis' is often useful in research. This may be an informed guess or hunch, for which the researcher does not yet have a fully developed rationale as described above. As well as bringing together, summarizing and integrating the researcher's thinking on the topic, which is valuable, such a guiding hypothesis can also give structure to the design, data collection and data analysis aspects of the study, and can expose other concepts in the researcher's thinking. In that sense, it is useful. But we should remember that research questions can do these functions as well. In particular, the sometimes noted 'focusing' function of a hypothesis is just as well fulfilled by a research question.

In short, I am against the idea that we should have hypotheses in research proposals *just for the sake of having hyphotheses*. Let us use them if appropriate, and not use them if not appropriate. Figure 2.1 showed a model of research built around research questions. This model can be modified for research which sets out to test hypotheses. The modified model is shown in Figure 3.1.

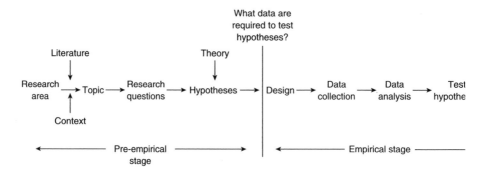

Figure 3.1   *Simplified model of research (with hypotheses)*

3.8   Review concepts and questions

Concepts

research area
research topic
general research question(s)
specific research question(s)
data collection questions
empirical criterion
hypotheses – relationship to theory

Questions

At the most general level:
What

- What is my research about?
- What is its purpose?
- What is it trying to find out or achieve?
- *Especially:* What questions is it trying to answer?

How

- How will my research answer its questions?

Why

- Why is this research worth doing?

More specifically:

- What is my research area? Have I clearly identified it?
- What is my topic? Have I clearly identified it and shown how it fits within the research area?
- What are my general research questions?
- What are my specific research questions?
- Does each specific research question meet the empirical criterion? Is it clear what data are required to answer each question?

4

The Role of Theory and Dealing with the Literature

The previous chapter dealt with an overall framework for developing proposals, and, as a practical and pedagogical device, focused on the central role of research questions. In this chapter, I look at four complementary issues. Two of them (perspectives and theory) concern the overall direction and orientation of the research; one (prestructured versus unfolding) concerns mostly design and methods; the fourth (the literature) is concerned both with the context of the research and with the way its research questions and strategy are developed.

These issues have particular prominence here because we are looking at quantitative and qualitative research together, and we are using the same general framework of research questions, design, data collection and data analysis to do that. They also come into focus because we are looking across social science research in general, including different areas and different research styles and traditions, as well as the two main different approaches. But the issues apply unevenly and in different ways across that range. Therefore not all will need explicit treatment in all proposals. Despite that, I think they are issues that should be routinely thought about in planning research. Doing so will expose hidden assumptions, strengthen the proposal, and prepare the researcher better, especially if defence of the proposal (or, ultimately, of the dissertation) is involved.

In planning research and developing proposals, I think of these as issues that occur around and alongside the central 'what', 'how' and 'why' questions of the previous chapter. In that sense, they give context and direction to the proposed research. In some respects, too, they may change the way the 'what' questions are asked and dealt with.

The main point I want to stress here is that the writer needs to put the reader in the picture as to which of these points apply in the proposed research, and in what way. That means, of course, that the writer has to figure out in the planning stage of the research which of these points apply, and in what way. Doing this and communicating this is an important clarifying task for the researcher, and an important safeguard against mistaken expectations on the part of the reader.

4.1 The perspective behind the research

Paradigm = a way of looking @ the world.

The issue here is whether there is a particular perspective, or philosophical position, or paradigm or metatheory, which lies behind and informs the research. The terms 'paradigm' and 'metatheory' now require a brief comment.

Paradigm here means a set of assumptions about the social world, and about what constitute proper techniques and topics for inquiring into that world. Put simply, it is a way of looking at the world. It means a view of how science should be done, and is a broad term encompassing elements of epistemology, theory and philosophy, along with methods.[1] Examples of general paradigms within social research are positivism, post-positivism, critical theory and constructivism. More detailed examples and classifications of paradigms are given by Guba and Lincoln (1994).

Some writers use the term *metatheory* similarly, to describe ideas about conceptions of science: 'Different thinkers, especially philosophers (of science) have suggested different ideas of what a scientist should and can do. Such thoughts about what is scientifically possible and what is not, are called metatheories' (Higgs, 1995: 3). Examples of metatheories considered by writers in the philosophy of education are logical empiricism (and post-empiricism), critical rationalism, critical theory, phenomenology, hermeneutics and systems theory.

The paradigms and metatheories noted above can also be thought of as 'perspectives' (or 'positions') which might lie behind a piece of social research. I will use the broader, more general (and less formidable!) term *perspective* here, to describe the idea that there might be a particular paradigm or metatheory or philosophical position behind the research. There are still other perspectives than those noted as paradigms and metatheories above which might apply in a piece of research, especially if it is qualitative. Examples are feminism, post-modernism, symbolic interactionism, semiotics, ethnomethodology, discourse analysis and conversation analysis.[2]

Adopting a particular perspective in a piece of research might influence the researcher in several ways. For example, it usually means making certain assumptions and adopting certain systems of meaning, and rejecting others. It might influence the researcher to focus on certain issues and to raise certain questions and problems for research. It might influence both the discourse and the methods of the research – for example, favouring the use of certain methods, and 'prohibiting' certain others. It might influence the way research questions are asked, with subsequent implications for methods. Finally, different perspectives often imply different sets of criteria for evaluating a piece of social research (see, for example, Denzin and Lincoln, 1994: 479–83).

This issue of perspective, perhaps more than any other, applies unevenly across different social science areas, and its role and importance may be interpreted differently in different areas. Thus it is more important in some areas than others, and sometimes, especially in some applied social research contexts, it is not seen as relevant at all. It may also be applied differently at different levels of higher degree work: for example, it is often seen as a more appropriate concern at doctoral level than at masters level. Again, some areas of social research are heterogeneous and pluralistic when it comes to perspectives and paradigms, whereas others are relatively homogeneous. And finally, of course, and partly as a result of these points, some areas are more subject to paradigm disputes and debates than are others. Thus educational research is both a heterogeneous and a contested area on these issues, whereas experimental psychology is homogeneous and relatively free of such debates.

An implication of this is that it is hard to write on this issue in a way that would apply to all social research areas. Despite this, I would suggest three straightforward points that can assist students in developing their proposals.

First, I do not believe that all social research *has* to begin or proceed from one of these perspectives. On the contrary, research may proceed from the more 'pragmatic' approach of questions that need answers, or problems that need solutions.

Second, and equally, a piece of social research *may well* proceed from some particular perspective, perhaps one of those mentioned above, or perhaps some combination of them. Examples would be a feminist study of participation in unions, a critical theory study of life in asylums, a constructivist study of curriculum development in science, and a post-positivist study of quality assurance procedures in education.

Third, if the second point applies, the proposal writer should identify that perspective early and clearly in the proposal. This is important in the interests of avoiding mistaken expectations on the part of readers.[3]

4.2 The role of theory

The previous section used the term 'metatheory' to refer to a particular paradigm or perspective which might inform a piece of research. This present section is about what we might call 'substantive theory' and the role it plays in the research. By substantive theory I mean a theory about a substantive issue or phenomenon, some examples of which are shown below. Usually, the function of such a theory is both to describe and to explain; an explanatory theory is one which not only describes but also explains the phenomenon of substantive interest. Thus theory, in this sense, is a set of propositions which together describe and explain the phenomenon being studied. These propositions are at a higher level of abstraction than the specific facts and empirical generalizations (the data) about the phenomenon. They explain the data by deduction, in the if–then sense.

Like metatheory, this question about the role of substantive theory is sometimes considered more appropriate at the doctoral level than at the masters level. This seems to be because a common criterion among universities for the award of the doctorate centres on the 'substantial and original contribution to knowledge' the study makes, and the 'substantial' part of that criterion is often interpreted in terms of substantive theory.

Some examples of substantive theories from different areas of social research are attribution theory, reinforcement theory, various learning theories and personal construct theory (from psychology); reference group theory and social stratification theory (from sociology); the theory of vocational personalities and career anchors (from occupational sociology); theories of children's moral development and of teacher career cycles (from education); and various leadership theories (from management and administration).

Thus the general question here, for the research proposal, is 'What is the role of (substantive) theory in this study?' We can look at this question under two subsidiary questions:

- Does the description–explanation distinction apply in the proposed project?
- Does the distinction between theory verification and theory generation apply?

4.2.1 Description versus explanation

Does the description–explanation distinction apply in the proposed study? This is one of those issues which does not necessarily apply to all studies, but is nonetheless a useful question to consider when designing the proposal.

Research, whether quantitative or qualitative, can be descriptive, or explanatory, or both. A *descriptive study* sets out to collect, organize and summarize information about the matter being studied. To describe is to draw a picture of what happened, or of how things are proceeding, or of what a situation or person or event is (or was) like, or means, or of how things are related to each other. It is concerned with making complicated things understandable. In social science, it often involves summarizing specific factual information into empirical generalizations (if the research has a nomothetic or generalizing bias), or summarizing details of events, characteristics, cases or processes (if the research has an ideographic or particularizing bias).

An *explanatory study*, on the other hand, sets out to explain and account for the descriptive information. It too is concerned with making complicated things understandable, but on a different level. It aims to find the reasons for things, showing why and how they are what they are.

Description is a more restricted purpose than explanation. We can describe without explaining, but we can't really explain without describing. Therefore explanation goes further than description; it is description plus something else. Broadly speaking, an explanatory study will be concerned with testing or verifying theory, or with generating theory, or with both of these.

One way to see the difference between description and explanation is to compare 'what' questions with 'why' or 'how' questions. A descriptive study asks, basically, 'What is the case or situation here?' An explanatory study asks, basically, 'Why is this the case or situation?' or 'How does (or did) this situation come about?' This description–explanation distinction applies to both quantitative and qualitative studies. For qualitative research, Maxwell (1996: 59) has a third category of questions: interpretive questions. Thus descriptive questions ask 'what', explanatory question ask 'why', and interpretive questions ask about the meanings of things for the people involved.[4]

In my opinion, both descriptive and explanatory studies have their place in research, and one is not necessarily better than the other. Rather, it is a question of assessing the particular research area or situation, and especially of assessing what stage the development of knowledge in that area has reached, and designing the emphasis of the study accordingly. Thus, for a relatively new research area (for example, how teachers use the internet in classrooms), it makes sense for research to have a descriptive emphasis. For a well worked research area (for example, the relationship between social class and scholastic achievement), where considerable descriptive information already exists, it makes sense for research to have an explanatory emphasis.

In some quarters, however, the value of a purely descriptive study might be questioned. There may well be a view, especially at the doctoral level, that a study should try to do more than 'just describe'. There is a good reason for this: explanatory knowledge is more powerful than descriptive knowledge. When we know why (or how) something happens, we know more than just what happens, and we can use the explanation for prediction. But, as a counter to that, and in addition to the example of a new research area given above, a very valuable step towards explanation can often be a careful and thorough description. A good first step in explaining why something happens is to describe exactly what happens. And careful descriptive work can be of great assistance in the development of more abstract concepts important in later theorizing. Also, some areas or styles of research have a different view on the merits of a descriptive study. An example is ethnography in anthropology (and in some applied social research areas), where 'full ethnographic description' may be the goal of the research. Another is Glaser's view of the Strauss and Corbin approach in grounded theory: that it is not true grounded theory, but rather 'full conceptual description' (see especially Glaser, 1992).

Explanation itself is a complex philosophical concept. The view of explanation I am using here emphasizes induction from specific facts or empirical generalizations to more general and abstract propositions. The empirical generalization is then a specific example of the more general proposition, which thereby 'explains' it. Another frequent and useful, but different, form of explanation is the 'missing links' form. Here, an event or empirical generalization is explained by showing the links which bring it about. Thus the relationship between social class and scholastic achievement might be explained by using cultural capital (Bourdieu, 1973) as the link between them. Or the relationship between social class and self-esteem might be explained by using the parent–child relationship as the link between them (Rosenberg, 1968: 54–82).[5]

To summarize, the questions for proposal development are:

- Is the proposed study descriptive, explanatory or both? In other words, does it aim to answer questions about 'what', or also about 'why' and 'how'?
- What is the logic behind the position taken, and how does that logic flow through the proposal?

4.2.2 Theory verification versus theory generation

This is another issue which may apply unevenly across different social science areas. It is linked to the previous section through the concepts of explanation and explanatory theory. Broadly speaking, the two main possible roles for substantive explanatory theory in a study are testing theory or generating theory. The first is usually called theory verification; the second is theory generation. This theory verification–generation distinction cuts across the quantitative–qualitative distinction. A theory verification study can be quantitative or qualitative or both; so can a theory generation study. Either can be appropriate, depending on the research area, topic or context. Neither is better than the other. At the same time, it is historically true that theory verification studies in social science research have more often been quantitative, and theory generation studies have more often been qualitative.[6]

Once again, I am using 'theory' here in the sense of substantive explanatory theory. In this sense, a theory is a set of statements which explains facts (observations, findings or empirical generalizations). It is at a more abstract level than the facts themselves. There is an if–then connection between the theory and the facts: if the theory is true, then the factual statements follow. These factual statements are hypotheses to be tested in a theory verification study.

A theory verification study aims to test a theory or, more accurately, to test propositions (that is, hypotheses) derived from the theory. This has been a very common model in social science areas which have traditionally emphasized quantitative research (such as psychology and some areas of management and education). Such a study starts with a theory, deduces hypotheses from it, and proceeds to test these hypotheses.

A theory generation study aims to generate or develop a theory to explain empirical phenomena or findings. Such a study typically starts with questions, moves to data and ends with a theory. This has been a common model in some qualitative research, especially where grounded theory is favoured (for example, nursing research).

This theory verification–generation distinction is really a matter of emphasis in a study. A theory verification study often ends up in theory modification or generation, especially if hypotheses are not confirmed. Similarly, a theory generation study will naturally use the processes of verification (and falsification) in constructing the theory. But, while the two may naturally get intertwined in doing the research, it is a good idea for a study to be clear at the proposal stage on which of the two is its main focus and objective.

A theory verification study has hypotheses for testing. Hypotheses are specific predictions about what is expected to be found in the data, paralleling research questions, and they should follow from (and be explained by) the theory. As noted earlier (Section 3.7.3), I see little point in having hypotheses without also showing the theory from which they follow.

Therefore the questions at proposal development stage are:

- If the purpose is explanatory, does the study focus on theory verification or theory generation?
- What is the logic behind this position and how does that logic flow through the proposal?
- If theory verification is the focus, what are the hypotheses and what is the theory behind them?

4.3 Prestructured versus unfolding

This issue is about the amount of structure and specificity which is planned into the research, especially in its research questions, its conceptual framework and design, and its data. As noted earlier (Section 2.4), it is about the timing of such structure. Across the whole field of empirical social science research, studies may vary from tightly preplanned and prestructured to almost totally unfolding, with many positions between. This is therefore a central issue to be clear about in planning the research, and in communicating that plan through the proposal. The distinction applies especially to the research questions, the design and the data, and it may also include the conceptual framework.

Some types of research are highly prestructured, with clear and specific research questions, a clear conceptual framework, a preplanned design and

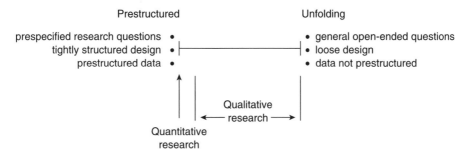

Figure 4.1   *Prestructured versus unfolding: the timing of structure*

precoded data. Some types of research, on the other hand, are not at all pre-structured. Specific research questions are not clear in advance, a general approach is described rather than a tightly prefigured design, and data are not prestructured. These things will emerge or unfold as the study progresses.

Figure 4.1 shows that these two descriptions represent the ends of a continuum, with varying degrees of prestructuring or unfolding along the continuum.

Once again, the point is not that one type is better than the other. Both have their place and both have their strengths and weaknesses. Rather than wanting to priv-ilege one over the other, it is better that we think of adopting the type of research which is most appropriate for the area, topic and purposes of a particular project.

For the proposal, it is likely that projects towards the left hand end of this continuum will be easier to describe, lending themselves more to a formula-like approach to proposal development. Towards the right hand end, the proposal writer has a different problem, because there is no detailed research plan with a specific set of steps. Here, however, I think the proposal should indicate:

- that the study (or some part of it) is of the unfolding, emerging type;
- why this is appropriate for the area, topic and approach;
- in general terms, how structure and specificity will emerge during the research – how research questions will be identified, how the design will be developed and how the analysis will uncover structure in the data.

In other words, an unfolding type of study does not imply an 'anything goes' type of proposal. Consider, for example, this statement from Eisner, writing about qualitative proposals in educational research:

Lest these comments be interpreted by some to mean that no planning is necessary in conducting qualitative research, or that 'anything goes,' as they say, I want to make it clear that this is not how my words should be interpreted. Planning is necessary. Nevertheless, it should not and cannot function as a recipe or as a script. Evidence matters. One has a responsibility to support what one says, but support does not require measured evidence. Coherence, plausibility, and utility are quite acceptable in trying to deal with social complexity. My point is not to advocate anarchy or to reduce the study of schools and classrooms to a Rorschach projection, it is to urge that the analysis of a research proposal or a research study should employ criteria appropriate to the genre. Professors who make such assessments should understand, as should graduate students, the nature of the genre, what constitutes appropriate criteria, and why they are appropriate. (1991: 241–2)

We return to this question in Section 6.3.

4.4 The literature

All social research has a relevant literature, and no research takes place in a vacuum. It is therefore part of the researcher's responsibility to:

- identify the literature which is relevant to the study and to be familiar with it;
- locate the present study in relation to the literature;
- determine how the literature will be handled in the proposal and, later, in the dissertation.

Each of these is now discussed.

4.4.1 Relevant literature

What literature is relevant to this project? In dealing with this question, reference to your research area, topic statement and general research questions is obviously a very good starting point. Basing your reading around your general research questions provides a way of organizing literature; some literature is centrally relevant, some is generally relevant, and some is background literature. Rudestam and Newton (2002: 64) have a Venn diagram using these ideas to guide the construction of a literature review. If you concentrate first on the research literature – mostly to be found in research journals, conference papers and proceedings, and dissertations – connections to the relevant theoritical, historical and contextual literature will normally build quickly. Access to major research library is therefore important, as is access to dissertation abstracts; as Burton and Steane (2004: 128) point out, others have gone before you. Articles in research journals usually include a brief literature review, and dissertations a more extensive one.

Some points to remember about identifying the relevant literature are:

- Different research areas and topics will have different quantities of relevant literature. In some areas the volume of literature will be vast, in some areas relatively small.
- More than one body of literature might be relevant, especially if your topic cuts across more than one substantive area.

- The levels of abstraction issue often arises. Be careful of saying, 'There is no relevant literature for my topic.' This statement may be true at a specific level, but not true at a more abstract level. Realize that connections to relevant literature may require you to raise the level of abstraction of your topic. Two examples of this are given in Box 4.1.
- As well as traditional literature searching methods, the internet today is an indispensable resource for locating relevant literature.

BOX 4.1   USING THE LITERATURE: LEVELS OF ABSTRACTION

Raising the level of abstraction of a specific topic helps to show its connections with the literature. As an example: assume the specific topic for the research is the educational performance of Aboriginal children in Narrogin, Western Australia. In all probability there is no literature or previous research on this specific topic. However, Aboriginal children are an indigenous ethnic minority group; Narrogin is a rural community. Now the search for relevant literature is broader: the educational performance of indigenous ethnic minority children in rural communities.

Bryant expresses a similar idea in the following tip:
Realize that if you choose to study a tiny subset of a population in a very specific setting, this does not mean you should neglect the research about your topic that may have been carried out for other populations in other settings. For example, studying the leadership behaviours of Hispanic men in small non-profit organizations in a single county in a single state does not mean you do not need to inform your readers about leaderships behaviours in non-profit organizations generally and of Hispanic men in general. (2004: 65)

4.4.2 Relationship between study and literature

What is the relationship of the proposed study to its relevant literature? This includes such questions as: where does the proposed study fit in relation to its relevant literature? What is its connection to that literature? How will the proposed research move beyond previous work or beyond what we already know?

There are several possible answers to these questions. For example, this study may fill a gap in the literature; it may sit in line with the main trends in the literature, seeking to extend these trends; it may take a quite different direction from those in the literature; it may aim to confirm, challenge or disconfirm other findings, as in a replication study; it may test or extend a theory from the literature; or it may use a theoretical framework or model from the literature. There are other possibilities as well, so the general question to be dealt with in the proposal is, 'What contribution will this study make to the literature?'

4.4.3 Using the literature

How will the proposed study deal with the literature? In particular, how will the argument in the proposal use the literature?

There are different ways a study may deal with its literature, and different expectations may apply for the use of the literature in the proposal. For example:

- The literature may be fully reviewed in advance of the research; the full literature review is part of the proposal and is included or attached (reviewing literature is discussed in the next section).
- The literature may be reviewed, but the review has not been done at proposal submission time; in this case, part of the review, a sample of the review, or themes to be used in the review, may be included with the proposal.
- The literature will be reviewed, analysed and incorporated as the study progresses, and perhaps especially when the study's data are being analysed and its findings are being discussed. An example of this is a grounded theory study. When this approach to the literature is proposed, it is worth giving a clear statement of it and justification for it, if only because of expectations sometimes held that the literature will be reviewed ahead of the research.

As to how the proposal itself uses the literature, one view on this matter is provided by Locke et al. (1993: 71–2), when they write that the proposal writer should place the research question(s) – or hypotheses – in the context of previous work in such a way as to explain and justify the decisions made for the proposed study, especially with respect to (1) how and why the research question or hypothesis was formulated in the present form, and (2) why the proposed research strategy was selected. They see no other role for the literature *in the research proposal*, and regard the heading 'review of the literature' as inappropriate in a proposal. Similar advice comes from Maxwell (1996). Clearly, this has the benefit of shortening the proposal. On the other hand there are certainly situations where a literature review is expected or required in the proposal, and in such cases it usually precedes the research questions or hypotheses. Thus the student needs to check departmental expectations on the question of literature review in the proposal. The following comments apply to those situations where reviewing literature is required as part of proposal development. They also apply, of course, to the literature review in the dissertation.

4.5 Reviewing literature

A good literature review demonstrates your mastery of your dissertation topic, and is much more than a summary of relevant literature. While summarizing literature is important, your review should go beyond mere summarizing in two main respects. First, reviewing literature requires the building of an argument. This, in turn, requires a synthesis of the literature, not merely a summary of it. Second, your review is expected to be critical, especially with respect to research literature. This means routinely examining and critiquing the methods used in reported research, with special reference to the generalizability or transferability of research findings (Bryant, 2004: 80). It also means taking an analytical approach in dealing with literature (Brink and Wood, 1994: 58), and critically reflecting on its organization, completeness, coherence and consistency.

Summarizing literature as you read is an important first step. Doing it systematically, with complete bibliographic details and organized filing, always pays later dividends, and it is wise to invest time early in your reading in developing an organized filing system. Once a sufficient overview of the relevant literature is achieved, summarizing needs to lead to the integration and synthesizing of literature. Burton and Steane (2004: 131) use the useful metaphor of tapestry to illustrate the idea of synthesizing literature, stressing the weaving together and integration of threads contained in previous writing on the topic. Synthesizing involves the covergence and divergence of findings, theories and implications, and Burton and Steane (2004: 131–2) further suggest the dialectical process of thesis–antithesis–synthesis as a framework for developing synthesis in a literature review.

Developing an organizing framework for dealing with the literature, as it is located and read, is part of reading critically and analytically, and the organizing framework you develop will often help with your own study's conceptual framework. It will also help to make your ultimate literature review both thematic (rather than merely a serialized or chronological summary of what others have done) and integrated with your study. Your study needs to be connected to its literature, so that there is some point to the literature review. It is best to avoid unintegrated chronological summaries; a literature review is not the same as an annotated bibliography.

A completed literature review needs a structure; the alternative to a structured review is an amorphous mass of unstructured writing, which makes it difficult for the reader to navigate and comprehend. Integration and synthesis of the literature will normally suggest a structure for writing the review. Thus sections and subsections within the review are useful, but should not be overdone. Also useful, and strongly recommended, is a short 'advance organizer' for the reader. Here the writer briefly describes the structure of the literature review to come, providing the reader with a 'road map' for navigating the material. Similarly important is how the literature review is finished off. Sound advice here is to lead back to the purpose and research questions of the study, showing at the same time how the present research relates to the literature just reviewed.

Good literature reviews are extremely valuable, tying a field together and showing us the state of knowledge in an area, its trends and its gaps. They show us 'where things are up to' in that area, what we already know and, just as important, what is contested and what we don't know. They are also difficult and time consuming to do. Therefore, if you find a good literature review, my advice is to use it, of course with appropriate acknowledgements.[7] In some research areas, the literature review will need to be selective. For some topics, the volume of related literature is so great that a dissertation literature review cannot be comprehensive, covering everything. In these cases, the researcher is forced to be selective. When that occurs, the writer should indicate the basis on which the selection is made, and why it is being done. Here is where previous reviews of the literature, if available and relatively contemporary, can be extremely valuable. It is worth remembering that completed dissertations normally contain a literature review. Finding a recent dissertation on (or close to) your topic can save you a lot of time and work.

Finally, there are some things to avoid in compiling a literature review. Box 4.2 shows four common problems.

BOX 4.2   IN REVIEWING LITERATURE, BE CAREFUL <u>NOT</u> TO:

- *Quote in excess.* Judgement, experience and the reactions of supervisor(s) about the amount of quoting are useful, but too many direct quotes, or direct quotes that are too long, raise doubts about your mastery of the literature. Rudestam and Newton have good advice. 'Restrict the use of quotations to those with particular impact or those that are stated in a unique way that is difficult to recapture' (2001: 59).
- *Rely too much on secondary sources.* At this level of work, you are expected, where possible, to study primary sources. Secondary sources are acceptable where the primary source is not available or accessible, or where the secondary source adds significantly to the discussion. Again, however, over-reliance on secondary sources raises doubts about your mastery of the literature for your topic.
- *Neglect practitioner-oriented literature.* While the research literature on your topic is obviously important, there is often practitioner-oriented literature which is relevant and useful. This applies particularly to fields such as business and management research where trade journals are important.
- *Give in to the temptation to include and report everything you know or have read.* Your review needs to be selective, on an appropriate basis. As Rudestam and Newton put it, 'build an argument, not a library' (2002: 59).

4.6 Review concepts and questions

Concepts
paradigm metatheory perspective substantive theory descriptive study explanatory study theory verification theory generation hypotheses – relationship to theory prestructured study unfolding study relevant literature literature review

Questions
Perspective • Is there a particular perspective (or paradigm, or metatheory) behind the research? *(Substantive) theory* • What is the role of theory in my study? • Does the description–explanation distinction apply? Is my study descriptive, explanatory or both? What is the logic behind my position? • Does the distinction between theory verification and theory generation apply? If my purpose is explanatory, is the focus on generalization or verification of theory? What is the logic behind my position? • If my focus is theory verification, what are the hypotheses and what is the theory behind them? *Prestructured versus unfolding* • To what extent is my study prestructured or unfolding? Does this apply differentially to different parts of my study?

Relevant literature

- What literature is relevant to my study?
- What is the relationship of my study to this literature?
- How will my study deal with the literature, and how does my proposal use the literature?

5
Methods

5.1 Introduction

For ease of presentation of the material in this chapter, I will assume at this point in the research planning process that we now have a stable set of specific research questions, connected with each other, integrated with general research questions and forming a coherent whole, and satisfying the empirical criterion. The proposal can now deal with the methods for the research. In other words, since we now know what data will be needed, we can focus on how to get the data, and on what to do with the data once collected.

This chapter does not cover research methods in detail. Rather, I deal now in general terms with the three main issues any piece of research must deal with, once it has settled on its research questions: *design*, *data collection* and *data* analysis. Since *sampling* is implicated in all three of these issues, but especially in design and data collection, I will discuss sampling in general terms also. The guiding question throughout this chapter is: *What needs to be said about each of these matters in the proposal?* Each section in the chapter therefore makes suggestions in answer to this question.

Before looking at these topics in the light of this question, I look again at the overriding question of quantitative data, qualitative data or both, and I end the chapter by looking at the general question of methodological expertise.

5.2 **Quantitative data, qualitative data or both?**

Obviously, this is a fundamental issue of design and method, and a major organizing principle for the methods section of the proposal. Sometimes the logic of a study, including the way research questions (or hypotheses) are framed, is clearly quantitative or clearly qualitative, and that logic flows through naturally into the design, sampling, data collection and data analysis.

As a quantitative example, perhaps the conceptualization of the problem and questions in the proposal is in terms of an experimental comparison, based on some intervention or treatment, with clear outcome variables in mind. This clearly involves quantitative methods and data. As a qualitative example, perhaps the research has been conceptualized as an ethnographic case study, focusing on interpretations, meanings and the cultural significance of some behaviour. Equally clearly, this involves qualitative data. Or, as a mixed-method example, perhaps a quantitative survey is to be followed by qualitative interviewing.

Quite often, however, the student researcher can get to the point of having research questions, and of now having to confront methodological issues, without clear implications from what has gone before about whether the data should be quantitative or qualitative. In other words, the research could be done either way. Hence the question arises: quantitative data (and methods), qualitative data (and methods), or both? Six suggestions for dealing with this choice are:

- Re-examine the research questions and the way they are phrased: what implications for data are there?
- Are we interested in making standardized comparisons, sketching contours and dimensions, quantifying relationships between variables and accounting for variance? These imply quantitative methods and data. Or are we more interested in studying a phenomenon or situation in detail, holistically and in context, focusing on interpretations and/or processes? These imply qualitative methods and data.
- What guidance do we find from the literature about this topic on this methodological question?
- What are the practical consequences of each alternative (including access to data and the need for resources)?
- Which way would we learn more?
- Which sort of research is more 'my style'?

Very often, the question (quantitative or qualitative?) focuses entirely on the data themselves, in which case it really becomes: to measure or not to measure? This is because measurement is the process of turning data into numbers, and is therefore the operation which differentiates quantitative data from qualitative data.

Often, too, this matter is the subject of some misconceptions, where students feel they must (or must not) develop or use measuring instruments. I strongly prefer a common-sense answer to the question 'To measure or not to measure?', based on an understanding of what measurement is, and of how it can help us in answering research questions and in building knowledge. When looked at this way, I think there are many 'ambiguous'[1] empirical research situations where measurement helps.

Dealing with this commonly occurring and often perplexing question ('Quantitative or qualitative data?', or, 'To measure or not to measure?') is often made easier by remembering these four practical points:

1   Get the research questions clear.
2   As far as possible, let questions dictate the nature of the data.
3   Measure if it is feasible and helpful to do so.[2]
4   Use both types of data, if appropriate.

Thus any proposal needs to be very clear on the extent to which the research will:

* use quantitative methods and data;
* use qualitative methods and data;
* combine the two types of methods and data.

If it combines the two approaches, it should be clear on which research questions involve quantitative methods and data, which involve qualitative methods and data, and which involve both. It should also be clear on the sort of combination that will be involved, given the various different models as to how this can be done (Tashakkori and Teddlie, 2002). It is very important that a mixed-method study has a clear logic underpinning the way the two types of data will be used.

On this question ('Quantitative, qualitative or both?'), perhaps more than any other issue, the proposal should demonstrate internal validity. Here, this means that its methods should match its questions, and the argument and logic of the proposal should be clear and internally consistent. In line with the passing of the 'paradigm wars' and of the associated quantitative–qualitative debate, there is an increasing tendency in a number of social science areas to combine the two approaches, bringing the two types of methods and data together (Thomas, 2003).

5.3 Design

I focus here on a view of the term 'research design' general enough to accommodate both quantitative and qualitative approaches. This general idea of design is one of situating the researcher in the empirical world. On a practical level, it means connecting the research questions to data. Design sits between the research questions and the data, showing how the research questions will be connected to the data, and what tools and procedures to use in answering them. Therefore it needs to follow from the questions, and to fit in with the data.

The design is the basic plan for a piece of empirical research, and includes five main ideas: strategy, conceptual framework, who or what will be studied, and the tools and procedures to be used both for collecting and for analysing empirical materials. Thus there are five main questions for research design:

- What strategy will be followed?
- Within what framework?
- From whom will the data be collected?
- How will the data be collected?
- How will the data be analysed?

These questions overlap, especially the first two, and they are brought together in Chapter 6. Also the second question, in particular, is more typical of quantitative designs, although it does apply in some qualitative research. We will now look briefly at each of the five questions.

5.3.1 Strategy

What strategy will be followed? At the centre of the design of a study is its internal logic or rationale – the reasoning, or the set of ideas, by which the study intends to proceed in order to answer its research questions. The term 'strategy' refers to that. Thus, in quantitative research, the experiment represents a strategy, designed to achieve certain comparisons. So does the correlational survey, though it is conceptualized and designed differently. Similarly, in qualitative research, a multiple case study involves a strategy for setting up certain comparisons. Ethnography and grounded theory are strategies the qualitative researcher might use, and ethnomethodology, discourse analysis and life history are others. Answers to the question 'What strategy will be followed?' will thus differ according to whether the approach is quantitative or qualitative. Associated with this question of strategy is another important question: to what extent will the researcher manipulate or organize the research situation, as against studying it naturalistically? In other words, to what extent will the researcher intervene in the research situation, contriving it and constructing it for research purposes, as against studying it as it occurs naturally? Quantitative research design can vary from extremely interventionist to non-interventionist. Qualitative research design is generally non-interventionist.

Therefore, what needs to be said about the strategy in a proposal depends on whether a quantitative or qualitative study is proposed.

- If the study is quantitative, which quantitative strategy is proposed?
- If qualitative, which qualitative strategy is proposed?
- If there is a combination of quantitative and qualitative approaches, what is the proposed mixture of strategies?

Some of the most commonly used strategies are the experiment, the quasi-experiment and the correlational survey for quantitative research, and case studies, ethnography and grounded theory for qualitative research. Appendix 1 gives more complete lists of quantitative and qualitative research strategies.

Whether the strategy is quantitative or qualitative, the researcher needs to describe it procedurally as well as generically. 'Generically' means identifying the strategy in general terms – for example, case study, ethnography, survey or quasi-experiment. That description is necessary, but only part of what is required. 'Procedurally' means saying how the researcher will execute the general strategy. To quote from Dreher:

> In general, terms such as *ethnography, participant observation, grounded theory, and fieldwork* are not useful to a reviewer unless they are described procedurally, in relation to the specific proposal. For example, participant observation is perhaps the most pervasive technique used in ethnographic designs, yet we know that the investigator cannot participate and observe everywhere at the same time. Methodological choices must be made about where and when observations take place. Although some of these decisions necessarily are made in the actual process of the research, from the emerging data, the investigator should be able to provide reviewers with a general outline of observations that is consistent with the problem being researched. (1994: 289)

The point being made here in a qualitative context applies just as well to quantitative research strategies and designs.

5.3.2 Framework

Within what framework? Framework here means conceptual framework – the conceptual status of the things being studied, and their relationship to each other. Prespecified research questions are often accompanied by a clear conceptual framework, and developing and describing that framework can help in clarifying the research questions. The structure continuum (Figure 4.1) applies to the conceptual framework as well; it may be developed ahead of the study, or it may emerge as the study progresses. Quantitative designs typically have well developed prespecified frameworks, whereas qualitative designs show much more variability, from clear prespecified frameworks, to 'first approximations', to no prespecified framework at all.

For the proposal, therefore:

- If your study has a predetermined conceptual framework, the proposal should show it; this can often be done effectively using a diagram.
- If this conceptual framework is seen as only an initial version or approximation, for modification as the study progresses, this should be noted in the proposal.
- If you have an unfolding study, where a conceptual framework will be developed during the research, this too should be noted and explained.

5.3.3 Sample

From whom will the data be collected? This question concerns sampling for the research. In this form, the question is biased towards quantitative studies. The more general question 'Who or what will be studied?' (Denzin and Lincoln, 1994) covers both quantitative and qualitative approaches.

All empirical research involves sampling: in the words of Miles and Huberman, 'You cannot study everyone everywhere doing everything' (1994: 27). The researcher thus needs to think through the sampling aspects of the study in preparing the proposal.

It is best if the sampling plan is seen as part of the internal logic of the study, rather than as an afterthought to be considered when data collection is close. This means it needs to fit into the study's logic, to follow from it and to be consistent with it. This is an overriding general principle about sampling, whatever type of research is involved. After that, it is difficult to suggest detailed rules about sampling, since the appropriate sampling plan for a study depends very much on what the study is trying to find out, and on its strategy for doing that.

Thus, for quantitative research, the sampling may be probabilistic (if representativeness is important) or purposive (if, for example, the point of the research is to study a relationship between variables). For qualitative research, many different sampling strategies are used. Table 5.1 shows some of the possibilities.

For the proposal, therefore, the researcher needs to see sampling as part of the planning process for the research, to select among sampling possibilities in line with the logic of the study, and to indicate the sampling plan in the proposal.

If the study is quantitative, the proposal should describe:

- the sampling strategy, especially whether it is purposive, representative or both, and what claims will be made for the generalizability of findings;
- how big the sample will be;
- how it will be selected.

This description of the sampling plan should include justification of the sample size, since there are established methods for determining appropriate sample size in quantitative research. This is a technical matter, which essentially involves balancing cost and access against the level of precision required in relation to the variability of the population on the characteristics being measured. Also, the power of the statistical test to be used needs to be considered (Lipsey, 1990 ; Moser and Kalton, 1979) and many computer packages now include this (Schofield, 1996).

If the study is qualitative, the proposal should similarly describe:

Table 5.1   *Sampling strategies in qualitative inquiry*

Type of sampling	Purpose
Maximum variation	Documents diverse variations and identifies important common patterns
Homogeneous	Focuses, reduces, simplifies, facilitates group interviewing
Critical case	Permits logical generalization and maximum application of information to other cases
Theory based	Finds examples of a theoretical construct and thereby elaborates and examines it
Confirming and disconfirming cases	Elaborates initial analysis, seeks exceptions, looks for variation
Snowball or chain	Identifies cases of interest from people who know people who know what cases are information-rich
Extreme or deviant case	Learns from highly unusual manifestations of the phenomenon of interest
Typical case	Highlights what is normal or average
Intensity	Examines information-rich cases that manifest the phenomenon intensely, but not extremely
Politically important cases	Attracts desired attention or avoids attracting undesired attention
Random purposeful	Adds credibility to sample when potential purposeful sample is too large
Stratified purposeful	Illustrates subgroups, facilitates comparisons
Criterion	Considers all cases that meet some criterion, useful for quality assurance
Opportunistic	Follows new leads, takes advantage of the unexpected
Combination or mixed	Features triangulation, flexibility, meets multiple interests and needs
Convenience	Saves time, money and effort, but at the expense of information and credibility

Source: Miles and Huberman (1994: 28)

- the sampling strategy, including what intention (if any) there is for the generalizability of findings;
- the extent of the proposed sample;
- how sample units will be chosen.

Qualitative sample sizes tend to be small, with no statistical grounds for guidance. The sample size here is usually a function of the purpose of the study in the light of its sampling frames and of practical constraints. For some qualitative strategies too, there is no predetermined sample size. An example is grounded theory, where theoretical sampling – successive sampling of data guided by the theroretical trends emerging from the analysis – guides the work.

Such a strategy should be indicated.[3] If a case study is involved, the basis of case selection should be made clear, as should the basis of within-case sampling. If sampling of documentary or other qualitative material is proposed, its basis needs to be shown.

5.3.4 Data collection: instruments, procedures

How will the data be collected? This question asks about the instruments and procedures to be used in data collection. Once again, we need to differentiate this section according to whether the data are quantitative or qualitative. We get quantitative data from counting, scaling or both. Qualitative data are most likely to be words, which we get by asking (interviewing), watching (observation) or reading (documents), or some combination of these three activities.[4]

Instruments: quantitative data

Quantitative data collection instruments are questionnaires, standardized measuring instruments, *ad hoc* rating scales or observation schedules. Whichever of these is involved, this question often arises in planning research: will I use an existing measuring instrument, or will I develop instruments (in whole or in part) specifically for this study? Either choice, or some combination of the two, can be acceptable, depending on the particular study. Each alternative has implications for what is included in the proposal. Thus:

- If the decision is to use existing data collection instruments, a brief description of their history, their use in research and their psychometric characteristics should be included.
- If the decision is to construct an instrument(s) specifically for this study, an outline of the steps involved in doing that should be given, showing what pretesting is involved.[5]

Instruments: qualitative data

The question of instruments for qualitative data collection is both more contentious, and more difficult to summarize. There is a range of possibilities here. At one end of the range, the idea of an 'instrument' to collect qualitative data, with its connotations of standardization and quantification, is quite inappropriate. Instead, in this sort of research, the researcher is seen as the primary instrument for data collection and analysis. Qualitative data are mediated through this human instrument, rather than through other instruments (Creswell, 1994: 145).[6]

At the other end of the range, qualitative data collection instruments may begin to resemble quantitative ones. Examples would be the questionnaire for a qualitative survey, where open-ended questions are involved, or the schedule for qualitative interviews, where standardization across respondents is involved. Here, the same question arises as above, namely: do I use instruments already developed, or will I develop my own for this research? It is more likely that the qualitative researcher will develop instruments than use those developed by others. But either way, similar considerations apply to the proposal. If others' instruments are to be used, their background and previous use should be sketched. If instruments are to be developed for this study, it is appropriate to indicate the steps to be followed in developing them.

Additional possibilities for data in qualitative studies include documents, diaries and journals, other written materials, and non-written qualitative data such as audiovisual materials or artefacts.

Thus, for the proposal:

- A general plan for the qualitative fieldwork should be shown. If the researcher is the 'instrument' for data collection, it is appropriate for the proposal to indicate this.
- If interviews are involved, what type of interviews and especially what degree of structure and standardization are proposed? If standardized interview schedules are to be used, how will they be developed and pretested?
- Similarly, if qualitative questionnaires are proposed, what will be the degree of structure and standardization? How would they be developed and (if appropriate) pretested?
- The same considerations apply for observational data: what degree of structure and standardization is proposed, and how would proposed schedules be developed and pretested?
- If documents are to be used, which ones and why? Are there sampling or access considerations?
- If diaries, journals, critical incident reports or other qualitative materials are involved, how would the collection of these, including any sampling aspects, be organized? For diaries, journals and critical incident reports, what directions would be given to participants?

Procedures

Procedures refers to the actual process of data collection, over and above any instruments proposed. If instruments are involved, the question here is how the instruments will be used or administered. In other words, what will be the actual data collection procedures? If fieldwork is involved, how would it be carried out?

Some examples can indicate the sorts of issues involved:

- If tests or rating scales are to be used, how will they be administered (face-to-face? one-to-one or group administration? by mail? by telephone? by the internet?)?
- If interviews are involved, where will the interviews be conducted (at the office? at home? somewhere else?)? When will they be done (working

hours? outside working hours?)? How will the recording be done (by taking notes? by reconstruction after the interview? by tape recorder?)?
- If observation is involved, will it be overt or covert? How will you do it? How will observational data be recorded?

While the proposal may not answer all procedural questions, it should none-theless indicate an awareness of the procedural and methodological choices ahead in the research.

5.3.5 Data analysis

How will the data be analysed? After design and data collection, the other main methodological question concerns what will be done with the data once they have been collected. What methods of analysis will be used?

Quantitative data analysis involves statistics with well established and well documented techniques. Qualitative data analysis has been a rapidly developing field in the past 20 or so years, and there are now many different data analysis varieties and possibilities for research.

For the proposal, you should indicate, at least in general terms, what analytic techniques you propose to use in order to analyse the data you will collect. The proposal should also indicate what computer programs (if any) will be used in the analysis, whatever the type of data. In my experience, data analysis is an area where students will often need to seek expert advice, because of the issue of methodological expertise.

5.4 The question of methodological expertise

A recurrent question now arises, for both quantitative and qualitative approaches: how much methodological expertise should the student researcher be expected to show, at the proposal stage? By 'methodological expertise', I mean expertise in the methods or techniques proposed. This question is prob-ably most acute and most visible at the data analysis stage, but it can involve other areas as well (for example, sampling, measurement, interviewing skills). Here are two examples of it:

- A quantitative survey is proposed, focusing on the relationships between different variables (this is the correlational survey). The researcher, quite appropriately, proposes to use multiple regression analysis as the main data analysis approach and technique. To what extent should we expect that the researcher should know the technical aspects of regression analysis at the proposal stage?
- A qualitative study is proposed, with the objective of generating a substan-tive theory of the phenomenon being studied. The researcher, again quite

appropriately, proposes to use grounded theory as the main data analysis approach and technique. To what extent should we expect the researcher to know the technical aspects of grounded theory analysis at the proposal stage?

Here again, different universities and departments may have differing views on this matter. It is wise, therefore, to check relevant expectations with the department where you work. My view on this now is different from the view I held (say) 20 years ago. Today (in contrast to then), I would not require the candidate to demonstrate methodological mastery of a technique at the proposal stage. If it can be demonstrated, well and good, but I believe it is unrealistic today to require it. However, as a minimum, I think it is reasonable at the proposal stage to require the candidate to:

- have thought about what is required for the data analysis stage of the work;
- have developed – perhaps with expert assistance – at least a general idea of what technique(s) would be required and how they would be applied;
- be able to show how that fits in with the overall logic of the study.

In other words, I think it is sufficient for the candidate's knowledge to be at a logical rather than a technical level *at the proposal stage*. I think that translates into a statement such as: 'I can see that I will need such-and-such a technique (for example, multiple regression analysis, or grounded theory) to analyse my data, because it will answer my research questions by showing how these independent variables relate to the dependent variables (regression analysis) or by enabling me to identify abstract grounded core concepts around which a theory can be built (grounded theory).' Such a statement can be made by a student who has not yet developed technical mastery of the data analysis method, but has a logical understanding of how it operates and where it can be used. Developing this logical level of understanding is important, and a significant part of the learning which should occur through proposal preparation.

In short, I think it is acceptable for the student not to have developed technical mastery at the proposal stage, ahead of the research. My reasoning is that the student will develop that mastery on the way through the research, and should be able to demonstrate it after completing the research. But having said that, it is surely all to the good, and to be encouraged, if the student can develop technical mastery ahead of the research.

5.5 Ethical issues

There is a much increased and still growing concern for ethical issues in social research today, stimulated by the growth in the use of qualitative methods. All research has ethical dimensions, and a good starting point for dealing with the ethical issues in the proposal is to realize that there are numerous stakeholders in your research. In addition to yourself, these include your supervisor(s), your university, your participants, and your examiners and other readers. Your goal should be to complete your dissertation with you and your university in good standing with your participants, and with your findings contributing to the advancement of knowledge or of professional practice (Burton and Steane, 2004: 59).

A researcher's ethical responsibilities include the overarching principles of academic integrity and honesty, and respect for other people. In developing a proposal they also include thinking through the ethical issues involved in your particular project, knowing and complying with your university's require-ments regarding ethical issues, and writing your proposal (and, ultimately, your dissertation) with ethical issues in mind.

Ethical issues in planning and executing the research centre on access,[7] consent and participants' protection. Since researchers cannot demand access to people, situations or data for research purposes, assistance and permission are necessarily involved. Thus, if the overall integrity, quality and worthiness of the research are conveyed by the proposal itself, the main ethical issues to be considered, and the questions central to them, are:

- *Informed consent.* Do the people I wish to study have full information about the research, including why and how they have been chosen to participate? Is their consent freely given? What about if children are involved? Rudestam and Newton (2002: 266–73) list 11 elements of informed consent, and Steane (2004: 64) points out that informed consent is not always a straightforward issue, especially in qualitative research.
- *Confidentiality and anonymity.* How will the information be safeguarded and the identity of people or institutions be protected? How will anonymity be preserved, for people and institutions? Much of the discussion in the research ethics literature concerns personal confidentiality, but Le Voi (2002: 155) points out that commercial confidentiality may also be involved, as when research is carried out with the cooperation or sponsorship of com-mercial organizations. The same point applies to professional organizations.
- *Ownership of data and conclusion.* After collection and analysis, who owns the data and the conclusions? How will the research results be reported and disseminated?
- *Use and misuse of results.* What obligations do I have to help my findings be used appropriately, and not to be misused (Miles and Huberman, 1994: 290–7)?
- *Honesty and trust.* What is my relationship with the people I am studying?
- *Reciprocity.* What do participants gain from my research?

- *Intervention and advocacy.* What do I do if I see harmful, illegal, wrongful behaviour during my research?
- *Harm and risk.* What might this research do to hurt the people involved? Health and safety issues can be involved in some types of research, and in all cases, the principle of non-maleficence (no harm) takes precedence.
- *Conflict of interest.* Steane (2004: 66) points out that questions of power and reliance, along with benefit and trust, are involved in some research situations, and need to be handled with care.

Ethical issues are also involved in academic writing, and acknowledging the work of others is part of academic honesty and integrity. In particular plagiarism, defined as 'fraudulently presenting ideas as your own when they are not' (Le Voi, 2002: 155), is to be avoided. In addition to avoiding plagiarism, the academic writer should also strive for bias-free writing, with no discrimination or oppression towards any group of people implied in the language or materials used. Rudestam and Newton (2002: 276–8) have several useful tips for avoiding bias in writing.

In most situations today, the submission of a research proposal requires a completed ethics checklist, which may have a separate format. It is especially important, therefore, that you check practices, guidelines and requirements on this matter in your department and university.

5.6 Review concepts and questions

Concepts
quantitative data (and methods)
qualitative data (and methods)
internal validity
design
strategy
conceptual framework
sample, sampling plan
data collection instruments
data collection procedures
data analysis
access
ethical issues
quality of data

Questions

- Will my study use quantitative methods and data, qualitative methods and data, or both?
- What strategy(ies) will my study use?

  - If the study is quantitative, which quantitative strategy is proposed?
  - If qualitative, which qualitative strategy is proposed?
  - If there is a combination of quantitative and qualitative approaches, what is the proposed mixture of strategies?

- Does my study have a conceptual framework?

  - Can this be shown in a diagram?
  - Is this an initial version, for modification as the study progresses?
  - Will my study develop a conceptual framework?

- Who or what will be studied?
- From whom will data be collected? Whether quantitative or qualitative:

  - What is the sample plan?
  - How big will the sample be (and why)?
  - How will sample units be selected?

- How will I collect the data?

  - If existing instruments are to be used, what is known about them?
  - If data collection instruments are to be developed, what steps will be followed?
  - If qualitative fieldwork is involved, what is the data collection plan?
  - What data collection procedures will be used?

- How will these procedures ensure that data of the best quality will be obtained?
- How will I analyse my data?

  - What computer packages are involved?

- How will I obtain consent and access to the people, situations and/or information required for the research?
- What ethical issues are involved in the proposed data collection procedures and how will they be handled?
- What other ethical issues are involved in my research and how will they be handled?

6
Writing the Proposal

6.1 Introduction

What should the research proposal as a finished product look like? What content should it include? What structure and sections might it have? This chapter deals first with these questions, bringing together what has been said in previous chapters, especially Chapter 5. It then comments on qualitative proposals, and discusses academic writing.

In the literature, there are several descriptions of proposals, with suggestions and recommendations for proposal sections and headings. Sometimes these are written for social science research in general: examples are Madsen (1983), Behling (1984), Mauch and Birch (1989) and Peters (1997). Sometimes they are written for specific areas: examples here are Tornquist (1993) and Brink and Wood (1994) for nursing research, Borg and Gall (1989) and Krathwohl (1998) for educational research, Coley and Scheinberg (1990) for research in human services and the helping professions, Gitlin and Lyons (1996) for health research and human service professionals, Parsigian (1996) for media projects and Hamper and Baugh (1996) for business research.

In addition, there is literature on 'grantsmanship' (research proposals for grant applications: see, for example, Gilpatrick, 1989; Lauffer, 1983; 1984), and literature on proposal preparation and development from within particular research approaches. Thus Marshall and Rossman (1989) and Maxwell (1996) write on proposals for qualitative research, while Locke et al. (1993) write mainly about proposals for quantitative research.

By contrast, the description of the research proposal given in this chapter aims to be general enough to suit different social science areas, and to cover quantitative, qualitative and mixed-method approaches to research. It is written primarily with the dissertation student in mind, but I believe it has application also to the non-university context.

Before the proposal's sections and structure are discussed, it is worth noting again four points from previous chapters:

1 Keep the framework of three overarching questions discussed in Chapter 3 in mind, since this will be what most of your readers are expecting your proposal to deal with. These are:

   (a) *What* is this research trying to find out; what questions is it trying to answer?
   (b) *How* will the proposed research answer these questions?
   (c) *Why* is this research worth doing?

2 Review again the five issues raised in Chapters 4 and 5. As noted there, they are not necessarily all applicable in any one project, but they are useful things to think about in planning the research and preparing the proposal. They are:

   (a) the perspective behind the research;
   (b) the role of theory;
   (c) prestructured versus unfolding research;
   (d) the relevant literature;
   (e) whether the study is to be quantitative, qualitative or both.

   When they do apply, how they are dealt with in the proposal is a matter of judgement for the writer: for example, whether they need separate sections, or can be interwoven throughout other sections.

3 Quoting Maxwell, remember that the form and structure of the proposal are tied to its purpose: 'to explain and justify your proposed study to an audience of nonexperts on your topic' (1996: 100–1).

4 The proposal itself needs to be presented as an argument. Seeing it as an argument means showing its line of reasoning, its internal consistency and the interrelatedness of its different parts. It means making sure that the different parts fit together, and showing how the research will be a piece of disciplined inquiry. As an argument, the proposal should show the logic

Table 6.1   *Checklist of headings for research proposals*

Title and title page
Abstract
Introduction: area, topic and statement of purpose
Research questions:
   General
   Specific
Conceptual framework, theory, hypotheses
The literature
Methods:
   Design: strategy and framework
   Sample
   Data collection: instruments and procedures
   Data analysis
Significance
Limitations and delimitations
Ethical issues: consent, access and participants' protection
References
Appendices

Notes

1   In some types of research, the research questions would come after the literature section.
2   In some situations, sections on costs (budget), risk management and timetable are required.
3   A table of contents coming immediately after the title page is helpful to readers.

behind the proposed study, rather than simply describing the study. In so doing, it should answer the question of why this approach, method and design have been chosen for this study.[1]

6.2 Proposal headings

To make the proposal clear and easy for the reader to follow, it will need an organizing framework or structure. This section gives a suggested set of headings for writing and presenting the research proposal. A checklist is given in Table 6.1.

A problem in suggesting a general set of headings for proposals is the variation in headings, format and length of required documents across different areas of university research. There appear to be two extremes in university practice. Some universities (and some degrees) have institution-wide requirements, where the proposal covers the same headings in all disciplines. Other universities (and degrees) have department- or area-specific requirements and headings.

Institution-wide formats are usually, and necessarily, more general. For example, they often use the broad heading 'aims' (or 'objectives'), rather than the more specific 'research questions' focus emphasized here. Again, the broad heading 'research plan' might be used, rather than the more specific term 'research methods'. Where these broader terms apply, the headings shown in Table 6.1 can easily be clustered accordingly.

The focus in this book on empirical research in social science means that a common set of proposal headings should be broadly useful across areas. At the same time, there needs to be room for variability in proposal format, to reflect the variability in research approaches, while accommodating the general expectations a reader will have when reading the proposal. These headings address those expectations, but it follows that they are not necessarily the only sections or headings, nor is their suggested order the only one that could be used. Therefore, this description is not meant to be prescriptive, and the researcher should feel at liberty to vary this material as appropriate. But that should be done against the background of readers' expectations (see Chapter 2), and any guidelines from your department and/or university. Even if these particular headings are not used, the content they point to should be contained in the proposal, in some clear, easy-to-follow format.[2]

Some of these sections apply to both quantitative and qualitative research, whereas some are more directly applicable to one approach than the other. The writer's judgement is needed to decide which sections are appropriate, in which order, and which might be omitted or combined. But, as with the issues discussed in Chapter 4, the full list is useful to think about in proposal preparation, and is also useful for developing full versions of the proposal; where shorter versions are required, a good strategy is to prepare the full version, then summarize it. Also, the full version of the proposal, outlined here, will be useful when it comes to writing the dissertation itself.

It is easier in many respects to suggest proposal guidelines for a quantitative study, since there is greater variety in qualitative studies, and many qualitative studies will be unfolding rather than prestructured. An unfolding study cannot be as specific in the proposal about its research questions, or about details of the design. When this is the case, the point needs to be made in the proposal. Unfolding qualitative proposals are discussed again in Section 6.3.

Some proposals require the definition of terms. This occurs when terms are used which may not be understood by people outside the field of study, or when specialized technical terms are used, or when there is a need to define one or more terms clearly so that misunderstanding does not occur (Creswell, 1994: 106). Quantitative research in particular has a clear tradition of defining its variables, first conceptually and then operationally. Whether or not a separate section is required for any definition of terms is again a matter of judgement; it can often easily be incorporated into other sections. But the conceptual and operational definition of variables in quantitative research is often best done in a separate section, perhaps under methods.

In the two sections following, I make some comments about abstracts and introductions. In the other main sections (research questions, conceptual framework, literature, methods), I bring together the points made in earlier chapters.

6.2.1 Abstract and title

An abstract is a brief summary, whether of a proposal or of a finished study. It is *not* the introduction to a proposal or study, but rather a summary of it. It functions like the executive summary in the business context, giving readers a brief overview of all essential elements of the proposal.

Abstracts play an important role in the research literature, and they are required in proposals (usually), in dissertations and in research articles in most refereed journals. Abstract writing is the skill of saying as much as possible in as few words as possible. For a proposal, the abstract needs to deal with two main issues: what the study is about and aims to achieve (usually stated in terms of its research questions), and how it intends to do that.[3] The abstract should give an overview not just of the study itself, but also of the argument behind the study.

For most of us, abstract writing is a skill which needs to be developed, since we typically use many superfluous words when we speak and write. Together with the title, the abstract is written last, since it is difficult to summarize what has not yet been written.

Examples of abstracts of proposals are difficult to find, since they are not collected and published. On the other hand, examples of abstracts of completed studies can be found in several places: in completed dissertations, at the start of articles in many top class research journals, and in compilations of research such as *Dissertation Abstracts International*, and the various collections of abstracts in different social science areas.

Titles also have importance in the research literature indexing process. Therefore a title should not just be an afterthought, nor should it use words or phrases which obscure rather than reveal meaning. Extending the point about abstract writing, the title should convey as much information as possible in as few words as possible.

6.2.2 Introduction: area, topic and statement of purpose

There are many ways a topic can be introduced, and all topics have a background and a context. These should be noted in the introduction, which sets the stage for the research. A strong introduction is important to a convincing proposal. It is the lead-in, to help the reader follow the logic of the proposal. Its purpose is not to review the literature, but rather to show generally how the proposed study fits into what is already known, and to locate it in relation to present knowledge and practice. Creswell (1994: 41) suggests four key components for introductions: (1) establishing the problem leading to the study, (2) casting the problem within the larger scholarly literature, (3) discussing deficiencies in the literature about the problem, and (4) targeting an audience and noting the significance of this problem for the audience.

In addition, I think the introduction should also contain a clear identification of the research area and topic, and a general statement of the purpose of the research.[4] These can lead later into general and specific research questions. Particular features of the proposed study, and important aspects of its context, can also be identified here, as appropriate: for example, if personal knowledge or experience form an important part of the context, or if preliminary or pilot studies have been done, or if the study will involve secondary analysis of existing data (Maxwell, 1996).

Especially for qualitative proposals, two other points might apply here. One is the first general issue raised in Chapter 4: is there a particular perspective behind this research? This would need to be noted here, to inform the reader early in the proposal. The other is the third issue raised in Chapter 4: where on the structure continuum is the proposed study? This strongly influences later sections of the proposal. If a prestructured qualitative study is planned, the proposal can proceed along similar lines to the quantitative proposal. If an unfolding study is planned, where focus and structure will develop as the study proceeds, this point should be made clearly, again to inform the reader. In the former case, there will be general and specific research questions. In the latter case, there will be more general orienting research questions.

The introduction should be strong and engaging. Various logical structures are possible, but a progression from more general to more specific issues, culminating in stating the topic and research questions for this study, often works well. Whatever structure you choose, make sure your introduction actually does introduce your topic, and sets the stage for what follows. In my experience, it is a mistake for the introduction to go on too long, especially about the background to the research, and it is a good idea to get to the point of your research, stated as purpose in the introduction and leading on to research questions, as soon as is possible.

An excellent illustration of an introduction, with edited comments, is given by Creswell (1994: 45–8). Four others, also edited, are given in Locke et al. (1993: 185–296), and others in Gilpatrick (1989: 57–60).

6.2.3 Research questions: general and specific

The nature and central role of research questions were discussed in Chapter 3. In the proposal outline suggested here, they can follow from the statement of purpose given in the introduction. If your research questions fit into the general-to-specific framework described in Chapter 3, presenting them in the proposal in this section should be quite straightforward. Remembering the empirical criterion for research questions in Section 3.6, it should be clear what data are required to answer each specific research question.

The point about this section is to tell the reader what questions the research is trying to answer, or what questions will initiate the inquiry in an unfolding study. This section is often what proposal readers turn to and concentrate on first, in order to get as clear a picture as possible of the purpose of the research. This reinforces the comments in Chapter 3 about the central role of research questions. It also implies that an emerging, unfolding type of study needs to indicate here what general questions will initiate the research, and how they might be refocused and refined as the study progresses.

6.2.4 Conceptual framework, theory and hypotheses

There is wide variation in the applicability of this section, given the range of studies possible across the quantitative and qualitative approaches. If a conceptual framework is involved, it is a matter of judgement whether it goes here, or in the methods section later in the proposal. Theory and hypotheses are included if appropriate, as explained in Chapter 3. If theory is involved, it may be included in the literature review section, rather than here.

Thus, as noted in Chapter 4:

- If your study has a predetermined conceptual framework, the proposal should show it; this can often be done effectively using a diagram.
- If this conceptual framework is seen as only an initial version or approximation, for modification as the study progresses, this should be noted when the framework is presented.
- If you have an unfolding study, where a conceptual framework will be developed during the research, this too should be noted and explained.
- The role of theory in the proposed study should be made clear. In particular, is it theory verification or theory generation? If a theory verification study is proposed, hypotheses and the theory behind them should be shown.

6.2.5 The literature

The proposal needs to identify the body of literature which is relevant to the research, to indicate the relationship of the proposed study to the relevant literature, and to indicate how the literature will be dealt with in the proposed study. These three possibilities were noted in Chapter 4:

- The literature is reviewed comprehensively in advance of the study, and that review is included as part of the proposal, or is attached.
- The literature will be reviewed comprehensively ahead of the empirical stage of the research, but that review will not be done until the proposal is approved. In this case, the nature and scope of the literature to be reviewed should be indicated.

- The literature will deliberately not be reviewed prior to the empirical work, but will be integrated into the research during the study, as in a grounded theory study. In this case too, the nature and scope of the literature should be indicated.

For some qualitative proposals, the literature may be used in sharpening the focus of the study, and to give structure to its questions and design. If so, this should be indicated, along with how it is to be done. In all cases, the researcher needs to identify the relevant literature, and to connect the proposed study to the literature. In general, I agree with the advice of Locke et al. (1993) and Maxwell (1996) that the function of the literature *in the proposal* is to locate the present study, and to explain and justify the directions it proposes to take.

6.2.6 Methods

Design: strategy and framework

At this point, the overall approach to be taken in the research – quantitative, qualitative or both – becomes decisive. While this might well have been indicated earlier in the proposal, it is nonetheless useful to make it clear here (again, if necessary). Whichever approach applies, the proposal should identify the basic strategy behind the research. Thus:

- If the study is quantitative, what strategy is proposed?
- If qualitative, what strategy is proposed?
- If there is a combination of quantitative and qualitative approaches, what is the proposed mixture of strategies?

A clear statement of the strategy helps to orient the reader, shows the logic of the research and leads naturally to a description of the design.

The design sits between the research questions and the data, and can now detail the implementation of the strategy. For example, if an experiment is planned, this section gives details of the proposed experimental design. If a case study is planned, this section gives details of the case study design – single or multiple, cross-sectional or longitudinal, and so on.

For conventional quantitative designs, the conceptual framework may be shown here instead of earlier. In qualitative studies, the location of the study along the structure continuum is particularly important for its design. Qualitative strategies such as case studies, ethnography and grounded theory may overlap, or elements of these may be used separately or together. This means it will be difficult to compartmentalize such a study neatly. That is not a problem, but it should be made clear that the proposed study uses elements of different strategies. Qualitative studies vary greatly on the issue of predeveloped conceptual frameworks, and the position of the study on this matter should be indicated. A fully or partly predeveloped framework should be shown. Where one will be developed, it needs to be indicated how that will be done. This will interact with data collection and analysis, and may be better dealt with there.

Sample

Chapter 5 stressed the need to think about sampling in the study as part of the planning process for the research, to select among sampling possibilities in line with the logic of the study, and to indicate the sampling plan in the proposal. The rationale behind the sampling plan needs to fit in with the logic of the study, and to be briefly described. Whatever the approach, the basic idea in this section is to indicate who or what will be studied, and why.

  If the study is quantitative, the proposal should indicate:

- the sampling strategy, especially whether it is purposive, representative or both, and what claims will be made for the generalizability of findings;
- how big the sample will be, and why;
- how it will be selected.

If the study is qualitative, the proposal should similarly indicate:

- the sampling strategy, including what intention (if any) there is for the generalizability of findings;
- the extent of the proposed sample;
- how sample units will be chosen.

If a case study is involved, the basis of case selection should be made clear, as should the basis of within-case sampling. If sampling of documentary or other qualitative material is proposed, its basis needs to be shown.

Data collection: instruments

As indicated in Chapter 5, the two matters to be considered within data collection are the instruments (if any) which will be used, and the procedures for administering the instruments or, more generally, for collecting the data. This section deals with instruments, and the next with procedures.

  For quantitative data collection:

- If the decision is to use already existing data collection instruments, a brief description of their history, their use in research and their basic psychometric characteristics (especially reliability and validity information, if available) should be included.
- If the decision is to construct an instrument(s) specifically for this study, an outline of the steps involved in doing that should be given, showing what pretesting is involved.

For qualitative data collection:

- A general plan for any qualitative fieldwork should be shown; if the researcher is the 'instrument' for data collection, the proposal should indicate this.
- If interviews are involved, what type of interviews and, especially, what degree of structure and standardization are proposed? If standardized interview schedules are to be used, how will they be developed and pretested?
- If qualitative questionnaires are proposed, what degree of structure and standardization is involved? How would they be developed and (if appropriate) pretested?
- Similar considerations apply for observational data: what degree of structure and standardization is proposed, and how would proposed schedules be developed and pretested?
- If documents are to be used, which ones and why? Are there sampling or access considerations?
- If diaries, journals, critical incident reports or other qualitative materials are involved, how would the collection of these, including any sampling aspects, be organized? For diaries, journals and critical incident reports, what directions would be given to participants?

Data collection: procedures

For both quantitative and qualitative approaches, the proposal needs to indicate:

- how the data will be collected;
- how the proposed procedures are arranged to maximize the quality of the data.

Issues of access and ethics may be dealt with here, if they apply especially to data collection procedures, or in the section on ethical issues and consent, access and participants' protection, if they apply more generally.

Data analysis

The objective in this section is to indicate how the data will be analysed. Quantitative proposals should indicate the statistical procedures proposed. Similarly, the qualitative proposal needs to show how its data will be analysed, and how the proposed analysis fits with the other components of the study. If applicable, both types of proposal should indicate what computer use is planned in the analysis of the data. As noted in Chapter 5, this is an area where you may well need the help of an expert.

6.2.7 Significance

Here, the proposal should indicate the significance of the proposed study. Synonyms for 'significance' here might be justification, importance, contribution or intended outcomes of the study. They all address the third general question of Chapter 3: why is this study worth doing? While the particular topic and its context will determine a study's significance, there are three general areas for the significance and contribution of a study: to knowledge in the area, to policy considerations and to practitioners (Marshall and Rossman, 1989). The first of these, contribution to knowledge, is closely tied to the literature in the area, and is often interpreted as theoretical contribution. If the study has the clear objective of theory generation or verification, indicating this contribution is straightforward.

6.2.8 Limitations and delimitations

'Limitations' refer to limiting conditions or 'restrictive weaknesses' (Locke et al., 1993: 18) which are unavoidably present in the study's design. Any study has limitations, and they should be noted in the proposal, which should argue nonetheless for the importance of this work. 'Delimitations' means defining the limits of or drawing the boundaries around a study, and showing clearly what is and is not included. This is sometimes useful in avoiding misunderstanding by the reader.

6.2.9 Ethical issues: consent, access and participants' protection

All social research involves consent, access and associated ethical issues, since it is based on data from people and about people. Section 5.5 shows a range of different ethical issues which might arise in research. Some ethical issues are present in almost all projects (for example, anonymity and confidentiality of data, the use of results), while others are much more project-specific (for example, intervention and advocacy). The researcher needs to anticipate the particular ethical issues involved in the proposed project, and to indicate in the proposal how they will be dealt with.

6.2.10 References

This is a list of the references cited in the proposal.

6.2.11 Appendices

These may include any of the following: letters of introduction or permission, consent forms, measuring instruments, questionnaires, interview guides, observation schedules, and examples of pilot study or other relevant work already completed (Maxwell, 1996).

6.3 Qualitative proposals

Qualitative studies vary greatly, and in many, the design and procedures will evolve during the research. As noted earlier, this obviously means that the proposal writer cannot specify exactly what will be done, in contrast to many quantitative proposals. When this is the case, the proposal can explain the flexibility the study requires, and show how decisions will be made as the study unfolds. Together with this, as much detail as possible should be provided. Review committees have to judge the quality, feasibility and viability of the proposed project, and the ability of the researcher to carry it out. The proposal itself, through its organization, coherence and integration, its attention to detail and its conceptual clarity, can inspire confidence in the researcher's ability to execute the research.

On the one hand then, for some types of qualitative research especially, we do not want to constrain too much the structure of the proposal, and we need to preserve flexibility. On the other hand, as pointed out in Section 4.3, this does not mean that 'anything goes'. Eisner writes as follows about qualitative research in education:

> Qualitative research proposals should have a full description of the topic to be investigated, a presentation and analysis of the research relevant to that topic, and a discussion of the issues within the topic or the shortfalls within the research literature that make the researcher's topic a significant one. They should describe the kinds of information that are able to be secured and the variety of methods or techniques that will be employed to secure such information. The proposals should identify the kinds of theoretical or explanatory resources that might be used in interpreting what has been described, and describe the kind of places, people, and materials that are likely to be addressed.
>
> The function of proposals is not to provide a watertight blueprint or formula the researcher is to follow, but to develop a cogent case that makes it plain to a knowledgeable reader that the writer has the necessary background to do the study and has thought clearly about the resources that are likely to be used in doing the study, and that the topic, problem, or issue being addressed is educationally significant. (1991: 241–2)

This elaborates Eisner's earlier comments (see Section 4.3) that 'evidence matters' and 'planning is necessary'. I want now to develop these points further, focusing both on proposals for qualitative research in general, and in particular on those with unfolding rather than prestructured elements. This sort of proposal is probably the most difficult to write, but the following points can guide the writing. They fit in with the headings shown in Table 6.1, though some modifications are required.

First, there should still be an identification of the research area and topic, and an introduction to those which places them in context and describes any necessary aspects of the background to the study. Second, there still needs to be an identification of the relevant literature, a connection of the proposed study to that literature, and an indication of how the research itself will deal with the literature. Third, there needs to be an assessment of the proposed study's significance and contribution, including its contribution in relation to the literature.

Fourth, when it comes to research questions, it is likely that only general guiding and starting research questions will be identified in such a proposal, supported by statements as to why this is appropriate and as to how more specific questions to direct the investigation will be identified as the research proceeds. As a matter of proposal presentation strategy, it is a good idea to indicate possible (or likely) research questions as the study unfolds, while pointing out that they are first approximations, to be revised and changed as the study proceeds. It is usually not difficult to make an intelligent first approximation to the sorts of research questions that might arise, through anticipating and trying to imagine or simulate the research situation. For some research also, some small scale empirical exploration (or pilot study) may be possible in developing the proposal. Where possible, this is very helpful in keeping things grounded.

Fifth, when it comes to design and methods, there should be clear statements in the proposal about the general research strategy envisaged, about the sorts of empirical materials to be targeted (at least initially), and about the general plan for collecting and analysing them. As before, the description of methods should not stop at a general identification of the research strategy. The proposal needs also to indicate awareness of the procedural and methodological choices ahead of the researcher in implementing the general strategy, and the basis on which those choices will be made. This was the distinction made in Section 5.3.1 between general and procedural descriptions of methods. Terms describing qualitative research strategies such as the case study, or participant observation, or grounded theory, or an interview-based study are necessary, but they are generic descriptions, identifying an approach and a strategy in general terms. The execution of any of these in research involves numerous procedural and methodological choices. Thus the 'interview-based study', for example, involves choices about such matters as the selection of interview respondents, approaches to them, the establishment of trust and rapport, physical arrangements for the interview (time, place, etc.), recording procedures, the type of interview, the nature of the questions and the role (if any) of an interview schedule and pretesting. The qualitative proposal does not need to be able to answer all such questions. Indeed, many of them may well be unanswerable, at proposal stage. But the proposal should indicate awareness of such upcoming methodological choices, and the basis on which they will be made.

Sixth, the other proposal headings listed (abstract and title, limitations and delimitations, ethical issues, references and appendices) apply, as appropriate, as before.

Writing the proposal for a qualitative study can be more complicated, given the less prestructured nature of most such research. The writer should indicate early in the document the unfolding nature of the proposed research and why such an approach is appropriate for this study on this topic in this context at this time. The need to preserve flexibility, the unfolding nature of the study, and the ways in which this research will follow a path of discovery can be strongly stated. Against that background, it is good advice to develop likely research questions and issues of design and methods as far as possible in the proposal, indicating what methodological choices will be involved and the basis on which they will be made.

6.4 Academic writing

Academic writing is required in proposals and dissertations for higher degrees in universities. Despite some discipline-specific conventions and preferences, there are widely held expectations for the general characteristics of academic writing, which are now briefly described.

Academic writing relies on logical argument, on the development and interconnection of ideas, and on internal consistency and coherence. For this reason, it depends heavily on well organized paragraphs with topic sentences, which are appropriately interconnected with each other. Two things which stand out very clearly to the experienced reader of academic writing (especially of proposals and dissertations) are the lack of connection between different points and, even worse, the inconsistency between different points. Among other things, the need for the logical development and interconnection of ideas requires us to be careful about the overuse of dot or bullet points. Occasionally they are fine, for clarity and emphasis. But their overuse is a mistake: interconnected argument cannot be built using only separate points.

The language of academic writing for research purposes should be dispassionate, precise and unambiguous, and consistent. *Dispassionate* means that the purpose of academic writing in proposals and dissertations is to inform, not persuade. Thus your proposal is not the place to 'grind your axe', or to pursue your favourite hobby horse, or to persuade others about a conclusion you have already reached. For this reason, dispassionate and unemotional language is expected. *Precise* means that accurate and unambiguous language is part of the careful approach which scholarship requires, with thorough attention to detail. In the same vein, conclusions should be based on evidence, and in line with academic honesty, the writer should clearly identify when speculation goes beyond evidence. *Consistent* means that terms should be used consistently (as well as precisely). Avoid the substitution of one term for another when the same thing is meant by both terms. This just creates confusion for the reader.

Similarly, academic writing in a scholarly context needs to be appropriately formal. This means avoiding slang, jargon and colloquialisms. It also means taking special care with – and not overdoing – the use of abbreviations and acronyms. Students often have a problem here. If the everyday discourse in the environment where they are working or studying makes heavy use of abbreviations and acronyms, there is the understandable temptation to write this way in the proposal. This, however, makes it difficult for the reader unfamiliar with that environment. A good rule is to write for the unfamiliar reader. Then phrases can be used in full the first time they occur, with acronyms and abbreviations thereafter. But even when that is done, an equally good rule is not to overdo the use of acronyms and abbreviations.

6.4.1 Strategies to help with academic writing

It is understandable that the beginning research student may see the prospect of writing a proposal – and later a dissertation – as formidable and daunting. The following four well known strategies can help reduce the level of difficulty of the writing task from formidable to manageable.

1 Develop a structure for the document that has to be written. The structure will have sections and subsections, and, up to a point, the more detailed the structure the better. One way to do this is to plan a table of contents for your document early in the process of writing; it may need several versions, and can be revised as you proceed. Once you have sections and subsections, you have modularized your writing task. Instead of one formidable task (writing the proposal, or the dissertation), you now have a series of manageable ones (writing the introduction, or the literature review, or the data collection subsection of the methods section). This chapter has described a structure for writing the research proposal.
2 Set deadlines, both for the whole document and for different main sections. Using the due date for submission of proposal or dissertation, first schedule time for revisions. This gives you the date by which you need to have completed a first draft. Then work backwards from that date to develop self-imposed deadlines for completing the draft of each main section.
3 If possible, write every day, preferably at the same time each day, for (roughly) the same length of time each day, and in the same place. This builds important conditioned associations between writing and the place and time of day. It also helps overcome the common problems of inertia, procrastination and writer's block.
4 When each daily writing session ends, make yourself a note about what to do next. This helps to deal with the problem of discontinuity – sitting down to write the next day, and spending the first period, usually in frustration, trying to pick up the threads from the previous session.

Together, these strategies can help you build writing momentum, which is necessary to get significant documents written. They also, by modularizing, make the task manageable. They should take you to a position of having a complete draft of your proposal with time for the necessary revisions. It is important now to stress that academic writing requires revision. Every successful academic writer understands the importance of revising what is written. Put bluntly, when it comes to academic writing, nobody gets it right the first time. When you read good academic writing, you can be sure that it has gone through the revision process, and usually more than once.

The main tasks in the revision process will typically focus on tidying up the use of language (often shortening by removing unnecessary verbiage), attending to details of grammar, punctuation, format and presentation, ensuring internal consistency and building connections between the different parts. Once again, it is good to have a deadline for revisions. Sometimes, students without deadlines get trapped in endless cycles of revisions, in a fruitless quest for perfection.

Two other strategies can help, if circumstances permit. The first is the 'drawer treatment' (Cryer, 2000: 158). This means putting a completed draft aside (in a drawer – or computer) for at least a few days, with the idea of returning to it refreshed and with a clearer view as final revisions are done. The second is to read your work aloud (Ward, 2002: 102). This helps you identify and correct sentences which are too long and complex, and other awkward structures. It also helps you to achieve writing which flows, and is therefore easier to read.

7
Tactics

7.1 Introduction

I believe there is no one way to develop a research proposal, and I have seen how much difference there is between the way different researchers proceed.[1] But I have also found that some strategies and tactics are consistently useful, especially for student researchers coming to proposal development for the first time. This chapter presents these. Before that, however, I restate five general tactical considerations, which I think should stay in the proposal writer's mind throughout the process of proposal development. They follow on from what has been said in previous chapters.

7.2 General tactical issues

1   Keep an overall focus on the three general questions:

    (a) *What* am I trying to find out?
    (b) *How* am I going to do it?
    (c) *Why* is this worth doing?

2 Put the 'what' question before the 'how' question. As far as possible, make research methods dependent on research questions, rather than questions dependent on methods. Remember that how you ask questions has implications for the methods to use in finding answers to them.

3 Realize that you will almost certainly have to revisit both questions (the 'what' and the 'how' questions) several times before you get the proposal right. The process is an iterative one, whether the proposal is quantitative, qualitative or mixed method. Whereas the research proposal, as a product, is expected to be neat, tidy, well structured and interconnected, showing clarity and internal consistency, the process, by contrast, is usually messy, iterative, stop–start, and often punctuated with tensions, hesitations and contradictions. The same is true of much of research itself.

4 The importance of feedback: throughout the process of putting your proposal together, you will need reactions and feedback from various quarters – friends, fellow students, and especially supervisors (see Section 7.4.2). Make it easy for them to give you feedback which helps. Two ways you can do that are to provide them with draft documents which are easily understood, and to raise directly with them – preferably attached to your drafts – questions and matters on which you would like their reaction.

5 Modularizing: student researchers are often daunted by the task of producing a finished research proposal. It can seem formidable. But, like other formidable tasks, it loses much of its sting when broken down into smaller, specific, component tasks. To do that requires an outline, and Chapter 6 suggests sections for that outline. Once the outline is in place, even if provisionally, you can begin assembling and categorizing your notes into these sections and organizing these into points to be made. From this basis, the writing itself can begin. Modularizing the work this way is one of the great benefits of having a structured outline, with sections (or modules). That outline itself may well be developed iteratively.

Against the background of these general considerations, I now have some specific tactical suggestions to add to those discussed in Section 3.7.

7.3 Departmental guidelines

No matter how obvious it seems, an important tactical issue right at the start of proposal development is to find out what departmental and/or university guidelines, regulations and policies apply, both to the proposal and to the final dissertation. Locke et al. note that there will usually be three main sources of regulation: 'Normally, the planning and execution of student research are circumscribed by existing departmental policy on format for the final report, university regulations concerning thesis and dissertation reports, and informal standards exercised by individual advisors or study committees' (1993: 5–6).

They point out also that there is wide variation in specificity between departments and universities. Some regulations are very explicit ('the proposal may not exceed 25 typewritten pages', or 'the proposal will conform to the style established in the *Publication Manual* of the American Psychological Association'), whereas others are very general ('the research topic must be of suitable proportions', or 'the proposal must reflect a thorough knowledge of the problem area').

As well as checking on departmental and/or university and/or dissertation committee regulations and guidelines regarding the proposal, it is useful to find out about the process of proposal evaluation and approval in your department, and, if possible, to consult previous successful proposals. You can learn a lot from reading these, and it too usually makes your task seem less formidable.[2]

Time and length guidelines might be laid down, and increasingly, universities are placing size limits on proposals and dissertations. Two main reasons for this are that the sheer volume of research going on today demands some limit on the size of proposals (and dissertations), and that a strong argument can be made that it is good discipline to be able to describe the proposed research (or completed project) in a certain limited number of words or pages. According to this argument, it is important to develop the skill to say what you need to say about your research within these limits of time and length.

On the other hand, to give a full treatment of all the issues raised in this book (including, as appropriate, those in Chapter 4) may well require a proposal document which might exceed these limits. What to do in these cases? My advice for this situation is to prepare a full version, along the lines described here, and then to summarize it down to the required length. This shows the review committee that you have done a thorough job in proposal preparation (you can indicate in your shortened version that a full version is available, and perhaps also include parts of it as an appendix). But also, the full version of the proposal will be an important contribution to the final dissertation itself. After the proposal is approved and the research is executed, you will have to report it in a dissertation. That dissertation is expected to be a full and detailed report of the research, though again, it will be expected to conform to size limits. Much of what is written in the full version of the proposal can be imported directly into the final dissertation.

7.4 Getting started

As noted, it is important to be clear about the formal requirements of both faculty and university for developing and submitting your research proposal. It is also important to learn about the process for evaluation and approval of your proposal. Sometimes these things can be learned through organized orientation experiences for beginning research students. At other times, the learniing may have to be empirical through your questioning and discussion with

other students. When starting on your research journey in a university department, be sure to check also on what research training is provided, and on what
research methods courses are available. Familiarize yourself also with the dissertation library, and if relevant, the proposal library.

7.4.1 Area, topic and research questions

Getting started in developing a proposal means either being able to identify a
research area and topic, and moving towards general and specific questions
within that topic, or knowing the specific research question(s) of interest, and
being able to locate those within more general questions, a topic and an area.

Many writers have discussed ways of getting started in research, and the
sources and types of research areas and topics. Thus Locke et al. (1993: 48)
suggest that research questions emerge from three broad sources: logic, practi-
cality and accident. As good practical advice for beginning research students,
they also recommend the benefits of conversing with peers, listening to profes-
sorial discussions, assisting in research projects, attending lectures and conferences, exchanging papers and corresponding with faculty and students at other
institutions. Neumann (1994: 110) suggests seven ways of selecting topics: personal experience, curiosity based on something in the media, the state of knowledge in a field, solving a problem (often associated with professional
experience), 'social premiums', personal values and everyday life. Gitlin and
Lyons (1996: 36) discuss seven different sources of ideas for funding: clinical or
professional experience, professional literature, interaction with others, societal
trends, legislative initiatives, public documents and agency goals and priorities.

In addition to the journal and dissertation literature, work experience
and workplace issues and the media, experts or authorities – especially professional associations – will often make pronouncements about research needs.
Consultancy work you might have been involved in is another possible source
of research areas and topics, as are your previous studies. And in some areas –
for example, business and management – trade sources will be useful.

Characteristics of good topics include access, achievable in time, value and
suitable scope (Gill and Johnson, 2002: 15). Two don'ts to remember in selecting
a topic are:

- Don't select a topic to solve a personal issue (Bryant, 2004: 18).
- Don't use your dissertation to 'grind an axe'.

7.4.2 Supervision and supervisors

Supervision is of central importance to the dissertation student and the dissertation experience, as is choosing a supervisor – assuming you have that
choice. Factors to consider about prospective supervisors in making the choice
include:

- *Area of research.* What research area(s) does this person work in, and how does that area relate to your proposed area? A perfect match is not necessary, but some intersection or overlap is desirable.
- *Methodological background and expertise.* What are the person's methodological preferences, and areas of expertise, especially on the central methodological issue for empirical research of quantitative, qualitative or mixed method? Important related questions are: do you know your own position on this, and the reasons for it? Is there compatibility between your methodological position and that of a prospective supervisor?
- *Supervision record.* Is there a track record of successful supervision? Departmental and university records will help here, as will consultations with other students. Sometimes tactful direct discussion of this is possible, but at other times more discreet and less obtrusive methods are better. Of course, this question needs to be de-emphasized or put aside if the staff member is very young, or has only recently begun academic work.
- *Supervision style* (especially with respect to flexibility and independence). This can usually only be determined by direct discussion with the supervisor, and by consulting other students with whom that supervisor has worked. Supervision styles can vary from very directive and prescriptive on the one hand, to very flexible and student centred – aimed at encouraging independence – on the other. While on this topic, a good piece of general advice is not to become too dependent on your supervisor. Supervisors are generally not there to tell you what to do, and the university tradition for postgraduate dissertation work is one of independent study's under supervision.
- *Availability.* As academic workloads (often including travel) increase, availability becomes more and more important. There is no point in having an expert supervisor who is seldom available for consultation and feedback.
- *Approachability.* Initial contacts and discussions are important here, as are the experiences of other students. While approachability is desirable, Marshall and Green have a timely list of what your supervisor is not: among other things, your supervisor is *not* 'your boss, your employer, your colleague, your best friend, your editor, your search engine, your wet nurse' (2004: 27).

When approaching possible supervisors, it is useful to prepare by thinking about your motivations for doing a research degree, your proposed area of research, your methodological orientations and preferences (with reasons), and the type of relationship you believe you would prefer with a supervisor.[3]

Once the choice of supervisor has been made, there is the question of managing the ongoing relationship. Relevant issues here include the frequency (and form) of meetings and discussions, supervisor expectations for the form and content of work to be submitted, and student expectations for the turnaround time and level of feedback for submitted work. These are best dealt with in direct discussion early in the supervision relationship.

Of course it is possible for things to go wrong, and how disagreements and disputes are handled becomes important. Most universities will have a code of supervisory practice, and it is important for the student to be aware of this. In extreme cases, the relationship may break down completely, or become dysfunctional. Change of supervision then becomes necessary.

7.4.3 The 'two-pager'

Often a good way to formalize getting started; after some period of work, is to write *no more than two pages* describing, as clearly and directly as possible, what the proposed research is trying to find out, and how it will do it. Students usually have some difficulty doing this. I find that common faults are for the one or two pages to expand to five, six or ten, and for the focus to be on the context, background and literature around the issue rather than the central issue itself – the 'what' and the 'how' of the proposed research. These things – the context, background and literature – of course have their place. But the value of this exercise, at this point, is in forcing a confrontation with the central questions of 'What am I trying to find out?' and 'How am I going to do it?' and in that order. Limiting this document to two pages is a deliberate strategy to get past the context and background.

Like other stages in proposal development, getting satisfactory and stable answers to these questions is inevitably an iterative process. It takes several tries, and almost nobody gets it right the first time. In any case, the two-pager is a work-in-progress document. Its function is to see where your thinking is up to, so you can take it to the next stage. Its benefit is to get systematic thinking started, and to ensure an early focus on writing, with these central questions in mind.

As a supervisor, I most often find that discussing a first attempt at this two-pager with the student leads naturally to a second (and sometimes third and fourth) attempt, and that these attempts progressively produce a clearer initial statement. Once that is in place, even if tentatively, it provides the springboard for the next stage of thinking, reading and discussing. You can see what you need to do next.

7.4.4 The ideas paper

Another useful strategy, sometimes instead of the two-pager, sometimes alongside it, is to write an ideas paper, which sets out to sketch the context and background to the proposed topic, and which probably deals also with some of the main themes in the literature. A primary purpose here is to identify main issues, points or themes, with a view to proceeding more or less deductively from these to general and then to specific research questions. When progress is not deductive but more interactive, moving backwards and forwards between general and specific issues, the ideas paper can have value in stimulating this.

The trick is not to let it become the main focus of this stage of work, but to use it to lead into the central 'what' and 'how' questions.

What I call here an 'ideas paper' is sometimes called a 'preliminary discussion paper' or a 'discussion and concept paper' (Gilpatrick, 1989: 45, 101; Maxwell, 1996: 24, 47–8). These labels and interpretations are often valuable for the researcher who focuses on the problem rather than the question (see Section 2.6). Whatever they might be called, such papers will normally bring the benefits of helping you to sort out your ideas on a topic, indicating and perhaps starting to draw on relevant literature and bringing into focus what you already know about the topic, perhaps from an experiential base.

7.4.5 Working deductively

If you are stuck, or are having trouble organizing your ideas and making them systematic, referring again to the hierarchy of concepts in Chapter 3 can help. From the most general to the most specific, that hierarchy is: research area, research topic, general research questions, specific research questions, data collection questions. We can develop from that hierarchy a simple set of deductive steps for developing a research proposal. Thus, for example, a six-step model is to:

- select a research area;
- develop one or more topics within that area;
- select one from among these topics to keep your project manageable;
- develop research questions, general and specific, for this topic;
- determine what data would be required to answer each specific research question;
- select research design, data collection and data analysis procedures in order to do this.

The value of this sort of thinking is not as a lockstep, formula-like approach to research planning. Rather, it is a useful 'fallback' frame of reference for an overloaded or confused research planner. And you do not have to start this process from the top and work down. You can start from the middle – for example, with a particular specific research question of interest – and then move up and down the set of steps, up and down the hierarchy of concepts as appropriate.

7.5 The value of discussion

Ultimately, in its written form, the proposal goes to some wider audience. At that stage, as noted earlier, the ideal completed proposal is a stand-alone document, able to be read and understood (and, in due course, approved) by a mixture of expert and non-expert readers. A valuable step, on the way to that, is discussing your developing ideas. Discussing is itself a process, in miniature, of taking your work to a wider audience.

Discussion with whom? In my opinion, with anybody at all that you find helpful – but especially with your supervisor(s), with other research students and/or colleagues and/or others working in similar areas, and with non-expert friends, acquaintances and so on. This last type of discussant, being non-expert, might play the very valuable role of the 'naïve inquirer'. As Bryant points out: 'The more widely you converse about your topic, the clearer you will be about it' (2004: 13). Such discussion includes brainstorming, which can help in topic identification and development.

Discussing your developing proposal has several benefits for your work:

- It is a step towards writing things down; both discussing your ideas with others and writing them down force you to think about structuring and representing your ideas so that they can be understood by others.
- It is a part of the clarification/communication process; you have both to plan and design a piece of research, and communicate that plan to others.
- It brings feedback from others, which is often important in clarification.
- It may suggest aspects of, or perspectives on, your topic that have so far escaped you.
- Discussion with experts may suggest literature you need to consult; discussion with non-experts may suggest aspects of the context or situation you need to take into account.

7.6 The value of writing it down

'Like the turtle, we progress only with our necks stuck out.' This is often good advice on proposal development. Translated, it means: have a go at writing your ideas down, especially if you are stuck, or if you are at a point where you have done quite a lot of reading and thinking and it is time to try to capture, consolidate and perhaps order your ideas. You do this sort of writing 'as best as you can see things at the moment', knowing that this is a draft, a step on the way to a finished product. This exercise will throw up points and issues that need more thought, discussion or reading. But its main value is in clarifying your thinking. As with discussion, the structuring and representation of ideas are involved here, as is the relationship between thinking and writing. The main value here of the concrete activity of writing it down, for someone else to read, is in clarification. This is an example of 'writing to learn' or 'writing to discover'. More accurately, it is an example of writing in order to sort things out. It is useful to regularize and formalize such writing into a research journal, which continues during the dissertation.

7.7 **Three common dilemmas**

This section deals with three dilemmas which often occur as students develop proposals. The first is the problem of several topics at once; the second is getting to closure versus getting to closure too quickly; and the third is focusing on the context, background and literature versus focusing on the research questions. I think of these as tensions in the research planning process, which are almost inevitable as work on the proposal progresses.

7.7.1 Several topics at once

One common problem students experience is selecting a research area and topic, and getting the development of the proposal started. But another common problem is finding that there is more than one topic (or proposal, or project) emerging, as the student continues to work. There are two main versions of this problem. One is deciding among possible research areas and topics. The other is deciding among possible research questions, after the area and topic have been selected.

A situation frequently encountered is where the student can see more than one, and perhaps several, attractive research areas and questions. These may be related to each other, or they may be rather unconnected and discrete. This situation is most common early in the process of developing the proposal. As Brink and Wood say: 'Perhaps the hardest task of all is deciding on one well-defined topic. There is so much to do that it is hard not to want to do it all at once' (1994: xii).

Faced with this problem, one strategy to consider is to develop more than one idea, as a possible proposal, up to a certain point. Most of the time, none of us can see clearly, up-front and in advance of a certain amount of work, where any one topic or set of questions might lead. Therefore, instead of trying to make judgements too early, it is better to push ahead with more than one topic for a period of time, in order to see where each leads: what type of study each leads to, how feasible and 'doable' each is, how each fits with the interests, preferences and situation of the student, and so on. The two-pager is helpful here. Of course there comes a time when judgements are needed as to future directions, and decisions have to be made. The point here is that keeping the options open for a time, while more than one area is explored, is often good policy.

The second aspect of this problem is when we discover, through the question development stage, that an initial apparently quite straightforward topic has much more in it than first meets the eye. This is by no means uncommon, and we usually only get to see this by developing the topic and its questions to a reasonable extent.

What generally happens after a period of question development (see Section 3.7.1) is that the project has expanded, sometimes greatly. This can cause anxiety, but for most projects it should happen. In fact, if it doesn't, we should probably be concerned, since it may be a sign of insufficient question development work. Therefore, it is to be encouraged, within reason, as an important stage. Probing, exploring, and seeing other possibilities with a topic can be valuable before reaching closure on the specific directions for a project.

When a small set of starting questions has multiplied into a larger set, disentangling and ordering are required. Disentangling is necessary because one question will often have other questions within it. Ordering involves categorizing, and the grouping of questions together. This will soon become hierarchical, and general and specific research questions begin to be distinguishable from each other.

The final stage then involves bringing the project down to size, since it has usually become too big. In fact, it probably suggests a research programme with several research projects by now. How is this trimming done? It involves deciding which questions are manageable within the practical constraints of this project, and which seem the most central and important. There are of course limits around any project – even if that project involves a substantial grant and a team of researchers. The principle here is that it is better to do a smaller project thoroughly than a larger project superficially. Trimming a project down to size is a matter of judgement, and experience in research has a big role to play here. Once again, therefore, this stage is best done in collaboration with others. This stage is sometimes called delimiting the project. This means drawing the boundaries around it, and showing what is not in the project, as well as what is (see Section 6.2).

How many research questions should there be? There are practical limitations on any one project, and, as noted, it is better to have a small job done thoroughly than a large job done only superficially. More than about three or four general research questions, assuming that each is subdivided into (say) two or three specific questions, is testing the upper limit of what can be done in one study.

7.7.2 Getting to closure versus getting to closure too quickly

Many higher degree programmes combine course work and a research dissertation. Completing the coursework is not normally the problem for most higher degree students. Completing the dissertation sometimes is.[4] The first major step in completing the dissertation is to complete the research proposal, and have it accepted.

For some students, the process of choosing a research area and topic, pondering its complexities, mastering its literature, and formulating questions and methods to guide the investigation can take too long. Indeed, as with the dissertation itself, there is a time limit usually imposed on this stage of the work. This reflects the view noted earlier, that part of the task is to get the job (proposal or dissertation) done within a certain period of time, and to get the story told within a certain number of words.

This means that there is a point at which, after an appropriate period of time, consideration and work, it is necessary to make decisions and complete the proposal. It is necessary to 'get to closure'. It helps in doing this to remember:

- that there is no such thing as a perfect research proposal (or dissertation);
- that it is appropriate to be aware of, and to make the reader aware of, difficulties, problems and limitations, while not being overly defensive about the research;
- that not all of the issues which might arise in a piece of research have to be dealt with in the proposal; some might well be dealt with after acceptance of the proposal, in the execution stage of the research itself. In these cases, they should be noted in the proposal;
- that emergent and unfolding designs will naturally be less definitive at the proposal stage than those which take a highly preplanned and prestructured approach.[5]

However, while some students have trouble getting to closure, there is also the opposite problem of getting to closure too quickly. That is why the phrase 'after an appropriate period of time' was used above. During this planning stage, there is some benefit to hastening slowly. Since research questions do not usually come out right the first time, several iterations are often required, and we only reach a full answer to the question 'What are we trying to find out?' after careful thought. This question development stage needs time – time to see the possible questions buried in an area and to see related questions which follow from an analysis of particular questions. The theme in Section 3.7.1 was the importance of the pre-empirical, setting-up stage of the research; the decisions taken here will influence what is done in later stages. This does not mean that the decisions cannot be varied, as when iteration towards the final research questions goes on during the early empirical stages of the project. But varying them should not be done lightly if considerable effort has been invested in reaching them during the set-up stage.

7.7.3 Focus on context, background and literature versus focus on research questions

Clearly, both context, background and literature on the one hand, and research questions on the other, are necessary in the finished proposal (or dissertation). So it is not a question of one of these things or the other. The issue here is about the focus on each, and especially about the timing of the focus on each, in developing the proposal.

On the one hand, focusing too much on the context, background and literature too early in the process of research planning can result in lengthy essays on these topics, delaying (sometimes almost indefinitely) the proposal itself. It can also strongly affect the direction of the research, not always beneficially. On the other hand, focusing only on the research questions runs the risk of unnecessary, uninformed and inappropriate duplication of research, and/or of decontextualizing the research.

The solution, as usual, is a matter of judgement, in how the two things are balanced and integrated. Some of both is essential, and I do not believe a formula can be prescribed for general use. With some topics, approaches and students, it is appropriate to focus heavily on research questions and methods until major directions for the research have been set. With others, it is important to get the context, background and literature integrated into the thinking early.

At the same time, I often feel that the danger of a student being overwhelmed by, or at least strongly influenced by, the literature especially, and to a lesser extent being preoccupied with matters of context and background, can be worse than the danger of developing research questions in isolation from literature, context and background. I think this is especially true in applied social science and professional areas, where the student often brings important knowledge[6] to the research. I do not believe that knowledge should be ignored.

That is why I usually recommend focusing initially on the 'what' and 'how' of the research, and then fitting context, background and literature around that. But the process is, overall, interactive. And, for most proposals, the writer moves backwards and forwards between the context–background–literature and the research questions, as the proposal develops.

7.8 The importance of clarity

Finally, and as noted several times already, your proposal will be much more convincing if it is clear. Recapping what has been said about academic writing in Section 6.4, two main ideas are involved in achieving this:

- *Organizing for understanding.* The proposal will be easier for readers to understand, especially in the stand-alone context described, if it is structured in a logical and coherent way. This means there should be clearly identified sections, which together cover the material expected, and which are suitably interconnected with each other. It also means that, as a writer, you are putting yourself in the position of the reader, and anticipating reader reactions.
- *Writing for clarity.* Writing for the academic research context demands both acceptable scholarly format, and clarity. Both, and especially the latter, take time. Good writing, in this context, is invariably the result of drafting and redrafting, sharpening and shortening. I agree with the phrase used by Locke et al. (1993: 46) when they suggest the need for 'semantic and conceptual hygiene'. Your thinking in a research situation needs to be systematic, organized and disciplined. Your writing needs to reflect that. Semantic and conceptual hygiene should lead on to linguistic hygiene.

8
Examples of Proposals

This chapter includes five examples of proposals – two quantitative, two qualitative and one mixed method. Two are from educational research and the other three are from social medicine, management–business and nursing. A caveat is now required. I have tried to write this as a general book for developing social science research proposals, without wishing to favour one style or type or approach over others. Since space reasons make it impossible to have proposals for all different types of research in this one book, any selection runs the risk of appearing to favour one sort of research over another, or of suggesting a 'template' for students to follow (Maxwell, 1996: 116). That is not intended. Rather, the five proposals are included as examples of best practice, and they are included here without comment. They illustrate many of the points made in earlier chapters.

I have retained the sections and section headings of the original proposals, rather than trying to standardize them into a common set of headings. Different universities, and sometimes different departments within the one university, vary in proposal format requirements. At the same time, each proposal included here meets – in one way or another – the reader's expectations described in Section 2.2 and covered in the general set of headings given in Table 6.1. At doctoral level, universities often ask candidates in their proposal to address the way in which the proposed research will meet the doctoral criterion of a 'substantial and original contribution to knowledge', and that section is included here, where it applies. Other proposal headings less relevant to this book are omitted from the versions of the proposal shown here, as are details of references, for space reasons.[1]

Aside from these omissions, the five proposals are presented in full. Coming after them is a list of examples of other proposals in the literature. This list gives an idea of the range and diversity of proposals, with titles included where available to indicate the area and topic of the research.

8.1 Quantitative proposal: education

Name of candidate: *Nola Purdie*
Degree: Doctor of Philosophy, The University of Western Australia

A. Proposed study

(i) Title

A cross-cultural investigation of the relationship between student conceptions of learning and their use of self-regulated learning strategies.

(ii) Aims

For a variety of reasons there is an increasing number of overseas students, particularly from south-east Asian countries, who are being educated in Australian schools. Differences in schooling and cultural traditions lead to different understandings of what learning actually is and to the strategies students use to regulate their own learning. Although it is not possible to speak with accuracy of an 'Asian' culture, it is, nevertheless, possible to identify several cultural characteristics that strongly influence understandings and practices related to education and learning that appear to be common across a number of Asian countries (Biggs, 1991; Garner, 1991; Hess & Azume, 1991; Thomas, 1990). In particular, concepts of filial piety and self-control, and an emphasis on rote memorization as a way of learning, contrast strongly with the qualities of independence of thought, verbal assertiveness, and learning through the development of meaning which are promoted as desirable behaviours in Australian students. If Australian teachers are to cater successfully for students from other cultures, it is important that we develop a better understanding of what these students actually think learning is and how they go about doing it.

This research, therefore, aims to determine if cultural differences in understandings about the nature of learning and the strategies used by students to perform a range of academic tasks do exist. Specifically, the research will compare the conceptions of learning and the use of self-regulated learning strategies of Australian secondary school students for whom English is a first language with those of students from two different south-east Asian countries (hereafter referred to collectively as Asian students). The research will test the hypothesis that what students understand by learning will, to a certain extent, determine their use of self-regulated learning strategies.

It is expected that the experience of schooling in Australia will cause changes in understandings about the nature of learning and the use of learning strategies. To investigate these changes, comparisons will be made between Asian students before they have been exposed to schooling in Australia and Asian students who have had several years of education in Australia and for whom English is a second language. The relationship between the level of English language proficiency of the Asian students and their use of self-regulated learning strategies will also be explored.

(iii) Substantial contribution to knowledge

The proposed research represents a substantial and original contribution to knowledge in that a cross-cultural perspective will be taken with respect to the investigation of students' conceptions of learning and their use of learning strategies. The research project will extend and integrate theory and findings from several areas of research relating to student learning. Self-regulated learning theory, developed through research from Western participants, will be applied to participants from two different south-east Asian countries. The motivational component of self-regulated learning will be explored with a view to expanding the already established output notion of what prompts students to engage in self-regulated learning to include an input component. Finally, theory that suggests that second language competence may be a factor in student use of self-regulated learning strategies will be tested.

(iv) Theoretical framework

Introduction
The importance of self-regulation in learning has now been firmly established (Bandura, 1989; Zimmerman, 1990b). In contrast to investigations of student achievement that focus on student ability as the key factor in learning, self-regulation theory focuses attention on *why* and *how* students become initiators and controllers of their own learning. *How* students self-regulate has largely been explained by the degree to which a student is aware of and uses appropriately specific strategies to achieve their academic goals. The *why* of self-regulation has been explained in terms of motivational processes that are dependent on learning outcomes which have either tangible or intangible personal implications. 'Behaviorally oriented approaches focus on tangible outcomes such

as material or social gains, whereas cognitively oriented approaches emphasize intangible outcomes such as self-actualization, self-efficacy, or reduced cognitive dissonance' (Zimmerman, 1990, p. 11).

The proposed research seeks to extend this view of motivational causation to include another component. In current theory, outcomes, both tangible and intangible, are considered to be the prime motivators of self-regulation in learning. A theory will be developed that posits inputs as an important, additional motivational factor. Specifically, input is that which students bring to academic tasks thereby prompting them to be proactive and systematic controllers of the learning process. In contrast to outcomes, where the focus is on a future-oriented actuality, inputs are derived from past experiences and are very much active in the present. Although there are bound to be several different sources of inputs, this research will focus on just one – student conceptions of learning. It will be argued, and subsequently tested, that what students understand by learning will, to a certain extent, determine their use of self-regulated strategies.

Self-regulated learning

Many studies have established the relationship between achievement, strategy use, and verbal self-efficacy in self-regulated learning (e.g. Bandura, 1982; Schunk, 1984; Zimmerman & Martinez-Pons, 1986; 1990) but this research has used Western participants for whom English is their first language. There are two potential problems with generalizing from these studies to second language users from a non-Western background. First, there may not be cross-cultural conceptual equivalence regarding the notion of self-regulated learning; and second, competence in the use of English may influence a student's ability to use self-regulated strategies, particularly those which are, in part, dependent on the four macro language skills of speaking, listening, reading and writing.

Self-regulation theory evolved out of an understanding of self-control as the product of socialization processes aimed at the development of moral standards of conduct (Bandura, 1977). Zimmerman (1990) noted Bandura's later extension of this theory to include a goal related aspect. A person's goals and expectations are seen to provide the motivational stimulus to the self-control of behaviour which is directed at effecting changes in self or situation.

One current theory of self-regulated learning perceives students to be self-regulated learners to the extent that they are metacognitively, motivationally and behaviourally active participants in their own learning processes (Zimmerman, 1986). This theory proposes that self-regulated learning involves three key elements: use of self-regulated learning strategies, self-efficacy perceptions of performance skill, and commitment to academic goals (Zimmerman, 1990). Self-regulated learning strategies involve agency, purpose and instrumentality self-perceptions by a learner and are aimed at acquiring information and skill. Furthermore, this theory proposes triad reciprocal causality among three influence processes: personal, behavioural, and environmental (Bandura, 1986; Zimmerman, 1989).

Based on this view of self-regulated learning, a structured interview for assessing student use of self-regulated learning strategies was developed (Zimmerman & Martinez-Pons, 1986). The Self-Regulated Learning Interview Schedule (SRLIS) has been used to correlate student strategy use with academic achievement (Zimmerman & Martinez-Pons, 1986); with teacher ratings of students' use of self-regulatory strategies, and students' verbal achievement (Zimmerman & Martinez-Pons, 1988); and with student perceptions of both verbal and mathematical efficacy (Zimmerman & Martinez-Pons, 1990). It is planned to use a form of the SRLIS, modified to cater for cross-cultural differences in educational context, to assess the strategy use of subjects in the proposed research project.

Conceptions of learning

Students' conceptions of learning have been found to be one component of the skill of self-regulated learning (Säljö, 1979). According to Säljö, when students perceive learning to be a reproductive process, the responsibility for transmitting an already existing body of knowledge into the head of the learner lies with an external source. In contrast, however, when learning is viewed as a meaning-centred process, the learner is more likely to assume responsibility for construing knowledge by proactively initiating and regulating the (re)construction process.

Six distinctly different conceptions of learning have been identified in research (Marton, Dall'Alba & Beatty, 1993; Säljö, 1979). These six different conceptions (increasing one's knowledge, memorizing and reproducing, applying, understanding, seeing something in a different way, and changing as a person) have been used in research to demonstrate that students from different cultures do conceive of learning in different ways (Marton, 1992; Watkins & Regmi, 1992). There are two aspects to a person's conception of learning: a way of seeing *what* is learned and a way of seeing *how* it is learned (Marton, Dall'Alba & Beatty, 1993). The implications for self-regulation learning theory with regard to the *how* of learning are clear. *How* a student perceives learning to occur will determine the set of strategies selected to achieve the desired outcome.

There is some evidence to suggest that students from different cultures do understand learning in different ways (Watkins & Regmi, 1992). If this is so for students from south-east Asian countries who are being schooled in Australia, then there are obvious implications for teachers and the classroom practices adopted by them.

Second language competence and self-regulated learning

Research findings that verbal achievement and verbal efficacy are correlated significantly with strategy use (Zimmerman & Martinez-Pons, 1988; 1990) are particularly pertinent to this proposed study. It is hypothesized that second language users, who are not yet fully competent in their second language, will be disadvantaged in their use of self-regulated strategies because of assumed weaknesses in verbal ability and verbal efficacy. Of the 14 strategies identified by Zimmerman and Martinez-Pons (1986), half (self-evaluation, organizing and transforming, seeking information, keeping records and monitoring, rehearsing and memorizing, seeking social assistance – from peers, teachers, and adults, reviewing records – tests, notes and textbooks) require students to use one or more of the macro skills of speaking, listening, reading and writing in the target language. Depending on the level of development in these four skills, students will be variously disadvantaged in their attempts to employ strategies that require direct use of one or more of the macro skills in their second language.

The interaction between language proficiency and the use of self-regulated strategies is further complicated by the verbalizations or private speech of students. Such speech is directed towards the self in order to facilitate the execution of a task. It has been shown to improve coding, storage, and retention of information thereby aiding the process of future retrieval and use (Denney, 1975; Schunk, 1986); verbalization can improve students' self-efficacy for performing tasks (Schunk, 1986) which in turn can promote task motivation and learning (Schunk, 1985); by using self-reinforcement and coping with verbalizations, students may be better able to maintain a positive task orientation and cope with difficulties (Michenbaum & Asarnow, 1979). These findings all point to the key role of verbalization in developing self-regulated learning in students.

Another potential problem for second language users lies in the area of the use of the social strategies of self-regulated learning (i.e. seeking assistance from peers, teachers, and other adults). In this respect, not only is there the problem of limited oral proficiency which could well discourage students from attempting to use these strategies but there is also the possibility of conflict arising out of different cultural and educational backgrounds. For some second language users, it is perceived to be inappropriate behaviour to seek personal assistance from the teacher. Furthermore, even though the seeking of assistance from peers may be viewed as acceptable behaviour by second language users, and is a previously highly practised activity for some (Tang, 1990), lack of confidence in their ability to approach peers successfully, to be clearly understood and to correctly understand their responses may be too strong a deterrent to the use of this strategy.

Finally, there is some research that suggests that studying in a second language will influence a student's approach to learning (Watkins, Biggs & Regmi, 1991). Students less confident in a second language tend to rely more on rote learning whereas those with greater confidence are low on surface and high on deep approaches to learning. This suggests that an increase in second language competence will be associated with an increased ability to employ self-regulated learning strategies in the execution of academic tasks.

(v) Research questions

1   What self-regulated learning strategies are used by Asian students in their native educational settings?
2   Do the self-regulated learning strategies of Asian students change when they become learners in Australian schools, using English as a second language? If so, in what ways?
3   What do Asian students actually understand by the term 'learning'?
4   Do the conceptions of learning held by Asian students change when they become students in Australian schools?
5   What is the relationship between students' conceptions of learning and their use of self-regulated strategies?
6   What, if any, are the differences between the conceptions of learning and the use of self-regulated learning strategies of Asian and Australian students?
7   Does the level of English language competence of Asian students in Australian schools affect their use of self-regulated learning strategies?

B. Research plan

(i) Methods and approaches

Study 1

Purpose

The purpose of this study is to design an interview schedule that is appropriate for use with both Australian secondary school students and students from two different Asian countries. In order for an interview schedule to provide reliable and valid information, a number of factors need to be kept in mind. Segall (1986) noted the following as important considerations in the construction of a cross-cultural interview schedule: efficiency with relation to time and cost; the construction of a set of questions which serve a purpose, which are unambiguous, which allow the interviewer to insert probe questions to obtain more elaboration of answers already given, and which make it easy for the respondent to answer; the use of translation techniques that will maximize correct interpretation of responses; and the development of appropriate coding and scoring systems.

Using the above guidelines for the construction of a reliable and valid instrument, an interview schedule, based on that developed by Zimmerman and Martinez-Pons (1986; 1990), will be designed. This interview schedule will assess the different categories of self-regulated learning strategies (self-evaluation; organizing and transforming; goal-setting and planning; seeking information; keeping records and monitoring; environmental structuring; self-consequences; rehearsing and memorizing; seeking peer, teacher or adult assistance; reviewing tests, notes, and texts; and other).

A number of different learning contexts will be identified both from the Zimmerman and Martinez-Pons studies and from pilot interviews with newly arrived Asian students and students who are accustomed to the Australian secondary school learning environment. This will ensure that learning contexts will be valid for all participants taking part in this research. The following is an example of a learning context that could be described:

> Imagine your teacher is discussing with your class the influence of twentieth-century developments in technology on the lives of people today. Your teacher says that you will be tested on the topic the next day. Do you have a method that you would use to help you learn and remember the information being discussed? What if you are having trouble understanding or remembering the information discussed in class?

> (adapted from Zimmerman & Martinez-Pons, 1990)

Zimmerman and Martinz-Pons (1986) described procedures for the coding of protocols which resulted in an interrater agreement level of 86%. Three different scoring procedures – strategy use, strategy frequency and strategy consistency – were developed to summarize the categorical data obtained. A pilot study using a small group of students from Perth metropolitan schools will be used to check the appropriateness of these procedures and refine them where possible. This group of students will include representatives of the three types of students used for this research and who are described in the following two studies.

Study 2
Purpose
This study will investigate conceptions of learning and the use of self-regulated strategies of Asian students from two different countries before they have been exposed to schooling in Australia.

Participants
The participants will be 60 newly arrived Asian students who are about to commence an intensive English language programme prior to entry into upper secondary (Years 11 and 12) education in Perth. Costs associated with the translation of interview data make it impossible to include students from a large number of Asian countries. Students from two Asian countries will be selected from Perth schools, depending on availability at the time of the study. In order to ensure that responses to questions in the interview schedule are based on the learning strategies students have developed for use in their

native learning environments rather than strategies that have been influenced by exposure to other learning environments, it is important that students have not had previous schooling in a non-native learning environment.

Procedures

The self-regulated learning interview schedule developed in Study 1 will be presented separately to each student in his or her native language by trained interviewers. The interviewers will have been acquainted with the nature and purpose of the study and trained to present the interview schedule in such a way as to elicit from students answers that are as fully elaborated as possible. A number of different learning contexts will be described to students and they will be asked to indicate the methods they would normally use in the situations described.

Students will also be asked to respond to the question 'What do you actually understand by learning?'

Student responses to questions will be recorded by the interviewer who will later translate these into English. All interviews will be tape-recorded to enable subsequent checking of responses.

Data analysis

Coding and scoring procedures developed in Study 1 will be applied to student responses to the self-regulated learning interview schedule.

Using methodology described by Marton and Säljö (1984), responses to the question about conceptions of learning will be analysed and coded according to the six levels: increasing one's knowledge; memorizing and reproducing; applying; understanding; seeing something in a different way; and changing as a person. Briefly, this approach to the analysis of the transcripts will involve the identification and grouping, on the basis of similarities, differences and complementarities, students' responses to the question 'What do you actually understand by learning?'

Multiple regression analyses will be used to determine if there is an association between learning strategy use and conceptions of learning. For instance, do students who use more self-regulated learning strategies tend to understand learning more in the last three ways as opposed to the first three ways?

Study 3

Purpose

The purpose of this study is to investigate the use of self-regulated strategies by two groups of secondary school students: native speakers of English; and Asian students whose second language is English, who have been studying in Australian schools for at least two years, and who have achieved at least an intermediate level of competence in the use of English. Patterns of strategy use of these two groups and the group of students from the second study will be compared in order to establish if differences exist between the groups.

The study will also investigate the conceptions of learning held by the native speakers of English and the Asian students. These will be compared with the conceptions of students in the first study.

Finally, the study will investigate the relationship between the two levels of English language proficiency (intermediate and advanced) and the patterns of self-regulated learning strategy use of the Asian students.

Participants

Ninety Year 12 students studying at Perth metropolitan high schools will be used for this study. Thirty will be native speakers of English and 60 will be non-native English speakers from similar Asian language backgrounds to those in the second study. They will have been studying in Australian schools for at least two years. Half of the non-English speaking background students will be at an 'intermediate' level of language proficiency and half will be at an 'advanced' level. Students will be assigned to proficiency groups according to language test scores and on teacher recommendation.

Procedure

The question 'What exactly do you understand by learning?' and the self-regulated learning interview schedule will be presented (in English) to students in a similar manner to that used in Study 2. Depending on information gained from Study 2 with respect to the category 'other', further categories of strategy will be added , or, if no new strategies did emerge, this category will remain as 'other'.

Data analysis

Responses to the strategy interview schedule and the question about conceptions of learning will be coded and scored as for Study 2. As the data will be frequency counts, log linear analysis will be used to assess differences in strategy use and conceptions of learning across the four groups.

(ii) What efforts have been made to ensure that the project does not duplicate work already done?

An extensive search of the literature has been undertaken since February, 1993. Searches on ERIC and Psychlit, and an examination of recent editions of CIJE and bibliographies obtained from key journal articles, have produced a large collection of readings related to self-regulated learning and conceptions of learning. Although these two areas have been well researched, a cross-cultural perspective has not been applied. Furthermore, the two areas have been researched independently of each other and no evidence of linking theory and findings in the manner proposed in this research has been found.

(iii) Confidentiality

All information pertaining to participants will remain the property of the researcher and will not be used for any purpose except for execution of this study. Students' names will not be used other than for organization of the raw data.

8.2 Qualitative proposal: education

Name of candidate: *Ron Chalmers*
Degree: Doctor of Philosophy, The University of Western Australia

A. Proposed study

(i) Title

The inclusion of children with a severe or profound intellectual disability in regular classrooms: how teachers manage the situation.

(ii) The research aim

The aim of this study is to use grounded theory methods to develop a theory about how primary school teachers in rural schools in Western Australia manage the situation of having a child with a severe or profound intellectual disability included in their classroom during the course of one school year.

Currently, in Western Australia, children with intellectual disabilities are taught in a variety of educational settings by teachers from a wide range of backgrounds. The vast majority of children with a severe or profound intellectual disability attend education support schools, centres or units. In rural and remote areas of the state where education support facilities do not exist, a relatively small number of children with this level of disability (35 primary school students in 1994) attend their local school and are included in a regular classroom. This study will focus on regular classroom teachers in country schools who are called upon to include a child with a severe or profound intellectual disability in their class.

The study will be limited to primary school teachers because, unlike their secondary school colleagues, they have the responsibility for the total educational programme and the duty of care for their class of students throughout the school day. Inclusion in secondary schools typically involves numerous teachers and a variety of classroom settings. Furthermore, the number of children with a severe or profound intellectual disability that are currently included in the regular classrooms of secondary schools is extremely small.

The study will use the criteria set by the Education Department of Western Australia to define severe and profound intellectual disability. The Department, utilizing the criteria for determining levels of severity developed by the Australian Council of Education Research, estimates that 0.1% of the population have a severe disability, and 0.05% of the population have a profound disability. A severely disabled child is described as having 'an IQ in the range 25 to 39, minimal speech and poor motor development, an inability to learn functional academic skills, and a capacity to profit from systematic habit-training' (de Lemos, 1993, p. 22). A profoundly disabled child is described as having 'an IQ below 24, minimal capacity for functioning, some motor or speech development, and a requirement of complete care and supervision' (de Lemos, 1993, p. 22).

In this proposal, the terms inclusive education and inclusion will be used deliberately in preference to the term integration. Inclusion will refer to situations in which a student with a disability is 'embedded within the normative educative pathways within the classroom and school' (Uditsky, 1993, p. 88), and in which the regular classroom teacher is responsible for the student's education. In contrast, in the Western Australia education system, the term integration is used to describe situations in which children with disabilities are located in education support units or centres, are the responsibility of education support teachers, and spend only parts of the school day in regular classrooms. In the wider education community the term integration has been used to describe many different types of placement. Terms such as physical integration, systematic integration, reciprocal integration, and associative integration are used to describe particular strategies for increasing the level of interaction between children with disabilities and their non-disabled peers. Each one of these forms of integration is something other than inclusive education as defined for this study.

(iii) The research context

The move towards the integration and inclusion of children with intellectual disabilities into mainstream education has been a feature of Western education systems for the past 15 years. This development has been largely the result of 'intensive advocacy for integration of people with disabilities into all areas of community life' (Sobsey & Dreimanis, 1993, p. 1).

Integrated or inclusive education contrasts markedly with the response of Western societies to the education of children with disabilities in earlier decades. At the turn of the last century the vast majority of children with intellectual disabilities were considered ineducable and subsequently excluded from any form of formal education (Galloway, 1985; Uditsky, 1993). In many countries there was no distinction made between children with intellectual disabilities and people with mental disorders. At the end of World War II, special education became a feature of public education in many countries (Barton & Tomlinson, 1986; Booth, 1981). Children with disabilities began to gain access to formal education, but only within the confines of special education systems.

The pressure for inclusion has come primarily from the parents of children with disabilities, educators and other community advocates (National Institute on Mental Retardation, 1981: Stainback, Stainback & Bunch, 1989). These groups have used powerful moral, social and political arguments in support of their case. One of the most persuasive arguments is that all children gain through inclusion. Studies indicate that, given proper guidance, students can learn in inclusive settings to understand, respect, be sensitive to, and grow comfortable with the individual differences and similarities amongst their peers (McHale & Simeonsson, 1980; Voeltz, 1980, p. 182). Stainback and Stainback (1985) observe that:

> there are many nonhandicapped persons who realise a tremendous range of emotional and social benefits from their involvements with persons who experience severe handicaps.

Advocates for inclusion also contend that segregated education leads to segregation in adult life, and that inclusion in education has the opposite effect. The assertion here is that positive attitudes toward people with disabilities are developed when disabled and non-disabled children interact at school, and that these attitudes are sustained in adult life (see, for example, Bricker, 1978; Snyder, Apolloni & Cooke, 1977).

Inclusion in education has also been portrayed as a human rights issue. The arguments used to enhance the participation rates of racial minorities and females in education have been used as the basis for promoting the inclusion of children with disabilities in schools. The landmark Victorian Report of the Ministerial Review of Educational Services for the Disabled (Collins, 1984) proposed that the development of policy be underpinned by five guiding principles. Significantly, the first principle was that every child has a right to be educated in an ordinary classroom in a regular class.

A number of commentators, including Bilken (1985) and Keogh (1990), have observed that the strength of the inclusive education movement has come from the values that underpin the cause rather than from the findings of studies into the outcomes of inclusion. According to Conway (1991), the introduction of policies intended to encourage inclusion has occurred not as an outcome of empirical research but as a result of changes in public attitudes about the way the wider community responds to people with disabilities.

It should not be inferred from this that there has been a dearth of research into aspects of inclusive education. The research literature in this field of education is extensive. The vast majority of this research has been characterized by the application of traditional quantitative methodologies. Experiments and questionnaire surveys in large-N studies have been the norm. The findings from quantitative research conducted during the past 15 years have contributed significantly to the field of special education and, more specifically, to the segregation–inclusion debate. Curriculum design, resourcing teacher training, administrative arrangements and efficacy research have been favoured areas for investigation.

There are, however, increasing calls for more qualitative research in this field of education (Biklen & Moeley, 1988; Hegarty & Evans, 1989; Patton, 1990; Salisbury, Palombaro & Hollowood, 1993; Stainback & Stainback, 1989). Hegarty (1989, p. 110) stated that there are 'many topics in special education that are best explored by means of qualitative methods of inquiry'. These include investigations into pupils' and teachers' perspectives and experiences of particular education programmes; clarifying the implications of various policy options; evaluating innovations; and providing detailed accounts of various forms of special education provision.

Despite these calls, Vulliamy and Webb (1993, p. 190) observed that:

> There have been relatively few published qualitative research studies on the theme of special education, despite the prominent impact of qualitative research on educational research more generally.

More research of this kind is needed to gain a greater understanding of the phenomenon of inclusive education from the perspectives of the people involved (teachers, parents, school administrators and students) in their natural settings. We need 'in-depth, penetrating investigation that strives for relational understanding of all the various factors that comprise and affect the object of the … study' (Wolf, 1979, p. 5). The development of theories about inclusion, grounded in data gathered from teachers and other school-based personnel, contribute significantly to this field of education, inform teachers who find themselves in similar situations in the future, and guide the development of policy for the education of students with disabilities.

There are clear indications that an increasing number of Australian children with intellectual disabilities will be educated in regular classrooms (see DEET, 1993; Education Department of Western Australia, 1992) and, correspondingly, that an increasing number of Western Australian primary school teachers will experience the phenomenon of inclusive education. Given that the outcomes of inclusion initiatives depend on the beliefs, values and attitudes of teachers (Cohen & Cohen, 1986), in the Western Australian context there needs to be a greater understanding of what teachers think and believe about this phenomenon, and how these thoughts and beliefs change over time.

(iv) This study's substantial and original contribution to knowledge

The aim of this study is to use grounded theory methods to build theory about a specific aspect of education where no theory currently exists. To date there is very little knowledge and no explanatory theory about the way primary school teachers in rural and remote schools manage inclusion. An extensive search of the research literature has failed to identify studies that have examined this particular phenomenon. The theory that will be generated from this study will be an original contribution to the knowledge base of the emerging field of inclusive education.

The importance of inclusive education in the 1990s

A number of recent developments indicate that the education of students with disabilities is one of the most important issues facing the Western Australian school system. In December 1992 the then Ministry of Education established the Task Force on the Education of Students with Disabilities and Specific Learning Difficulties in response to 'growing parent concerns about the problems faced by children with disabilities' (Ministerial Task Force, 1993, p. v). The Task Force report listed 60 recommendations to government. Many of these recommendations relate specifically to the role of the teacher in educating students with disabilities. In February 1994 the Minister for Education responded to the report. The Minister announced that the education of students with disabilities and specific learning difficulties would be a priority for the next three years and that schools will be required to reflect this in their school development plans. Additional resources ($6 million over the next triennium) will be allocated to implement recommendations in the Task Force report.

A recent Commonwealth Government report entitled *Project of National Significance: Students with Disabilities in Regular Classrooms* (1993) reinforces the importance for school systems and educational researchers of examining the role of the teacher in the inclusion of children with disabilities. The study outlined in this present proposal is therefore both relevant and timely. The findings will make a significant contribution to the understanding of an aspect of education that has become a priority in the current decade.

Research into aspects of inclusive education in Western Australia

The limited research conducted in Western Australia into aspects of inclusive education has tended to focus on children with mild to moderate intellectual disability (see, for example, Bain & Dolbel, 1991; Roberts & Naylor, 1994; Roberts & Zubrick, 1992). The inclusion of students with severe or profound disability has not attracted the attention of the local research community. This trend is consistent with the research focus in other education systems and in other nations. Within the context of the Western Australian education system this study will break new ground because it will focus exclusively on situations where the most disabled students are being included in regular classrooms.

The descriptors used by the Western Australian Education Department to categorize a child as severely or profoundly intellectually disabled are significantly different to the descriptors used to categorize a child as mildly or moderately intellectually disabled. Findings from the relatively substantial amount of research conducted into aspects of inclusive education for children with mild to moderate disabilities may not be relevant for an understanding of inclusion for students with more severe disability who present with a range of different functional characteristics. The findings from this study will go some way towards addressing this imbalance in the research focus.

The use of grounded theory

A preliminary examination of the research literature has failed to identify research studies that have used grounded theory methods to examine the way teachers manage the situation of having a child with a disability included in their class. This study is therefore uniquely placed to generate theory, grounded in data collected from rural schools in Western Australia, about this particular phenomenon.

It is anticipated that the theory that emerges from this study will be comprehensible and make sense to those teachers who will be studied. Also, the nature of grounded theory is such that the emergent theory 'will be abstract enough and include sufficient variation to make it applicable to a variety of contexts related to that phenomenon' (Strauss & Corbin, 1990, p. 23). In other words, the theory developed from this research will be of use to other teachers involved with inclusion, as well as other groups such as school administrators, educational policy makers, and members of the wider educational research community.

Grounded theory has been used extensively as a research methodology in sociology, and in nursing and related fields. It has been used less widely in education. This study will provide an opportunity for observations to be made about the applicability of this mode of research in education, and more specifically in the field of inclusive education.

B. The research plan

(i) The research questions

The central question of this research is as follows:

How do primary school teachers manage the situation of having a child with a severe or profound intellectual disability included in their classroom for a period of one year?

The study, and especially the data gathering process, will be guided by the following eight questions:

1   What are teachers' expectations of what is going to be involved when they realize they will have a child with a severe or profound intellectual disability in their class for the year, and what philosophical standpoint do they have about inclusion?
2   What are teachers' perceptions of the expectations of the school principal, other teachers and parents of them regarding their management of the inclusion situation? How do these perceptions change over the course of the year?
3   How does the teacher organize the classroom and education programme to accommodate the child with the severe or profound intellectual disability, and how does this change over the course of the year?
4   What are the characteristics of the relationship between the teacher and the rest of the children in the class, and how does this relationship develop over the course of the year?
5   What are the characteristics of the relationship between the teacher and the rest of the school staff, and how does this relationship develop over the course of the year?
6   How does the teacher manage the interaction between the child with the severe or profound intellectual disability and other students in the class?
7   What are the characteristics of the relationship between the teacher and the parents of the child with a severe or profound intellectual disability, and how does this relationship develop during the year?
8   What relationships develop between the teacher and the parents of non-disabled children in the class? What are the characteristics of these relationships and how do they change over the course of the year?

(ii) The research method

Research design

This study will use grounded theory methodology. Grounded theory is a research method that offers a comprehensive and systematic framework for inductively building theory. A grounded theory is one that is discovered, developed, and provisionally verified through systematic data collection and analysis of data pertaining to a particular phenomenon (Strauss & Corbin, 1990). The careful and precise application of this method will ensure that the theory to emerge from this study will meet the criteria of good science: generalizability, reproducibility, precision, rigour, and verification (Corbin & Strauss, 1990).

A number of the basic features of grounded theory make it an appropriate method for this research. These include:

1   Grounded theory methodology specifically includes analysis of process. Within grounded theory methodology the term process is used to describe 'the linking of sequences of action/interaction as they pertain to the management of, control over, or response to, a phenomenon' (Strauss & Corbin, 1990, p. 143). Process is the analyst's way of accounting for or explaining change. An important aspect of this research will be to monitor the way teachers manage inclusion over the entire school year. The research questions have been constructed to guide data collection and analysis in ways that will highlight and account for any changes in teacher management as well as the ways teachers manage changing conditions that may occur during the year. In this way process will be analysed both as progressive movement characterized by phases or stages, and as 'non-progressive movement, that is as purposeful alterations or changes in action/interaction in response to changes in conditions' (Strauss & Corbin, 1990, p. 52). The first conceptualization of process will involve an analysis of the conditions and corresponding actions that move the teacher from one phase or stage of management to another. The conceptualization of process as non-progressive will involve analysis of the adjustments taken by teachers in response to changing conditions throughout the year.

2   Grounded theory methodology directly links macroscopic issues to the phenomenon under investigation. This mode of research requires that broader, contextual issues, that are shown to influence the phenomenon under study, be given appropriate recognition in the development of theory. Rather than focusing the investigation by disregarding these broader conditions, every effort will be made to acknowledge and account for them.

3   Grounded theory makes its greatest contribution in areas in which little research has been done. As stated previously, little research has been conducted specifically into aspects of the management of the inclusion of children with severe or profound intellectual disabilities in regular classrooms. Most of the research in this field has tended to focus on children with mild to moderate disabilities (for example, Center & Curry, 1993; Chambers & Kay, 1992; Deno, Maruyama, Espin & Cohen, 1990; Roberts & Zubrick, 1992), and on integration, mainstreaming, or some other form of placement that differs from inclusion (for example, Biklen, 1985; Center et al., 1988; Taylor, 1988). The paucity of research about inclusion means that many of the variables relevant to the concepts of this phenomenon are yet to be identified. Grounded theory is an appropriate methodology for this study as it will generate theory that can be used as a precursor for further investigation of this phenomenon and related issues. Other qualitative research techniques, quantitative methods, or a combination of both, can then be used in subsequent studies to test, verify or extend the qualitative hypotheses that emerge from this initial research.

The study population

The population for this study will be all primary school teachers in Western Australian country schools who, in the 1995 school year, have a child with a severe or profound intellectual disability included in their class. Information provided by the Social Justice Branch of the Education Department of Western Australia indicates that in 1994 there are 25 Government school teachers in this situation. It is anticipated that in 1995 this number will increase to approximately 28. Within the non-Government school systems (Catholic Education Commission and the Association of Independent Schools) there are approximately 10 teachers in this situation in the current year. This number is not expected to increase in 1995. It is therefore estimated that the total population for this study will be 38 teachers.

The study sample

It is estimated that approximately 25 of the 38 teachers in the study population will be in school districts in the southern half of Western Australia. For logistical reasons the gathering of data for this study will be restricted to these southern districts (Esperance, Albany, Manjimup, Bunbury North, Bunbury South, Narrogin, Peel, Northam and Merredin). Of the 25 teachers that remain as candidates for this study, it is likely that a small proportion are unlikely to accept the invitation to become involved. This leaves a field of approximately 20 teachers.

Six teachers will be selected, at random, to provide the first body of data. This will be the initial sample group. Subsequent data collection will be guided by the theoretical sampling principle of grounded theory. Where necessary, data will be gathered from all 20 teachers if theoretical saturation on any particular category has not been achieved at an earlier stage.

In this study other decisions about the sampling process will be made during the research process itself. In a grounded theory study theoretical sampling cannot be fully planned before the study commences.

Data collection

In this study data gathering methods will include semi-structured interviews, teacher diaries, observations, and document analysis. Data will be gathered from the initial sample group in a cyclical process as outlined in the timetable below.

- Semi-structured interviews (round 1), December 1994–January 1995
- Teacher diary entries (5 days), term 1, 1995
- Semi-structured interviews (round 2), end of term 1, 1995
- Observations of teachers; 2 days per teacher (round 1), early term 2, 1995
- Teacher diary entries (5 days), early term 3, 1995
- Semi-structured interviews (round 3), early term 3, 1995
- Observations of teachers; 2 days per teacher (round 2), term 3, 1995
- Teacher diary entries (5 days), term 4, 1994
- Semi-structured interviews (round 4), term 4, 1995.

This timetable is a tentative plan for data gathering. In grounded theory studies data gathering and analysis are tightly interwoven processes; data analysis guides future data collection. Therefore, changes may be made to this provisional timetable if the analysis of data collected early in the school year indicates a need to adopt a different sequence of data gathering processes.

The precise timing of interviews, diary entries and observations will also depend on events in individual schools. It may be possible to anticipate, at the start of the school year, crucial events or periods in the school calendar that are likely to influence the way the teacher responds to the phenomenon of inclusion. These may include the first parents' meeting, the annual swimming carnival, or the first class excursion. As far as possible, data gathering activities will be timed to coincide with, or immediately follow, these school events.

Semi-structured interviews will be used as the primary means of data collection. Initially, arrangements will be made to interview each of the teachers in the initial study sample on four occasions during the course of the school year. These interviews will be tape recorded. The first round of interviews will be structured to gather data about the widest possible range of issues associated with the phenomenon under study. The research questions will guide the data gathering process. The structure and content of subsequent interviews will be determined after the data analysis process has commenced. The second, third and fourth rounds of interviews will be used to (a) gather new data about known concepts and categories that will have been developed about the phenomenon, (b) gather new data about the phenomenon, and (c) involve the teachers in a process of testing and verifying data and the emerging theory.

Each of the teachers included in the initial study sample will be requested to maintain a tape recorded diary for three periods during the year. On each of these occasions, the teacher will be encouraged to make entries into a handheld micro tape recorder for a period of five days (one school week). Every effort will be made to ensure that the teacher is comfortable with the tape diary technique and that they are clear about the purposes of this data gathering procedure.

Tape diaries serve a number of purposes (Burgess, 1984, p. 203). Firstly, these diaries provide first-hand accounts of situations to which the researcher may not have direct access. Secondly, they provide insiders' accounts of situations. Finally, they provide further sampling of informants, of activities and of time which may complement the observations made by the researcher.

In this study, diary entries will (a) provide the researcher with information about critical incidents that relate to the phenomenon under investigation, (b) serve as a record of the teachers' perceptions of their experiences with inclusion, (c) act as a triangulation strategy, and (d) stimulate and direct the data gathering process in subsequent interview sessions. The value of the link between the analysis of diary data and subsequent interviews is highlighted by Burgess (1984, p. 203) when he states that:

in cases where the researcher obtains an informant's diary, it may be scanned for data that needs to be elaborated, discussed, explored and illustrated, all of which are tasks that can be conducted in an interview.

Teachers will be encouraged to keep the tape recorder with them (at home, in the car, as well as at school) throughout the five days to record as much information as possible about their experiences in managing inclusion. They will be given a brief overview of critical incident technique and encouraged to report critical incidents. They will also be advised to record their thoughts, feelings, beliefs and attitudes about these critical incidents and about the management of inclusion generally. It is anticipated that the data from each of the interviews will highlight categories that will provide a degree of focus for teachers as they use their tape diaries.

The decision to limit the periods of diary keeping to five days is based on the experiences of other researchers who have used diary techniques (see Sommer & Sommer, 1986). The primary objective is to gather the maximum amount of relevant data without the process becoming tedious for the teacher.

The third major data gathering technique will be observation. Direct observation of how individual teachers manage the inclusion of a child with a severe or profound intellectual disability will provide the data required to verify and corroborate the information gained through interviews and diary entries. It will also allow the researcher to find cases in which there is a mismatch between interview data and teacher behaviour; where teachers do not do or act as they say they do. This will ensure that the theory generated from this research is based on more than the perceptions of teachers. School-based observations will also allow the researcher to pursue and test out relationships between theoretically relevant categories.

Initially it is planned to conduct two rounds of observations of each teacher. Once again, this may change during the course of the year depending upon the categories that emerge. Similarly, decisions about matters such as participant versus non-participant observation, timing of observations, length of observations, questioning during observation, and data recording methods will be made on a site-by-site basis.

Data will be obtained from document analysis and interviews with other members of the school communities. Arrangements will be made to interview other members of the school staff at times throughout the year. It is not possible, prior to the commencement of the data gathering process, to predict the timing of these interviews or the actual staff members to be interviewed. Education Department and school documents will also be used as sources of data. It is anticipated that such documents will provide a 'rich source of information, contextually relevant and grounded in the contexts they represent' (Lincoln & Guba, 1985, p. 277).

A piloting exercise will be conducted during the fourth term of the 1994 school year. A teacher with a severe or profoundly intellectually disabled child included in their class in 1994 will be invited to (a) trial the teacher diary for one week, (b) respond to, and comment on, the draft interview schedule for the first round of semi-structured interviews, and (c) comment on their experiences with inclusion during the previous three terms. This process will fine tune the data gathering methods and heighten my theoretical sensitivity towards the phenomenon of integration. Theoretical sensitivity refers to the 'attribute of having insight, the ability to give meaning to data, the capacity to understand, and capability to separate the pertinent from that which isn't' (Strauss & Corbin, 1990, p. 42).

Analysis of the data

Analysing data by the grounded theory method is an intricate process of reducing raw data into concepts that are designated to stand for categories. The categories are then developed and integrated into a theory (Corbin, 1986). This process is achieved by coding data, writing memos, and diagramming.

In this study, data will be coded and analysed using the three coding methods of the grounded theory model: open coding, axial coding and selective coding. Open coding is the process of breaking down, examining, comparing, conceptualizing, and categorizing data. The aim of open coding is the development of categories. Axial coding involves re-building the data (fractured through open coding) in new ways by establishing relationships between categories, and between categories and their sub-categories. Selective coding involves selecting a core category, systematically relating it to other categories, validating those relationships, and filling in categories that need further development or refinement. It is through this process that all the interpretive work done over the course of the research is integrated to form a grounded theory.

Coding procedures, memo writing and diagramming will be used as data analysis strategies. Facts or incidents obtained from interviews, documents, or diary entries, will be coded in a systematic way. Memos will be written as records of analysis, and diagrams will be developed as visual representations of the relationships between concepts. Code notes, memos and diagrams will become progressively more detailed and sophisticated as the analysis moves through the three types of coding.

Throughout the data analysis process, the teachers and other participants in the research will be involved directly in verifying the data and the emerging theory.

(iii) Efforts made to ensure that the project does not duplicate work already done

During the past six months I have conducted an extensive review of the literature in the areas of special education, integration, and inclusive education. I have been unable to locate any research that utilizes grounded theory methodology to develop a theory about how primary school teachers manage the inclusion of children with severe or profound intellectual disabilities in their regular classroom.

(iv) Confidentiality

The informed consent of the following people will be obtained prior to the commencement of the study:

1   the principals of the nominated schools;
2   the appropriate officers from the Catholic Education Commission and the Association of Independent Schools;
3   the teachers chosen in the initial sample group;
4   the parents of the children with disabilities.

The informed consent of other teachers and parents (chosen in the wider sample group) will be sought at the time they are approached to participate in the study.

All data will be treated in a way that protects the confidentiality and anonymity of the teachers, parents and children involved in the study. Coding will be used during the gathering and processing of interview notes, tapes and transcripts.

8.3 Mixed-method proposal: social medicine

Name of candidate: *Claire Chinnery*
Degree: Master of Educational Studies, The University of Western Australia

Abstract

Research has demonstrated that the performance of emergency medical teams depends not only on the technical knowledge and skills of individual team members, but on generic competencies such as communication, leadership, and problem-solving. The goal of the present study is to identify factors that predict team performance in simulated cardiac arrest scenarios. The sample for the proposed study will comprise groups of health professionals attending training sessions at CTEC. Data will be collected from at least 60 teams, with approximately four members per team (total sample $n = 240$). During their standard debriefing sessions, all participants will complete a Team Composition and Process Questionnaire, which will include both closed- and open-ended questions on individual and team functioning during the scenario. Videotapes of the scenarios will then be analysed to determine the quality of each team's performance. Multiple regression analyses will be performed to test for relationships between scores on the Team Composition and Process Questionnaire and team performance ratings. Further, on the basis of the latter ratings, three poorly functioning teams will be selected for in-depth case study analysis. Videotapes for these three teams will then be analysed using the framework of activity theory to identify factors that contributed to the teams' poor task performance. The ultimate goal of the study is to provide information that may be used to improve training programmes in cardiac arrest resuscitation.

Introduction

Over the past few decades, significant efforts have been made to enhance the efficacy of training programmes in cardiac resuscitation.* Despite this, survival rates from cardiac arrest have remained relatively stable (Abella, Alvarado et al., 2005; Sanders & Ewy, 2005), even with the introduction of internationally recognized resuscitation guidelines (Sanders & Ewy, 2005). One possible reason for these poor outcomes is that health professionals fail to follow standard guidelines, resulting in delays or failures to provide the appropriate treatment (Abella, Alvarado et al., 2005; Abella, Sandbo et al., 2005; Aufderheide et al., 2004; Milander et al., 1995).

Traditionally, training for cardiac resuscitation has focused on disseminating technical knowledge and task-specific practical skills (e.g. knowledge of abnormal cardiac rhythms, appropriate use of a defibrillator). Recent perspectives on higher education have, however, highlighted the need for training programmes to foster generic competencies, as well as discipline-specific knowledge and skills. *Generic competencies* include non-technical skills that are important across all areas of a particular discipline (e.g. OECD, 2002). Given that health care delivery typically involves working as a member of a multidisciplinary team, generic competencies within this area would include skills such as communication, problem-solving, and leadership. In relation to cardiac arrest and similar medical emergencies, generic competencies may be critical for effective team performance for at least two major reasons.

First, rapid delivery of care is essential for successful resuscitation of the patient. It is generally accepted that to maximize patient survival, diagnosis and treatment should commence within three minutes of the arrest onset (Australian Resuscitation Council, 1998). Research has also indicated that as complexity in health care increases, so too do the number of errors made by health professionals (Australian Council for Safety and Quality in Health Care, 2001). In cardiac resuscitation, the need for rapid delivery, the complex and demanding nature of the treatment, and the severe implications of errors made in the delivery of the treatment, place considerable emphasis on the smooth functioning of the team managing the arrest.

Second, cardiac arrests are relatively rare. In one hospital in the UK, only 0.4% of patients were reported to have experienced a cardiac arrest (Hodgetts et al., 2002). This means that many individual health care professionals may have limited direct experience in managing cardiac arrests. Teams confronted with cardiac arrests will, therefore, often rely heavily on the distributed knowledge of all team members. By implication, the effective management of cardiac arrests will rely on factors such as the ability of team members to communicate their knowledge to others and coordinate their actions within an emergency timeframe.

Previous research on teamwork in medicine

Few studies have been conducted on the generic competencies needed by members of medical work teams in emergency situations. Of those that have, there has been an almost exclusive emphasis on the characteristics of team leaders and performance. For example, Cooper and Wakelam (1999) found that good leadership correlated positively with medical team performance in cardiac arrest situations. Several components of good leadership were identified. Overall, the ability to initiate a structure within the team was of primary importance, as it enabled the team members to work more effectively together and to perform the tasks required more efficiently. Attributes such as the ability to direct and command, to be flexible, to engender trust, and to give guidance and assistance where necessary, were found to be critical in establishing a team structure. Further key competencies of leaders included adherence to standard guidelines where appropriate, and the ability to display a positive attitude, motivate and encourage the team, decide how and when things should be done, and assign tasks to specific team members.

Other studies have supported the key facets of leadership suggested by Cooper and Wakelam (1999). In a questionnaire survey of 130 Resuscitation Training Officers in the UK, Pittman, Turner and Gabbott (2001) found that the ability to establish a team structure is important for the success of resuscitation teams. Using videotape evidence of cardiopulmonary resuscitation techniques, Mann and Heyworth (1996) also found that resuscitation tasks were performed more effectively when the team leader used standard guidelines. In a study of leadership in trauma teams, Ritchie and Cameron (1999) also ascribed many deficiencies in the performance of teams to a lack of assertive direction, poor enunciation of the overall plan, poor identification of the leader, and communication problems. In the latter study, failures by leaders to verbalize thought processes and to give clear verbal instructions were identified as particularly detrimental.

Recent research beyond medical emergencies, however, has suggested that focusing on leadership as a source of team success or failure may be too restrictive. This research has suggested that team performance may be influenced by a host of other factors such as cohesiveness, clear role divisions, and group composition factors such as gender, status and experience (e.g.

Allen, Arocha & Patel, 1998; Christensen et al., 2000; Hawryluck, Espin, Garwood, Evans & Lingard, 2002; O'Donnell, Adams, DuRussel & Derry, 1997; Pagliari & Grimshaw, 2002; Strom, Strom & Moore, 1999; Vinokur, Burnstein, Sechrest & M., 1985). As indicated above, some emergency medical situations such as cardiac arrest are relatively rare. As a result, even a team leader may have relatively limited experience in dealing with these situations, and thus will rely on the knowledge of other team members. Given this, effective team performance is likely to depend on a complex interplay between communication and coordination factors that do not stem solely from the actions of the team leader.

Furthermore, research within the field of medical emergencies has typically used an individualistic approach to examining team performance, rather than seeing the team as a unit of analysis. In such approaches, the assumption must be that improving the skills of individuals within the team will produce better performance by the team as a whole. While this approach has produced some insights into ways in which team performance can be improved, it has neglected overall group composition and interaction processes that may contribute to performance. The results of such research are likely to produce an overly simplistic picture of the factors that impact team outcomes. For example, much previous research suggests that team performance will hinge on characteristics of the leader. However, in emergency situations, actual (as opposed to nominal) leadership roles are often necessarily fluid. As a result, team performance cannot clearly be ascribed to only one individual within the team, as many will adopt a leadership role at different times in dealing with the emergency.

Activity theory and the study of medical emergencies

The shift to more process- and context-oriented accounts of team functioning invites the application of new tools for analysing the interactions that occur between team members. The conceptual framework provided by activity theory has clear implications for research in emergency team response contexts. From this perspective, teams are viewed *as activity systems* rather than collections of individual agents. In turn, the processes associated with responses to emergencies are viewed in terms of the activity of the team as a whole.

Activity theory has a long history within Soviet psychology, drawing on Vygotskian notions of tool mediation and sociocultural-historical theories of learning. Central to the sociocultural-historical approach is that it focuses on the analysis of the sociocultural context rather than on the individual in isolation. Vygotsky's followers identified the *activity* as the fundamental unit of analysis. An activity refers to a goal-oriented hierarchical system of actions and operations, mediated by cultural artefacts or tools. A fundamental assumption of this approach is that activities cannot be analysed meaningfully in isolation from their social contexts. As indicated by Leontiev

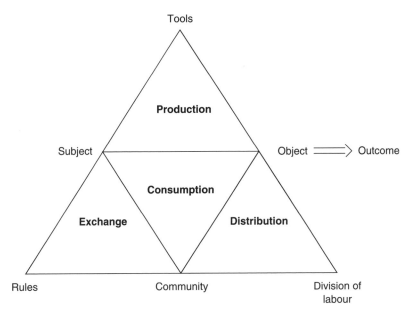

Figure 8.1 *Engeström's activity system model*

(1981), activity 'is not a reaction or aggregate of reactions, but a system with its own structure, its own internal transformations, and its own development' (p. 23).

These notions are further explicated and developed in the work of Engeström and his colleagues (e.g. Engeström, 1987; Engeström & Escalante, 1996). Engeström's conceptualization of activity theory emphasizes the mediating role of the community in an individual activity system. Engeström's model divides activity systems into several components (see Figure 8.1). In this model, the *subject* refers to the individual or group of individuals whose agency is chosen as the point of view in the analysis. The *object* refers to the ends towards which activity is directed (i.e. the activity that the members of the system transform into an outcome to satisfy certain needs). The *tools* mediate relationships between the subject and the object. The *community* comprises a group of interdependent people whose agency is directed at the object of the activity, and this group mediates the relationships between subject and object. The *rules* refer to the set of norms and conventions that regulate the relationships between subject and community. *Division of labour* mediates the relation between community and object, reflecting power and status within the community as well as the division of tasks between its members.

Changes within activity systems occur as a product of various inner *contradictions* that emerge within and amongst their constituent components (Engeström, 1996). *Primary* contradictions within the components of the system are responsible for the development of *need states* within the system. These need states can be resolved through the system evolving into an improved system that maintains the structure of the original by incorporating a new tool, rule, or division of labour that enables the need state to be met. Such a change is referred to as a *solution innovation*. More complex need states may have to be resolved through radical change that results in structural changes in the system. When a strong novel factor is introduced into a component of the system, it acquires a new quality, and *secondary* contradictions may appear between that component and existing components of the system. These contradictions may lead to the evolution of *tertiary* contradictions between the central form of the activity and a more advanced version of it. The activity system gradually transforms into this more advanced form to resolve the tensions that are created by such internal contradictions. These tensions may, therefore, prompt the creation of new approaches to achieving the object of the system through the development of new tools or structures that enable the system to function more cohesively.

Although the use of activity theory to analyse team processes is relatively new, this framework has been applied to examine the work of medical teams in a handful of recent studies. Engeström (2000) illustrated the potential use of activity theory to analyse interactions between nurses, physicians, and other members of medical teams in a Danish urgent care unit. A similar example is provided by Boreham, Shea and Mackway-Jones (2000), who focused on analysing the interdependencies that arise within teams in hospital emergency departments. Bardram (2000) also used activity theory to analyse the role of temporal coordination problems in hospital emergency work teams. More recently, Korpela et al. (2004) conducted an activity analysis of a medical team who were managing the treatment of a sick baby in an intensive care unit. A common theme that has emerged from all of these studies is that developing a collective understanding through the creation of shared knowledge is central to group effectiveness. Boreham et al. demonstrated further that failures to share knowledge in hospital emergency teams can have serious consequences. By implication, in order to achieve maximum effectiveness in a group situation, it is necessary to establish exactly what shared knowledge the group possesses, and assess whether this knowledge is being communicated in the most effective manner possible.

Summary and study rationale

At present, training of medical practitioners for emergency situations focuses primarily on improving technical knowledge and skills. Recent perspectives have, however, highlighted the need to include a secondary focus on generic competencies, as well as task-related knowledge and skills. This may be particularly true in emergency medical situations, where skills such as communication and problem-solving can impact performance dramatically. Further, although there has been some research on teamwork within emergency situations, it is necessary to examine the team as a whole, rather than focusing on characteristics of individuals (e.g. leaders) within the team.

In the present study, data collected during simulated cardiac arrests will be analysed to identify factors that predict team performance in emergency medical situations. A mixed-method approach will be used to address two primary research questions:

1   What are the key group composition factors (e.g. collective background experience, differentials in leadership characteristics) that predict the performance of teams in simulated cardiac resuscitation exercises? A quantitative survey approach will be used to address this goal.
2   What are the mediating links between such compositional factors and team performance? A case study approach will be used to address this goal, involving in-depth observations and analyses of the team interaction processes that occur in the simulated cardiac resuscitation exercises.

Method

Sample

The sample for the proposed study will be gathered from groups of health professionals attending training sessions at CTEC. Groups attending the centre normally include one or two doctors and three or four nurses. The groups participate in a number of emergency medical scenarios as part of their training. One of these scenarios is usually a cardiac arrest. Approximately three to four health professionals from the group would normally participate in the cardiac arrest scenario. It is expected that data collection will occur over approximately 9 months, which should allow access to at least 60 cardiac arrest scenarios (i.e. 60 teams, with approximately four members per team, total sample $n = 240$).

Setting

While simulated arrests are an accepted method of training, they have not been used extensively in research to date. In addition to the practical advantages of this approach, studying real cardiac arrests can be problematic because of the large number of factors that may impact outcomes in field situations. Many such factors will not be within the control of the team. For this reason, simulations provide a more suitable context for conducting controlled evaluations of specific team functioning and performance factors.

In the present study, all data will be collected in the high fidelity medical simulation facility at The University of Western Australia's Clinical Training and Education Centre (CTEC). The facility uses a sophisticated, computer-controlled manikin that is capable of responding to participant actions. The simulations will be conducted in a mock hospital setting with real hospital equipment. The simulated arrests will mimic real cardiac arrests as closely as possible, and participants will be asked to perform as they would in their normal professional roles.

Instruments

Team Composition and Process Questionnaire

Immediately following the simulated cardiac arrest, participants will be asked to complete the Team Composition and Process Questionnaire (see Appendix A [not reproduced]). Given that there was no established instrument available that could address the study goals, the researcher developed this questionnaire by drawing information from previous studies of group dynamics and performance outcomes. The questionnaire has two major components. The first includes a number of closed-ended subsections, designed to collect information on group demographics and perceptions of team processes. The second uses an open-ended format designed to collect qualitative information to explain relationships between group characteristics and performance at critical points during the scenario.

Previous research in team functioning has identified a number of performance predictors that were deemed to be potentially relevant in this study. At the most general level, these are typically divided into group composition and group process factors. Composition factors that have been found to predict team performance in some situations include gender mix, age differentials, and cultural diversity (e.g. Dailey, 2003). Numerous team process factors have also been identified as potential predictors of team performance. In this study, a small number of key components were selected for inclusion on the basis of previous research in group dynamics (e.g. Doel & Sawdon, 2003; Dunn, Lewandowsky & Kirsner, 2002; Riordan & Wetherley, 1999):

- team cohesiveness (e.g. task cohesion, interpersonal cohesion, conflict);
- team processes (e.g. communication, problem-solving, and metacognition/reflection);
- team structure (e.g. salience of the cooperative task structure, collective knowledge available, role divisions within the team, and coordination of team efforts);
- leadership efficacy (e.g. decision-making, role distribution, style, communication and exchange); and
- personal characteristics of team members (e.g. sense of membership in the team, awareness of roles, personal knowledge, assertiveness, and attitudes towards teamwork).

Appendix A [not reproduced] presents the full list of items to be used in all sections of the questionnaire. The demographic checklist will be used to derive the team composition variables of interest in the study. For the closed-ended section on team processes, items are listed under conceptual category headings. In the instrument used, the items from the different subsections in this component will be interspersed. The process questions in the open-ended component of the scale are organized according to critical incidents in the resuscitation scenarios. Thus, in this section, participants will be asked to report on their actions and thought processes at key junctures during the resuscitation effort (i.e. points at which actions taken or not taken can result in the survival or death of the patient). Information from the open-ended response section will be used to map participants' perspectives on their own and on their team's performance to actual performance ratings assigned by the researcher. These ratings will be assigned during observations of video data collected for each scenario.

Video observation protocol
As part of the standard training programme at CTEC, participants are videoed during the medical emergency scenarios. The videotapes are used to facilitate discussion during a debrief after each scenario. The videotapes are normally erased at the end of each training session. For the purposes of the proposed research study, however, the videotapes will be retained for further analysis. Explicit consent for using the tapes in this manner will be sought from all participants. Based on these videos, two measures will be applied:

(i) Cardiac arrest management Task Performance Index
Each group will be rated using a previously developed index of task performance in cardiac arrest (see Appendix B [not reproduced]). The index gives a numerical score to each team based on correct and timely use of the accepted protocol for management of cardiac arrest. The interrater reliability of the index will be estimated during the proposed using a sample of 5% of all videos. A criterion level of 85% agreement will be adopted before the observations proceed.

(ii) Team Process Transcriptions
Three low scoring groups with different kinds of profiles on the quantitative Team Composition and Process Questionnaire will be selected for the in-depth case study observations. Videos for these three groups will then be transcribed both for the actions taken and for interactions between team members in a running event record format (Heath & Vom Lehn, 2000).

Procedure
All groups attending training sessions at CTEC will be invited to participate in the study. Participants will be given verbal and written information relating to the study. Written consent will be obtained from those who wish to participate. Consent will state explicitly that videos will be

retained for the purpose of analysis by the researcher only, and that their anonymity will be preserved in the presentation of the study results. Trainers involved in running the training sessions will be briefed on the requirements of the study and will distribute the questionnaires following cardiac arrest scenarios. Each participant in the cardiac arrest scenario will be identified by a number pinned to his or her clothing and written on the questionnaire. This will enable correlation of data from questionnaires and video transcriptions. The completed questionnaires and videotape from each scenario will be sealed in an envelope and stored in a locked cupboard to be collected by the researcher for analysis.

Data analysis

Two different types of analyses will be used to address the two research questions.

Research question 1 will be addressed using quantitative analysis methods. To identify which group composition and process variables contributed significantly to predicting team performance, a multiple regression analysis will be performed. In this analysis, the criterion (dependent) variable will be group scores on the Task Performance Index. The unit of analysis will be team performance, rather than individual scores. The predictor (independent) variables will be the indices of team composition and process derived from members of each team. These will be combined (e.g. averaged) to form group-level indices for inclusion in the analysis. Using the summed scores for each of the dimensions in the Team Composition and Process Questionnaire, there will be four composition predictors (e.g. collective background experience of each team) and six process predictors (e.g. overall cohesiveness score). Given overall $n = 60$ (i.e. $n > 5$ cases per predictor), the statistical power of associated inferential tests will be within acceptable ranges.

Research question 2 will be addressed through qualitative analysis of the cases selected for this phase. To identify the mediating links between the group composition/process variables and team performance, data collected in the Team Process Transcriptions and the open-ended component of the Team Composition and Process Questionnaire will be integrated to identify potential explanatory themes that emerge with respect to group dysfunction.

As noted by Engeström (2000), activity theory does not offer ready-made techniques and procedures for research. Instead, it provides conceptual tools that must be applied according to the specifics and nature of the objective of the activity under scrutiny. Engeström does, however, present the following two principles for conducting an activity-based analysis:

1   Focus on a collective activity system as the unit of analysis. Once the collective activity system has been established, identify components and attributes of that system.

2 Identify all sources of contradictions 'within' and 'between' the various components of the collective activity system. According to Engeström, contradictions form the basis of new understandings about the activity system being investigated.

In this study, the event records will first be analysed for evidence of contradictions arising from tool use, divisions of labour, and application of rules based on the researcher's observations. The open-ended responses made by each participant will then be analysed to explore individuals' perspectives on the extent to which their performance was impacted by the tools available and the manner in which these were used, the adequacy of the rules they attempted to follow in the situation, and the divisions of labour within the team. Thus the analysis of the open-ended responses will lend itself to two levels of conclusions: one relating to the contradictions in the perspectives of individuals and observed events, the second relating to the inner contradictions between the components of the activity system.

In the observations of the videos, key dimensions will include conflict processes, role divisions and specializations, patterns of dominance and status, and task characteristic/group composition factors. A coding scheme will be developed to identify themes that emerge in the team exchanges and dialogues. This scheme will focus on the types of exchanges that occur in response to specific events in the teamwork context. For example, in coding the associated verbal exchanges, members' statements will be coded as initiations, elaborations, integrations, modifications, maintenance, clarification seeking, or disengagement bids. This method of structural analysis is well validated within the sociocultural-historical tradition.

Ethical considerations

Ethics approval will be sought from The University of Western Australia human ethics committee. As previously stated, all participants will be informed verbally and in writing about the study and participation will be on a voluntary basis. Written consent to participate will be obtained from those who volunteer and participants may withdraw from the study at any time. Raw data including videos, questionnaires, and transcripts will be stored securely for the appropriate period of time according to the requirements of the ethics committee.

Note

*A cardiac arrest occurs when a patient's heart ceases to beat in the organized manner required to circulate blood around the body. There are four disturbances of the normal heart rhythm that can cause cardiac arrest. Two of these, ventricular tachycardia and ventricular fibrillation, can be successfully reversed in the majority of patients if rapid detection and appropriate resuscitation occur. The other disturbances, asystole and pulseless electrical activity, are less amenable to treatment but can still be reversed in some cases. Hospital-based treatment of cardiac arrest includes cardiac compressions, defibrillation, advanced airway management and the administration of drugs. Together, these interventions are often called Advanced Life Support.

8.4 Quantitative proposal: management/business

Name of candidate: *Tim Mazzarol*
Degree: Doctor of Philosophy, Curtin University of Technology

1 Abstract

It is proposed to undertake a research study to examine the factors critical to the establishment and maintenance of sustainable competitive advantage for education service enterprises in international markets. A model of sustainable competitive advantage for service enterprises in international markets has been developed following an examination of current literature. This model will be tested via a survey encompassing all Australian institutions, and a further 100 overseas institutions drawn equally from the United States, United Kingdom, Canada and New Zealand. This will be supplemented by a detailed examination of approximately six Australian institutions using a case study approach.

The survey method will involve a mailout questionnaire designed to measure the responses of key decision makers in the sample institutions. This questionnaire will capture information reflecting the perceptions and practice of those guiding the export strategy of education institutions. It will serve as a means of evaluating the validity of the research model. Data analysis will be made using causal path analysis aided by computer packages such as LISREL and SPSS. The case studies will be undertaken via personal interviews with key decision makers within the selected institutions.

A pilot survey is currently being field tested, with a full survey to follow in late 1994, early 1995. The case studies will be undertaken in early 1995 via interviews. Data analysis will take place during 1995, with an anticipated completion of the thesis by late 1996.

Objectives

The overall objectives of this research may be summarized as follows:

1 Examine the effects of external environmental variables (industry and foreign market structure) on marketing strategies within education service exporters.

2 Evaluate the importance of specific marketing strategy outcomes to the generation of competitive advantage for education service providers within international markets.

3 Evaluate the ability of education service providers to generate barriers to the imitation of strategies offering competitive advantage.

4 Examine the long term market and financial performance of education service providers in international markets as an outcome of the interaction between marketing strategies (offering sources of competitive advantage), and the ability of the enterprise to sustain such advantage in the face of imitation.

2 Background

Australian schools and universities have educated foreign students for over 100 years, but until the mid 1980s, most of these students came to Australia through overseas aid programmes such as the Colombo Plan (DCT, 1993: 38). In 1985 the Federal Government opened the nation's education system to full-fee-paying foreign students with a view to tapping the estimated world student market of 1 million (Kemp, 1990). From an initial 4,503 in 1986, the size of Australia's intake of overseas students has grown rapidly to 47,882 in 1991 (AGB, 1992). These students generate hundreds of millions of dollars in export income via fees and services, and help support around 970 institutions (Industry Commission, 1991: 39).

Despite the relative success of Australia's education exports, concern has been expressed over the lack of comprehensive research into the marketing of such services (Marshall & Smart, 1991). A recent survey of international students and their advisers found their knowledge of Australia as an education destination mixed (AGB, 1992). There was a lack of knowledge about the country and its institutions even though quality was generally viewed as 'probably acceptable'. In some markets, notably Korea, Australia's image was quite poor (AGB, 1992). The problem was summarized as follows:

> Australia has no clear differentiation on product offerings, i.e. it is not perceived as the 'best' destination for any particular study disciplines. This contrasts with perceptions about the USA and the UK which have established particular discipline strengths in the minds of respondents. (AGB, 1992: 2)

Many of Australia's education exporters entered the market offering a relatively undifferentiated service, attractive primarily due to its low cost and generous work provisions within the visa regulations (Smart & Ang, 1992a; Industry Commission, 1991). The majority of Australia's overseas students have been drawn from a narrow range of markets. Malaysia and Singapore, for example, represent over two-thirds of the total students enrolled in Western Australia (DCT, 1993: 44). This poses long term sustainability problems should these markets experience a contraction due to political, social or economic change. Research also suggests that the world wide flow of students has declined rapidly since the 1980s (Kemp, 1990), raising additional questions about future industry growth.

3 Significance of This Research

This research is significant because it addresses a need – as outlined above – for comprehensive research into the international marketing of education. Past literature relating to the export of education has examined the economic or socio-political aspects of the industry rather than marketing (Smart & Ang, 1992b). Furthermore, despite a rapid growth in services marketing literature during the past decade (Fisk, Brown & Bitner, 1993), research into the international marketing of services remains limited (Nicoulaud, 1989; Dahringer, 1991; Erramilli & Rao, 1990; Erramilli, 1990; 1991).

Both services and international marketing are relatively new academic fields and were not given serious consideration prior to the 1970s (Terpstra, 1987; Berry & Parasuraman, 1993). With the growth in both international trade and the services sectors of most industrialized nations during the 1970s and 1980s (Blois, 1974; Plunkert, 1990; Roach, 1991; Terpstra, 1987), interest in these two fields grew. However, there remains a dearth of literature relating to the international marketing of services. It is hoped that this research will make a significant contribution to enhancing the level of knowledge in this area.

Of equal importance is how to develop strategies that will ensure the sustainability of competitive advantage for education service exporters so as to offer long term stability for this important industry. Academic research into sustainable competitive advantage for services industries remains at a rudimentary level with little applied research having been undertaken (Bharadwaj, Varadarajan & Fahy, 1993). Once again this research should make a significant contribution to enhancing the level of understanding relating to this.

Although the primary focus of this research will be on the education export industry, it is anticipated that the findings of this study will be applicable to most other services exporters. It is therefore the intention of this research to develop models and conclusions that will be generic to international services marketing.

Because it is proposed to survey virtually all Australian institutions engaged in the export of education, this study will provide valuable insights into the current perceptions and marketing practices of the industry. It has the potential to serve as a bench mark study of current practice. To this end it should prove of interest and value to practising managers and those seeking to implement international marketing strategies for education institutions.

4 Research methodology

4.1 The research model

Figure 8.2 illustrates a model of sustainable competitive advantage for service enterprises in international markets developed from a number of established theories relating to competitive advantage, international marketing and services marketing research (Aaker, 1989; 1992; Barney, 1986; 1991; Booms & Bitner, 1981; Cowell, 1984; Dahringer, 1991; Gronroos, 1990; Klein & Roth, 1990; Nicoulaud, 1987; Porter, 1980; 1985; Porter & Fuller, 1986; Porter & Millar, 1985).

As a model of sustainable competitive advantage it assumes that business and marketing strategies within the enterprise are determined by external environmental factors to which the enterprise responds. It is consistent with the theoretical framework offered by Porter (1980; 1985). An alternative perspective is that proposed by Bharadwaj, Varadarajan & Fahy (1993), which views the achievement of sustainable competitive advantage resulting from the enterprise selecting critical sources of competitiveness from among internal resources and skills.

The elements of the model can be briefly summarized as follows:

- *Industry structure.* Describes the external forces influencing the industry within which the enterprise operates. Porter (1980) defines these as: (1) barriers to entry; (2) supplier power; (3) buyer power; (4) threat of substitutes; (5) industry competitiveness.
- *Foreign market structure.* Includes tariff and non-tariff barriers to entry (Dharinger, 1991; Onkvisit & Shaw, 1988) as well as the degree of *psychic distance* (cultural similarity/dissimilarity) and *experience* (level of market knowledge/information) (Erramilli, 1991; Goodnow & Hansz, 1972; Klein & Roth, 1990).
- *Generic enterprise strategy.* This adopts Porter's (1985) theory that all enterprises must adopt one of three *generic* strategies in order to achieve a competitive advantage. These three strategies are: (1) *cost leadership* (competing via cost); (2) *differentiation* (competing via uniqueness); and (3) *focus* (competing via cost or differentiation within a niche market) (Porter, 1985).
- *External marketing strategy.* Describes the specific marketing strategies relating to the *marketing mix* which incorporates considerations of the following: (1) product/service development; (2) pricing; (3) distribution;

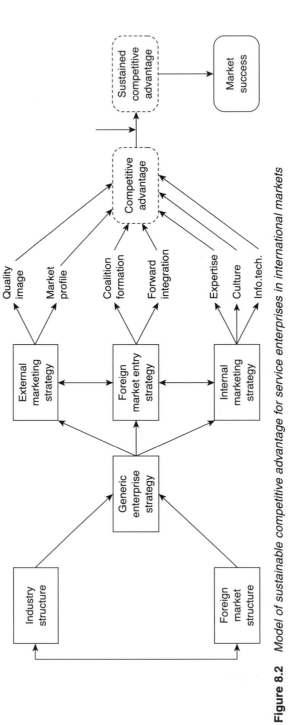

Figure 8.2 *Model of sustainable competitive advantage for service enterprises in international markets*

(4) promotion; and development of physical evidence of the service (buildings, equipment) (McCarthy, 1960; Booms & Bitner, 1981).

- *Foreign market entry strategy*. Describes the methods used to enter a foreign market. These are identified as: (1) direct export; (2) licensing; (3) franchising; (4) joint venture; (5) acquisition; and (6) management contracting (Cowell, 1984). Also examines the degree of control exercised by the enterprise over its marketing channel (Anderson & Coughlan, 1987).
- *Internal marketing strategy*. Describes the processes undertaken within the enterprise to foster an organizational culture that is both client service oriented (Flipo, 1985; Gronroos, 1990), and encouraging of innovation (Ansoff, 1987; Barney, 1986; Foster & Pryor, 1986; Ghemawat, 1986; Kanter, 1989). Also considers the enterprise approach to the recruitment and retention of experienced and talented staff, and their performance via various service delivery processes (Booms & Bitner, 1981; Lovelock, 1983; Thomas, 1978).
- *Outcomes*. The outcomes of enterprise marketing strategies identified within the model are considered of critical importance to the establishment of competitive advantage for services enterprises in international markets. These are: (1) quality of image; (2) market profile (consumer awareness or knowledge of enterprise) (Aaker, 1989; Hill & Neeley, 1988); (3) coalition formation (strategic alliances) (Dunning & Pearce, 1985; Ohmae, 1985; Porter & Fuller, 1986); (4) degree of forward integration into the marketing channel (Erramilli & Rao, 1990; Erramilli, 1990; Nicoulaud, 1987; Vanermere & Chadwick, 1989); (5) level of staff expertise and organizational learning (Winter, 1987); (6) organizational culture as client oriented and innovative (Quinn, 1980; 1985); and (7) effective use of information technology (Porter & Millar, 1985).
- *Barriers to imitation*. To ensure that competitive advantage is sustained it is suggested (Bharadwaj, Varadarajan & Fahy, 1993) that the enterprise erect barriers to the imitation of its strategies. A variety of possible barriers have been identified in the literature (Coyne, 1985; Dierickx & Cool, 1989; Lippman & Rumelt, 1982; Rumelt, 1984; 1987; Reed & Defillippi, 1990).
- *Market success*. The model assumes that the concepts *competitive advantage* and *sustainable competitive advantage* cannot be measured directly. Instead the measurement of market success is achieved via the dual outcomes of (1) market share and (2) profitability (financial performance).

4.2 Hypotheses

The relationships that will be tested in the model can be identified in the following hypotheses:

H1   Industry structure is a determinant of generic enterprise strategy adopted by a service enterprise seeking competitive advantage in international markets.

H2   Foreign market structure is a determinant of generic enterprise strategy adopted by a service enterprise seeking competitive advantage in international markets.

H3   Generic enterprise strategy is a moderating variable that determines:

    (a)   the external marketing strategy of the enterprise;
    (b)   the foreign market entry strategy of the enterprise;
    (c)   the internal marketing strategy of the enterprise.

H4   External marketing strategy is a moderating variable that enables the creation of sources of competitive advantage for a service enterprise within an international market.

H5   Foreign market entry strategy is a moderating variable that enables the creation of sources of competitive advantage for a service enterprise within an international market.

H6   Internal marketing strategy is a moderating variable that enables the creation of sources of competitive advantage for a service enterprise within an international market.

H7   The key intervening variables that strengthen the competitive advantage of a service enterprise within an international market are:

    (a)   quality of image;
    (b)   market profile;
    (c)   coalition formation;
    (d)   degree of forward integration into the export channel;
    (e)   organizational expertise and quality of staff;
    (f)   possession of a client-oriented/innovative culture;
    (g)   effective use of information technology.

H8   Sustainability of competitive advantage is only achievable if there are intervening variables which act as barriers to imitation. The most likely barriers are:

    (a)   the external marketing strategy of the enterprise;
    (b)   the foreign market entry strategy of the enterprise;
    (c)   the internal marketing strategy of the enterprise.

4.3 Sample plan

It is proposed to survey all education institutions in Australia that are accredited to the Department of Education, Employment and Training (DEET) as exporters. DEET maintains a Commonwealth Register of Institutions and Courses (CRICOS) listing all such institutions in Australia. DEET has provided a complete listing including telephone numbers and addresses. This listing includes around 1,000 institutions ranging from small training colleges to large universities. This will form the basis of the

Australian sample and has already proven of value in conducting the pilot study.

In addition to the Australian institutions, an additional 100 institutions in each of four overseas countries (USA, UK, Canada and New Zealand) will be sampled. Details of institutions within these countries are available from the various diplomatic and consular agencies located in Australia. Initial contact with the British Council, Canadian High Commission, US Consulate and New Zealand High Commission has proven fruitful in identifying suitable institutions likely to form a sample.

Non-English-speaking countries have been ignored due to the added complexities and cost of developing a foreign language survey. Traditionally, the primary competition to Australian education institutions are other English-speaking nations, although Germany, France and Japan are emerging as significant competitors in Australian markets (Smart & Ang, 1992b). Nevertheless, it is felt that sufficient validity within the sample will be achieved using the English-speaking nations alone.

Selection of the case study sample (estimated to be approximately six institutions) will be on the basis of size, institution type and relative experience within the international market. The aim will be to select a cross-section of institutions which represent these elements. A suggested case study sample would be likely to include: (1) a large university; (2) a commercial business/training college; (3) a private secondary school; (4) an English language college; (5) a TAFE/technical training college; (6) a specialist training institution (e.g. pilot training).

4.4 Instrumentation and data collection

A copy of the questionnaire as used in the pilot study is attached [not reproduced]. Prior to forwarding, a contact person within each institution is to be identified. A pre-paid envelope will be included with each questionnaire sent. Respondents will be offered a summary of findings from the study as a courtesy. This approach has been adopted in the pilot study with success.

4.5 Data analysis

Due to the relatively large number of variables in the research model, analysis will be made using causal path modelling (Saris & Stonkhorst, 1984). This will enable the relationships between the variables in the model to be solved as a multivariate regression equation, and will permit the examination of both observed and unobserved (latent) variables (Loehlin, 1992).

Data analysis will be facilitated using the LISREL computer software package operating in conjunction with SPSS (Byrne, 1989). Both software packages operate under the MS Windows environment on an IBM compatible PC. The LISREL package will allow a statistical comparison of the data and the research model (Byrne, 1989).

8.5 Qualitative proposal: nursing

Name of candidate: *Kay Price*
Degree: Doctor of Philosophy, The University of South Australia

1 Title

The construction of pain within a surgical ward.

2 Purpose of the study

Pain management is an aspect of post-operative care which is, or is perceived as, being poorly managed by health care professionals (e.g. U.S. Department of Health and Human Services, 1992; Owen, McMillan and Rogowski, 1990; Winefield, Katisikitis, Hart and Rounsefell, 1990; Edwards, 1990; Kilham, Atkinson, Bogduk, Cousins, Hodder, Pilowsky, Pollard and Quinn, 1988; Liebeskind and Melzack, 1987). This being despite a view heralded within the literature that advances in the understanding of pain mechanisms, the action of analgesic drugs and the development of sophisticated systems for drug delivery, mean that it is no longer necessary for the surgical client to suffer from unrelieved pain post-surgery (e.g. U.S. Department of Health and Human Services, 1992; Owen and Cousins, 1991; Kilham et al., 1988; Mather and Phillips, 1986). Unrelieved pain has personal, social and economic costs. For example, the experience of unrelieved pain has been linked to the surgical client experiencing complications, thus increasing their length of stay in hospital which ultimately requires the allocation of additional resources (e.g. Ready, 1991; Benedetti, 1990). While the experience of unrelieved pain has been recognized as an undesirable occurrence for surgical clients, the provision of appropriate pain management for surgical clients remains a contentious issue.

This study is based on the belief that a certain way of thinking and speaking about pain dominates the management of a surgical client's potential or actual experience of pain at the exclusion of (or silencing of) other ways of thinking and speaking. The potential or actual experience of pain has become a means through which dominant knowledge sources and power relations are maintained and produced through its management. Abercrombie, Hill and Turner (1988: 71) define a 'domain of language use that is unified by common assumptions' as a discourse. The notion of discourse and the way in which it shapes the form and content of language both written and spoken has been extensively explored by Foucault (1977). His notion of discourse and his analyses of discursive frameworks provide an understanding of the interplay between power, knowledge and discourses

(Cheek and Rudge, 1993). Pain and its management have become discursively constructed. Within this discursive construction exists the interplay of other discursive constructions which offer competing, potentially contradictory ways of positioning its author(s), all of which vary in authority (Gavey, 1989: 464). The 'authors' of these discursive constructions and the positioning they adopt in relation to other discourses in pain management need to be identified if effective management from a client-centred approach is to be a reality of practice.

Thus this study aims to explore and explicate:

1 the way in which pain is constructed within a surgical ward;
2 the effect(s) of this construction on nursing practice; and
3 the influences of this construction on client outcomes.

Guided by poststructuralist theory this critical study will, by using ethnographic techniques and discourse analysis, represent, interrogate, juxtapose and construct the experience of pain for surgical clients. In so doing, it is envisaged that client satisfaction with their pain management will be enhanced.

The objectives of this study are to:

1 explore the various construction(s) of pain within a surgical ward of an acute care hospital and within the literature;
2 interview nursing staff, doctors and clients in regard to the work they perform in acute pain management;
3 observe the clinical practices of nursing staff and doctors within a surgical ward as they relate to the acute pain management of a surgical client;
4 analyse the documentation that reflects the care provided to surgical clients in acute pain management;
5 articulate the influence on nursing practice in light of the above understandings; and thus
6 reflect a view that highlights the consequences of all of the above on client outcomes in acute pain management following surgery.

3 Background and preliminary studies

Research studies in acute pain management have generated the dominant view that post-surgical clients experience a high incidence of unrelieved pain (Owen, McMillan and Rogowski, 1990; Winefield, Katisikitis, Hart and Rounsefell, 1990; Carr, 1990; Donovan, Dillon and McGuire, 1987; Cohen, 1980). Unrelieved post-operative pain is considered a significant health problem (Cousins and Mather, 1989; Benedetti, 1990; Ready, 1991; Owen and Cousins, 1991). The focus of research reports has tended to concentrate on the attributes of medical and nursing staff as correlates to poor pain management (e.g. Bonica, 1980; Kilham et al., 1988; Mather and Phillips, 1986; McKingley and Bolti, 1990; McCaffery, 1990; McCaffery and Ferrell, 1991; 1992; 1994). As well, it has been stated that treatment options for post-operative pain would be ineffective in environments which had logistic and administrative hurdles (Owen et al., 1990: 306; Cousins and Mather, 1989: 355). The view that 'freedom' from acute pain without demand for such freedom has been suggested as a 'right' of surgical clients (e.g. Liebeskind and Melzack, 1988; Madjar, 1988).

There is literature which reflects the view that nursing has been constructed by powerful discourses including those of medicine and gender, thus marginalizing a nursing discourse (e.g. Cheek and Rudge, 1994; Parker and Gardner, 1992; Street, 1992; Bruni, 1989). Research by Street (1992: 2) into nursing practice has been described as a study in which:

> The culture of nursing is reclaimed ... as a site in which the intersection of power, politics, knowledge, and practice gives rise to the contested terrain of conflict and struggle.

Street (1992: 276) believed that nursing care was essentially nurturant and that her research would enable nurses 'to recognise the politics that constrain and oppress' the clinical practice of nurses.

What influence the view that a discourse of nursing has been marginalized has on nursing practice in routine acute pain management situations remains to be explored. It is known that acute pain management for surgical clients involves a number of health care professionals, predominantly medical and nursing personnel who share responsibility for the quality of care the surgical client receives, and the financial costs involved in the delivery of this care. As a consequence of this shared responsibility there is the potential for divergence of opinion as to how the surgical client is to be most appropriately managed, which will influence client outcomes as well as affect nursing practice. Further to this, studies into clients' participation in their own care (Strauss, Fagerhaugh, Suczek and Weiner, 1982) have revealed that the work of clients in hospitals is often unrecognized and taken for granted. While clients are judged on their ability to carry out certain 'tasks', this is conceived as participation in the work of health care professionals rather than the work of clients (Strauss et al., 1982; 979). It is unknown how nurses and doctors conceive the work of clients in acute pain management.

The predominant view within the literature on pain is that proposed scientific discoveries in pain management only await application by health care professionals (e.g. Owen et al., 1990) and that following universal acceptance pain management for clients will improve. The difficulty in accepting such a view is not a rejection of the achievements made, but the limited critique of the power that the dominant positivist, empiricist research tradition presumes and the effects this power exerts on the way of knowing promoted and the subsequent management of clients by health care professionals, particularly nurses.

Code (1991: 159) writes:

> Scientific achievement is at once wonderful and awful: it can never be evaluated merely as knowledge for its own sake, for there are always political implications.

The political implications of scientific achievements in pain management have received minimal debate within the literature reviewed on pain and its management. This is not surprising given that research in the main has evolved from the dominant positivist, empiricist research tradition. A noted exception to this is the early work of Fagerhaugh and Strauss (1977) who explored the politics of pain management from a grounded theory approach.

Fagerhaugh and Strauss (1977: 9) argued that pain management took place within an organizational and interactional context, and maintained that pain management had profoundly political aspects. They (Fagerhaugh and Strauss, 1977: 8–9) suggest that people enter highly politicized arenas when they enter hospital and that while staff make and enforce the 'basic rules', staff are neither all-powerful nor completely in control of all issues which affect clients. Consequently, they believed that medical and nursing care involved politicized action. As a result of their study, Fagerhaugh and Strauss (1977: 69) believed that a critical examination of pain management in routine situations was necessary so as to improve accountability of all concerned, and prevent the phenomenon of problem pain patients. It is significant to note that Fagerhaugh and Strauss (1977) did not address specifically the influence of power relations on pain management; rather they focused on personal pain philosophies of nurses and doctors as being a key determinant of client outcomes.

The theme 'politics of health-talk' has been researched by Fox (1993). In his study, Fox was interested in discourse and its consequences for power, control and knowledgeability. His interest was on discerning a difference between modern and postmodern theories of health, in particular the practical politics and ethics of health, and produced the view that generating new positions and resisting existing discourses was essential. Nettleton (1992), in her studies on dentistry, researched the technique of disciplinary power – the dental examination – as a means by which bodies are observed and analysed. In her study, Nettleton explored dental practices to show the relations between dental knowledge and dental power.

The definition of pain which is commonly cited in the literature is that 'pain is what the person says hurts' (Kilham et al., 1988). This definition assumes not only the authenticity of the experience as expressed by the person, but their ability to express the experience and for this to be heard (and/or observed) by nurses and doctors. Furthermore, Fox (1993: 144) writes about the 'politics of pain' and states that pain as a sensation has no meaning, the self is the pain and the self is the effect of the meaning. These perspectives require that an understanding of how pain is constructed by nurses, doctors and clients be undertaken. For as much as Fox (1993) and Nettleton (1992) have generated new viewing positions in relation to health and dentistry, thus resisting existing discourses, a similar situation needs to be explored in acute pain management.

Thus this study seeks to build upon the research of Fagerhaugh and Strauss (1977), by applying a poststructuralist framework to acute pain management for the surgical client. The interest of this study is to explore the social construction of pain by the major care providers in an acute post-operative ward, namely nurses and doctors.

4 Subjects: selection and exclusion criteria

The setting for this study will be a general adult surgical ward of an acute care public hospital. The actual location of the study setting will be negotiated with the hospital hierarchy and in full consultation with all staff members of the ward. Given the diversity of compounding factors which could influence the outcomes of this study, the setting will not be an orthopaedic ward given the likelihood of trauma causing the reason for surgery. Permission will be sought from the hospital hierarchy to locate the study within a ward that focuses on abdominal and/or thoracic surgery. Nursing, medical and client personnel working within such a setting will be invited to participate by consenting to being interviewed and observed in their work. The interactions (written and verbal) that take place in relation to the acute pain management of surgical clients will be the focus of the study. A perceived difficulty of the study will be the ability of surgical clients during the acute phase of their surgical admission, and the availability of medical and nursing staff to participate in the interview process.

As in all ethnographic studies, it will be necessary for the researcher to ensure the appropriateness and adequacy of information needed to achieve the aims of the study. It is difficult therefore to be precise about the selection and sample of informants. Control of the selection of informants may be necessary. In the event that interviews of any one group prove to be difficult, a survey by the use of a questionnaire will be adopted. Any additional informant identified by the researcher as having particular knowledge deemed as necessary for inclusion in the study will be approached to participate. These biases will be used as a 'tool' to facilitate the research study.

The decision to focus the study in an adult acute care public hospital has been based on the professional and personal experiences of the researcher.

These experiences have led to the belief that there are varying approaches to care in the management of children and adults in acute pain management. As well, that the role of medical and nursing personnel in the private sector is different to that of the public sector. It is envisaged that further research will follow from this study to address the basis for these beliefs.

While the success of the study depends upon the willingness of individuals to participate, if at any time such participation places an individual at risk or causes undue stress, participation will not be pursued. A particular concern of this researcher is not to interfere with the recovery of surgical clients and the nursing and medical practices needed to facilitate this recovery. If observations and/or interviews of either clients, nurses or doctors are deemed inappropriate, alternative methods (e.g. survey questionnaire) to gather information will be adopted.

5 Study plan and design

Ethnographic research techniques aim to generate descriptions for the purpose of analysis. Working from an insider's (nurses, doctors and surgical clients) knowledge and experience of acute pain management will provide the means for the exploration of how pain is constructed and how the construction of pain influences nursing practice and client outcomes. The question for this study is:

How is pain constructed within a surgical ward?

An ongoing review of the literature will take place throughout the study which will incorporate the following stages.

Stage 1

The first stage of this research will include:

1   Gaining human ethics committee approval for the research project.
2   Negotiating access to the setting for the study.
3   Meeting with the nursing and medical staff of the general surgical ward to discuss the research, its aims and objectives; to process consent; and to provide any additional information as requested. It will be particularly important to discuss with nursing and medical staff the role of the researcher during those times of observation on the ward. Ethical considerations are discussed in more detail in Section 7 of this proposal.
4   Seeking the consent of medical and nursing staff of the general surgical ward to be interviewed and observed (written and verbal) in their practice.
5   Establish rapport with the nursing and medical staff of the general surgical ward so as to establish guidelines for observation of their practices.

Stage 2

The second stage of the research (over a period of 4–6 months) will include:

1   Observation of nursing, medical and/or clients' work in acute pain management during: admission procedures; ward rounds (nursing and/or medical); nursing handovers; and direct client care by either nursing and/or medical staff to surgical clients. Section 7 of this proposal discusses ethical considerations in relation to the role of the researcher during observation. Observation of clients will encompass that time from admission to the surgical ward until discharge.

2   Selection and interview (formal and informal) of nursing and medical staff involved in client care and surgical clients admitted to the general surgical ward during the period of the study.

Interviews will mainly be informal and will occur at a time convenient to staff and clients during observation and at prearranged times during the course of the study. Surgical clients who give consent to participate in the study, dependent upon their health status, will be interviewed on admission, post-surgery and on discharge. The number of times a surgical client will be interviewed post-surgery will be dependent upon their length of stay in hospital and will take place at a time that has been mutually agreed by the client and nursing and medical staff.

Initially the interviews will be unstructured, and as the study progresses more structured interviews will be arranged with the consent of informants. With the permission of informants, interviews may be taped and transcribed. All information provided in the interviews and during observation will be treated in strictest confidence, and transcriptions of observations and interviews will be given to informants for review to ensure that their views have been accurately represented. The interviews will focus on the informants' views about: their feelings; events; and incidents that have occurred as related to acute pain management.

3   Review of nursing and medical documentation surrounding surgical clients' stay in hospital as it relates to acute pain management. Permission to access clients' case-notes will be obtained prior to the review of the same and pseudonyms will be used so as to ensure confidentiality.

4   Collation of data obtained from observation and interviews and the provision of such data to informants at regular interviews as is appropriate.

Stage 3

This stage of the study will occur concurrently with stage 2, and will include:

1   Analysis of documentation such as nursing care plans, client case-notes and related literature on acute pain management.

2   Analysis of observations of medical, nursing and clients' work in acute pain management.
3   Analysis through interviews of medical, nursing and clients' perceptions of acute pain management.
4   Interrelationship of all the analyses on the construction(s) of pain within the general surgical ward, and the potential implications for nursing practice and client outcomes.

6 Efficacy

Not applicable.

7 Ethical considerations

Informants' needs will take precedence over the actual process of the research. While the success of the study depends upon the willingness of individuals to participate, if at any time such participation places an individual at risk or causes undue stress, participation will not be pursued. A particular concern of this researcher is not to interfere with the recovery of surgical clients and the nursing and medical practices needed to facilitate this recovery. If observations and/or interviews of either clients, nurses or doctors are deemed inappropriate, alternative methods (e.g. survey questionnaire) to gather information will be adopted.

Gaining access to the study's setting will involve negotiations with hospital hierarchy so as to determine in which adult general surgical ward the study will be based. Following this determination, a meeting of the medical and nursing staff of the surgical ward will take place. Given the busy schedules of these personnel, it may be desirable to hold separate meetings with medical and nursing staff to discuss the study. At these meetings, it will be stressed that:

1   Participation in this study will be entirely voluntary for all informants.
2   At all times, every potential informant will have communicated to her/him the objectives of the research and any change that may occur in these objectives during the course of the study. An information sheet (Appendices 1 and 2 [not reproduced]), will be provided to all potential informants.
3   Continuous and negotiated permission to observe and/or interview medical staff, nursing staff and clients will take place. Consent, either written or verbal, will be obtained prior to any aspect of the study. Informants who wish to give written consent to observation of their practice/work in acute pain management and/or interviews at the beginning of the study will be informed that they can withdraw at any time during the study (Appendix 3 [not reproduced]).

Given the ongoing nature of the study, a proposal for process consent will be suggested. 'A process consent offers the opportunity to actualize a negotiated view and to change arrangements if necessary. A process consent encourages mutual participation' (Munhall, 1991: 267). The process consent will be discussed with all potential nursing and medical staff informants at the initial meeting. Arrangements to be negotiated will include:

1 lines of communication between the researcher, informants and hospital hierarchy;
2 location of interviews;
3 length of time for interviews;
4 how information will be treated (confidentiality and anonymity);
5 taping of interviews;
6 reviewing of transcripts;
7 what will be done with unanticipated findings;
8 how secrets and confidential information will be treated;
9 possibility of group interviews;
10 when and how progress of the study will occur and be reported;
11 publishing of findings;
12 presentation of the study's progress by the researcher to doctoral review panel.

It is important to highlight that the researcher will not be delivering care to clients. The Faculty of Nursing has a Clinical Facilitation agreement with hospitals and the conditions of this agreement will be adhered to by the researcher. As a registered nurse, the researcher will only intervene in emergency situations, that is, where the life and safety of the client is at risk. Consequently, it will be essential for the researcher to establish clear guidelines, as per the Clinical Facilitation agreement, with nursing and medical staff in relation to situations where the researcher observes what she perceives to be inappropriate (or unsafe) delivery of care to clients. Mechanisms for reporting action to be taken in such situations will be clarified at the first meeting and renegotiated with nursing and medical staff as is necessary.

It is envisaged that consent from surgical clients to be interviewed and observed will be negotiated at the time of the first interview and will involve renegotiation at all subsequent contacts. Permission will be sought from surgical clients to review their case-notes (Appendix 4 [not reproduced]). Where surgical clients consent to being interviewed, either informally or formally, this will be recorded in the field diary or at the beginning of the tape where consent has been given to tape the interview. Surgical clients who consent to being informants will be told that they can withdraw from the research at any time and that their participation is strictly voluntary. They may therefore suspend either observation and/or interview at any such time they wish. At the first meeting, it will also be discussed with the client the possibility of a situation arising (e.g. where the client may be in pain) which results in them being unable to give verbal consent to the observation. The client can indicate their consent (or otherwise) to the continuing of the observation without verbal consent on the understanding that this will be written into the field notes of the researcher at the time and discussed with them at a later date. In seeking validation from the client of the observation, the client will be immediately informed that the care given by nursing and/or medical staff was observed at a time that they were unable to give verbal consent. If before or on reviewing the transcript of the observation the client wishes that the observation not be included in the study, all references to the observation will be deleted.

Protecting the privacy of informants will be of paramount concern, as will non-exploitation of any informant. At all times, the provision of any information collected and/or analysed will be communicated to informants as is reasonably practicable and especially prior to any publication of the study. Pseudonyms will be used when retrieving information from clients' case-notes.

Tapes, field data, and transcripts used in the research will be kept in secure storage at The University of South Australia for a period of seven years after the completion of the research and then disposed of according to NH&MRC guidelines.

8 Drugs

Not applicable.

9 Safety and ecological considerations

Not applicable: there are no issues of personal safety or ecological considerations associated with the research.

10 Analysis and reporting of results

10.1 Analysis

Following a procedure adapted from the works of Cheek and Rudge (1994), Kellehear (1993), Clark and Wheeler (1992) and Denzin (1989), the analysis will involve:

1   *Assembling of material.* As an ongoing process, all available material (review of the literature and documentation, observation notes, and interview transcripts) will be assembled together and read to acquire a sense of the data, its textual and contextual dimensions.

2 *Isolating issues, topics and themes.* In the reading, the aim is to illuminate what was being said, taken-for-granted assumptions, and what was missing or de-emphasized. Significant statements will be extracted, by both the researcher and informants, and the meaning of such observation and interview data checked with informants. The meaning of extracted statements will be formulated and organized into themes.

3 *Comparing different accounts.* Comparison of different accounts/ elements/versions 'across and against each other' – a practice sometimes called 'intertextuality' (Game, 1991: 48; Cheek and Rudge, 1994) – will be done. Examination of 'deviant' accounts, with exceptions to patterned regularities, will be examined and checked with informants.

4 *Integrating all results.* Alternative interpretations will be advanced based upon the negative or deviant accounts and incorporated into a coherent descriptive text that attempts to deal with every instance of the focus under study (micro and macro levels). Validation of the descriptive results will be sought from informants.

5 *Moving from the descriptive into a critical discourse analysis.* Discourse analysis is a form of analysis that is attentive both to detail in text and context. It involves a careful reading of the descriptive text to elicit discursive patterns of meaning, contradictions and inconsistencies. Discursive themes and subject positions will be forwarded and discussed within the framework of poststructuralist theory. In using discourse analysis, the researcher accepts that the descriptive text is not static, fixed and orderly, but rather is fragmented, inconsistent and contradictory (Gavey, 1989: 467).

6 *Reviewing the final analysis.* The final analysis will be returned to the informants to seek their input into their understanding of the results.

10.2 Reporting of the results

The results will be reported to the:

- Faculty of Nursing, The University of South Australia as a doctoral thesis.
- Organization and informants involved in the form of a written report.
- Nursing and medical professions by conference presentations and articles presented to appropriate journals for publication.

8.6 Other proposals in the literature

- Four 'specimen proposals' are included in the book by Locke et al. (1993: 185–296). There is extensive and helpful editorial comment on each, and they cover a range of research approaches. The four proposals are:

  'The effects of age, modality, complexity of response and practice on reaction time' (experimental design).

'Returning women students in the community college' (qualitative study).

'Teaching children to question what they read: an attempt to improve reading comprehension through training in a cognitive learning strategy' (quasi-experimental design).

'A competition strategy for worksite smoking cessation' (funded grant).

- Brink and Wood (1994: 255–375) include four sample research proposals, without editorial comment. The first two are descriptive studies, the third is a correlational study, and the fourth an experimental study. They are:

  'Value orientations of Hutterian women in Canada'.
  'Eating patterns successful dieters use to maintain weight loss'.
  'The relationship between preterm infant sleep state disorganization and maternal–infant interaction'.
  'Patient controlled analgesia for total hip arthroplasty patients'.

- Madsen (1983: 109–54) has two sample proposals, the first historical, the second experimental. They are:

  'The Carnegie Institute of Washington, 1901–1904: Andrew Carnegie, Daniel Gilman and John Billings search for the exceptional man'.
  'An investigation of two methods of achieving compliance with the severely handicapped in a classroom setting'.

- Maxwell (1996: 116–37) reproduces, with commentary, a qualitative proposal entitled 'How basic science teachers help medical students learn: the students' perspective'.
- Maykut and Morehouse (1994: 165–77) include two shorter qualitative proposals, one on school climate, the other entitled 'An exploration of how children and adolescents with autism or autistic tendencies use facilitated communication in their lives'.
- Coley and Scheinberg (1990: 112–24) give the example, with critique, of a proposal for an intervention project where a community wants to address the problem of unintended adolescent pregnancy.
- Similarly, the proposal for an intervention project entitled 'A program to train interdisciplinary health care teams to work with the homeless' is presented and critiqued, as a case study, by Gitlin and Lyons (1996: 195–203).
- Gilpatrick (1989) gives a progressive commentary and critique, throughout her book, of five intervention projects in a funding context. They are:

  'Education for parents of infants discharged from intensive care'.
  'Ambulance staff training in emergency medical services'.
  'City children involved in the arts community'.
  'Writing skills for retention of graduate students'.
  'Development of leadership by women of color in the antiviolence movement'.

- Wallen and Fraenkel (1991: 267–87) critique two student research proposals in education. They are: 'The effects of individualized reading upon student motivation in grade four' and 'The effects of a peer-counselling class on self esteem'.
- Finally, O'Donoghue and Haynes (1997: 91–169) give six examples of proposals in education, with these titles:

  'Goal directed behaviour, reputation enhancement and juvenile delinquency.'
  'The inclusion of children with a severe or profound intellectual disability in regular classrooms: How teachers manage the situation'.
  'Teacher of all the Gods: The educational thought of Ki Hajar Dewantara'.
  'An analysis of emergence, development and implementation of Italian as a school subject in the curriculum of Western Australian secondary schools over the period 1968 to 1994'.
  'Ideal algebra word problem test design: an application of the Rasch model for partial credit scoring'.
  'Language, thought and reality: A critical reassessment of the ideas of Benjamin Lee Whorf'.

Appendix 1
Disentangling the Terms 'Perspective', 'Strategy' and 'Design'

There is sometimes confusion with the terms 'perspectives', 'strategy' and 'design'. This appendix suggests a way of ordering these terms, while acknowledging some inevitable overlap between perspective and strategy, and between strategy and design.

Perspective

In Chapter 4, I used *perspective* as a general term to refer to the paradigm, metatheory or philosophical assumptions behind a piece of research. Examples of perspectives are positivism, postpositivism, critical theory, constructivism, feminism and postmodernism. The perspective may or may not be made explicit in the research proposal or project. The research may start from a perspective such as one of these, or it may start from the pragmatic position of questions needing answers.

Strategy

Strategy can then be seen as something which is consistent with (or follows from) a perspective, which implements that perspective, and which, together with the perspective, leads to a set of research questions. In this sense, the strategy of the research is its internal logic or rationale – the set of ideas which will guide the study in answering its research questions (or testing its hypotheses). Both quantitative and qualitative approaches to research have a number of typical consistently used strategies.

Quantitative research strategies

The most common general strategies here, as shown in *Introduction to Social Research* (Punch, 2005), are the experiment, the quasi-experiment and the (correlational) survey. But there are others, most of which are more specialized. Examples are: normative surveys, longitudinal studies, time series analysis, panel studies, causal path studies, structural equation modelling, hierarchical linear modelling, event history analysis, facet design and analysis, Q methodology, cluster analysis, cohort analysis, mobility analysis, unidimensional scaling and multidimensional scaling, operations research and multiattribute evaluation.

Qualitative research strategies

Here, as usual, the situation is more diverse. Denzin and Lincoln (1994: 202–8) suggest the following main categories of qualitative strategy, noting that each has its own history and literature, its own exemplary works, and its own preferred ways for putting the strategy into motion: the case study; ethnography and participant observation; phenomenology; ethnomethodology and interpretive practice; grounded theory; the biographical method; the historical method; applied and action research and clinical models.

Janesick (1994: 212) has this list of qualitative research strategies, noting that it is not meant to include all possibilities: ethnography, life history, oral history, ethnomethodology, case study, participant observation, field research or field study, naturalistic study, phenomenological study, ecological descriptive study, descriptive study, symbolic interactionist study, microethnography, interpretive research, action research, narrative research, historiography and literary criticism.

Morse (1994: 224–5) has a slightly different list again: phenomenology, ethnography, grounded theory, ethnomethodology, discourse analysis and participant observation, qualitative ethnology and ethnoscience.

These overlapping lists show the many different strategies possible in qualitative research. As a judgement about which of these seem most common, and with space limitations applying, *Introduction to Social Research* concentrated on case studies, ethnography (including observation and participant observation) and grounded theory, but also gave some attention to the language-based strategies of narratives, ethnomethodology and conversation analysis, discourse analysis, semiotics, and documentary and textual analysis.

Design

To move now from strategy to design, for both quantitative and qualitative research, *design* can be seen as something which implements the strategy. It deals with the general question 'Who or what will be studied, and how?' and begins with the strategy selected. Thus, as shown in Chapter 5, it can be broken down into five more specific questions:

- What strategy will be followed?
- Within what framework?
- From whom will the data be collected?
- How will the data be collected?
- How will the data be analysed?

Each of these questions is discussed in Chapter 5.

Synthesis

A benefit of this way of seeing these terms is that it suggests the components which need to fit together to ensure the overall validity of a piece of research. When all of them apply, they are:

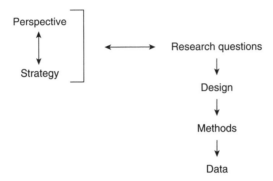

'When all of them apply' is a caveat referring to perspectives. Some research projects will start from (or be saturated with) a perspective, in which case all six components apply. But equally, many projects take the pragmatic position of questions requiring answers, in which case the five components of strategy, research questions, design, methods and data will apply. In these cases, a perspective is implicit rather than explicit. Sometimes, too, a perspective which is implicit at the start of a project may become much more explicit during the project.

Appendix 2
Questions to Guide Proposal Development

This appendix brings together the questions raised in earlier chapters. Together, they constitute a comprehensive checklist of questions to help students in proposal development. They are of three types.

First, there are the questions about the context for the proposal noted in Chapter 2:

- Who will read my proposal?
- What will their expectations be?
- What is the process for approval of my proposal?
- What departmental and/or university guidelines are there for my proposal and its presentation?

Second, there are the three general and overarching questions highlighted in Chapter 3:

What

- What is my research about?
- What is its purpose?
- What is it trying to find out or achieve?
- *Especially*: what questions is it trying to answer?

How

- How will my research answer its questions?

Why

- Why is this research worth doing?

Third, there is a set of middle range questions to help in proposal development. I call them 'middle range questions' because they sit between the general overarching questions above, and the many, much more specific and technical questions which can be asked of research. These specific and detailed questions were presented in Chapter 12 of *Introduction to Social Research* (Punch, 2005), and concern such technical details as the internal validity of the research design, or the reliability and validity of the data, or aspects of data collection or analysis methods. While they are sometimes appropriate questions to ask of proposals, these detailed questions are generally more applicable to completed projects and reports.

The following list brings together the questions from Chapters 3, 4 and 5. Naturally, there is some overlap between them, and this list consolidates and summarizes them. The more detailed versions of some of the questions can be consulted in the review sections at the end of Chapters 3, 4 and 5.

Questions to help in proposal development

Area, topic, purpose

1   What is my research area? Have I clearly identified it?
2   What is my topic? Have I clearly identified it, and shown how it fits within the research area?
3   What is the overall purpose of my research?

Background and context

4   Into what background and context does my research fit?

Research questions

5   What are my general research questions?
6   What are my specific research questions?
7   Does each specific research question meet the empirical criterion? That is, is it clear what data are required to answer each question?

Relevant literature

8   What literature is relevant to my study?
9   What is the relationship of my study to this literature?
10 How will my study deal with the literature?
11 How does my proposal use the literature?

Perspectives

12 Is there a particular perspective behind my research?

Substantive theory

13 What is the role of theory in my study?

  (a) Does the description–explanation distinction apply? If my purpose is explanatory, is the focus on theory verification or theory generation? What is the logic behind my position?
  (b) Does the distinction between theory verification and theory generation apply? What is the logic behind my position?

(c) If my focus is theory verification, what are the hypotheses and what is the theory behind them?

Prestructured versus unfolding

14   To what extent is my study prestructured or unfolding? Does this apply differentially to different parts of my study?

Methods and data

15   Will my study use quantitative methods and data, qualitative methods and data, or both?
16   What strategy(ies) will my study use?
17   Does my study have a conceptual framework?
18   Who or what will be studied?
19   From whom will data be collected? Specifically, what is the sampling plan, the sample size and the basis for sample selection?
20   How will I collect the data?
21   What instruments (if any) will be used? Will I use already existing instruments? If so, what is known about them? Will I develop instruments for this study? If so, using what steps?
22   What data collection procedures will be used?
23   How will these procedures maximize the quality of my data?
24   How will I analyse my data?
25   What computer packages will be involved?

Consent, access, ethics

26   What issues of consent are involved in carrying out my study, and how will they be dealt with?
27   What issues of access are involved in carrying out my study, and how will they be dealt with?
28   What other ethical issues are involved in carrying out my study, and how will they be dealt with?

Presentation

29   Does my proposal constitute a logical and coherent argument, with interconnected sections? Do its parts fit together?
30   Have I given enough information for readers to make the judgements shown in Chapter 2?
31   Have I been clear? Is the proposal well organized, easy to follow and clearly written?
32   Is my proposal presented in an appropriate scholarly form?

Notes

Chapter 1

1 I am indebted to Sandra Carrivick for this suggestion.
2 More accurately, qualitative research is a collection of ways of thinking about social reality. Whereas quantitative research is relatively homogeneous in its way of thinking, qualitative research is much more heterogeneous.
3 This is part of what is meant by the term 'paradigm' (see Section 4.1), involving assumptions about the nature of the reality being studied. As an example, quantitative research typically conceptualizes the world in terms of variables (which can be measured) and studies relations between these variables. Qualitative research, by contrast, often studies cases and processes, rather than variables.
4 This view might be described as a 'modified logical empiricist' view, with some additions from critical rationalism (see Higgs, 1995).

Chapter 2

1 I single this point out because of the frequency with which I find it occurs in research supervision. I am sure every supervisor is familiar with the following exchange:

   Supervisor (reacting, for example, to a proposal draft): 'This is not clear', or 'I cannot understand this.
   Student (in response): 'What I meant was …' and proceeds to clarify.
   The point is, of course, that the student will usually not be there to clarify what is written when the committee member is reading the proposal, or when a wider audience is involved. It is necessary to make the proposal clear in the 'stand-alone' sense.

2 'Naturalistic' refers here to research which does not contrive or manipulate the situation being studied, and which does not involve any intervention or treatment. It studies the world 'as it is'.

Chapter 3

1 A generalizing question seeks nomothetic knowledge – universalized law-like statements applying generally across a class of people, situations, events or phenomena. A particularizing question seeks ideographic knowledge – local, case-based, specific propositions.
2 This does not apply literally to all actual data collection questions which might be used in a study. Thus some data collection questions might themselves be quite general questions – for example, introductory or 'grand tour' questions in a qualitative research

interview. But the point being made here is that the role of most data collection questions in the research is to operate at the most specific level. As Maxwell (1996: 53) says, research questions identify what you want to understand; interview questions, as data collection questions, provide the data you need to understand these things. The same is true of survey questions. Being the most specific level of questions, the actual data collection questions will probably not be shown in the proposal.

3   Locke et al. (1993) give examples of this question development process, including inductively (p. 50) and deductively (p. 53). Maxwell (1996: 54–9), writing for qualitative research, makes distinctions between research questions (generalizing–particularizing, instrumentalist–realist, variance–process). He also (p. 50) gives an example of the development of research questions, and (pp. 61–2) gives an exercise to assist in this. Madsen (1983: 30–4) shows how to develop subsidiary (that is, specific) research questions from a general question.

4   The rephrasing needs to go further than just this, for the question to meet the empirical criterion completely. Also, of course, there are other ways of rephrasing the original 'should' question. This simple way has been used for illustration, but this way of rephrasing might well be part of any evaluative answer to the original question, even though it changes its meaning somewhat. Another way is to rephrase the 'should' question in terms of means–ends (or causes–effects). For example, 'Should nurses wear white uniforms?' might become 'What consequences does the wearing of white uniforms have (for example) on nurse–doctor–patient relationships, or on patients' attitudes?'

Chapter 4

1   Guba and Lincoln write as follows: 'A paradigm may be viewed as a set of *basic beliefs* (or metaphysics) that deals with ultimates or first principles. It represents a *worldview* that defines, for its holder, the nature of "the world", the individual's place in it, and the range of possible relationships to that world and its parts, as, for example, cosmologies and theologies do' (1994: 107).

2   There is some confusion and overlap of terms here: for example, it becomes difficult to separate paradigm, metatheory and perspective from strategy, and strategy from design. Thus Morse (1994: 224–5) sees semiotics as a paradigm, ethnomethodology and discourse analysis as strategies, and phenomenology as both paradigm and strategy. She also (p. 221) writes about 'paradigmatic perspectives'. One way to minimize this difficulty of demarcation is to use perspective as a broad term (including paradigm and metatheory), to see strategy as something which implements a perspective, and design as something which implements a strategy. Appendix 1 elaborates this use of perspective, strategy and design.

3   I realize that the issue of perspective (or paradigm) is always present even if implicitly, including in 'pragmatic' research, since assumptions about reality and strategies and methods of inquiry are always involved. I know too that a case can be made for insisting on the articulation of these assumptions in research proposals. But I have found that a strong emphasis on perspectives and paradigm issues can leave *beginning* research students confused, and bogged down. In my teaching, therefore, I now prefer most of the time to 'back into' the issue of perspective, letting it emerge as appropriate rather than insisting on or forcing its emergence. The question of the defence of that perspective, if

any is required, is a matter that appears to be department-specific (or perhaps university-specific). One department might insist on a detailed articulation and defence of the perspective adopted, whereas another might not. In view of this, it is good advice for the student to see 'how the land lies' on this issue in the department in question.

4   More completely, Maxwell (1996: 59–60) defines five categories of understanding in qualitative research: description, interpretation, theory (explanation), generalization and evaluation. The first three categories include most types of questions that qualitative researchers develop.

5   These are examples from quantitative research, where the concept of intervening variables is used to describe the links. In Maxwell's (1996: 58) terms, this type of explanation is variance theory explanation. But the logic works just as well with qualitative data (see Miles and Huberman, 1994: 222–8). In this case, it is termed process theory explanation.

6   Creswell (1994: 81–101) has a particularly useful discussion on the role of theory, showing its typical deductive structure for theory-testing quantitative research, and its typical inductive structure for theory-generating qualitative research.

7   Many books contain a section or chapter on locating and reviewing the relevant literature: examples are Bell (1993: 33–51), Borg and Gall (1989: 114–66) and Delamont et al. (1997: 51–66). Hart has written two valuable books with the titles *Doing a Literature Review* (1998) and *Doing a Literature Search* (2001). Creswell (1994: 20–40) has a chapter on the use of the literature in both quantitative and qualitative research. A specialized technique for reviewing and synthesizing research findings in an area is meta-analysis (Rosenthal, 1991).

Chapter 5

1   'Ambiguous' in the sense that the research question(s) could be addressed using either quantitative or qualitative data.

2   The distinction between the measurement of 'major' variables using established instruments, and measurement using researcher constructed, *ad hoc* rating scales, is useful here (see Punch, 2005: 87–90).

3   In my experience, however, it is still wise in such cases to anticipate questions about sample size.

4   In either approach, the proposal for the research may be to work (in whole or in part) with data which already exist. This is known as *secondary analysis* – the term used for the reanalysis of previously collected and analysed data. In such a case, the proposal should discuss instruments, procedures and sample as appropriate, in describing how the initial data were collected.

5   A general set of steps for doing this is shown in Punch (2005: 92–3).

6   As Punch (1994: 84) points out, much qualitative field research is dependent on one person's perception of the situation at a given point in time. That perception is shaped by personality and by the nature of the interaction with the researched. This makes the researcher his or her own 'research instrument'.

7   Bell (2000: 46–7) has a useful checklist for negotiating access, which points to some of the common ethical issues in social research. This is a subject of increasing importance in the social research methods literature.

Chapter 6

1 Maxwell (1996: 112–13) has an excellent example showing the structure of a dissertation proposal, as an argument with its own logic. Locke et al. (1993: 18) suggest three useful questions which address the logic of the proposed research, its topic and research question. First, what do we already know or do? (The purpose here, in one or two sentences, is to support the legitimacy and importance of the question.) Second, how does this particular question relate to what we already know or do? (The purpose here is to explain and support the exact form of questions or hypotheses that serve as the focus for the study.) Third, why select this particular method of investigation? (The purpose here is to explain and support the selections made from among alternative methods of investigation.)

2 Other lists of possible proposal headings are shown in the literature noted in the introduction to this chapter, and other proposal outlines are described by Morse (1994) and by Kelly (1998).

3 For a finished report (or dissertation), the abstract would need to deal with three issues: these two, and a third which summarizes what was found.

4 Creswell (1994: 56–67) gives examples of purpose statements for five different types of study: a phenomenological study, a case study, an ethnographic study, a grounded theory study and a quantitative survey.

Chapter 7

1 Despite this, some of the literature has diagrams and flowcharts of steps and stages to go through in developing a proposal. For example, Locke et al. (1993: 54–5) suggest 20 steps to a proposal, Coley and Scheinberg (1990: 18–27) describe nine steps, and Hamper and Baugh (1996: 17–24) also have a nine-step proposal preparation process.

2 For the same reason I would also recommend finding out about the process of dissertation examination in your department, and consulting previous dissertations.

3 In the PhD context, Marshall and Green (2004: 31–2) have a helpful list of 10 questions to ask prospective supervisors.

4 For this reason, a term often used is 'abd', which means 'all but the dissertation'.

5 Balancing these points, the writer needs to remember also that the proposal is an argument, and needs to be convincing and (within reason) confident. This is another tension which exists in the research planning process.

6 Or insights, or hunches, or relevant 'experiential data'.

Chapter 8

1 The sections omitted are timetable, scholars, facilities, estimated costs, appendices and research instruments.

Glossary

Readers using this book to support the Open University course EK310 'Research with Children and Young People' may also want to refer to the booklet *Key Research Terms* (2004) prepared by the course team. Where a term is in this glossary and also in the *Key Research Terms* booklet, page numbers to the latter entry are given after the abbreviation 'KRT'.

Accounting for variance   A central strategy in quantitative research; accounting for the variation in a dependent variable through studying its relationship with independent variables.

Action research   Using empirical procedures, in iterative cycles of action and research, to solve practical problems. (KRT 2)

Analysis of covariance   A statistical technique for investigating the difference between groups on some dependent variable after controlling for one or more covariates. (KRT 2–3)

Analysis of variance   A statistical technique for investigating differences between groups on some dependent variable. (KRT 3–4)

Audit trail (through the data)   Showing how the data were analysed to arrive at conclusions.

Axial coding   Discovering connections in the data between abstract concepts; used in grounded theory analysis; produces theoretical codes. (KRT 5)

Case study   A research strategy which focuses on the in-depth, holistic and in-context study of one or more cases; will typically use multiple sources of data.

Chi square   A statistical technique with many uses; a common use is to see whether variables in a cross-tabulation are related to each other. (KRT 5–6)

Coding   Placing labels or tags on pieces of qualitative data. (KRT 7–8)

Conceptual framework   A framework showing the central concepts of a piece of research, and their conceptual status with respect to each other; often expressed as a diagram.

Contingency table   Uses cross-tabulation to see if the distribution of one variable is related to (or contingent upon) the other variable. (KRT 10)

Continuous variable   A variable which varies in degree rather than in kind (e.g. height, level of income, level of achievement). Synonym is 'measured variable'.

Control variable   A variable whose effect we want to rule out, or control. Synonym is 'covariate'. (KRT 11)

Correlation   A statistical technique for showing the strength and direction of the relationship between two variables. (KRT 12)

Correlational survey   A quantitative survey where the focus is on studying the relationships between variables.

Covariate   See *control variable*. (KRT 12)

Cross-tabulation   Two variables are cross-tabulated against each other. (KRT 13–14)

Data   The general term for observable information about, or direct experience of, some aspect of the world; see *empirical, qualitative data, quantitative data*.

Data collection questions   The actual questions asked to collect the data; examples are survey questions in quantitative research, and interview questions in qualitative research; data collection questions follow logically from specific research questions.

Deduction   Moving downward in levels of abstraction, from more general and abstract to more specific and concrete; opposite of *induction*.

Definitions   A conceptual definition is the definition of a concept (or variable) in terms of other abstract concepts. This brings the need to find observable activities which are indicators of the concept; those activities constitute the operational definition of the concept. Construct *validity* is enhanced when there are tight logical links between the conceptual and operational definitions.

Deliberate (or purposive) sampling   The sample is drawn from the population in a deliberate or targeted way, according to the logic of the research.

Dependent variable   The variable seen as the 'effect' in a cause–effect relationship. Synonyms are 'outcome variable' in experimental design, 'criterion variable' in a correlational survey. (KRT 14)

Discourse   A system of language which draws on a particular terminology and which encodes specific forms of knowledge; often used to refer to systems of knowledge and their associated practices (Seale, 1998; Tonkiss, 1998). (KRT 14–15)

Discrete variable   A variable which varies in kind, not degree; its variance is in categories (e.g. eye colour, religious affiliation, country of birth). Synonyms are 'categorical variable', 'discontinuous variable'.

Empirical   Based on direct experience or observation of the world.

Empirical criterion (for a research question)   Is it clear what data are needed to answer this research question? If yes, the research question satisfies the empirical criterion. If no, further development of the research question is necessary.

Empiricism   Philosophical term to describe the epistemological theory that sees experience as the foundation or source of knowledge.

Ethnography   The preferred research strategy of anthropologists; seeks to understand the symbolic significance of behaviour, in its cultural context, to the participants; aims for a full cultural description of the way of life of some group of people. (KRT 15–16)

Ethnomethodology   Examines how people produce orderly social interaction in ordinary everyday situations; exposes the taken-for-granted 'rules' which constitute the infrastructure making everyday social interaction possible. (KRT 16)

Experiment   A predominantly quantitative research design where (1) one or more independent variables are manipulated to study their effect on a dependent variable and (2) participants are randomly assigned to treatment or comparison groups. (KRT 16)

Factor analysis   A family of statistical techniques for reducing the number of variables without loss of information.

Fact–value gap   The view that statements of fact and statements of value have no logical connection between them.

Focus group (interview)   A powerful method of qualitative data collection where a small group (six to eight) of people are interviewed as a group. (KRT 17–18)

Frequency distribution   A table or diagram showing the distribution of a set of scores. (KRT 19)

Grounded theory   A distinctive strategy for research which aims to discover or generate explanatory theory grounded in data. (KRT 20)

Grounded theory analysis   Specific procedures in the analysis of data for generating explanatory theory; focuses essentially on raising the conceptual level of (i.e. reconceptualizing) the data.

Hierarchy of concepts   A useful tool in planning and organizing research: area; topic; general research questions; specific research questions; data collection questions.

Hypothesis   A predicted answer to a research question.

Hypothetico-deductive model   The central strategy of theory verification research which stresses the empirical testing of hypotheses deduced from theory. A *hypothesis* is *developed* from a *theory* by *deduction* and then tested against data.

Independent variable   The variable seen as the 'cause' in a cause–effect relationship. Synonyms are 'treatment variable' in experimental design, 'predictor variable' in a correlational survey. (KRT 20)

Induction   Moving upwards in levels of abstraction, from more specific and concrete to more general and abstract; opposite of *deduction*.

Interaction   A technical term in quantitative research design; two (or more) independent variables may interact in their effect on a dependent variable. (KRT 21)

Internal validity of a proposal   Proposal as argument: the proposal should show strong internal consistency and coherence; all of its different parts should fit together. Especially, its methods should match its research questions; its argument and logic should be clear and consistent.

Latent trait   The trait (or variable) we want to measure is hidden; we measure it by inference from its observable indicators.

Measurement   The operation which turns data into numbers.

Member checking   The qualitative researcher checks the data and the analysis as it develops with the people being studied, who gave the data; typical in *grounded theory* research.

Memoing   Pausing, in qualitative analysis especially, to write down ideas about the data as they occur during coding and analysis.

Mixed-method research   Empirical research which brings together quantitative data (and methods) and qualitative data (and methods); there are many models for doing this.

Multiple causation   The idea that a particular 'effect' has multiple causes which are usually interrelated.

Multiple linear regression   A quantitative design and data analysis strategy with several independent variables and one dependent variable; aims to account for variance in the dependent variable.

Multivariate   More than one dependent variable.

Naturalism   The social world is studied in its natural state, rather than contrived for research purposes. (KRT 31)

Negative correlation   High scores on one variable go with low scores on the other variable (and vice versa).

Open coding   Concentrates on raising the conceptual level of the data. Guided by the question: what is this piece of data an example of? Used in *grounded theory analysis*; produces substantive codes. (KRT 31)

Operationalism   In quantitative research, the idea that the meaning of a concept is given by the set of operations necessary to measure it (see *definitions*).

Paradigm   A set of assumptions about the social world, and about what constitute proper techniques and topics for inquiring into that world; a set of basic beliefs, a world view, a view of how science should be done (ontology, epistemology, methodology).

Participant observation   The preferred strategy for doing ethnography; the researcher aims to be both observer of and participant in the situation being studied, in order to understand it. (KRT 34)

Population   The target group, usually large, about whom we want to develop knowledge, but which we cannot study directly; therefore we sample from that population.

Positive correlation   High scores on one variable go with high scores on the other variable (and vice versa). (KRT 34)

Positivism   In a loose sense, has come to mean an approach to social research that emphasizes the discovery of general laws, and separates facts from values; it often involves an empiricist commitment to naturalism and quantitative methods (Seale, 1998: 328).

Prestructured research   A research project with clear and specific research questions, a clear conceptual framework, a preplanned design and precoded data; see *unfolding research*.

Psychometric characteristics   A general term referring to the measurement characteristics of a quantitative research instrument; usually includes *reliability* and *validity*.

Purposive (or deliberate sampling)   The sample is drawn from the population in a deliberate or targeted way, according to the logic of the research.

Qualitative data   Empirical information not in the form of numbers (most of the time, though not always, this means words).

Qualitative research   Empirical research where the data are not in the form of numbers.

Quantitative data   Empirical information in the form of numbers (or measurements).

Quantitative research   Empirical research where the data are in the form of numbers.

Quasi-experiment   Naturally occurring treatment groups permit comparisons between the groups approximating those of true experimental design. (KRT 38)

Reactivity   The idea that the data being collected might be somehow changed or influenced by the data collection process itself.

Regression   A statistical technique for predicting scores on one variable from scores on another variable. (KRT 40–1)

Reliability (of data)   In quantitative research, the consistency of measurement: (1) consistency over time, i.e. test–retest reliability; (2) consistency within indicators, i.e. internal consistency reliability. In qualitative research, the dependability of the data. (KRT 41)

Representative sampling   A sampling strategy where each unit of the population has an equal chance of being selected in the sample; directed at generalization. (KRT 41)

Research questions   Organize the research by showing its purposes. General research questions guide the research by showing the general questions the research aims to answer; too general themselves to be answered directly; need to be made more specific. Specific research questions make the general research questions more specific; connect the general research questions to the data.

Sample   A smaller group which is actually studied, drawn from a larger population; data are collected (and analysed) from the sample, and inferences may then be made back to the population. (KRT 41–3)

Science as method   An empirical method for building knowledge where the objective is to develop and test theory to explain data. Theory generation research generates theory from data; theory verification research tests theory against data.

Secondary analysis   The reanalysis of previously collected and analysed data.

Selective coding   Used in grounded theory analysis; identifies the core category of a grounded theory, and raises the conceptual level of the analysis a second time. (KRT 43)

Semiotics   The science of signs; focuses on the process whereby something comes to stand for something else.

Sensitivity (of measurement)   The ability of a measuring instrument to produce (reliable) variance, to differentiate between the people being measured.

Social science   The scientific study of human behaviour; 'social' refers to people and their behaviour and to the fact that so much behaviour occurs in a social context; 'science' refers to the way that people and their behaviour are studied; see *science as method*.

Statistical inference   A set of decision making rules to assess the accuracy of the inference made from sample to population.

Statistically significant   Using inferential statistics to conclude that a particular result is very unlikely to have occurred by chance; such a result is therefore taken as real. (KRT 44, 46–7)

Structured interview   Interview questions are pre-established and have preset response categories. (KRT 47)

Survey   A research strategy involving the collecting of data from a range of respondents (usually a sample drawn from a population); may be quantitative, qualitative, or mixed method, depending on the nature of the data; usually involves a survey questionnaire.

***t*-test**   A statistical technique for investigating differences between two groups on some dependent variable; a special case of *analysis of variance*. (KRT 48)

Theoretical sampling   Consecutive cycles of data collection are guided by the theoretical directions emerging from the ongoing analysis (see Figure 3.1); typically used in *grounded theory* research. (KRT 47–8)

Theoretical saturation   The 'end-stage' of theoretical sampling in grounded theory research, when new data are not showing new theoretical elements, but rather confirming what has already been found.

Theoretical sensitivity A term used in grounded theory; being alive and sensitive to the theoretical possibilities in the data; the ability to 'see', with theoretical and analytic depth, what is in the data.

Theory Explanatory theory is a set of propositions which explain the data; the concepts in the propositions of the explanatory theory are more abstract than those in the data.

Theory generation research Empirical research where the objective is discovering or constructing theory to explain data; starts with data, ends with theory.

Theory verification research Empirical research where the objective is testing theory against data; starts with theory, uses data to test the theory (see *hypothetico-deductive model*).

Thick description The emphasis in qualitative research on capturing and conveying the full picture of behaviour being studied – holistically, comprehensively and in context.

Triangulation Using several kinds of methods or data to study a topic; the most common type is data triangulation, where a study uses a variety of data sources. (KRT 49)

Unfolding research A research project where specific research questions are not clear in advance, a general approach rather than a tightly prefigured design is used, data are not prestructured; these things will unfold as the study progresses; see *prestructured research*.

Univariate Only one dependent variable.

Unstructured interview Interview questions and response categories are not pre-established; interview questions are deliberately open-ended. (KRT 49–50)

Validity A complex term with many meanings, both technical and general. Three important technical meanings are: the validity of a measuring instrument; the validity of a research design; the truth status of a research report. (KRT 50)

Validity (of measurement) The extent to which a measuring instrument measures what it is supposed to measure. Content (or face) validity asks: how well does the measuring instrument sample from all areas of content in the conceptual description? Criterion related validity may be considered as: concurrent validity, which asks how the measuring instrument compares with another measure of the same construct; predictive validity, which asks how well it predicts later behaviour; and construct validity, which asks how well it conforms with theoretical expectations.

Value judgements Moral or ethical judgements; judgements of what is good or bad, right or wrong, etc.; usually made as terminal values, i.e. ends in themselves.

References

Aspin, D.N. (1995) 'Logical empiricism, post-empiricism and education', in P. Higgs (ed.), *Metatheories in Philosophy of Education.* Johannesburg: Heinemann. pp. 21–49.

Behling, J.H. (1984) *Guidelines for Preparing the Research Proposal,* rev. edn. Lanham, MD: University Press of America.

Bell, J. (1993) *Doing Your Research Project: A Guide for First Time Researchers in Education and Social Science*, 2nd edn. Buckingham: Open University Press.

Bourdieu, P. (1973) 'Cultural reproduction and social reproduction', in R. Brown (ed.), *Knowledge, Education and Cultural Change.* London: Tavistock. pp. 71–112.

Borg, W.R. and Gall, M.D. (1989) *Educational Research: An Introduction*, 2nd edn. White Plains, NY: Longman.

Brink, P.J. and Wood, M.J. (1994) *Basic Steps in Planning Nursing Research. From Question to Proposal,* 4th edn. Boston, MA: Jones and Bartlett.

Bryant, Miles T. (2004) *The Portable Dissertation Advisor.* Beverly Hills, CA: Sage.

Coley, S.M. and Scheinberg, C.A. (1990) *Proposal Writing.* Newbury Park, CA: Sage.

Creswell, J.W. (1994) *Research Design: Qualitative and Quantitative Approaches.* Thousand Oaks, CA: Sage.

Cryer, P. (2000) *The Research Student's Guide to Success,* 2nd edn. Buckingham: Open University Press.

Delamont, S., Atkinson, P. and Parry, O. (1997*) Supervising the PhD: A Guide to Success.* Buckingham: Open University Press.

Denzin, N.K. and Lincoln, Y.S. (eds), (1994) *Handbook of Qualitative Research.* Thousand Oaks, CA: Sage.

Dreher, M. (1994) 'Qualitative research methods from the reviewer's perspective', in J.M. Morse (ed.), *Critical Issues in Qualitative Research Methods.* Thousand Oak, CA: Sage. pp. 281–97.

Eisner, E.W. (1991) *The Enlightened Eye: Qualitative Inquiry and the Enhancement of Educational Practice.* New York: Macmillan.

Gill, J. and Johnson, P. (2002) *Research Methods for Managers,* 3rd edn. London: Sage.

Gilpatrick, E. (1989*) Grants for Nonprofit Organizations: A Guide to Funding and Grant Writing.* New York: Praeger.

Gitlin, L.N. and Lyons, K.J. (1996) *Successful Grant Writing.* New York: Springer.

Glaser, B. (1992) *Basics of Grounded Theory Analysis.* Mill Valley, CA: Sociology Press.

Guba, E.G. and Lincoln, Y.S. (1994) 'Competing paradigms in qualitative research', in N.K. Denzin and Y.S. Lincoln (eds), *Handbook of Qualitative Research.* Thousand Oaks, CA: Sage. pp. 105–17.

Hammersley, M. (1992) 'Deconstructing the qualitative–quantitative divide', in J. Brannen (ed.), *Mixing Methods: Qualitative and Quantitative Research.* Aldershot: Avebury. pp. 39–55.

Hamper, R.J. and Baugh, L.S. (1996) *Handbook for Writing Proposals.* Lincolnwood, IL: NTC Publishing Group.

Hart, C. (1998) *Doing a Literature Review.* London: Sage.

Hart, C. (2001) *Doing a Literature Search*, 2nd edn. London: Sage.

Higgs, P. (1995) 'Metatheories in philosophy of education: introductory overview', in P. Higgs (ed.), *Metatheories in Philosophy of Education.* Johannesburg: Heinemann. pp. 3–17.

Janesick, V.J. (1994) 'The dance of qualitative research design: metaphor, methodolatory, and meaning', in N.K. Denzin and Y.S. Lincoln (eds), *Handbook of Qualitative Research.* Thousand Oaks, CA: Sage. pp. 209–19.

Kelly, M. (1998) 'Writing a research proposal', in C. Seale (ed.), *Researching Society and Culture.* London: Sage. pp. 111–22.

Krathwohl, D.R. (1998) *Methods of Educational and Social Science Research: An Integrated Approach.* New York: Longman.

Lauffer, A. (1983) *Grantsmanship,* 2nd edn. Beverly Hills, CA: Sage.

Lauffer, A. (1984) *Grantsmanship and Fundraising.* Beverly Hills, CA: Sage.

Lefferts, R. (1982) *Getting a Grant in the 1980s,* 2nd edn. Englewood Cliffs, NJ: Prentice-Hall.

Le Voi, M. (2002) 'Responsibilities, rights and ethics' in S. Potter (ed.), *Doing Postgraduate Research.* London: Sage. pp. 153–164.

Lipsey, M.W. (1990) *Design Sensitivity.* Newbury Park, CA: Sage.

Locke, L.F., Spirduso, W.W. and Silverman, S.J. (1993) *Proposals that Work,* 3rd edn. Newbury Park, CA: Sage.

Madsen, D. (1983) *Successful Dissertations and Theses: A Guide to Graduate Student Research from Proposal to Completion.* New York: Jossey-Bass.

Marshall, S. and Green, N. (2004) *Your PhD Companion.* Oxford: How to Books.

Marshall, C. and Rossman, G.B. (1989) *Designing Qualitative Research.* Newbury Park, CA: Sage.

Mauch, J.E. and Birch, J.W. (1989) *Guide to the Successful Thesis and Dissertation,* 2nd edn. New York: Marcel Dekker.

Maxwell, J.A. (1996) *Qualitative Research Design. An Interactive Approach.* Thousand Oaks, CA: Sage.

Maykut, P. and Morehouse, R. (1994) *Beginning Qualitative Research: A Philosophic and Practical Guide.* London: Falmer.

Meador, R. (1991) *Guidelines for Preparing Proposals,* 2nd edn. Chelser, MI: Lewis.

Miles, M.B. and Huberman, A.M. (1994) *Qualitative Data Analysis,* 2nd edn. Thousand Oaks, CA: Sage.

Miner, L.E. and Griffith, J. (1993) *Proposal Planning and Writing.* Phoenix, AZ: Oryx.

Morse, J.M. (1994) 'Designing funded qualitative research', in N.K. Denzin and Y.S. Lincoln (eds), *Handbook of Qualitative Research.* Thousand Oaks, CA: Sage. pp. 220–35.

Moser, C.A. and Kalton, G. (1979) *Survey Methods in Social Investigation,* 2nd edn. Aldershot: Gower.

Neumann, W.L. (1994) *Social Research Methods: Qualitative and Quantitative Approaches,* 2nd edn. Boston: Allyn and Bacon.

O'Donoghue, T. and Haynes, F. (1997) *Preparing Your Thesis/Dissertation in Education: Comprehensive Guidelines.* Katoomba, NSW: Social Science Press.

Parsigian, E.K. (1996) *Proposal Savvy: Creating Successful Proposals for Media Projects.* Thousand Oaks, CA: Sage.

Peters, R. L. (1997) *Getting What You Came For: The Smart Student's Guide to Earning a Master's or a PhD,* rev. edn. New York: Noonday.

Punch, K. (2005) *Introduction to Social Research,* 2nd edn. London: Sage.

Punch, M. (1994) 'Politics and ethics in qualitative research', in N.K. Denzin and Y.S. Lincoln (eds), *Handbook of Qualitative Research.* Thousand Oaks, CA: Sage. pp. 82–97.

Rosenberg, M. (1968) *The Logic of Survey Analysis.* New York: Basic Books.

Rosenthal, R. (1991) *Meta-Analytic Procedures for Social Research.* Thousand Oaks, CA: Sage.

Rudestam, K.E. and Newton, R.R. (1992) *Surviving Your Dissertation.* London: Sage.

Schofield, W. (1996) 'Survey sampling', in R. Sapsford and V. Jupp (eds), *Data Collection and Analysis.* London: Sage. pp. 25–56.

Schumacher, D. (1992) *Get Funded!* Newbury Park, CA: Sage.

Seale, C. (ed.) (1998) *Researching Society and Culture.* London: Sage.

Steane, P. (2004) 'Ethical Issues in Research', in S. Burton and P. Steane (eds), *Surviving Your Thesis.* London: Routledge, pp. 59–70.

Tashakkori, A. and Teddlie, C. (2002) *Handbook of Mixed Methods in Social and Behavioural Research.* Thousand Oaks, CA: Sage.

Thomas, R. M. (2003) *Blending Qualitative and Quantitative Research Methods in Theses and Dissertations.* Thousand Oaks, CA: Sage.

Thomas, R. Murray (2003) *Blending Qualitative and Quantitative Research Methods in Theses and Dissertations.* London: Sage.

Tonkiss, F. (1998) 'Analyzing discourse', in C. Seale (ed.), *Researching Society and Culture.* London: Sage. pp. 245–60.

Tornquist, E.M. (1993) *From Proposal to Publication: An Informal Guide to Writing About Nursing Research.* San Francisco: Addison-Wesley Publishing Company.

Wallen, N.E. and Fraenkel, J.R. (1991) *Educational Research: A Guide to the Process.* New York: McGraw-Hill.

Ward, A. (2002) 'The Writing Process', in S. Potter (ed.), *Doing Postgraduate Research.* London: Sage. pp. 71–116.

Index